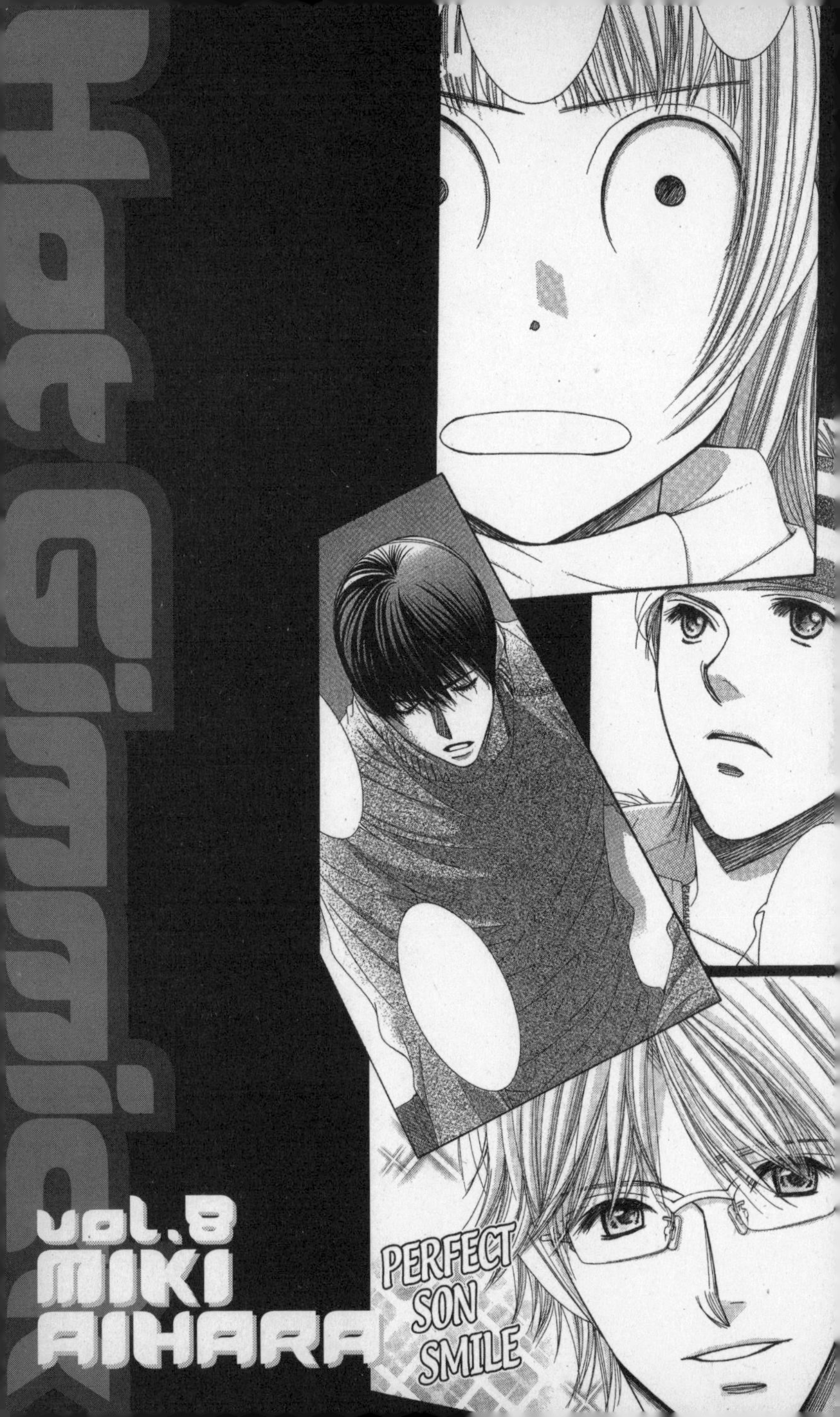
Hot Gimmick
vol.8
MIKI
AIHARA
PERFECT
SON
SMILE

HOT GIMMICK
CONTENTS

Chapter 33

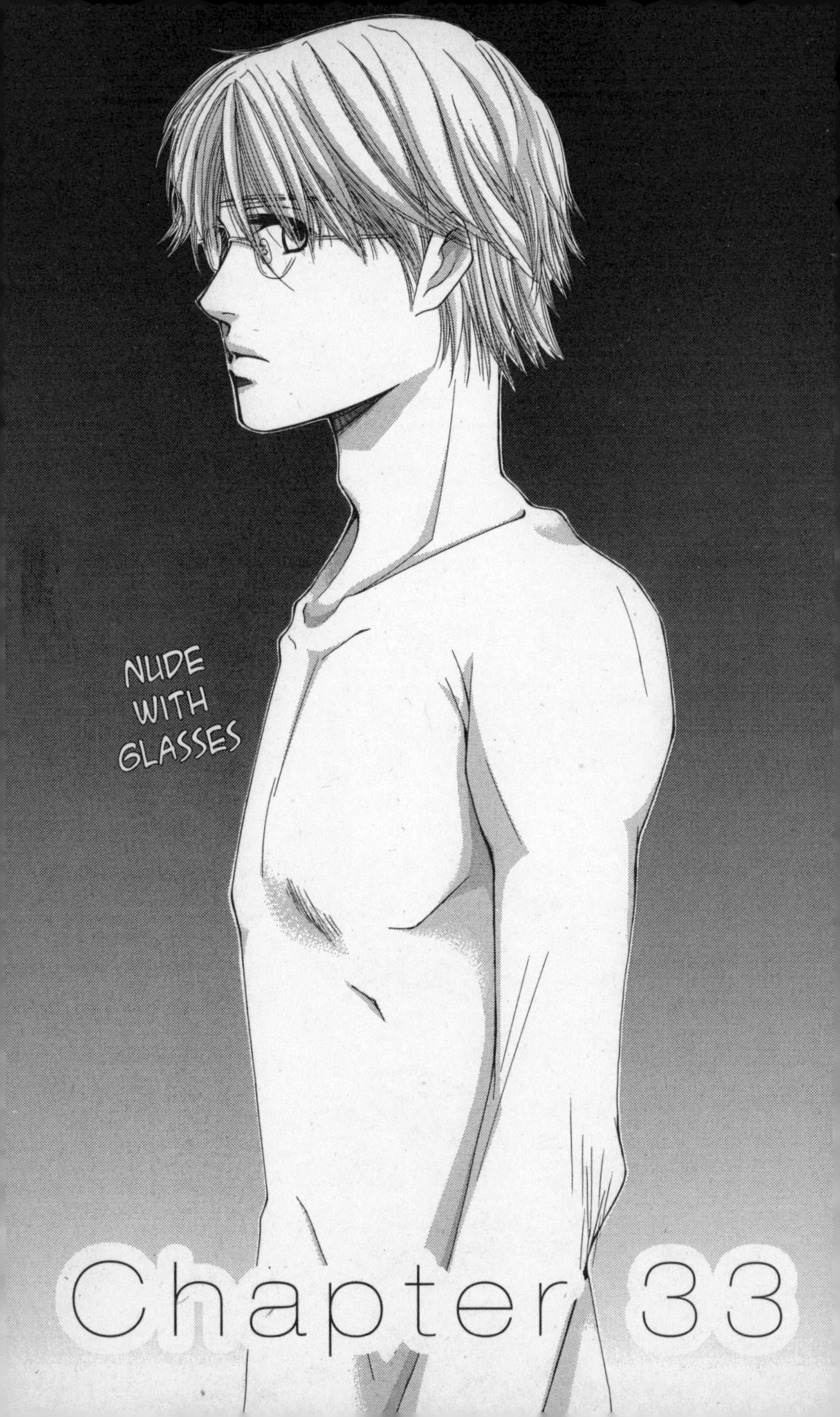
NUDE WITH GLASSES

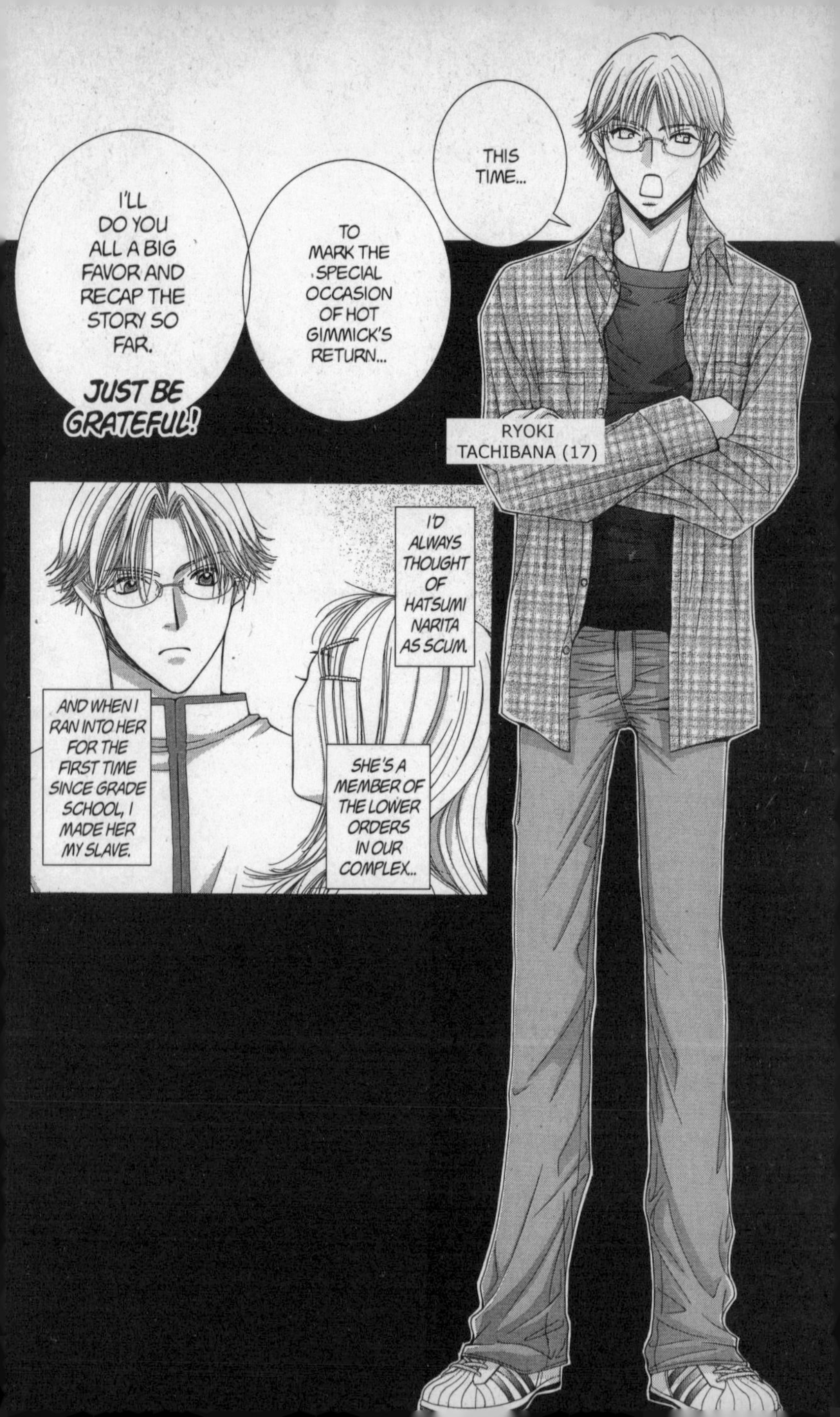
THIS TIME...
TO MARK THE SPECIAL OCCASION OF HOT GIMMICK'S RETURN...
I'LL DO YOU ALL A BIG FAVOR AND RECAP THE STORY SO FAR.
JUST BE GRATEFUL!
RYOKI TACHIBANA (17)
I'D ALWAYS THOUGHT OF HATSUMI NARITA AS SCUM.
SHE'S A MEMBER OF THE LOWER ORDERS IN OUR COMPLEX...
AND WHEN I RAN INTO HER FOR THE FIRST TIME SINCE GRADE SCHOOL, I MADE HER MY SLAVE.

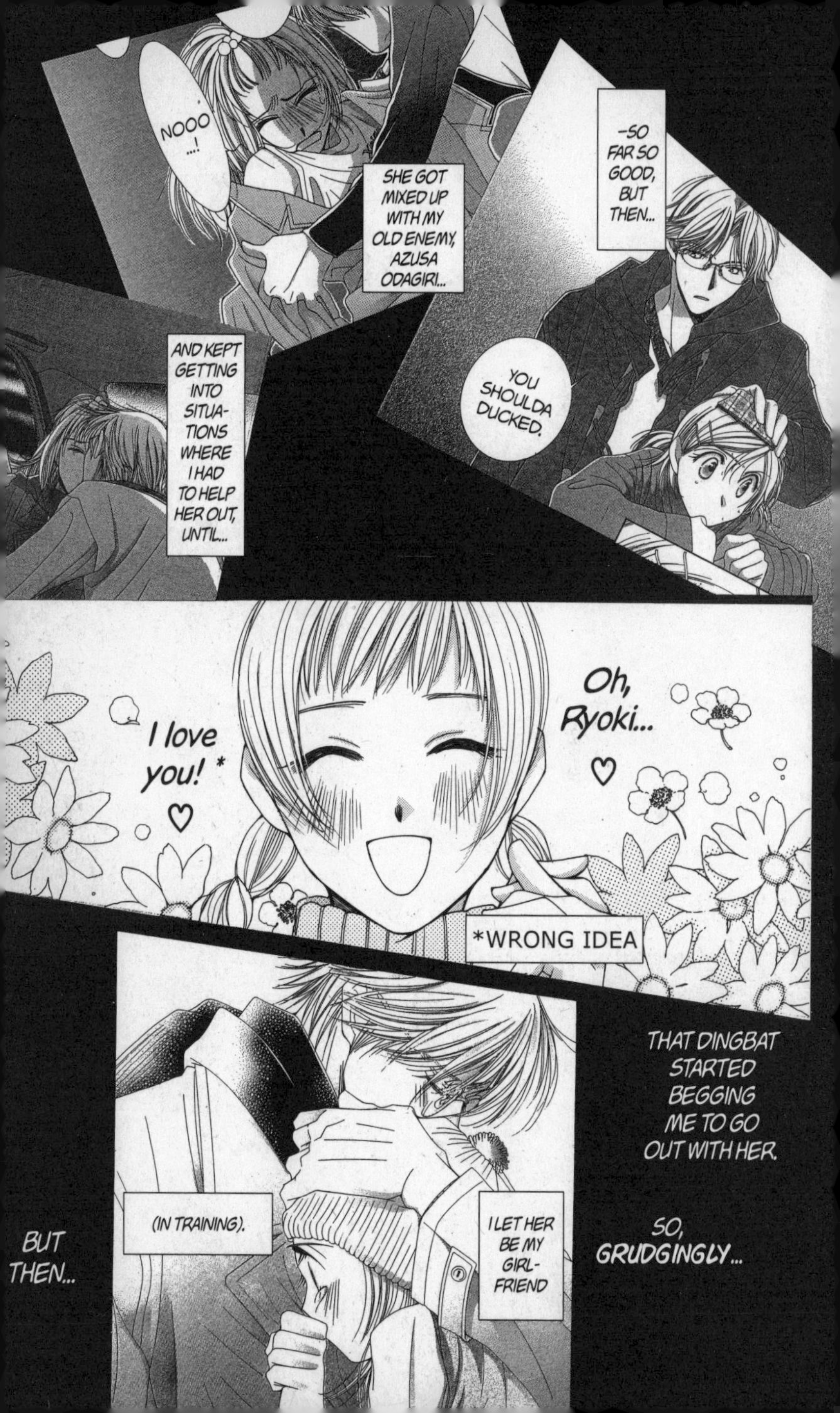

–SO FAR SO GOOD, BUT THEN...
YOU SHOULDA DUCKED.
NOOO ...!
SHE GOT MIXED UP WITH MY OLD ENEMY, AZUSA ODAGIRI...
AND KEPT GETTING INTO SITUA-TIONS WHERE I HAD TO HELP HER OUT, UNTIL...
Oh, Ryoki... ♡
I love you! * ♡
*WRONG IDEA
THAT DINGBAT STARTED BEGGING ME TO GO OUT WITH HER.
SO, GRUDGINGLY...
I LET HER BE MY GIRL-FRIEND
(IN TRAINING).
BUT THEN...

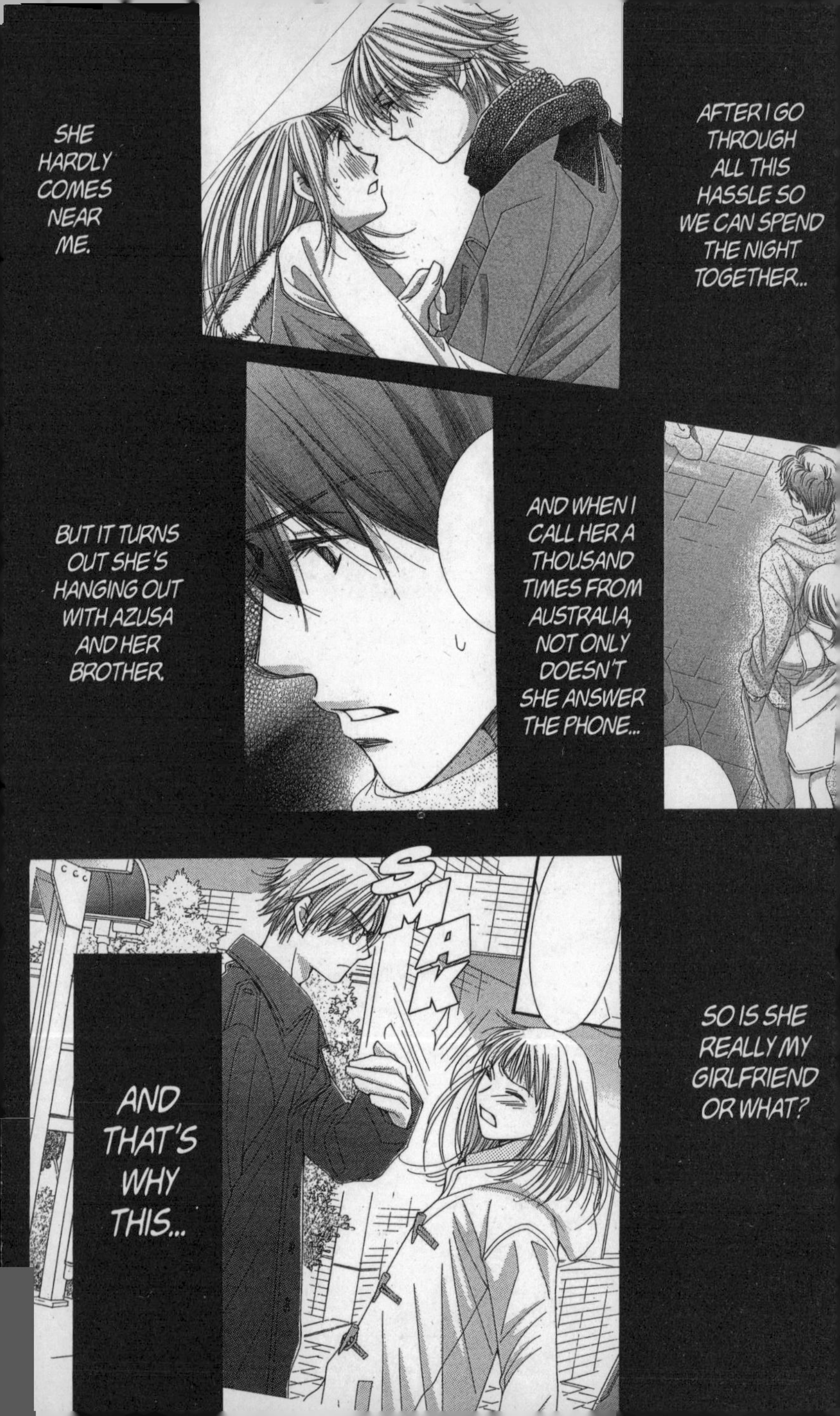
AFTER I GO THROUGH ALL THIS HASSLE SO WE CAN SPEND THE NIGHT TOGETHER...
SHE HARDLY COMES NEAR ME.
AND WHEN I CALL HER A THOUSAND TIMES FROM AUSTRALIA, NOT ONLY DOESN'T SHE ANSWER THE PHONE...
BUT IT TURNS OUT SHE'S HANGING OUT WITH AZUSA AND HER BROTHER.
SO IS SHE REALLY MY GIRLFRIEND OR WHAT?
SMAK
AND THAT'S WHY THIS...

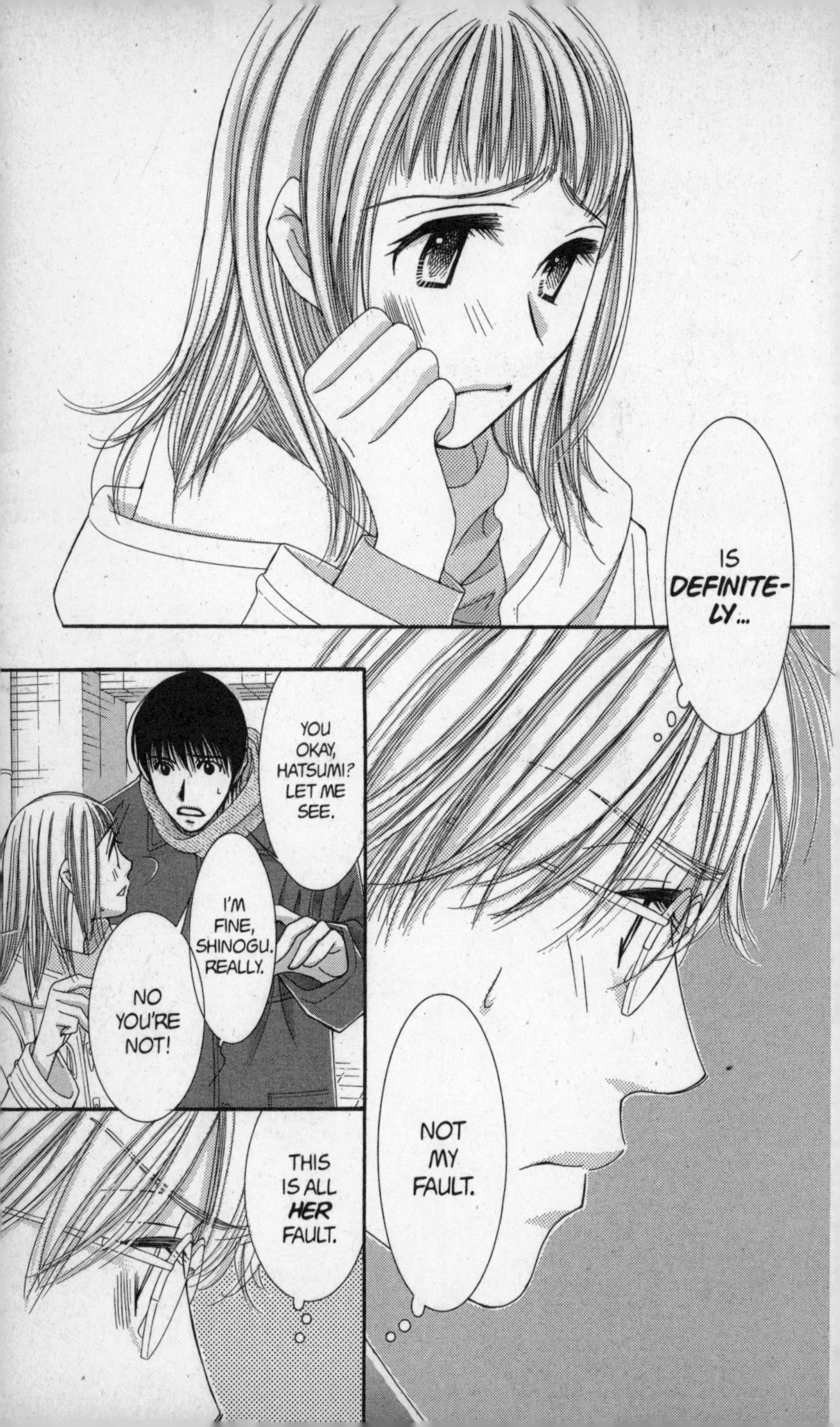
IS DEFINITE-LY...
NOT MY FAULT.
YOU OKAY, HATSUMI? LET ME SEE.
I'M FINE, SHINOGU. REALLY.
NO YOU'RE NOT!
THIS IS ALL HER FAULT.

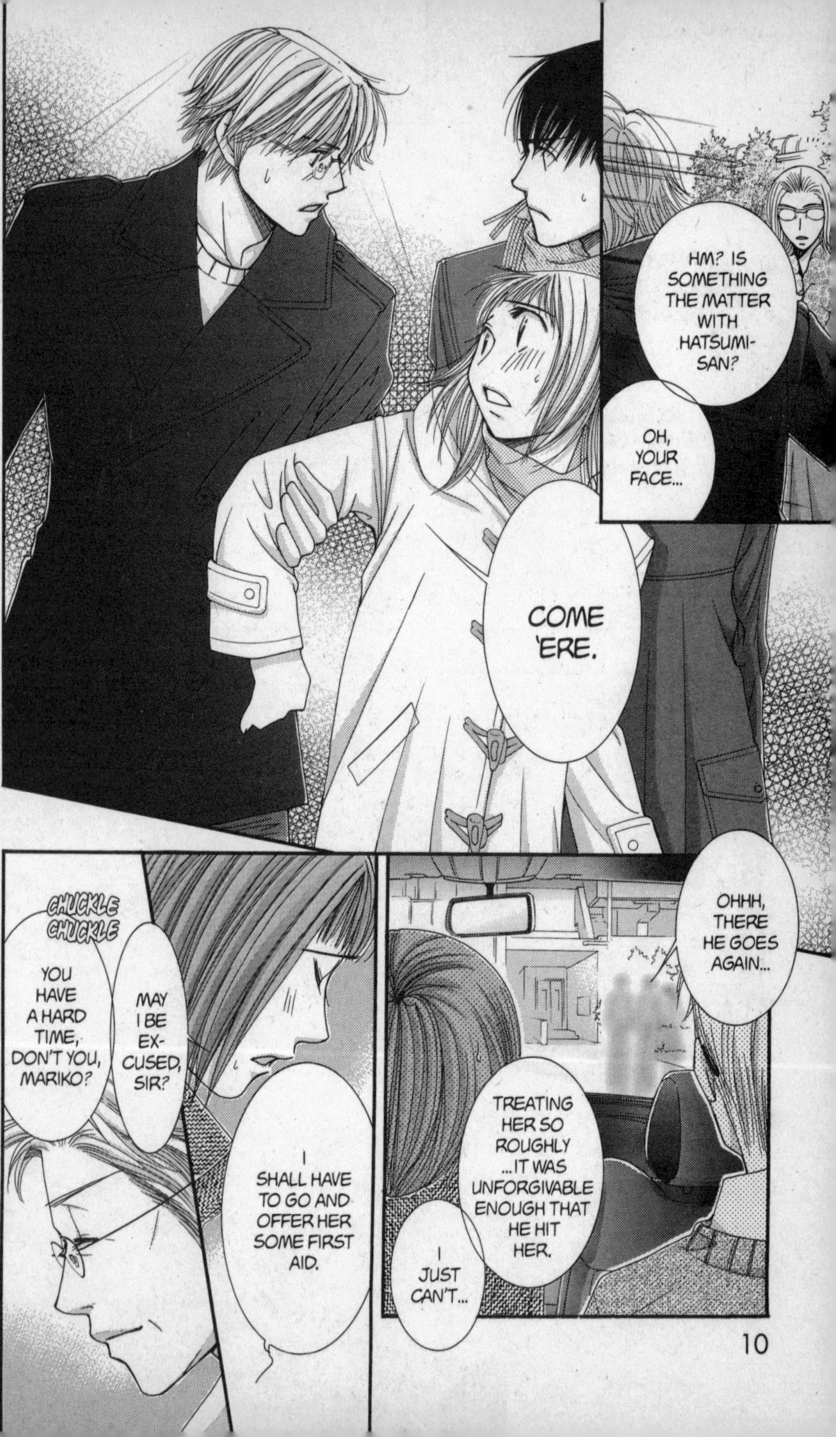
HM? IS SOMETHING THE MATTER WITH HATSUMI-SAN?
OH, YOUR FACE...
COME 'ERE.
OHHH, THERE HE GOES AGAIN...
TREATING HER SO ROUGHLY ...IT WAS UNFORGIVABLE ENOUGH THAT HE HIT HER.
I JUST CAN'T...
MAY I BE EX-CUSED, SIR?
I SHALL HAVE TO GO AND OFFER HER SOME FIRST AID.
CHUCKLE CHUCKLE
YOU HAVE A HARD TIME, DON'T YOU, MARIKO?

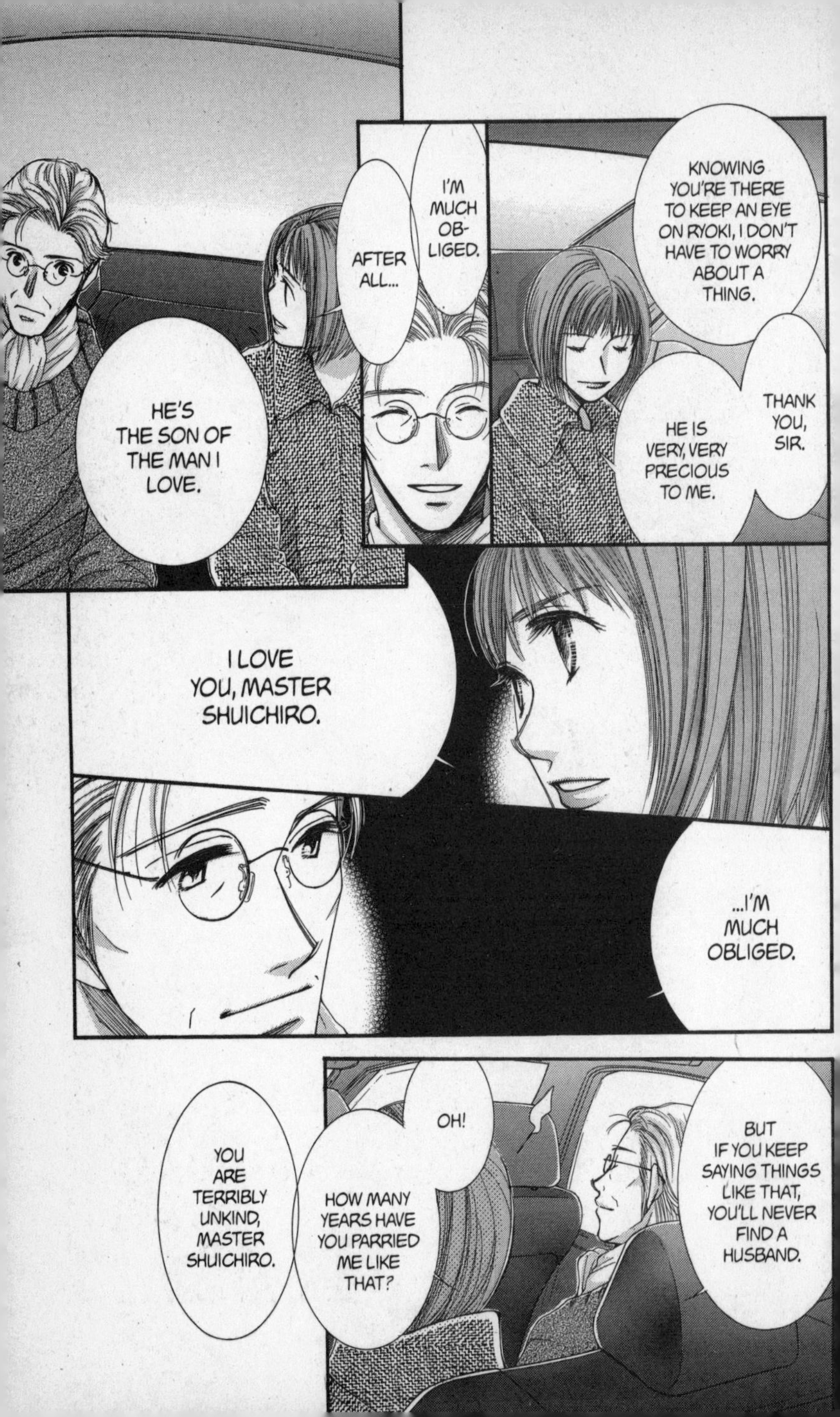
KNOWING YOU'RE THERE TO KEEP AN EYE ON RYOKI, I DON'T HAVE TO WORRY ABOUT A THING.
THANK YOU, SIR.
HE IS VERY, VERY PRECIOUS TO ME.
I'M MUCH OB-LIGED.
AFTER ALL...
HE'S THE SON OF THE MAN I LOVE.
I LOVE YOU, MASTER SHUICHIRO.
...I'M MUCH OBLIGED.
BUT IF YOU KEEP SAYING THINGS LIKE THAT, YOU'LL NEVER FIND A HUSBAND.
OH!
HOW MANY YEARS HAVE YOU PARRIED ME LIKE THAT?
YOU ARE TERRIBLY UNKIND, MASTER SHUICHIRO.

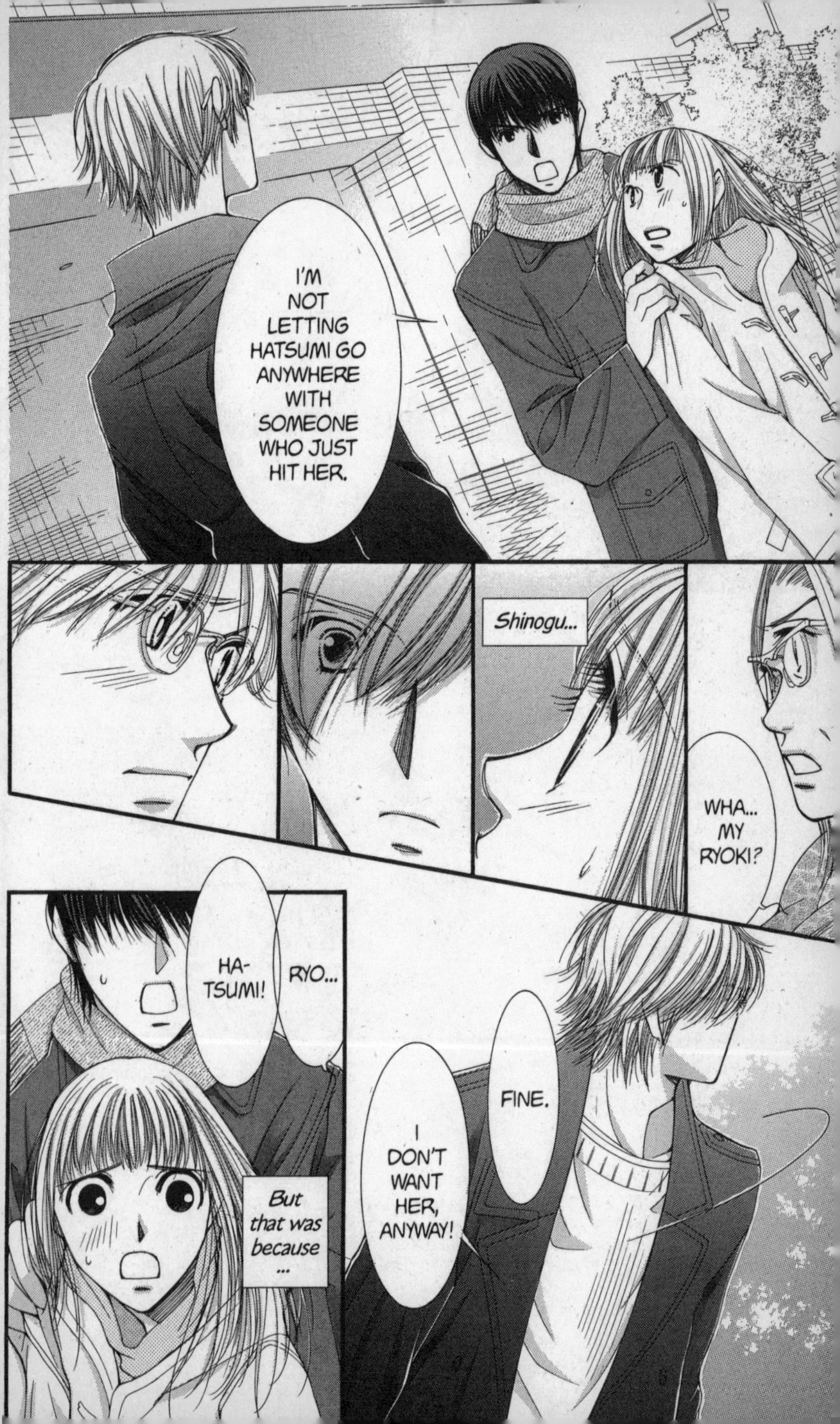
I'M NOT LETTING HATSUMI GO ANYWHERE WITH SOMEONE WHO JUST HIT HER.
WHA... MY RYOKI?
Shinogu...
FINE.
I DON'T WANT HER, ANYWAY!
RYO...
HA-TSUMI!
But that was because ...

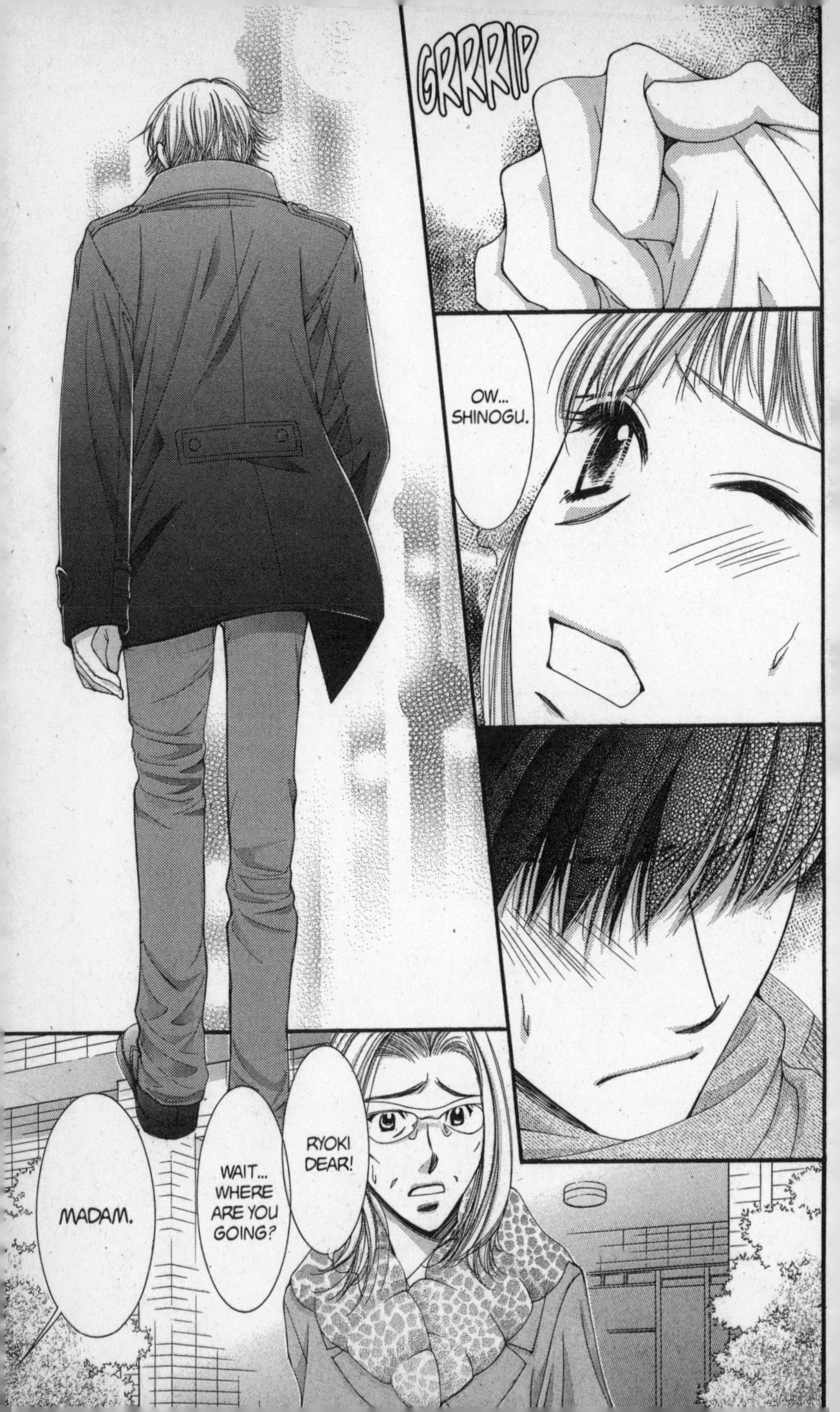
GRRRIP
OW... SHINOGU.
RYOKI DEAR!
WAIT... WHERE ARE YOU GOING?
MADAM.

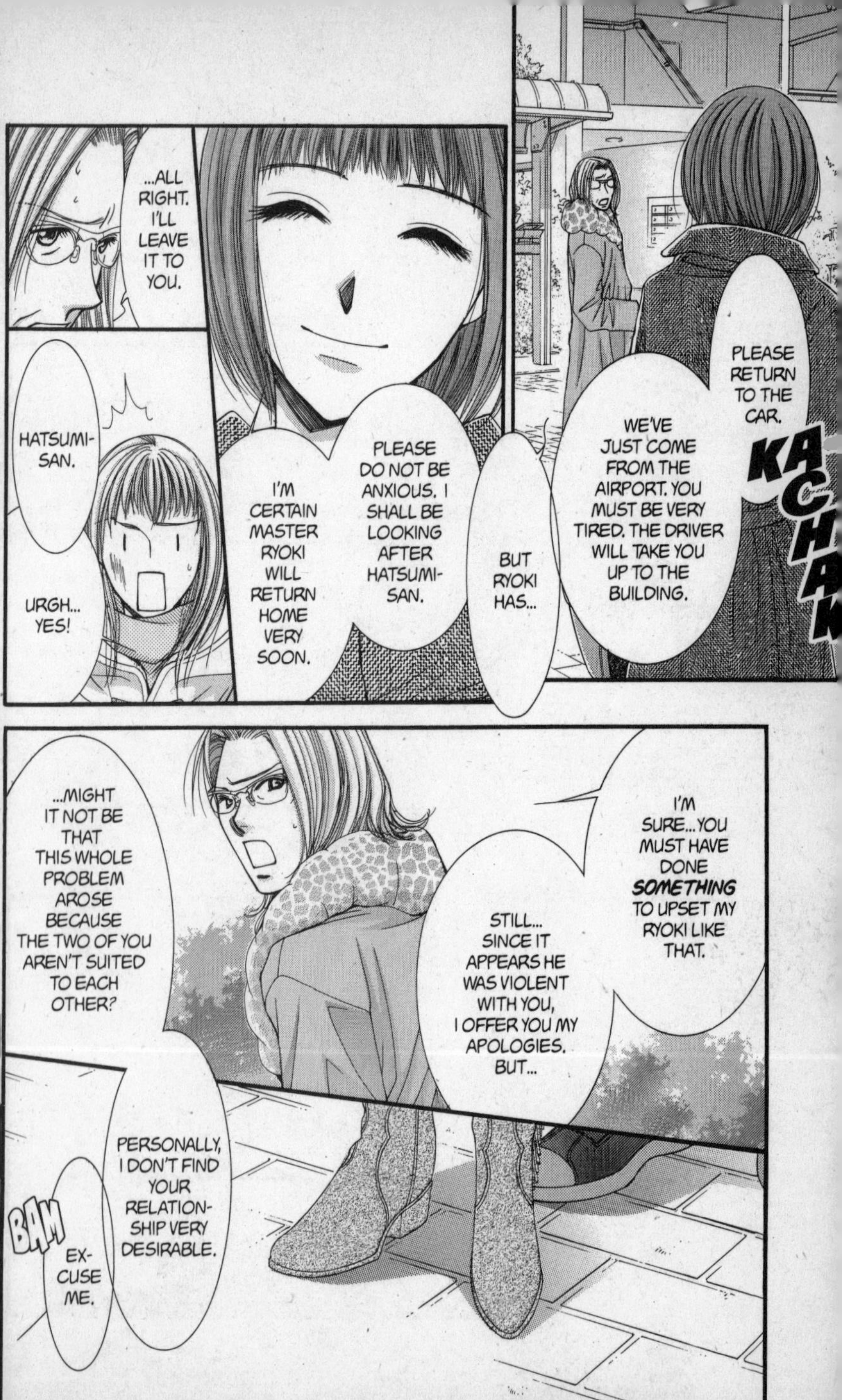
PLEASE RETURN TO THE CAR.
KACHAK
WE'VE JUST COME FROM THE AIRPORT. YOU MUST BE VERY TIRED. THE DRIVER WILL TAKE YOU UP TO THE BUILDING.
BUT RYOKI HAS...
PLEASE DO NOT BE ANXIOUS. I SHALL BE LOOKING AFTER HATSUMI-SAN.
I'M CERTAIN MASTER RYOKI WILL RETURN HOME VERY SOON.
...ALL RIGHT. I'LL LEAVE IT TO YOU.
HATSUMI-SAN.
URGH... YES!
I'M SURE...YOU MUST HAVE DONE ***SOMETHING*** TO UPSET MY RYOKI LIKE THAT.
STILL... SINCE IT APPEARS HE WAS VIOLENT WITH YOU, I OFFER YOU MY APOLOGIES. BUT...
...MIGHT IT NOT BE THAT THIS WHOLE PROBLEM AROSE BECAUSE THE TWO OF YOU AREN'T SUITED TO EACH OTHER?
PERSONALLY, I DON'T FIND YOUR RELATION-SHIP VERY DESIRABLE.
EX-CUSE ME.
BAM

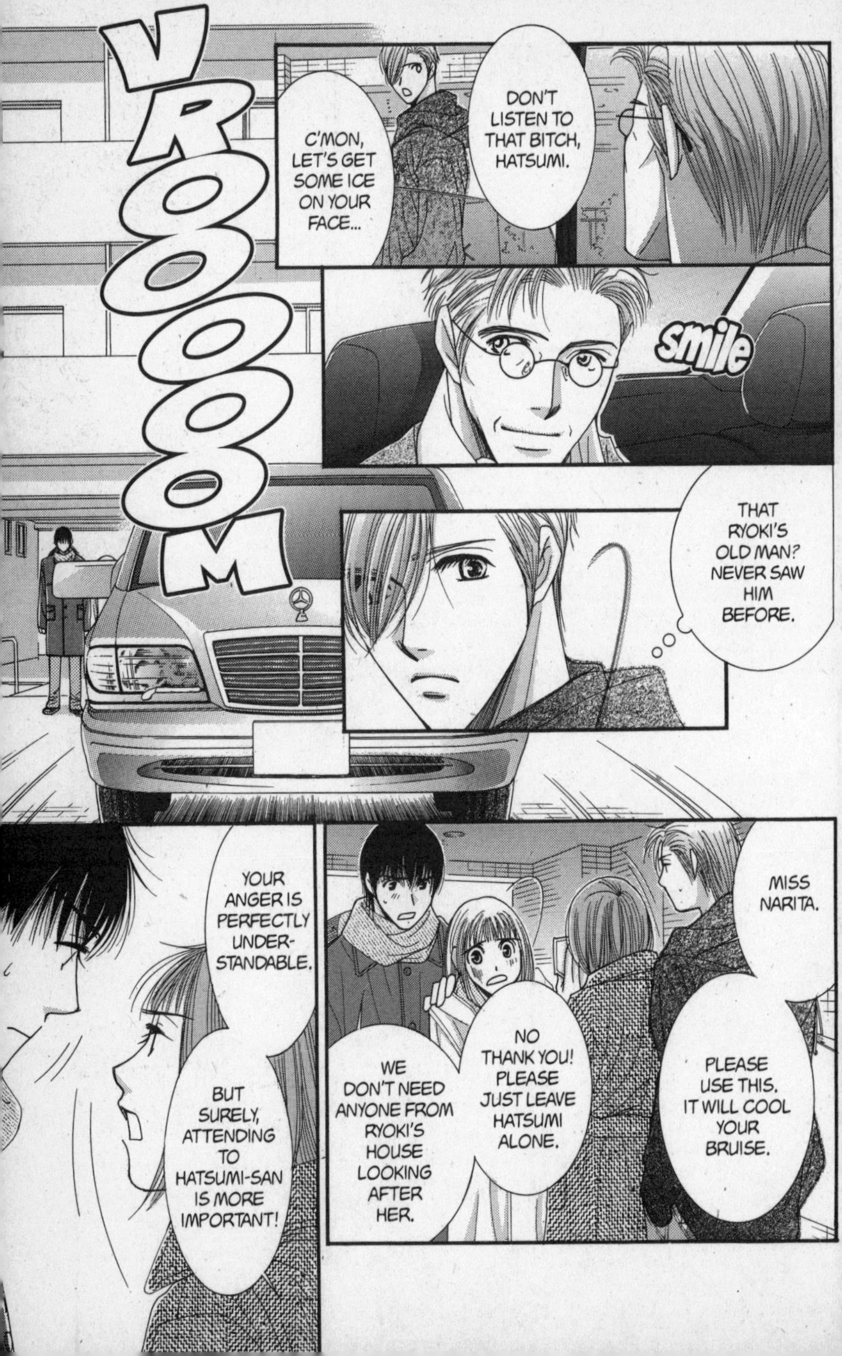
DON'T LISTEN TO THAT BITCH, HATSUMI.
C'MON, LET'S GET SOME ICE ON YOUR FACE...
smile
THAT RYOKI'S OLD MAN? NEVER SAW HIM BEFORE.
VROOOOOM
MISS NARITA.
PLEASE USE THIS. IT WILL COOL YOUR BRUISE.
NO THANK YOU! PLEASE JUST LEAVE HATSUMI ALONE.
WE DON'T NEED ANYONE FROM RYOKI'S HOUSE LOOKING AFTER HER.
YOUR ANGER IS PERFECTLY UNDER-STANDABLE.
BUT SURELY, ATTENDING TO HATSUMI-SAN IS MORE IMPORTANT!

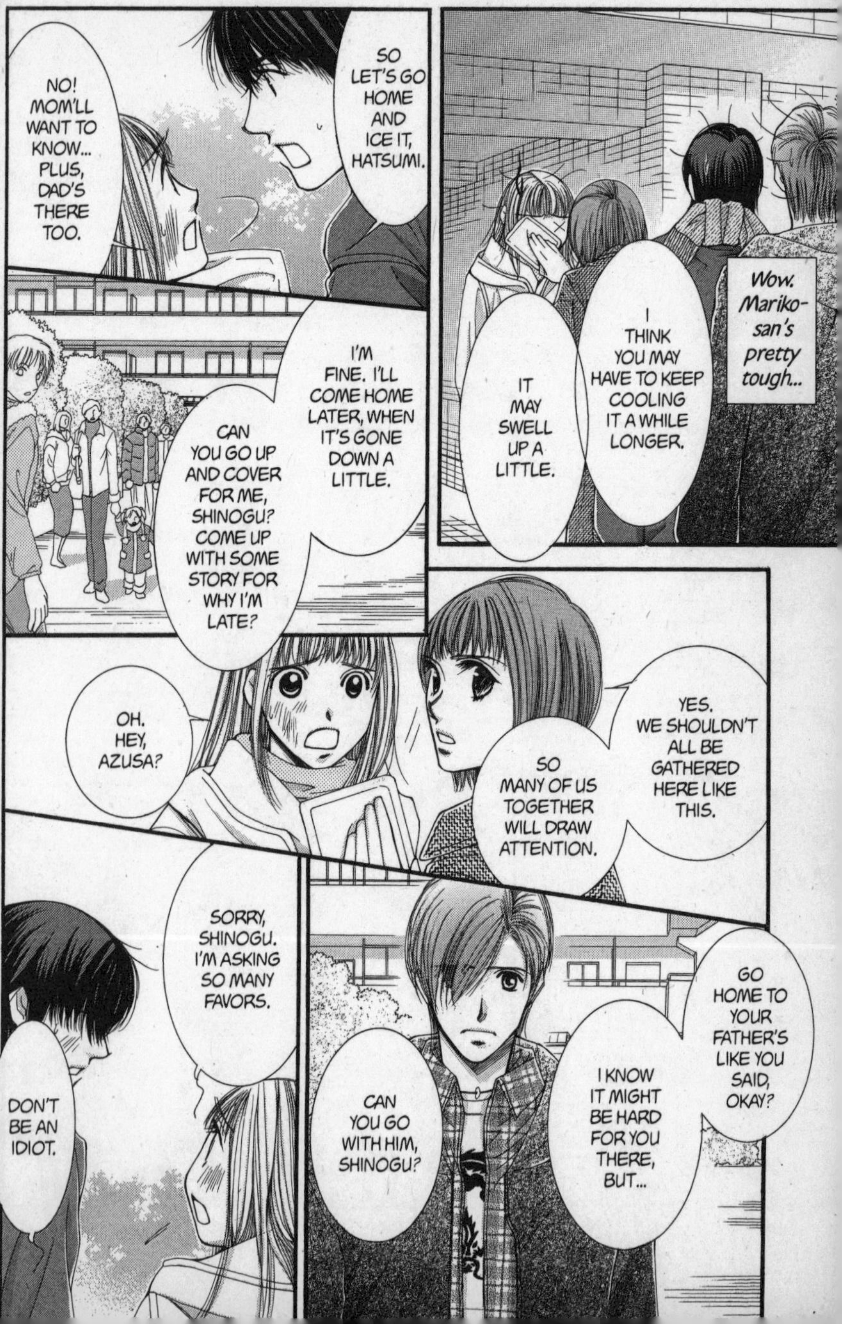
Wow. Mariko-san's pretty tough...
I THINK YOU MAY HAVE TO KEEP COOLING IT A WHILE LONGER.
IT MAY SWELL UP A LITTLE.
SO LET'S GO HOME AND ICE IT, HATSUMI.
NO! MOM'LL WANT TO KNOW... PLUS, DAD'S THERE TOO.
I'M FINE. I'LL COME HOME LATER, WHEN IT'S GONE DOWN A LITTLE.
CAN YOU GO UP AND COVER FOR ME, SHINOGU? COME UP WITH SOME STORY FOR WHY I'M LATE?
YES. WE SHOULDN'T ALL BE GATHERED HERE LIKE THIS.
SO MANY OF US TOGETHER WILL DRAW ATTENTION.
OH. HEY, AZUSA?
GO HOME TO YOUR FATHER'S LIKE YOU SAID, OKAY?
I KNOW IT MIGHT BE HARD FOR YOU THERE, BUT...
CAN YOU GO WITH HIM, SHINOGU?
SORRY, SHINOGU. I'M ASKING SO MANY FAVORS.
DON'T BE AN IDIOT.

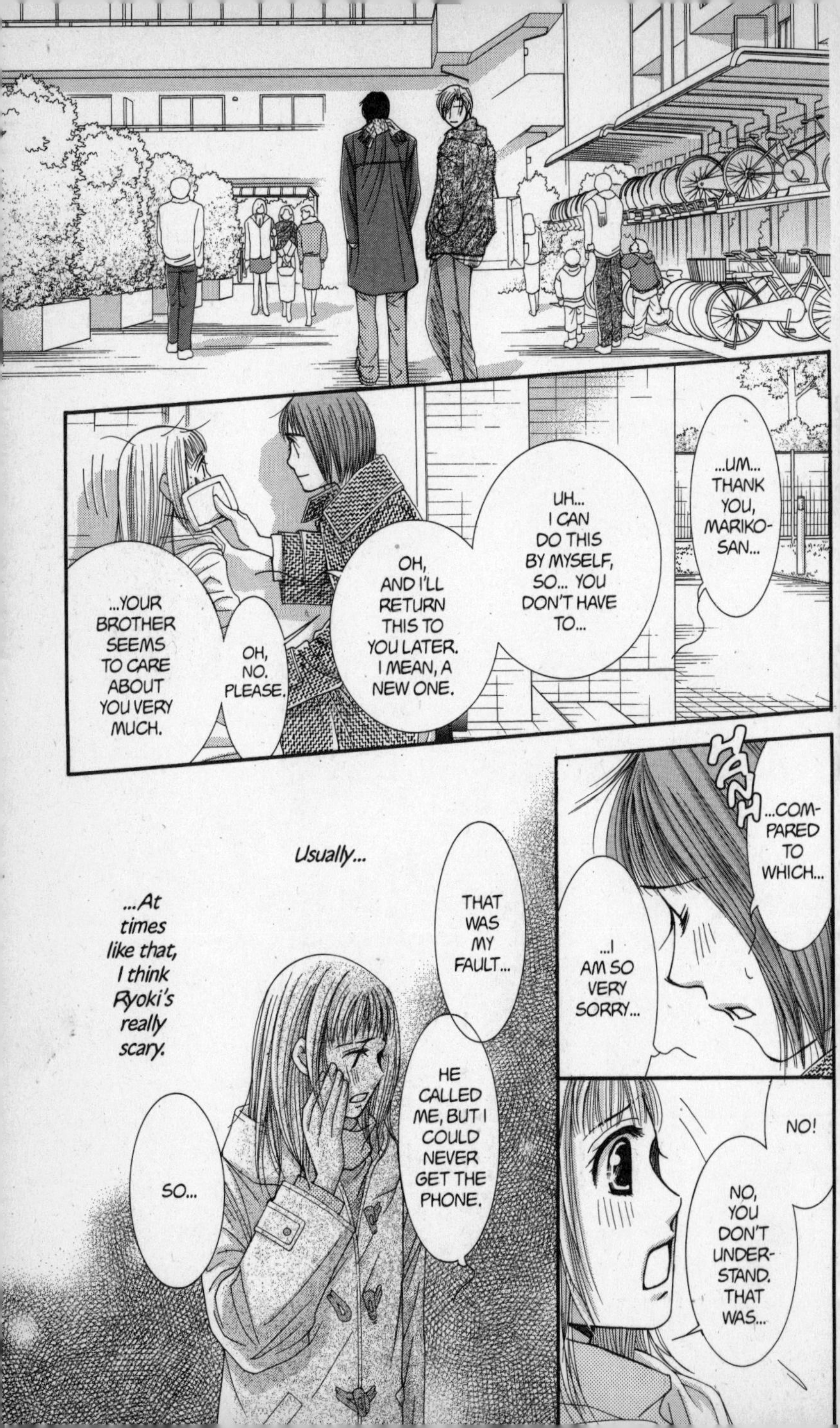

...UM... THANK YOU, MARIKO-SAN...
UH... I CAN DO THIS BY MYSELF, SO... YOU DON'T HAVE TO...
OH, AND I'LL RETURN THIS TO YOU LATER. I MEAN, A NEW ONE.
OH, NO. PLEASE.
...YOUR BROTHER SEEMS TO CARE ABOUT YOU VERY MUCH.
...COMPARED TO WHICH...
...I AM SO VERY SORRY...
NO!
NO, YOU DON'T UNDERSTAND. THAT WAS...
THAT WAS MY FAULT...
HE CALLED ME, BUT I COULD NEVER GET THE PHONE.
SO...
Usually...
...At times like that, I think Ryoki's really scary.

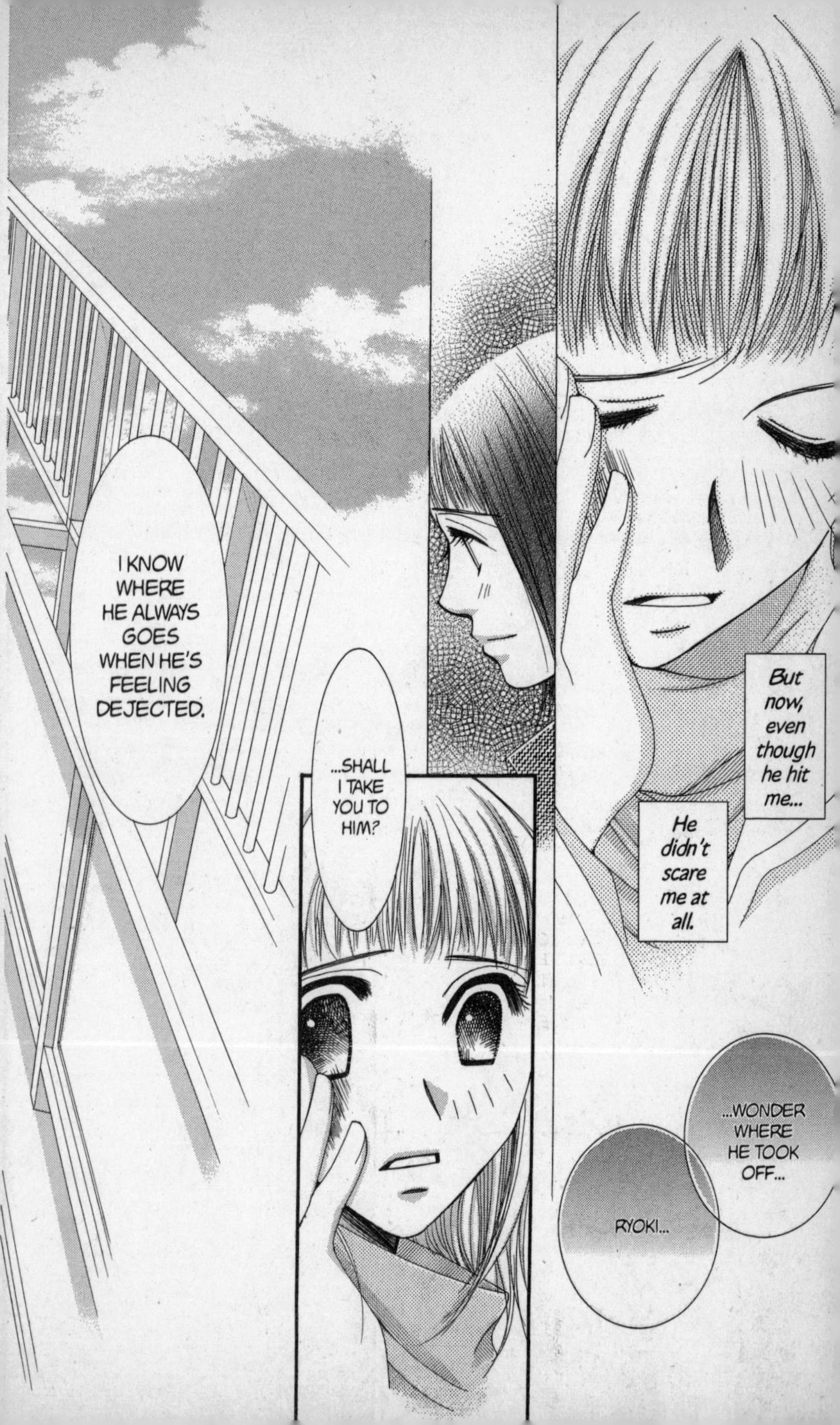
But now, even though he hit me...
He didn't scare me at all.
...WONDER WHERE HE TOOK OFF...
RYOKI...
...SHALL I TAKE YOU TO HIM?
I KNOW WHERE HE ALWAYS GOES WHEN HE'S FEELING DEJECTED.

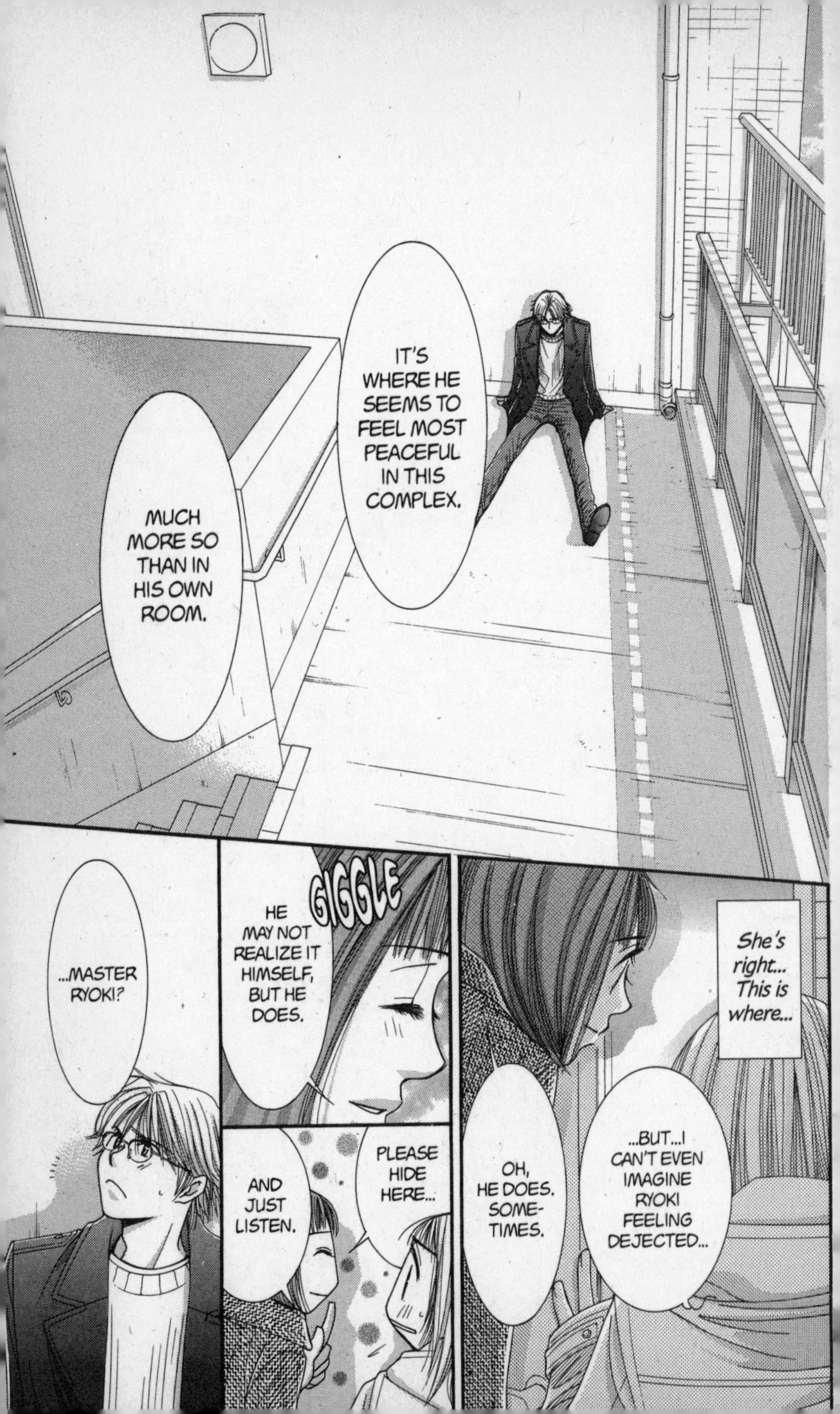
IT'S WHERE HE SEEMS TO FEEL MOST PEACEFUL IN THIS COMPLEX.
MUCH MORE SO THAN IN HIS OWN ROOM.
She's right... This is where...
...BUT...I CAN'T EVEN IMAGINE RYOKI FEELING DEJECTED...
OH, HE DOES. SOME-TIMES.
GIGGLE
HE MAY NOT REALIZE IT HIMSELF, BUT HE DOES.
PLEASE HIDE HERE...
AND JUST LISTEN.
...MASTER RYOKI?

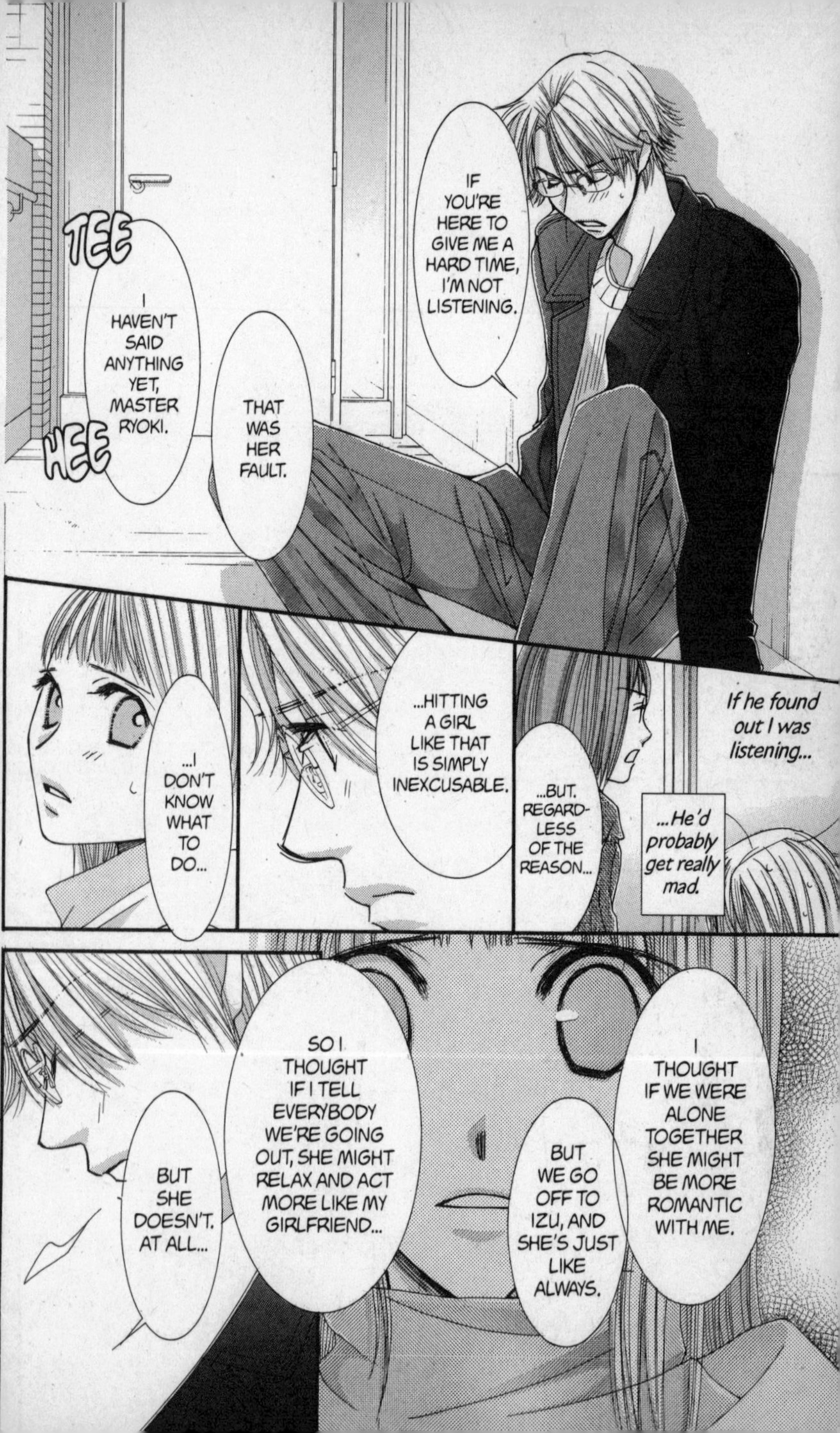
IF YOU'RE HERE TO GIVE ME A HARD TIME, I'M NOT LISTENING.
THAT WAS HER FAULT.
I HAVEN'T SAID ANYTHING YET, MASTER RYOKI.
TEE HEE
If he found out I was listening...
...He'd probably get really mad.
...BUT. REGARDLESS OF THE REASON...
...HITTING A GIRL LIKE THAT IS SIMPLY INEXCUSABLE.
...I DON'T KNOW WHAT TO DO...
I THOUGHT IF WE WERE ALONE TOGETHER SHE MIGHT BE MORE ROMANTIC WITH ME.
BUT WE GO OFF TO IZU, AND SHE'S JUST LIKE ALWAYS.
SO I THOUGHT IF I TELL EVERYBODY WE'RE GOING OUT, SHE MIGHT RELAX AND ACT MORE LIKE MY GIRLFRIEND...
BUT SHE DOESN'T. AT ALL...

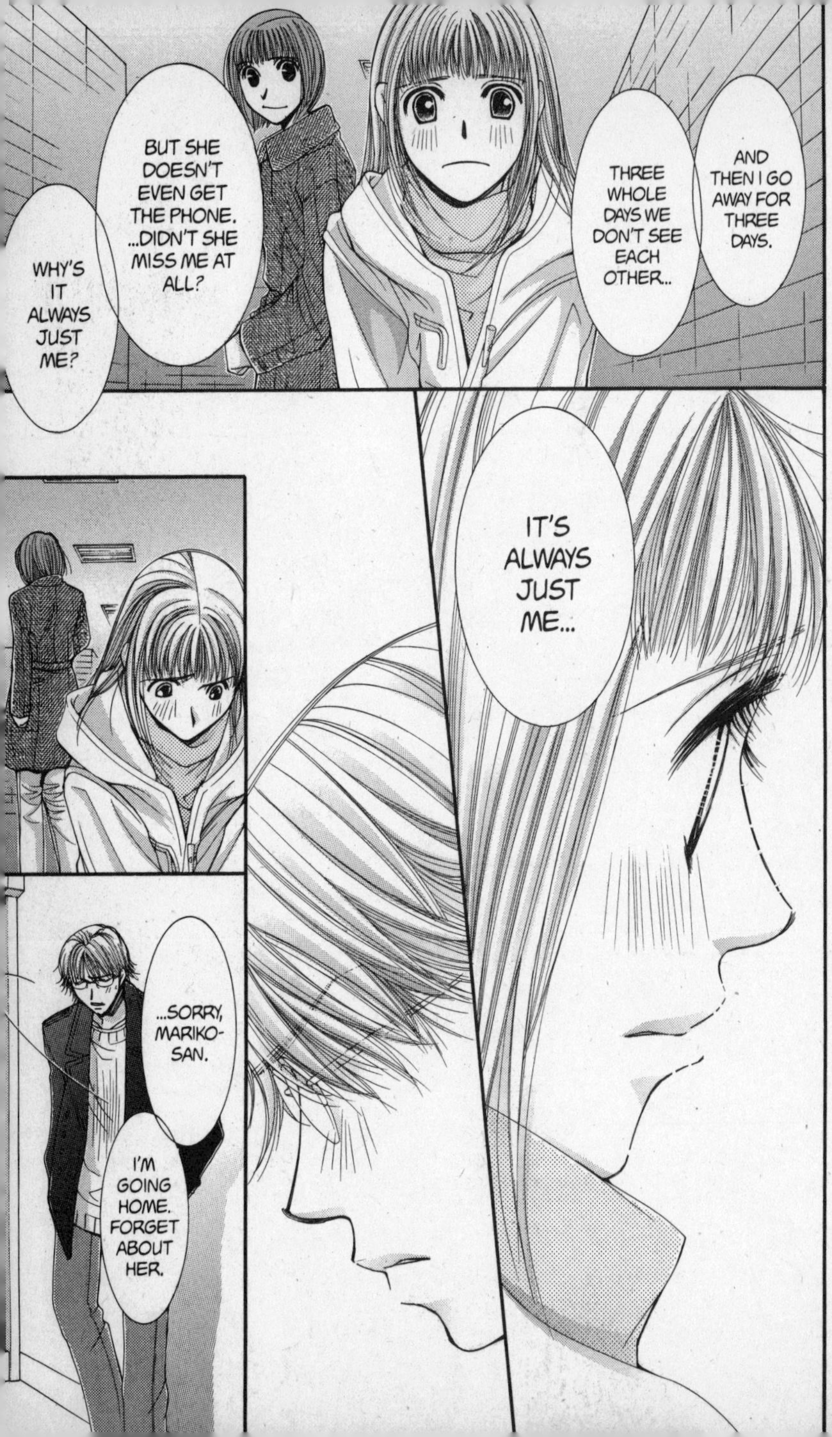
AND THEN I GO AWAY FOR THREE DAYS.
THREE WHOLE DAYS WE DON'T SEE EACH OTHER...
BUT SHE DOESN'T EVEN GET THE PHONE. ...DIDN'T SHE MISS ME AT ALL?
WHY'S IT ALWAYS JUST ME?
IT'S ALWAYS JUST ME...
...SORRY, MARIKO-SAN.
I'M GOING HOME. FORGET ABOUT HER.

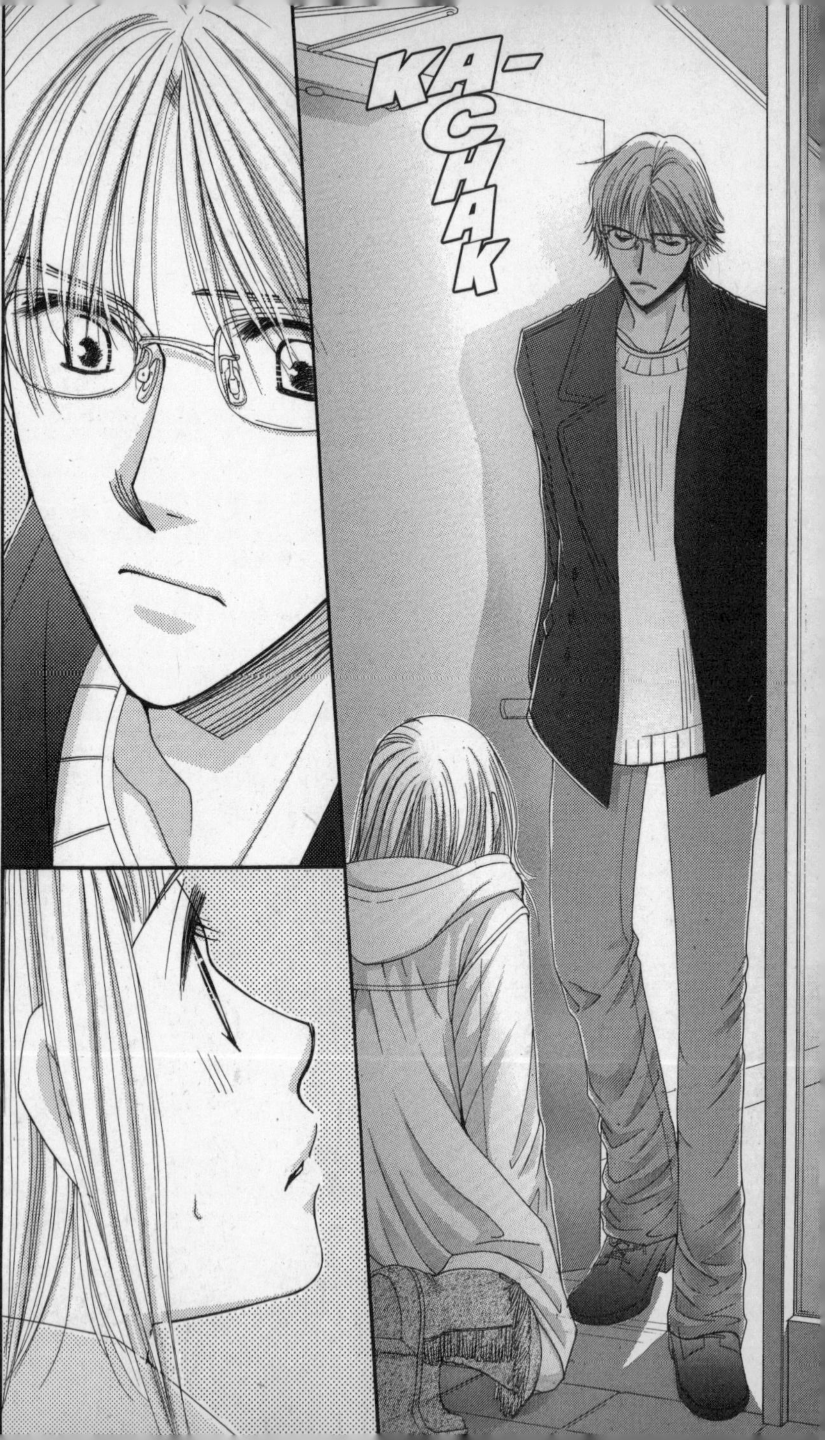
KA-CHAK

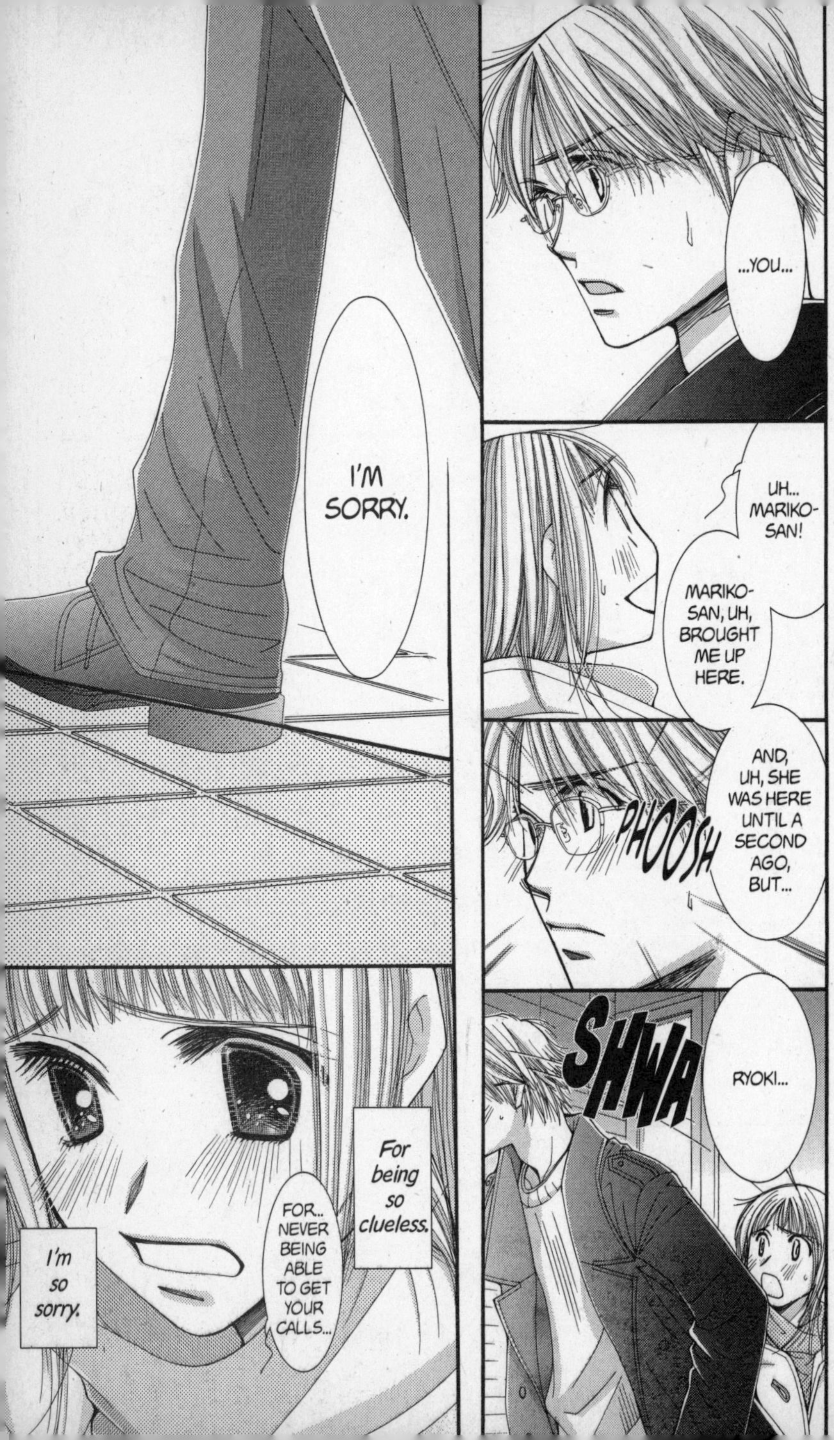
...YOU...
UH... MARIKO-SAN!
MARIKO-SAN, UH, BROUGHT ME UP HERE.
PHOOSH
AND, UH, SHE WAS HERE UNTIL A SECOND AGO, BUT...
SHWA
RYOKI...
I'M SORRY.
For being so clueless.
FOR... NEVER BEING ABLE TO GET YOUR CALLS...
I'm so sorry.

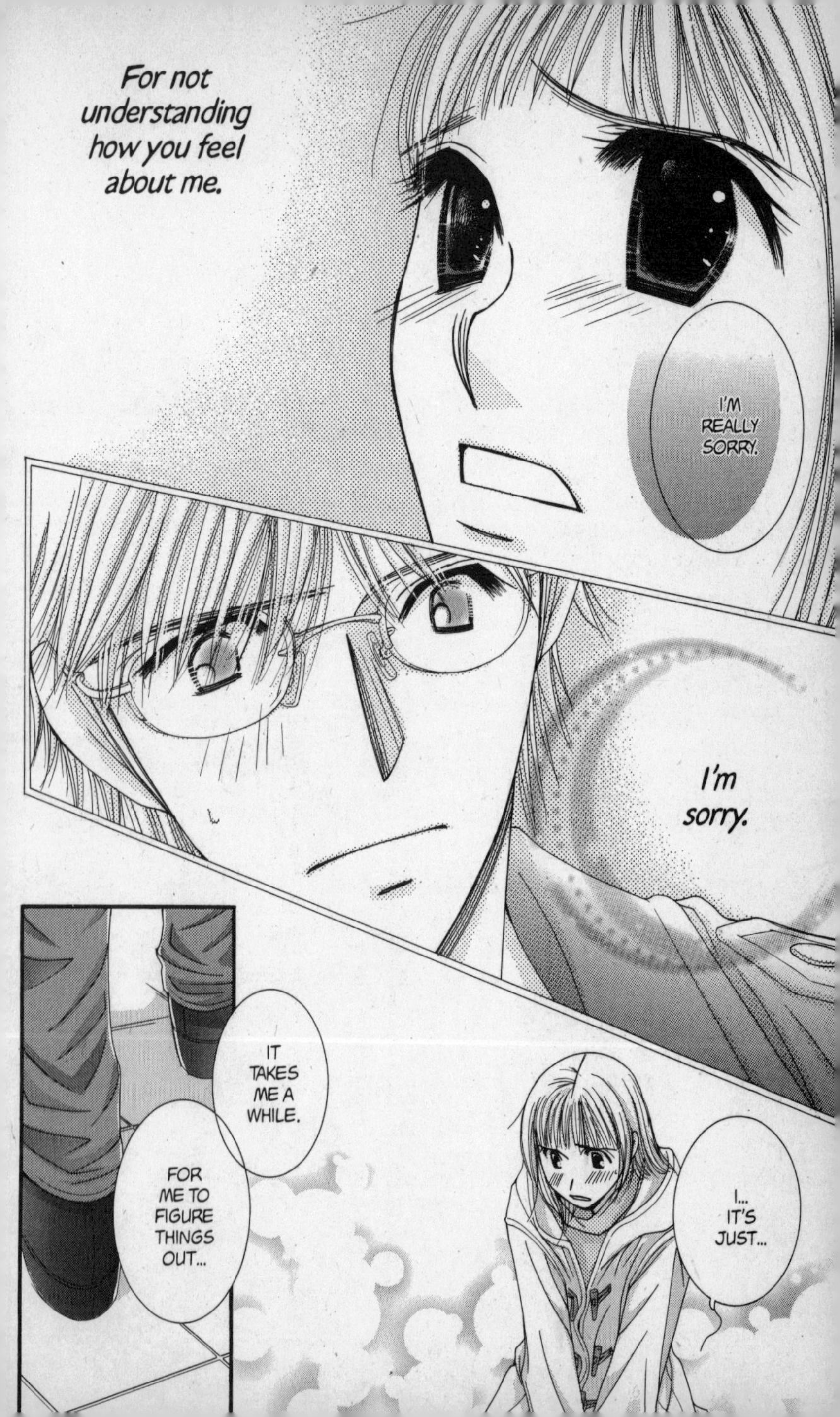
I'M REALLY SORRY.
For not understanding how you feel about me.
I'm sorry.
I... IT'S JUST...
IT TAKES ME A WHILE.
FOR ME TO FIGURE THINGS OUT...

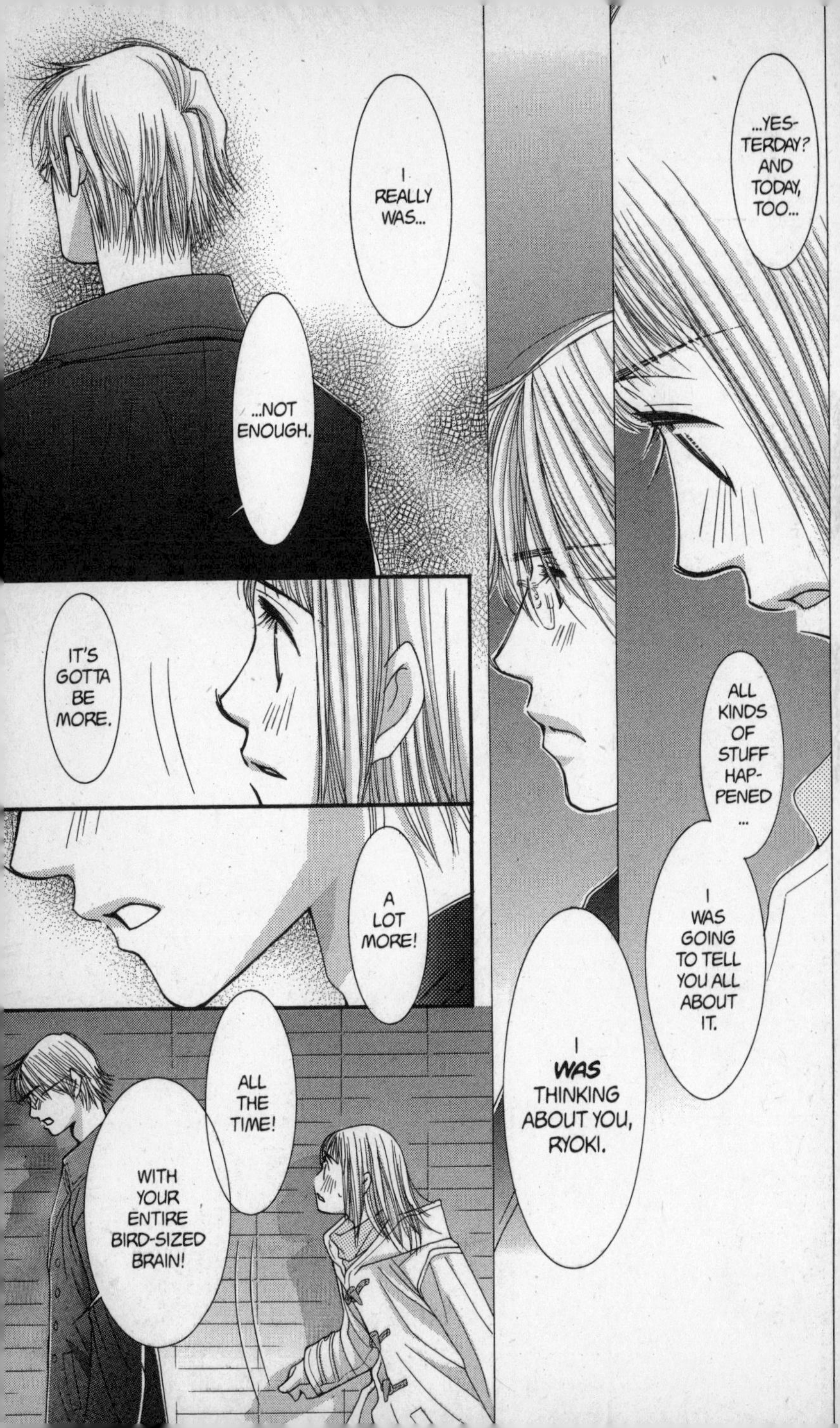
...YES-TERDAY? AND TODAY, TOO...
ALL KINDS OF STUFF HAP-PENED ...
I WAS GOING TO TELL YOU ALL ABOUT IT.
I *WAS* THINKING ABOUT YOU, RYOKI.
I REALLY WAS...
...NOT ENOUGH.
IT'S GOTTA BE MORE.
A LOT MORE!
ALL THE TIME!
WITH YOUR ENTIRE BIRD-SIZED BRAIN!

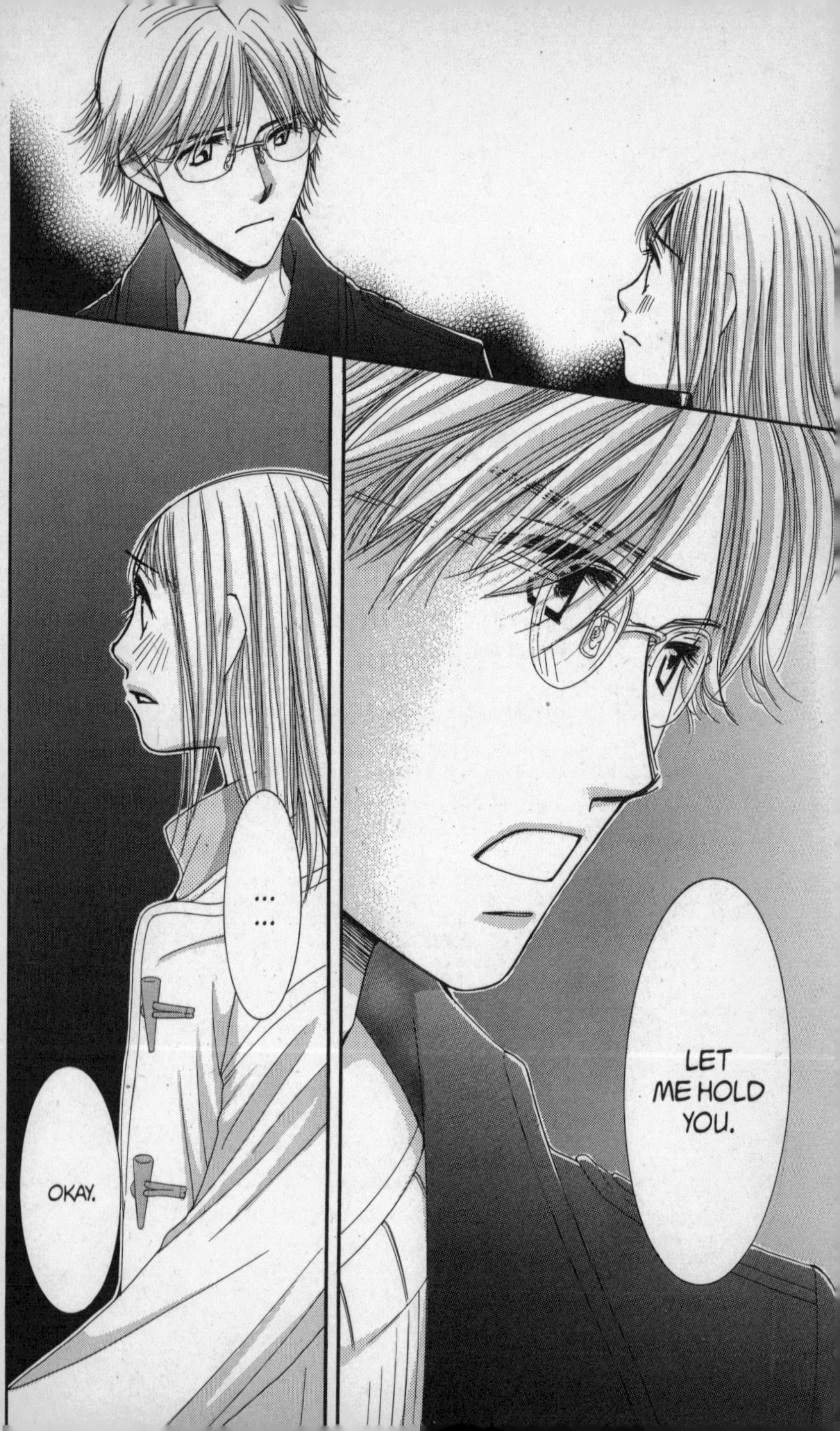
LET ME HOLD YOU.
... ...
OKAY.

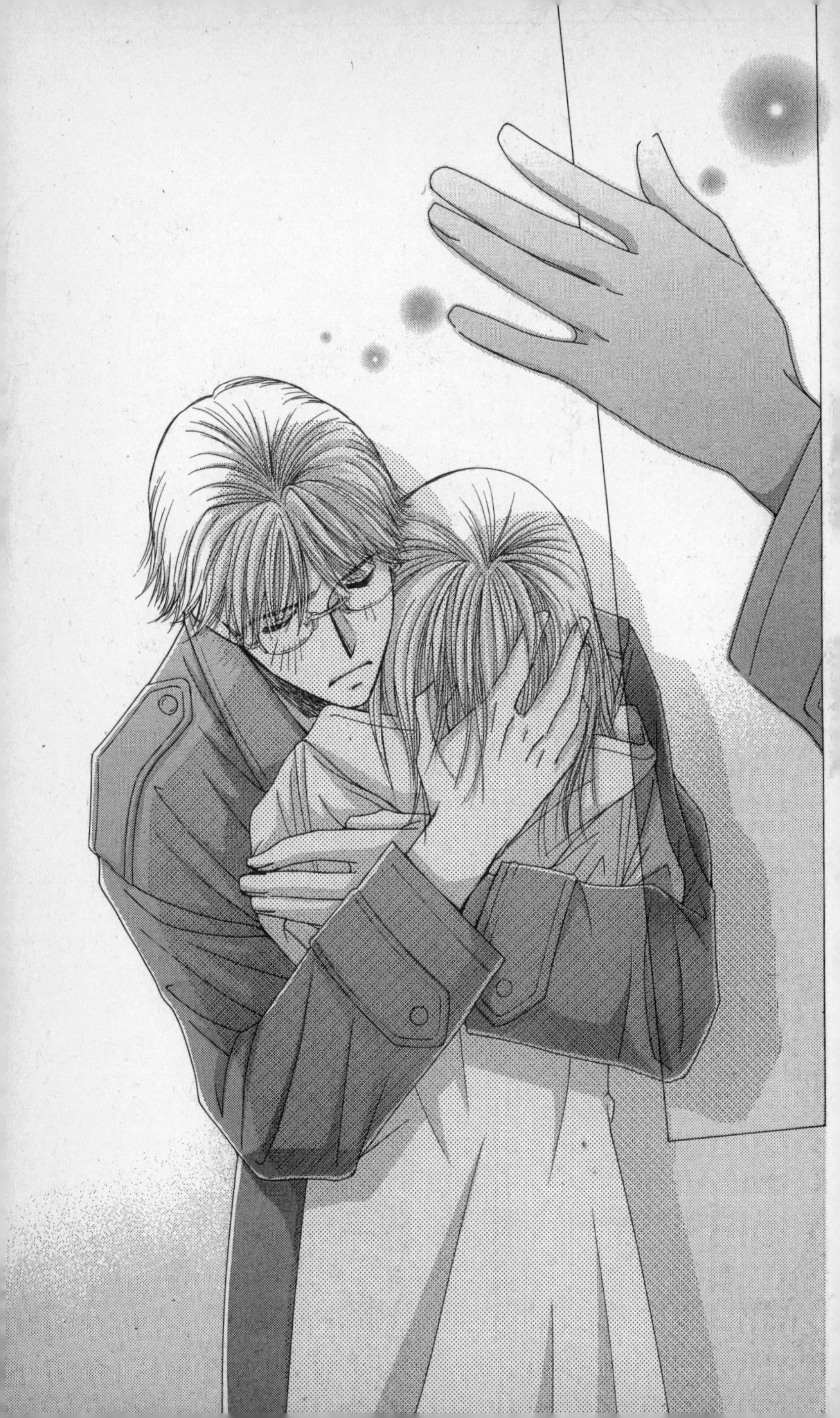

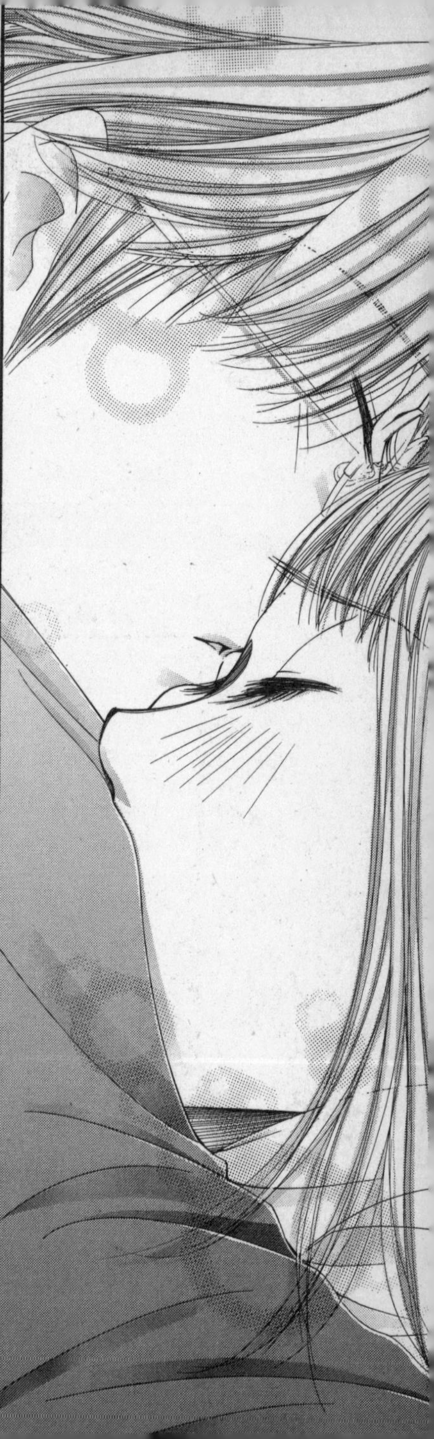

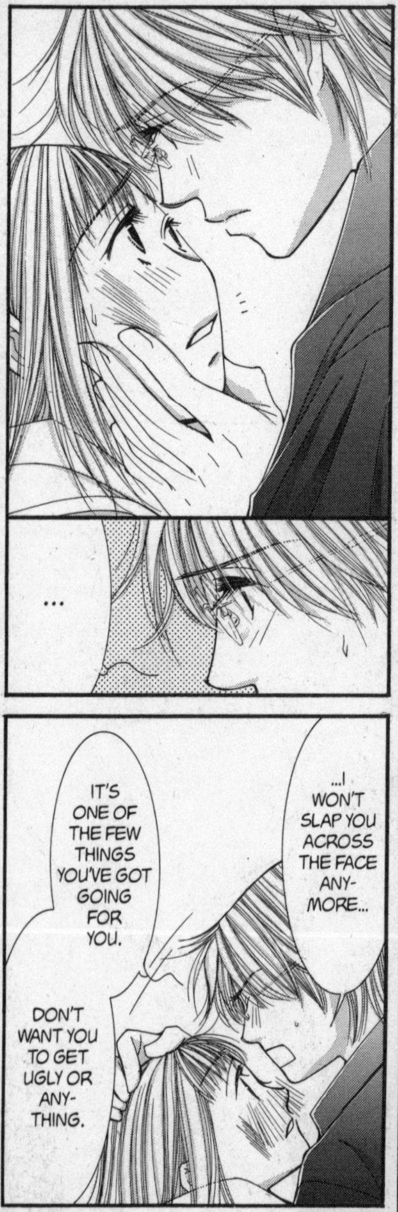
...
...I WON'T SLAP YOU ACROSS THE FACE ANY-MORE...
IT'S ONE OF THE FEW THINGS YOU'VE GOT GOING FOR YOU.
DON'T WANT YOU TO GET UGLY OR ANY-THING.

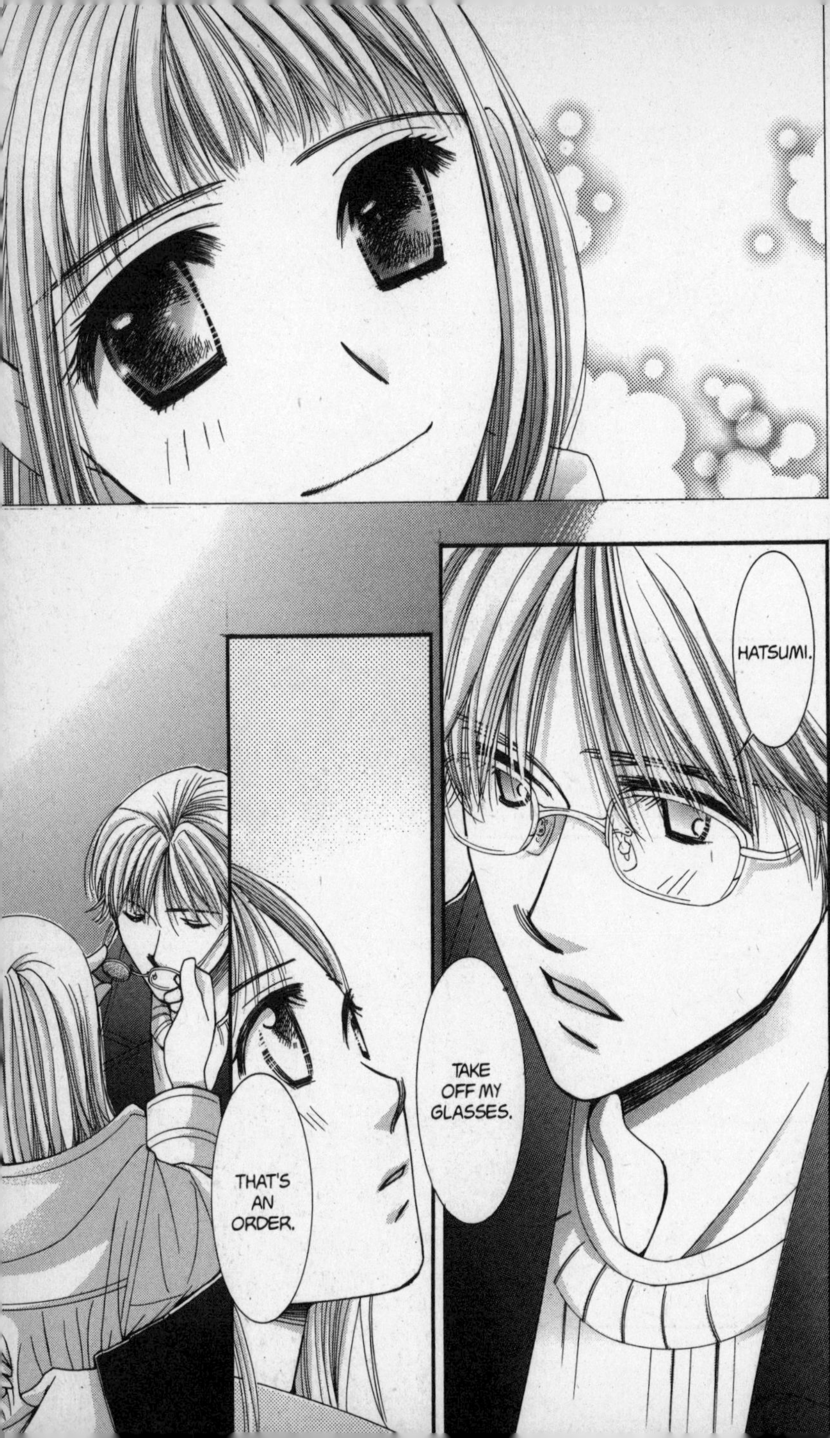
HATSUMI.
TAKE OFF MY GLASSES.
THAT'S AN ORDER.

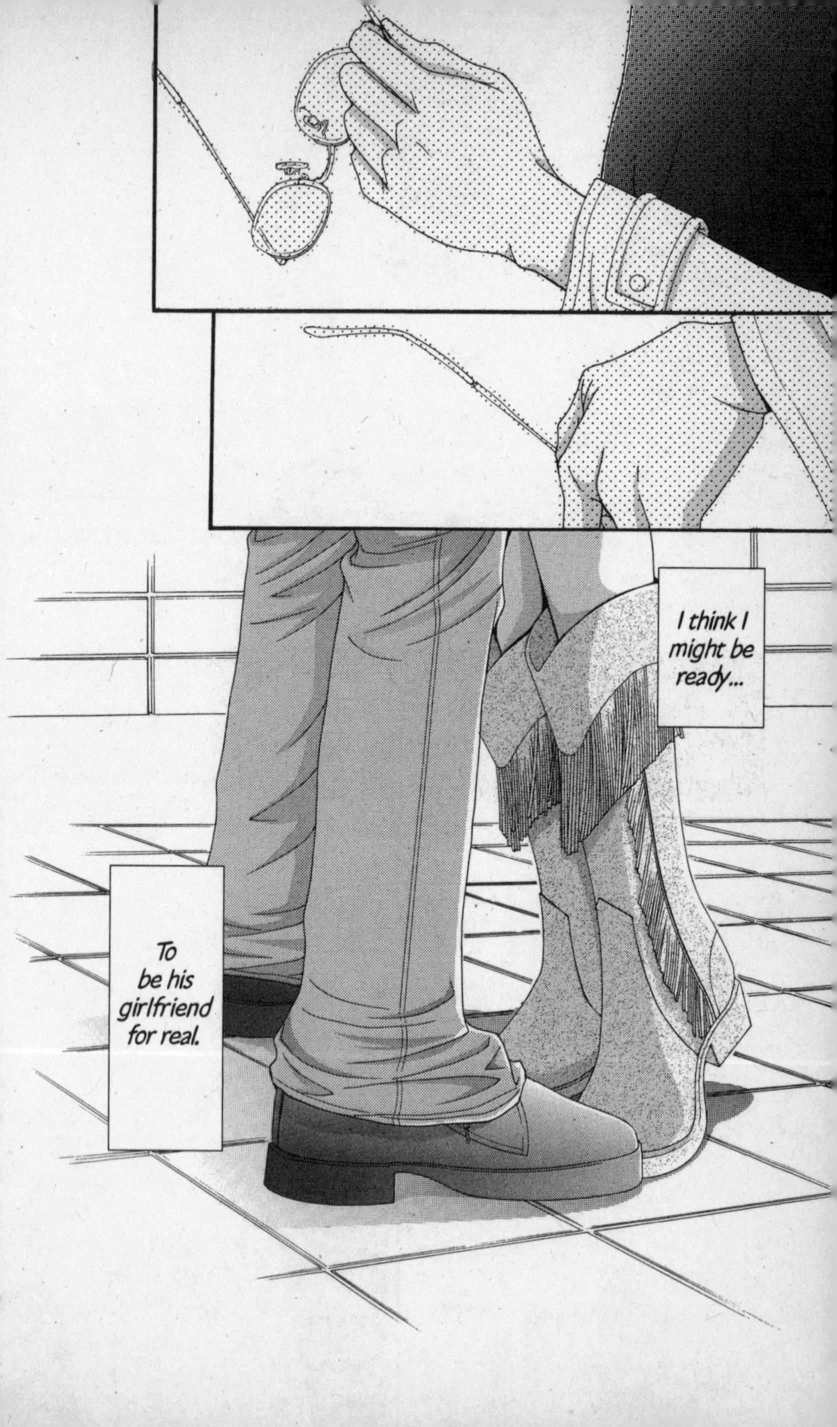
I think I might be ready...
To be his girlfriend for real.

hot gimmick

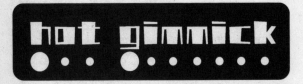

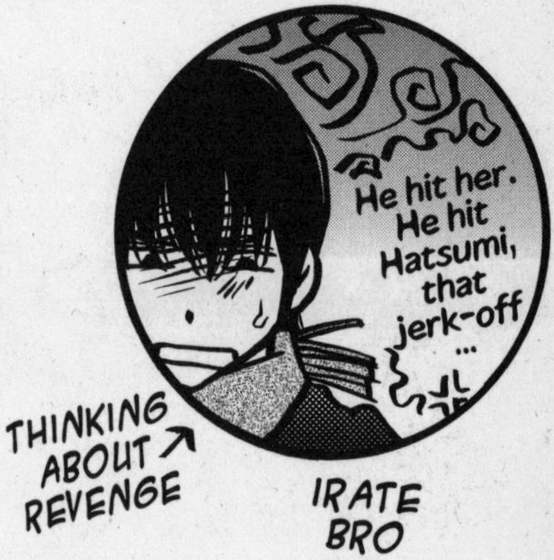
He hit her. He hit Hatsumi, that jerk-off ...
THINKING ABOUT REVENGE
IRATE BRO

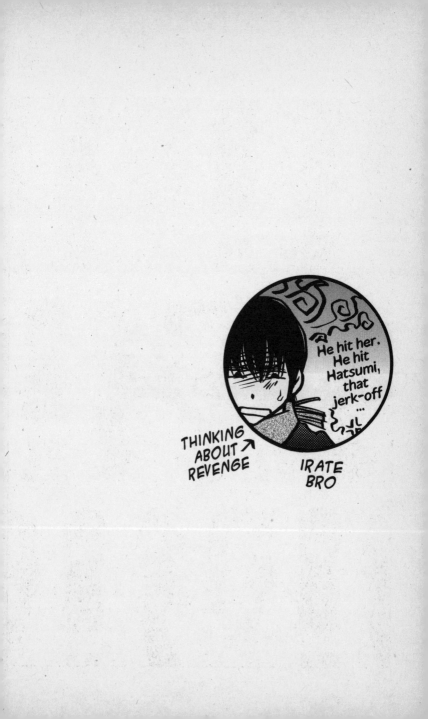

Chapter 34

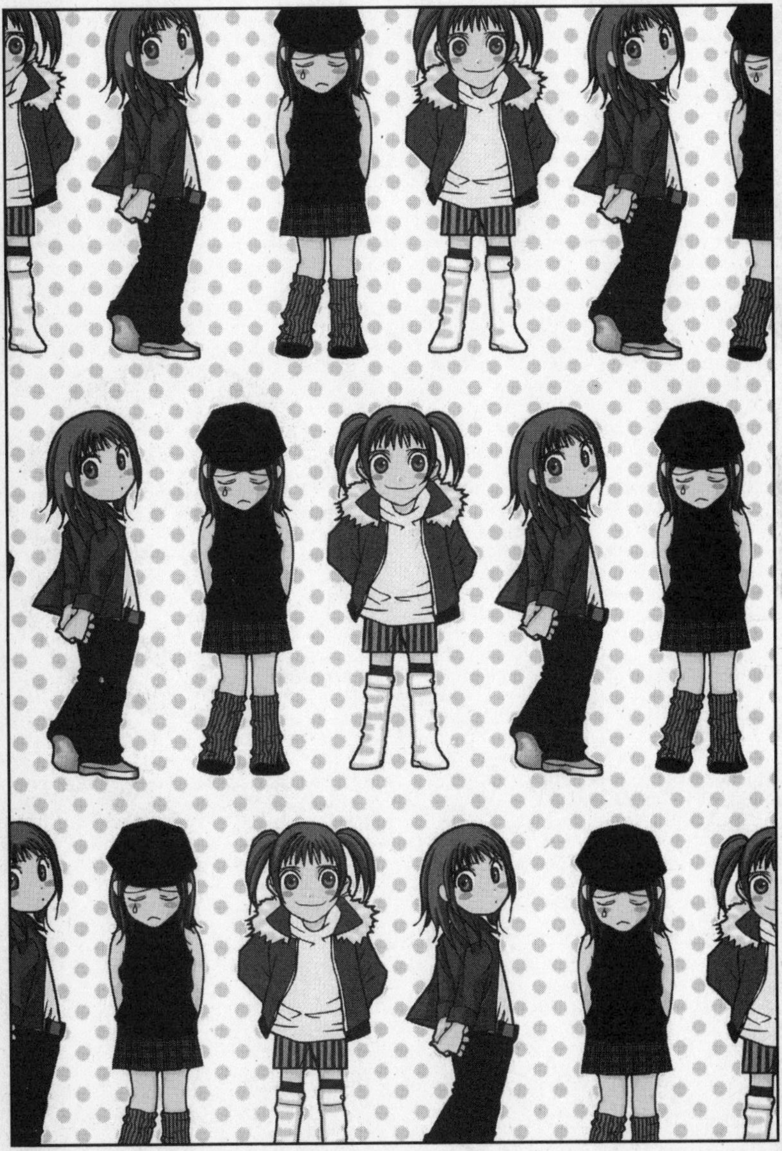

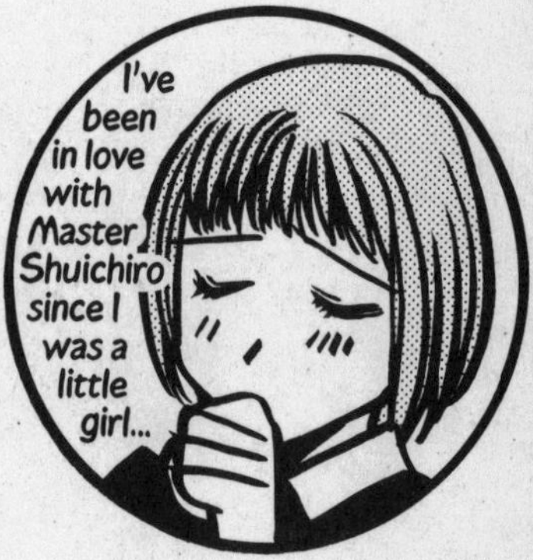
I've been in love with Master Shuichiro since I was a little girl...

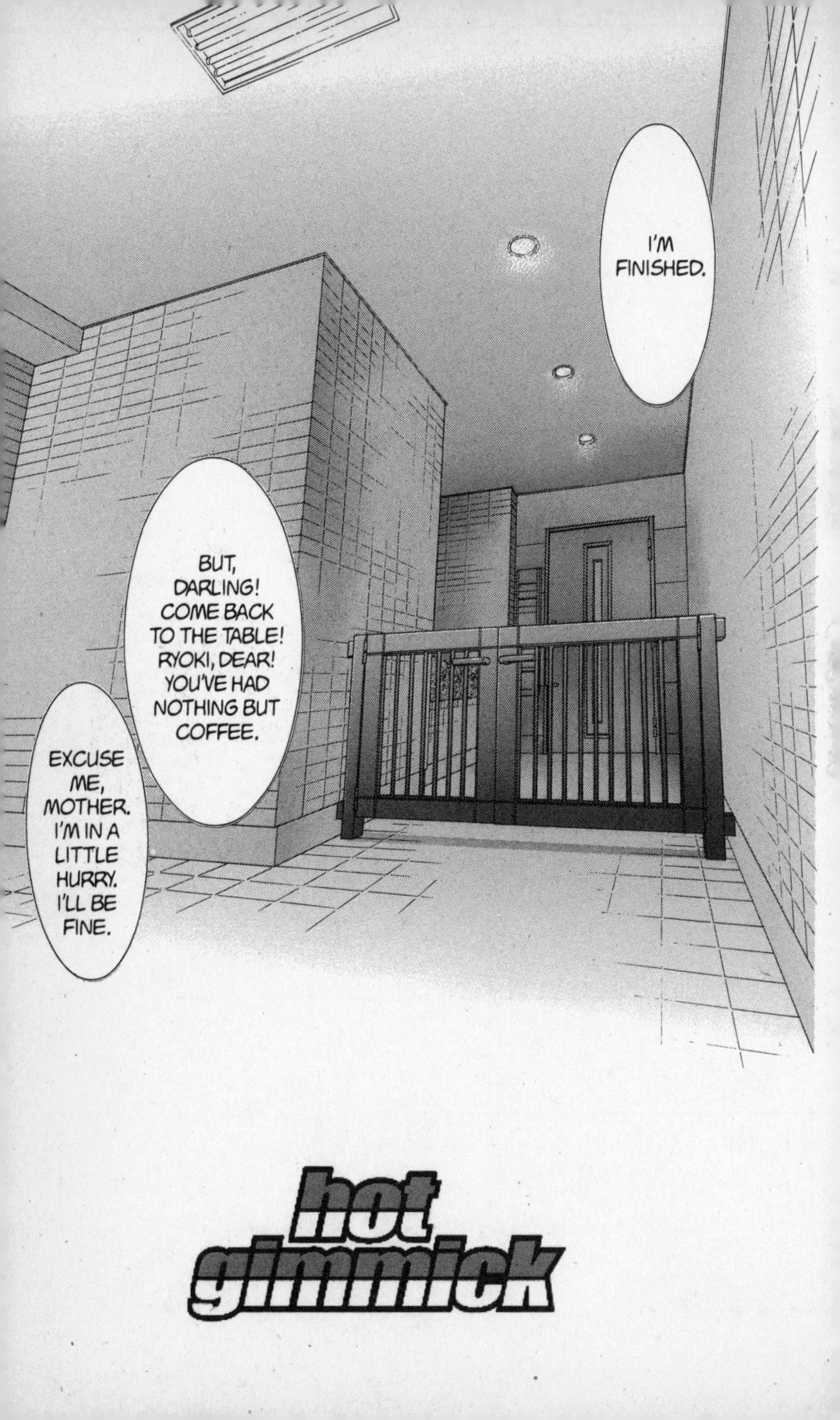
I'M FINISHED.
BUT, DARLING! COME BACK TO THE TABLE! RYOKI, DEAR! YOU'VE HAD NOTHING BUT COFFEE.
EXCUSE ME, MOTHER. I'M IN A LITTLE HURRY. I'LL BE FINE.
hot gimmick

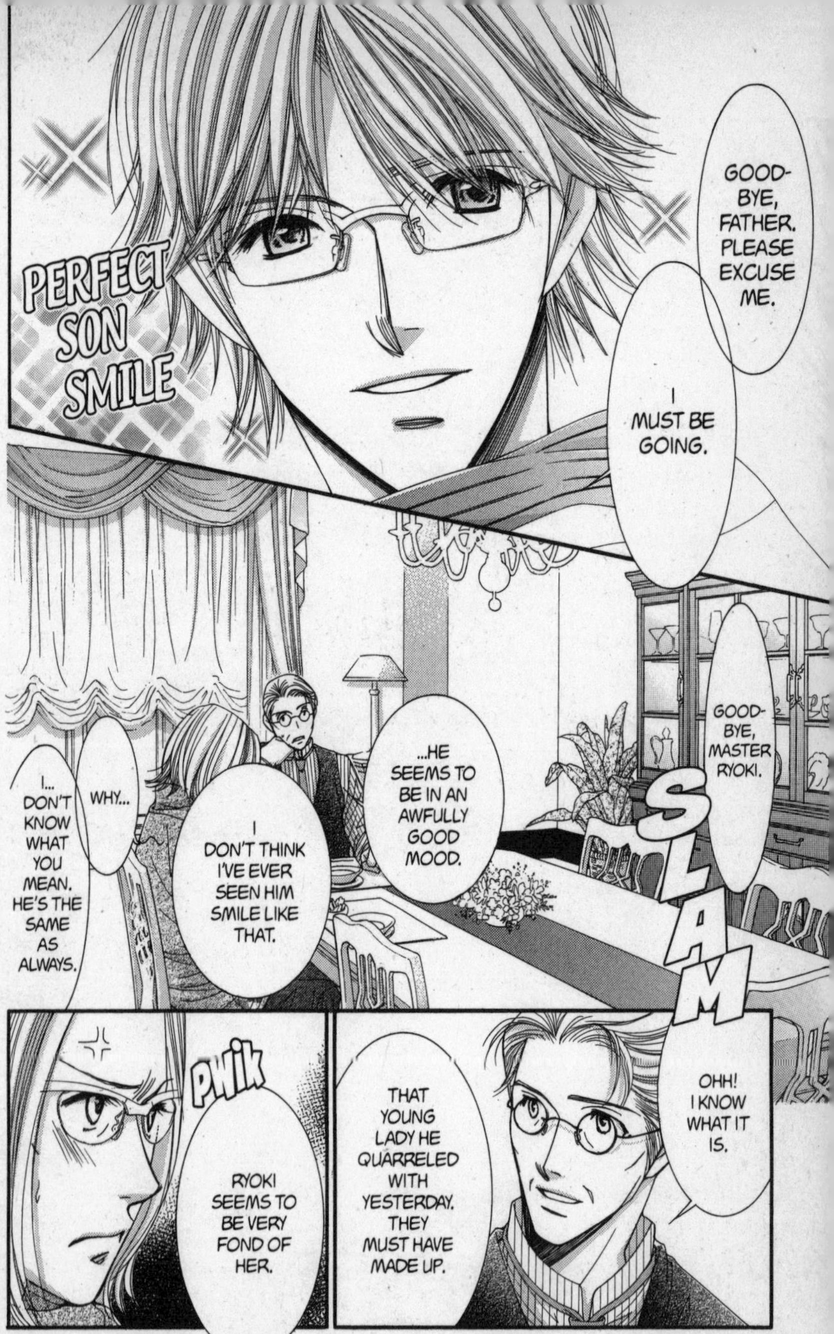

GOOD-BYE, FATHER. PLEASE EXCUSE ME.
I MUST BE GOING.
PERFECT SON SMILE
GOOD-BYE, MASTER RYOKI.
SLAM
...HE SEEMS TO BE IN AN AWFULLY GOOD MOOD.
I DON'T THINK I'VE EVER SEEN HIM SMILE LIKE THAT.
WHY...
I... DON'T KNOW WHAT YOU MEAN. HE'S THE SAME AS ALWAYS.
OHH! I KNOW WHAT IT IS.
THAT YOUNG LADY HE QUARRELED WITH YESTERDAY. THEY MUST HAVE MADE UP.
PWIK
RYOKI SEEMS TO BE VERY FOND OF HER.

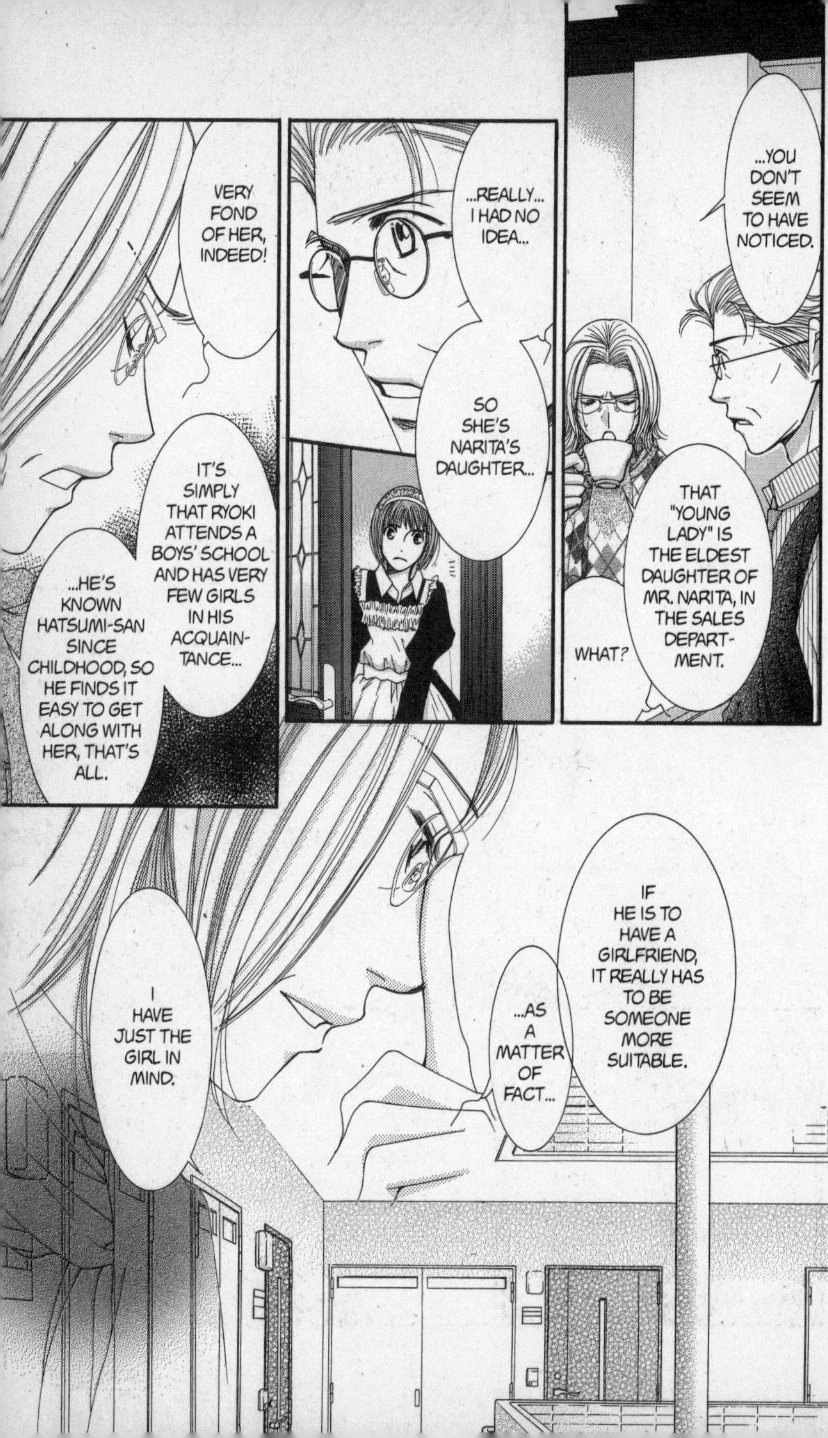
...YOU DON'T SEEM TO HAVE NOTICED.
THAT "YOUNG LADY" IS THE ELDEST DAUGHTER OF MR. NARITA, IN THE SALES DEPARTMENT.
WHAT?
...REALLY... I HAD NO IDEA...
SO SHE'S NARITA'S DAUGHTER...
VERY FOND OF HER, INDEED!
IT'S SIMPLY THAT RYOKI ATTENDS A BOYS' SCHOOL AND HAS VERY FEW GIRLS IN HIS ACQUAIN-TANCE...
...HE'S KNOWN HATSUMI-SAN SINCE CHILDHOOD, SO HE FINDS IT EASY TO GET ALONG WITH HER, THAT'S ALL.
IF HE IS TO HAVE A GIRLFRIEND, IT REALLY HAS TO BE SOMEONE MORE SUITABLE.
...AS A MATTER OF FACT...
I HAVE JUST THE GIRL IN MIND.

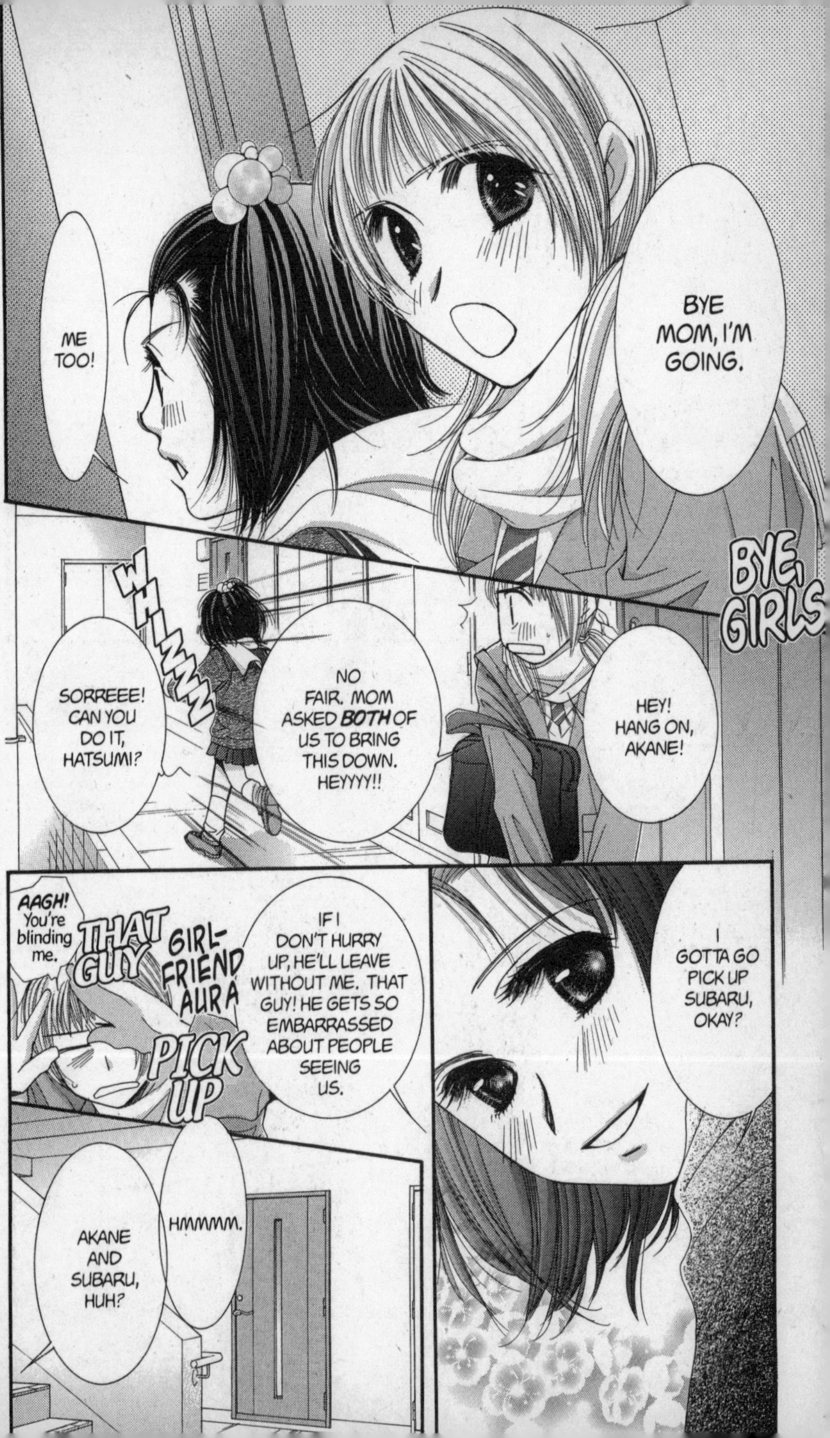
BYE MOM, I'M GOING.
ME TOO!
BYE, GIRLS
HEY! HANG ON, AKANE!
NO FAIR. MOM ASKED **BOTH** OF US TO BRING THIS DOWN. HEYYYY!!
WHINNNN
SORREEE! CAN YOU DO IT, HATSUMI?
I GOTTA GO PICK UP SUBARU, OKAY?
IF I DON'T HURRY UP, HE'LL LEAVE WITHOUT ME. THAT GUY! HE GETS SO EMBARRASSED ABOUT PEOPLE SEEING US.
GIRL-FRIEND AURA
PICK UP
THAT GUY
AAGH! You're blinding me.
HMMMM.
AKANE AND SUBARU, HUH?

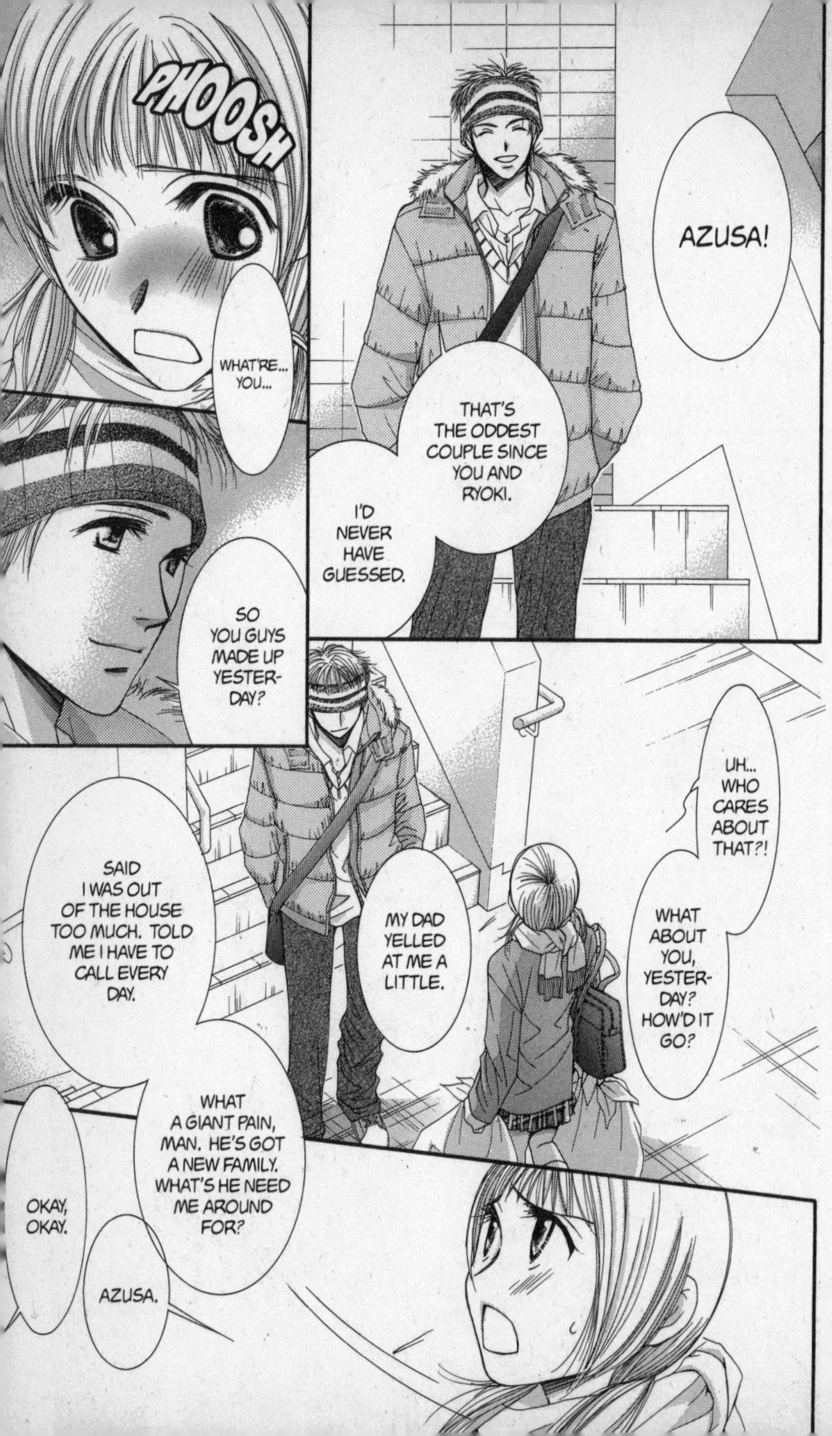
AZUSA!
THAT'S THE ODDEST COUPLE SINCE YOU AND RYOKI.
I'D NEVER HAVE GUESSED.
PHOOSH
WHAT'RE... YOU...
SO YOU GUYS MADE UP YESTER-DAY?
UH... WHO CARES ABOUT THAT?!
WHAT ABOUT YOU, YESTER-DAY? HOW'D IT GO?
MY DAD YELLED AT ME A LITTLE.
SAID I WAS OUT OF THE HOUSE TOO MUCH. TOLD ME I HAVE TO CALL EVERY DAY.
WHAT A GIANT PAIN, MAN. HE'S GOT A NEW FAMILY. WHAT'S HE NEED ME AROUND FOR?
OKAY, OKAY.
AZUSA.

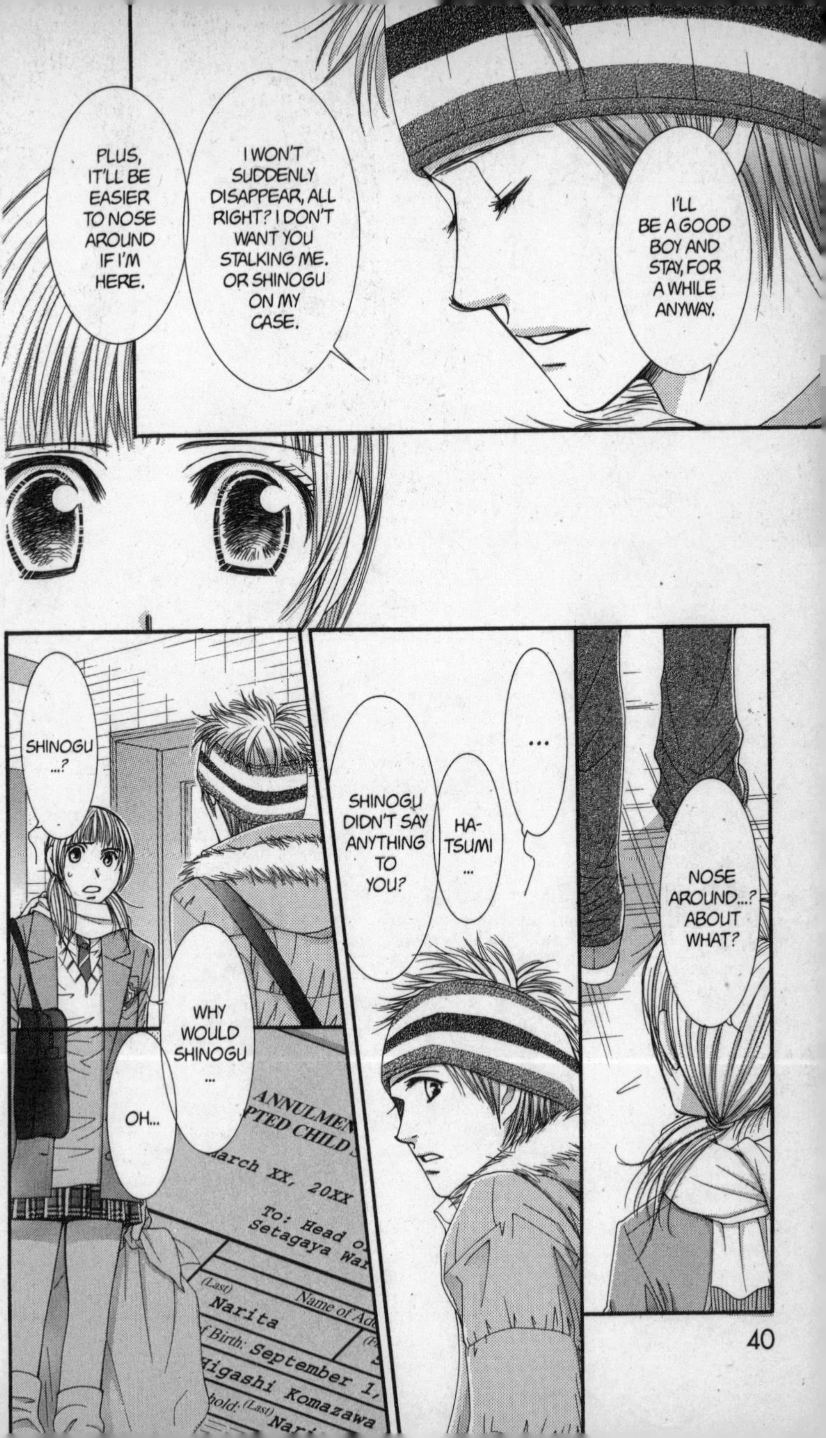
I'LL BE A GOOD BOY AND STAY, FOR A WHILE ANYWAY.
I WON'T SUDDENLY DISAPPEAR, ALL RIGHT? I DON'T WANT YOU STALKING ME. OR SHINOGU ON MY CASE.
PLUS, IT'LL BE EASIER TO NOSE AROUND IF I'M HERE.
NOSE AROUND...? ABOUT WHAT?
...
HA-TSUMI...
SHINOGU DIDN'T SAY ANYTHING TO YOU?
SHINOGU...?
WHY WOULD SHINOGU...
OH...
March XX, 20XX
(Last)
Narita
Birth: September 1,
Higashi Komazawa

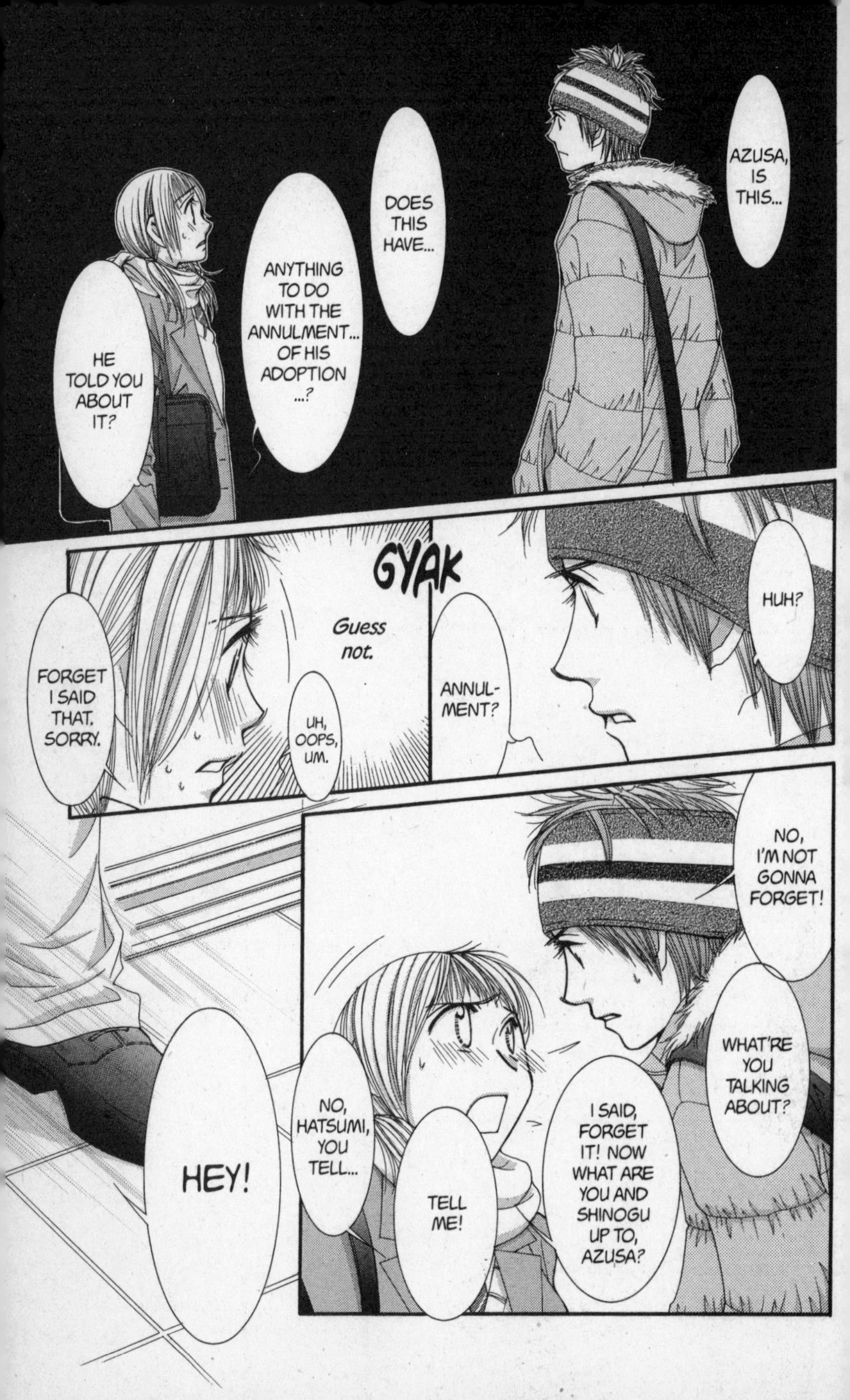
AZUSA, IS THIS...
DOES THIS HAVE...
ANYTHING TO DO WITH THE ANNULMENT... OF HIS ADOPTION ...?
HE TOLD YOU ABOUT IT?
HUH?
ANNUL-MENT?
GYAK
Guess not.
UH, OOPS, UM.
FORGET I SAID THAT. SORRY.
NO, I'M NOT GONNA FORGET!
WHAT'RE YOU TALKING ABOUT?
I SAID, FORGET IT! NOW WHAT ARE YOU AND SHINOGU UP TO, AZUSA?
TELL ME!
NO, HATSUMI, YOU TELL...
HEY!

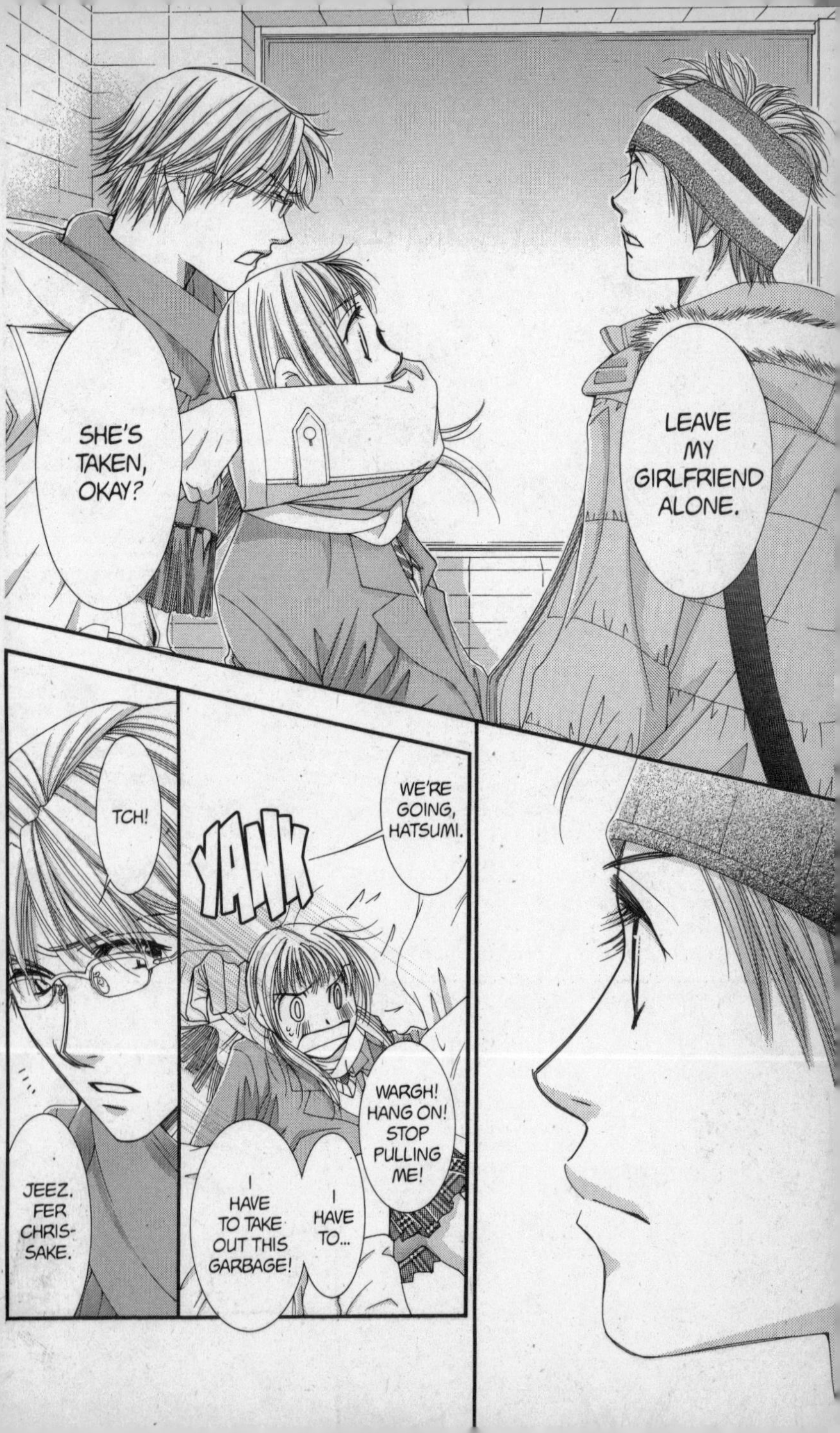
LEAVE MY GIRLFRIEND ALONE.
SHE'S TAKEN, OKAY?
WE'RE GOING, HATSUMI.
YANK
WARGH! HANG ON! STOP PULLING ME!
I HAVE TO...
I HAVE TO TAKE OUT THIS GARBAGE!
TCH!
...
JEEZ. FER CHRIS-SAKE.

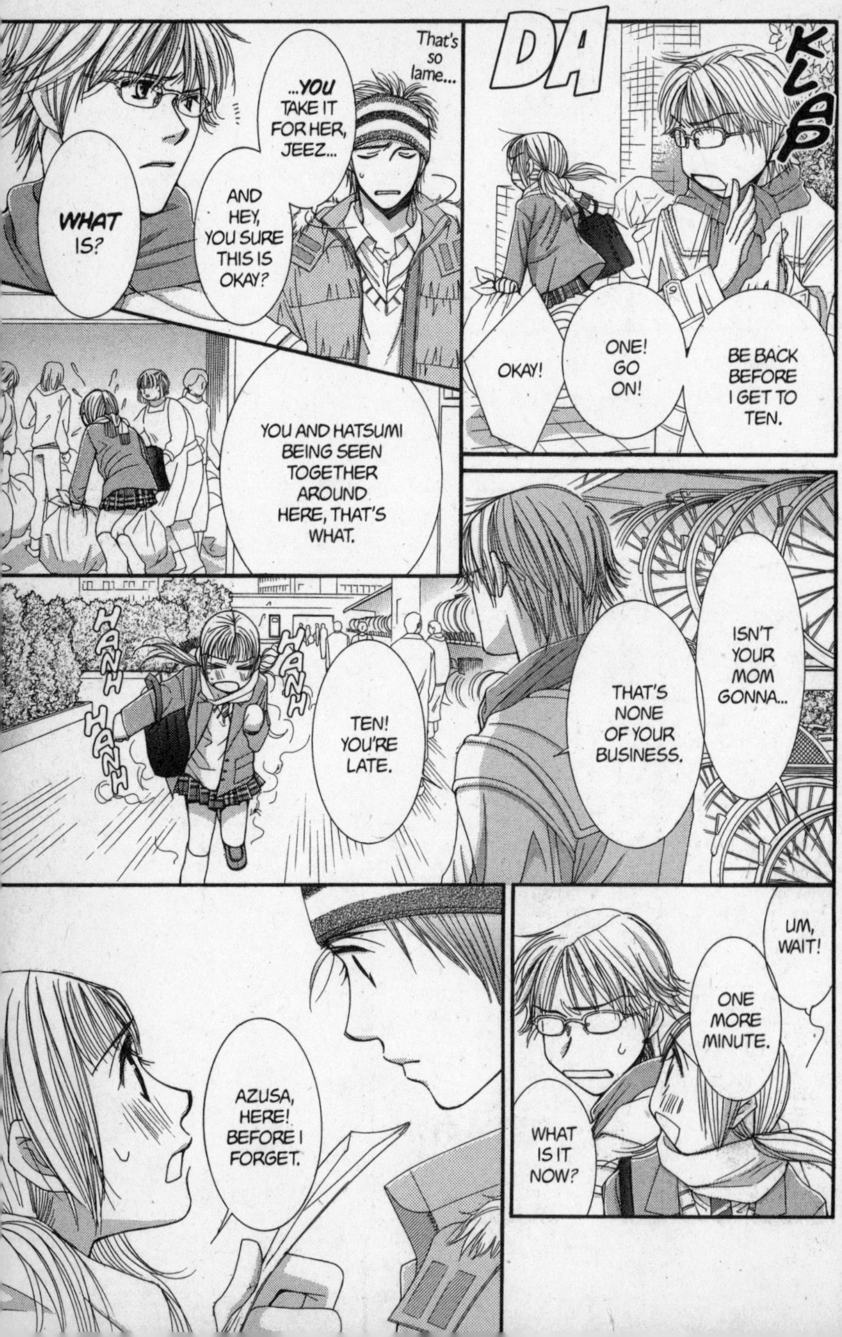
DA
KLAP
BE BACK BEFORE I GET TO TEN.
ONE! GO ON!
OKAY!
That's so lame...
...YOU TAKE IT FOR HER, JEEZ...
AND HEY, YOU SURE THIS IS OKAY?
WHAT IS?
YOU AND HATSUMI BEING SEEN TOGETHER AROUND HERE, THAT'S WHAT.
ISN'T YOUR MOM GONNA...
THAT'S NONE OF YOUR BUSINESS.
HANH HANH
HANH
TEN! YOU'RE LATE.
UM, WAIT!
ONE MORE MINUTE.
WHAT IS IT NOW?
AZUSA, HERE! BEFORE I FORGET.

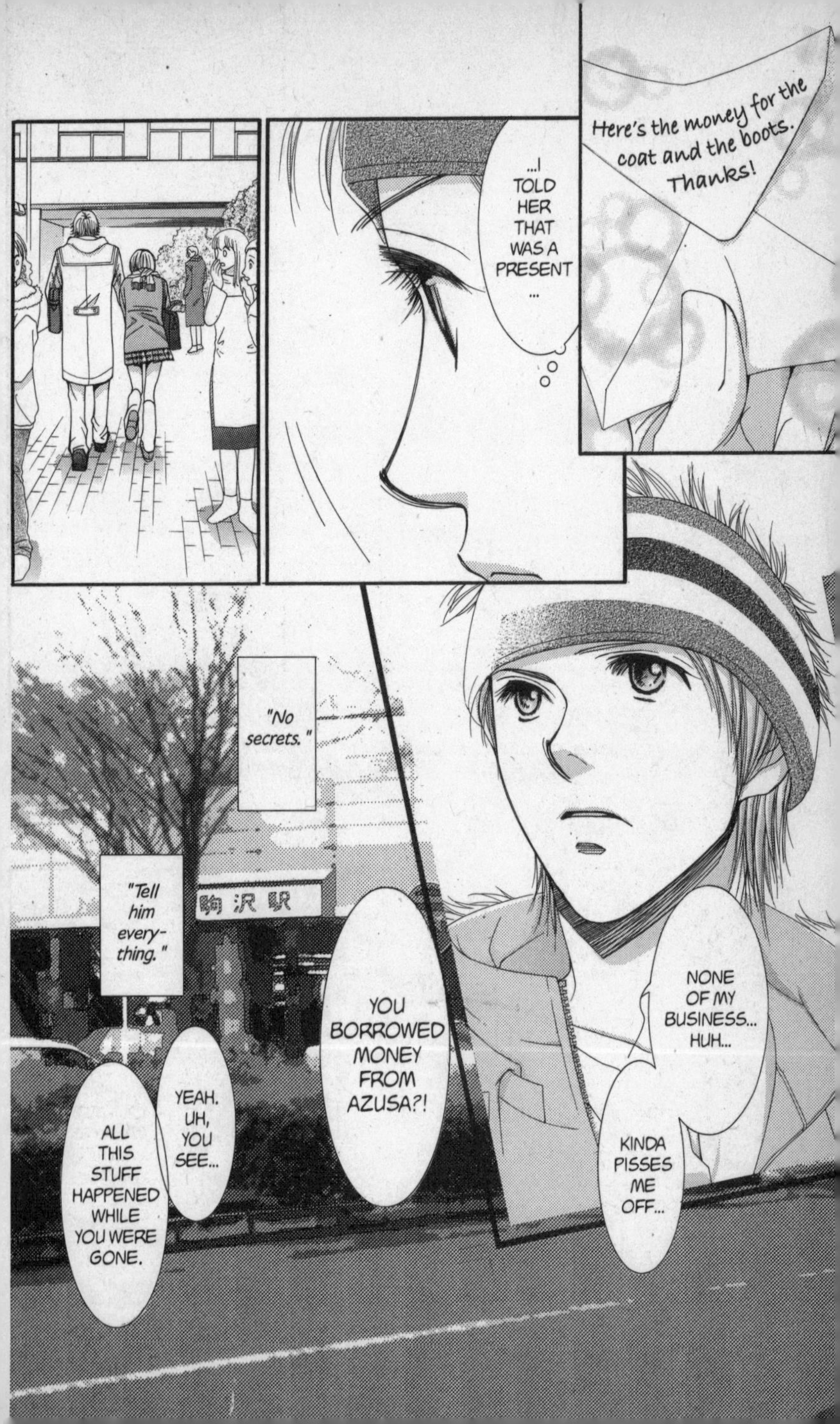
Here's the money for the coat and the boots. Thanks!
...I TOLD HER THAT WAS A PRESENT ...
NONE OF MY BUSINESS... HUH...
KINDA PISSES ME OFF...
"No secrets."
"Tell him every-thing."
駒沢駅
YOU BORROWED MONEY FROM AZUSA?!
YEAH. UH, YOU SEE...
ALL THIS STUFF HAPPENED WHILE YOU WERE GONE.

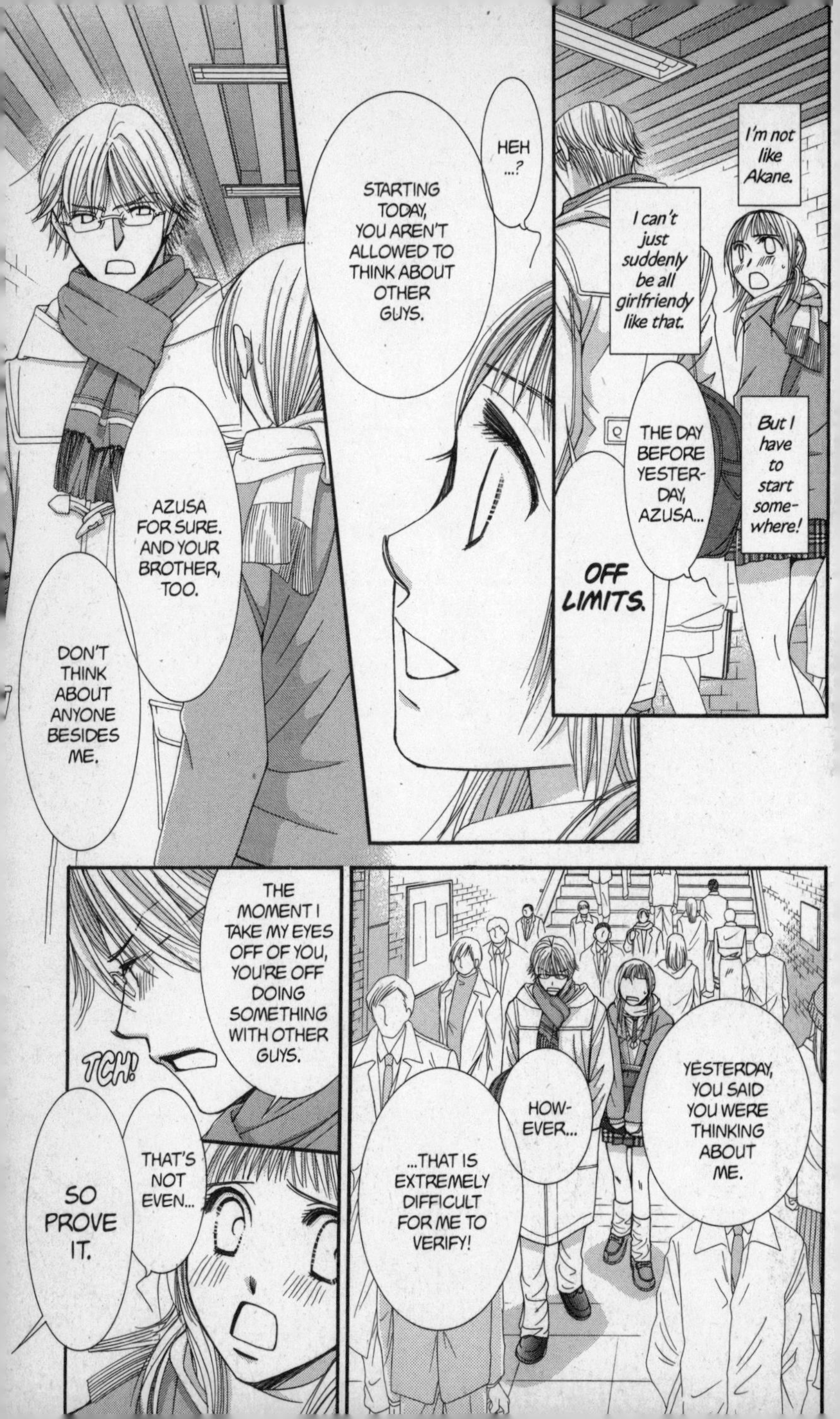
I'm not like Akane.
I can't just suddenly be all girlfriendy like that.
But I have to start somewhere!
THE DAY BEFORE YESTERDAY, AZUSA...
OFF LIMITS.
HEH ...?
STARTING TODAY, YOU AREN'T ALLOWED TO THINK ABOUT OTHER GUYS.
AZUSA FOR SURE. AND YOUR BROTHER, TOO.
DON'T THINK ABOUT ANYONE BESIDES ME.
YESTERDAY, YOU SAID YOU WERE THINKING ABOUT ME.
HOW-EVER...
...THAT IS EXTREMELY DIFFICULT FOR ME TO VERIFY!
THE MOMENT I TAKE MY EYES OFF OF YOU, YOU'RE OFF DOING SOMETHING WITH OTHER GUYS.
TCH!
THAT'S NOT EVEN...
SO PROVE IT.

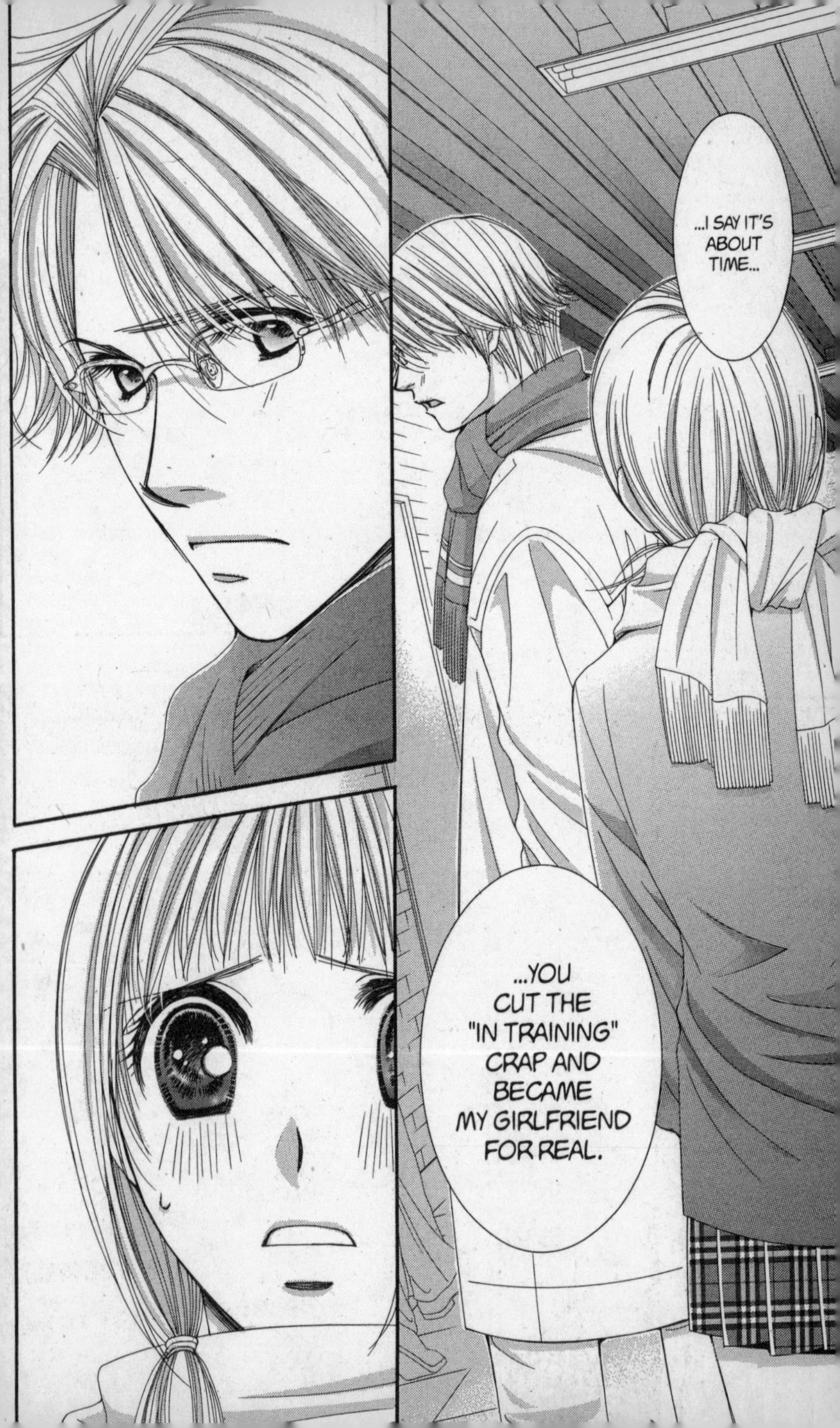
...I SAY IT'S ABOUT TIME...
...YOU CUT THE "IN TRAINING" CRAP AND BECAME MY GIRLFRIEND FOR REAL.

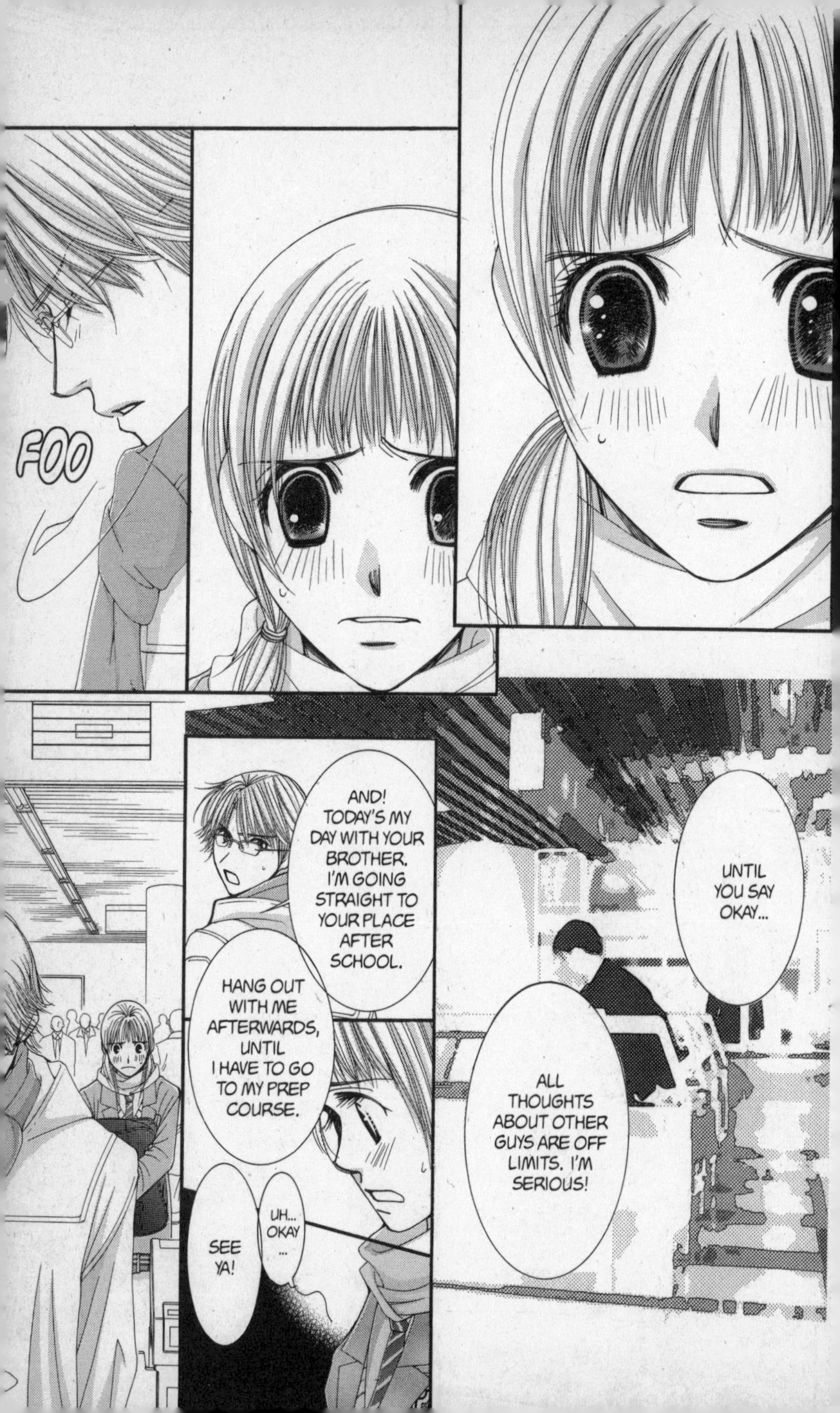
FOO
UNTIL YOU SAY OKAY...
ALL THOUGHTS ABOUT OTHER GUYS ARE OFF LIMITS. I'M SERIOUS!
AND! TODAY'S MY DAY WITH YOUR BROTHER. I'M GOING STRAIGHT TO YOUR PLACE AFTER SCHOOL.
HANG OUT WITH ME AFTERWARDS, UNTIL I HAVE TO GO TO MY PREP COURSE.
UH... OKAY ...
SEE YA!

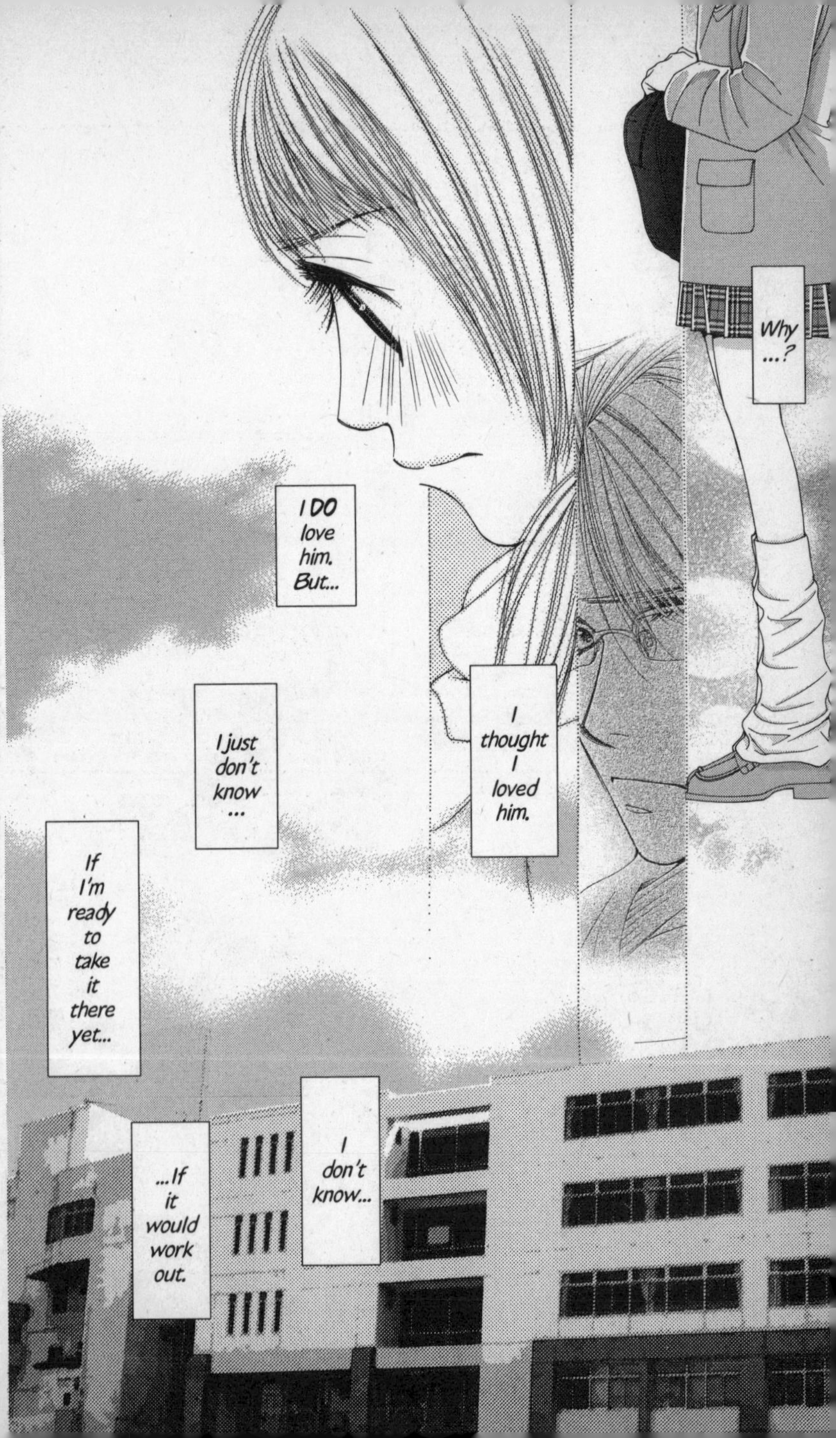
Why ...?
I thought I loved him.
I DO love him. But...
I just don't know ...
If I'm ready to take it there yet...
I don't know...
...If it would work out.

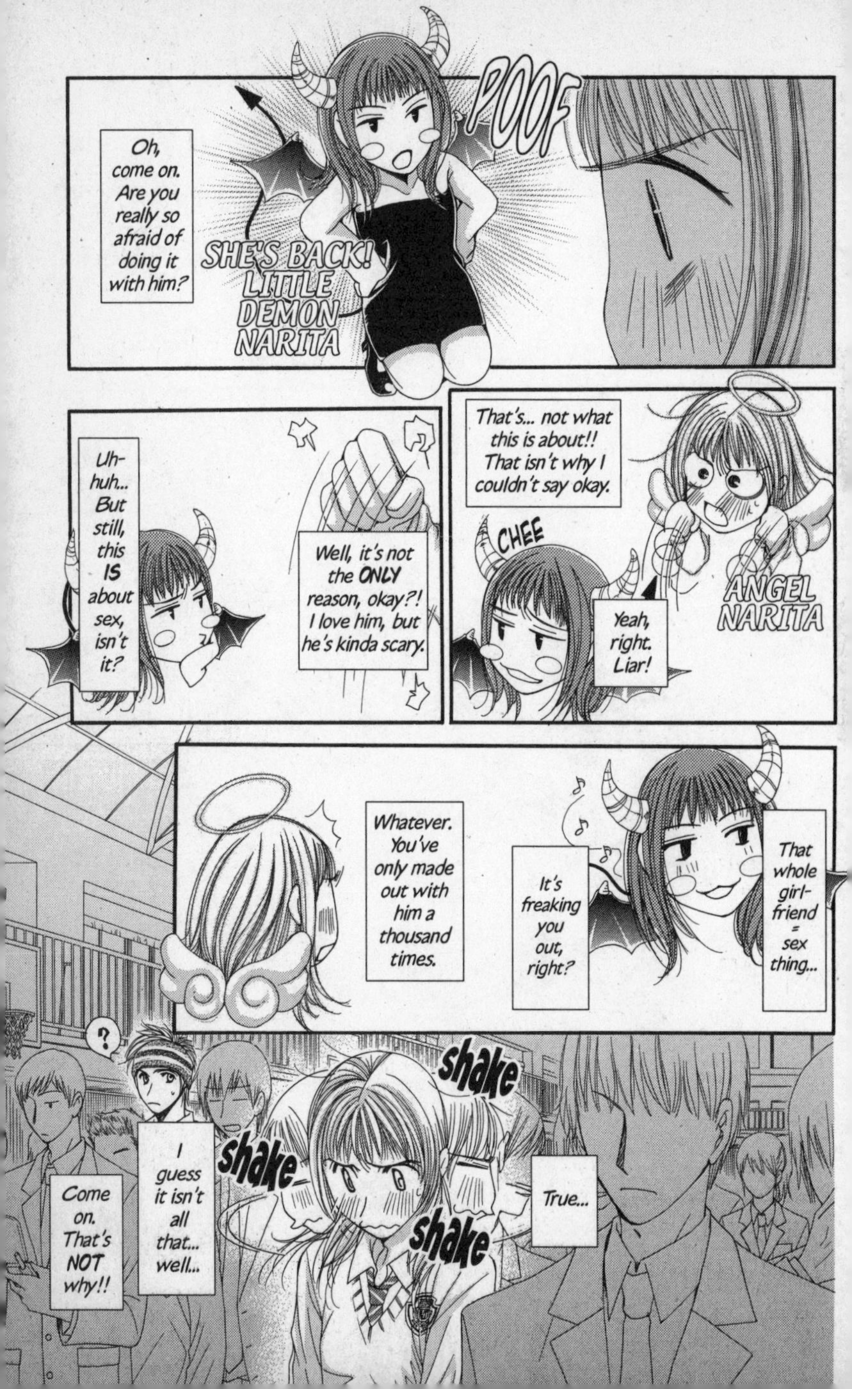
POOF
Oh, come on. Are you really so afraid of doing it with him?
SHE'S BACK! LITTLE DEMON NARITA
That's... not what this is about!! That isn't why I couldn't say okay.
CHEE
ANGEL NARITA
Yeah, right. Liar!
Well, it's not the ONLY reason, okay?! I love him, but he's kinda scary.
Uh-huh... But still, this IS about sex, isn't it?
That whole girl-friend = sex thing...
It's freaking you out, right?
Whatever. You've only made out with him a thousand times.
shake
True...
shake
shake
I guess it isn't all that... well...
?
Come on. That's NOT why!!

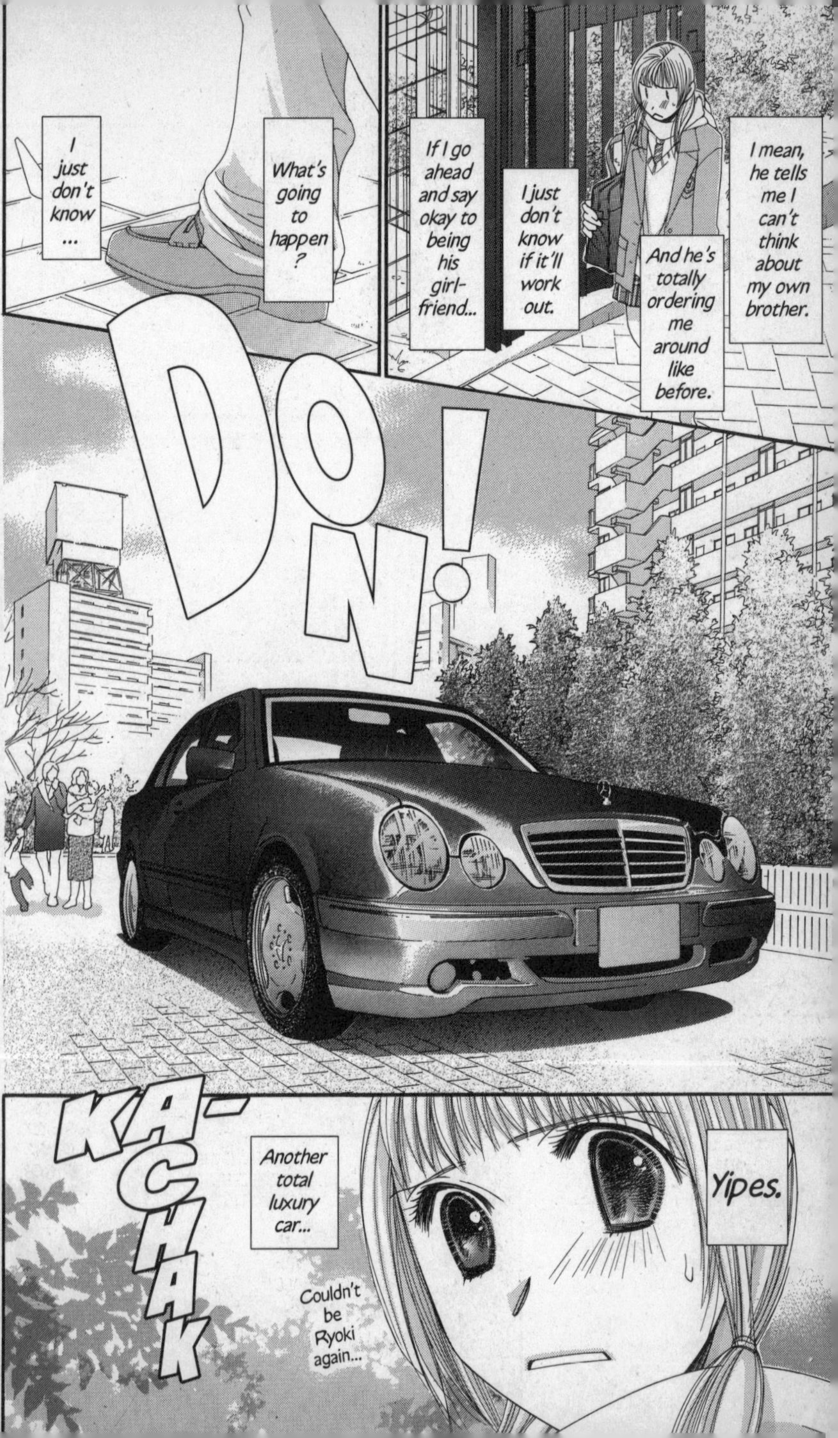
I mean, he tells me I can't think about my own brother.
And he's totally ordering me around like before.
I just don't know if it'll work out.
If I go ahead and say okay to being his girl-friend...
What's going to happen?
I just don't know...
DON!
Yipes.
Another total luxury car...
Couldn't be Ryoki again...
KA-CHAK

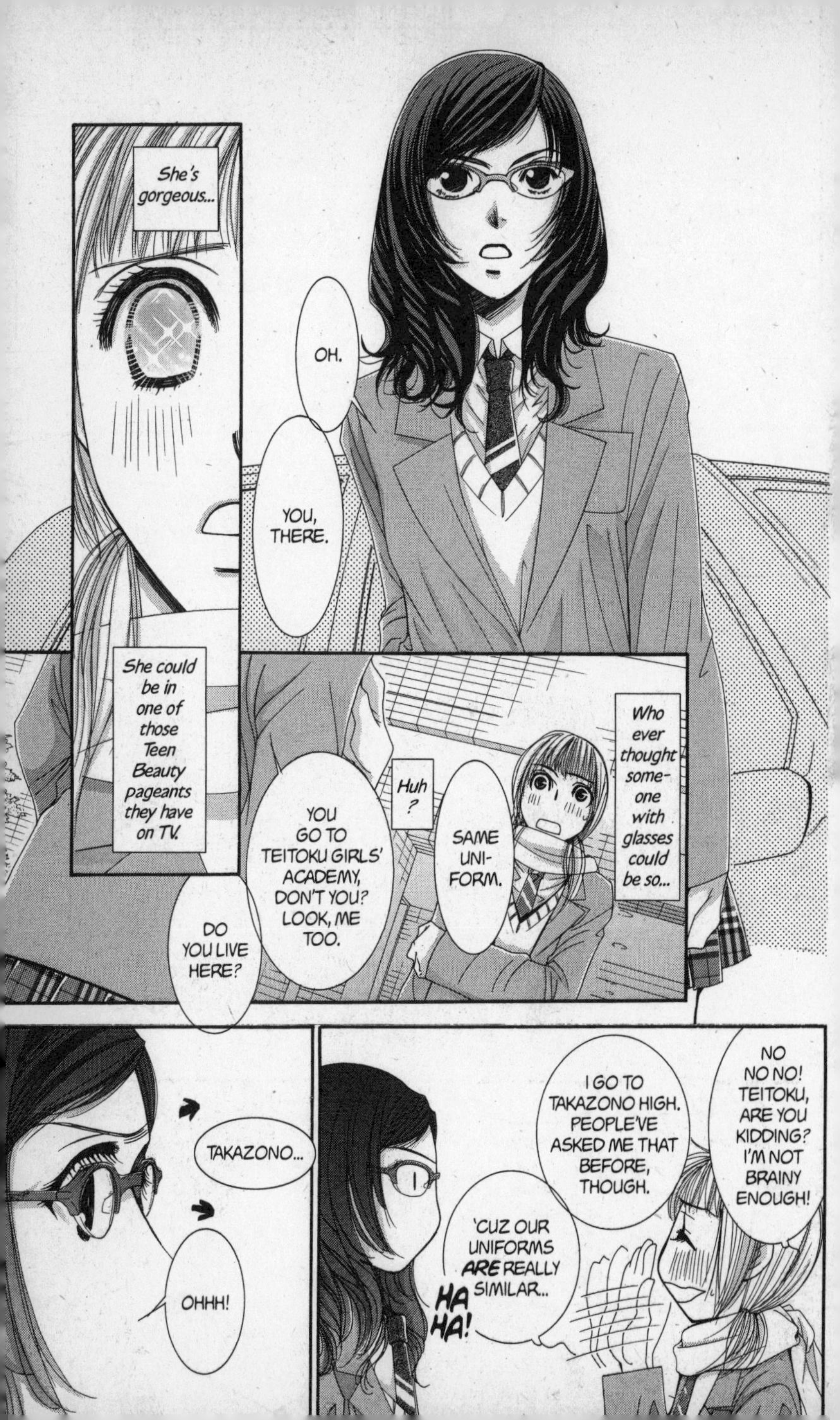
OH.
YOU, THERE.
She's gorgeous...
She could be in one of those Teen Beauty pageants they have on TV.
Who ever thought some-one with glasses could be so...
SAME UNI-FORM.
Huh?
YOU GO TO TEITOKU GIRLS' ACADEMY, DON'T YOU? LOOK, ME TOO.
DO YOU LIVE HERE?
NO NO NO! TEITOKU, ARE YOU KIDDING? I'M NOT BRAINY ENOUGH!
I GO TO TAKAZONO HIGH. PEOPLE'VE ASKED ME THAT BEFORE, THOUGH.
'CUZ OUR UNIFORMS ARE REALLY SIMILAR...
HA HA!
TAKAZONO...
OHHH!

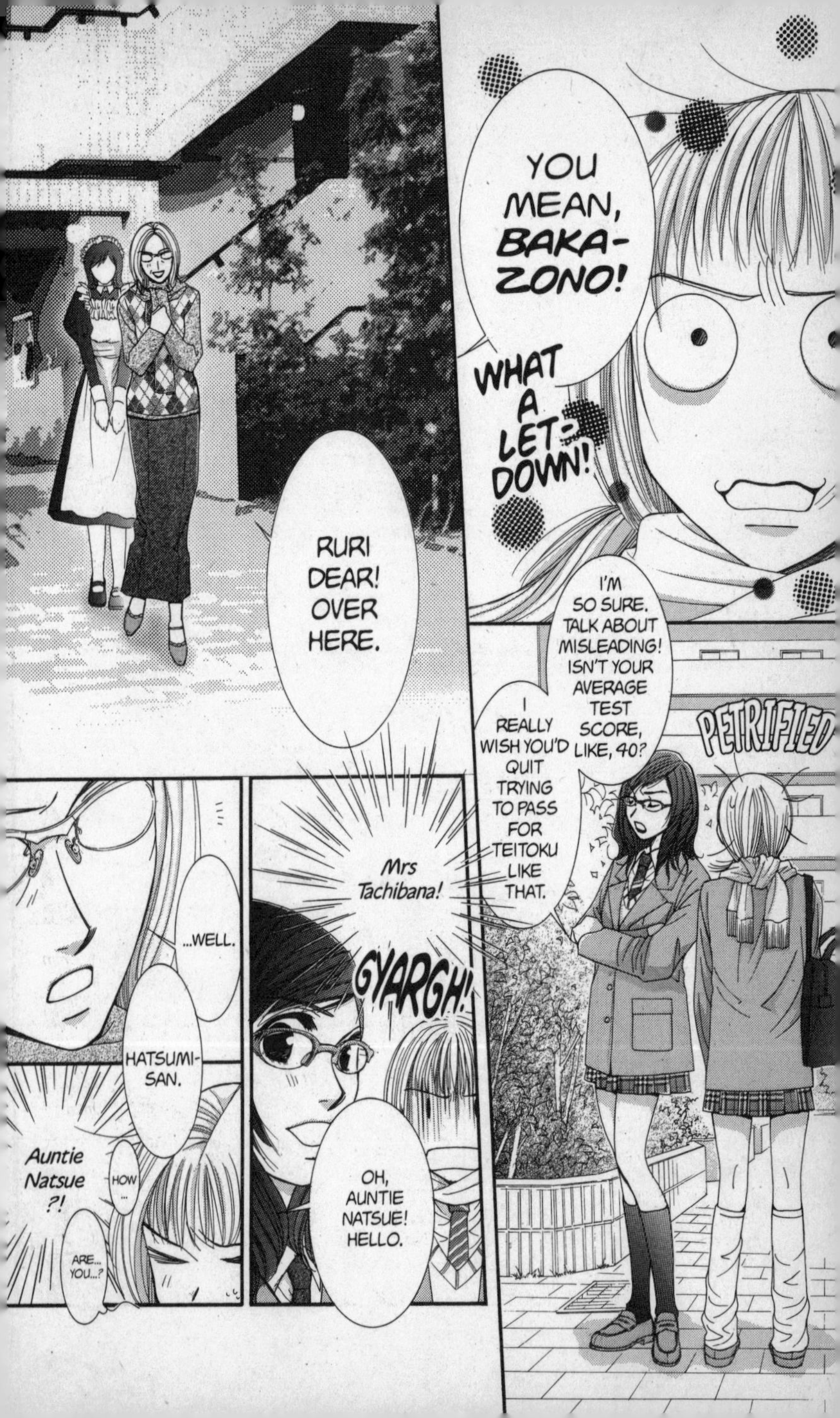
YOU MEAN, BAKA-ZONO!
WHAT A LET-DOWN!
PETRIFIED
I'M SO SURE. TALK ABOUT MISLEADING! ISN'T YOUR AVERAGE TEST SCORE, LIKE, 40?
I REALLY WISH YOU'D QUIT TRYING TO PASS FOR TEITOKU LIKE THAT.
RURI DEAR! OVER HERE.
Mrs Tachibana!
GYARGH!
OH, AUNTIE NATSUE! HELLO.
...WELL.
HATSUMI-SAN.
Auntie Natsue?!
HOW...
ARE... YOU...?

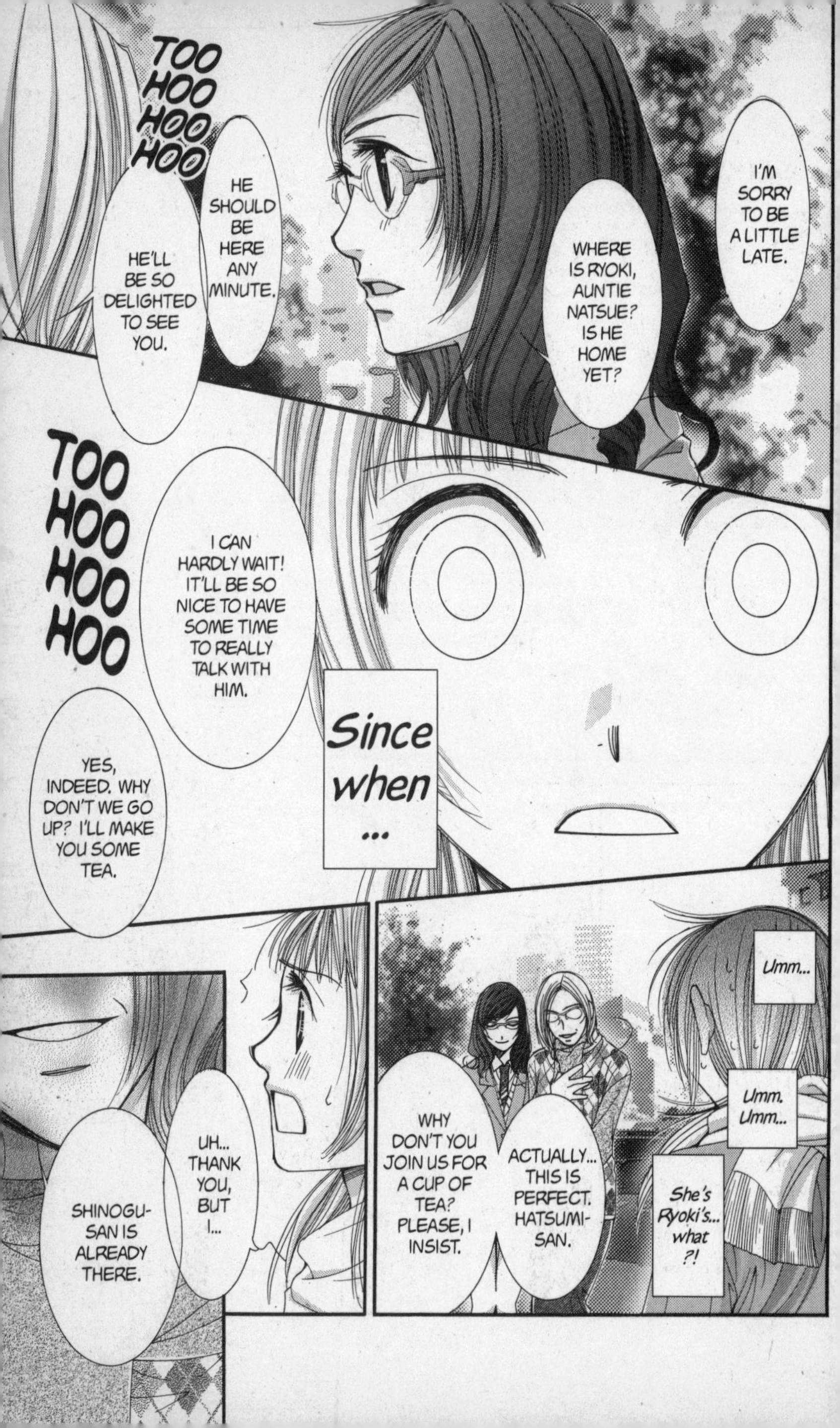
I'M SORRY TO BE A LITTLE LATE.
WHERE IS RYOKI, AUNTIE NATSUE? IS HE HOME YET?
TOO HOO HOO HOO
HE SHOULD BE HERE ANY MINUTE.
HE'LL BE SO DELIGHTED TO SEE YOU.
Since when ...
I CAN HARDLY WAIT! IT'LL BE SO NICE TO HAVE SOME TIME TO REALLY TALK WITH HIM.
TOO HOO HOO HOO HOO
YES, INDEED. WHY DON'T WE GO UP? I'LL MAKE YOU SOME TEA.
Umm...
Umm. Umm...
She's Ryoki's... what ?!
ACTUALLY... THIS IS PERFECT. HATSUMI-SAN.
WHY DON'T YOU JOIN US FOR A CUP OF TEA? PLEASE, I INSIST.
UH... THANK YOU, BUT I...
SHINOGU-SAN IS ALREADY THERE.

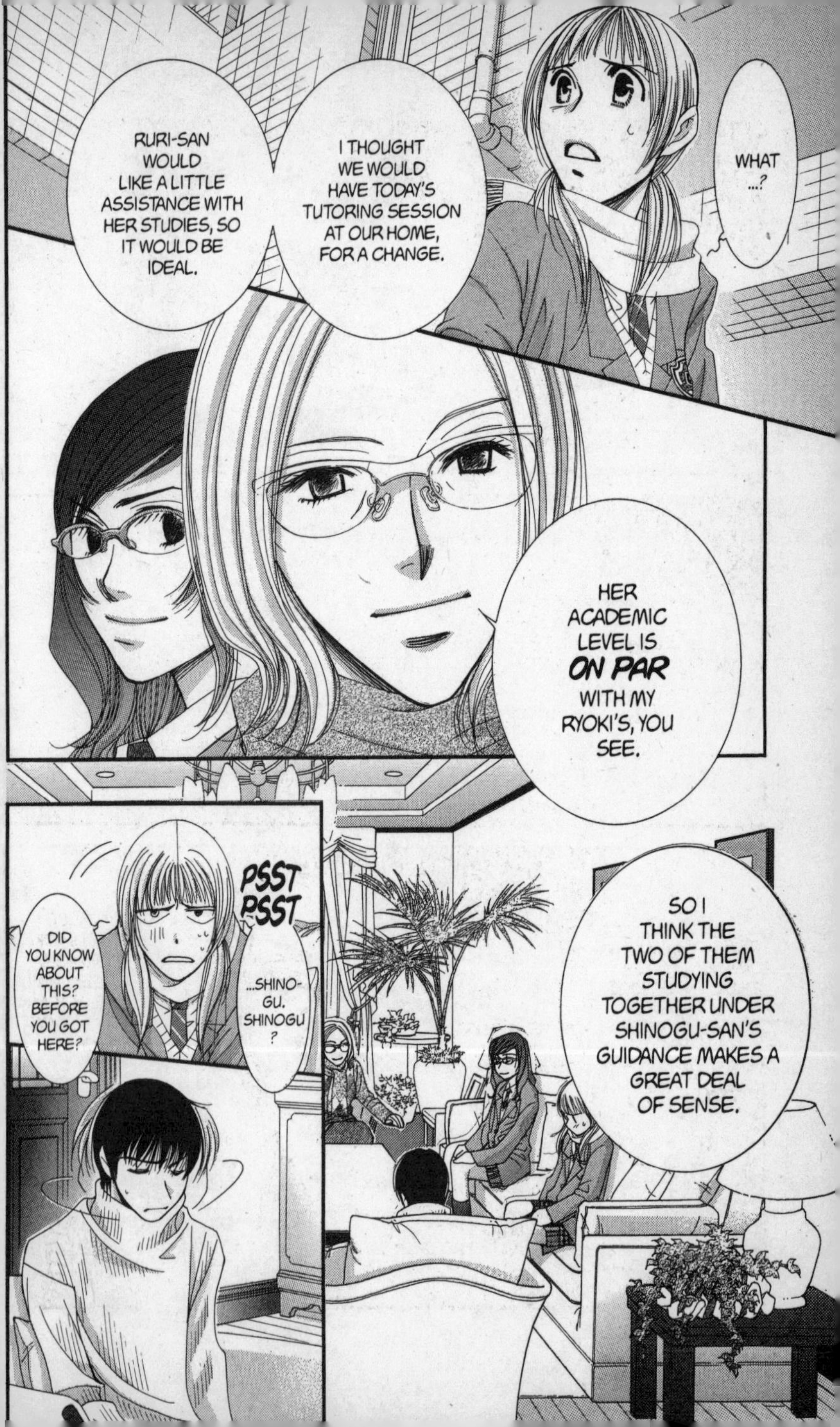
WHAT ...?
I THOUGHT WE WOULD HAVE TODAY'S TUTORING SESSION AT OUR HOME, FOR A CHANGE.
RURI-SAN WOULD LIKE A LITTLE ASSISTANCE WITH HER STUDIES, SO IT WOULD BE IDEAL.
HER ACADEMIC LEVEL IS ON PAR WITH MY RYOKI'S, YOU SEE.
SO I THINK THE TWO OF THEM STUDYING TOGETHER UNDER SHINOGU-SAN'S GUIDANCE MAKES A GREAT DEAL OF SENSE.
PSST PSST
...SHINOGU. SHINOGU?
DID YOU KNOW ABOUT THIS? BEFORE YOU GOT HERE?

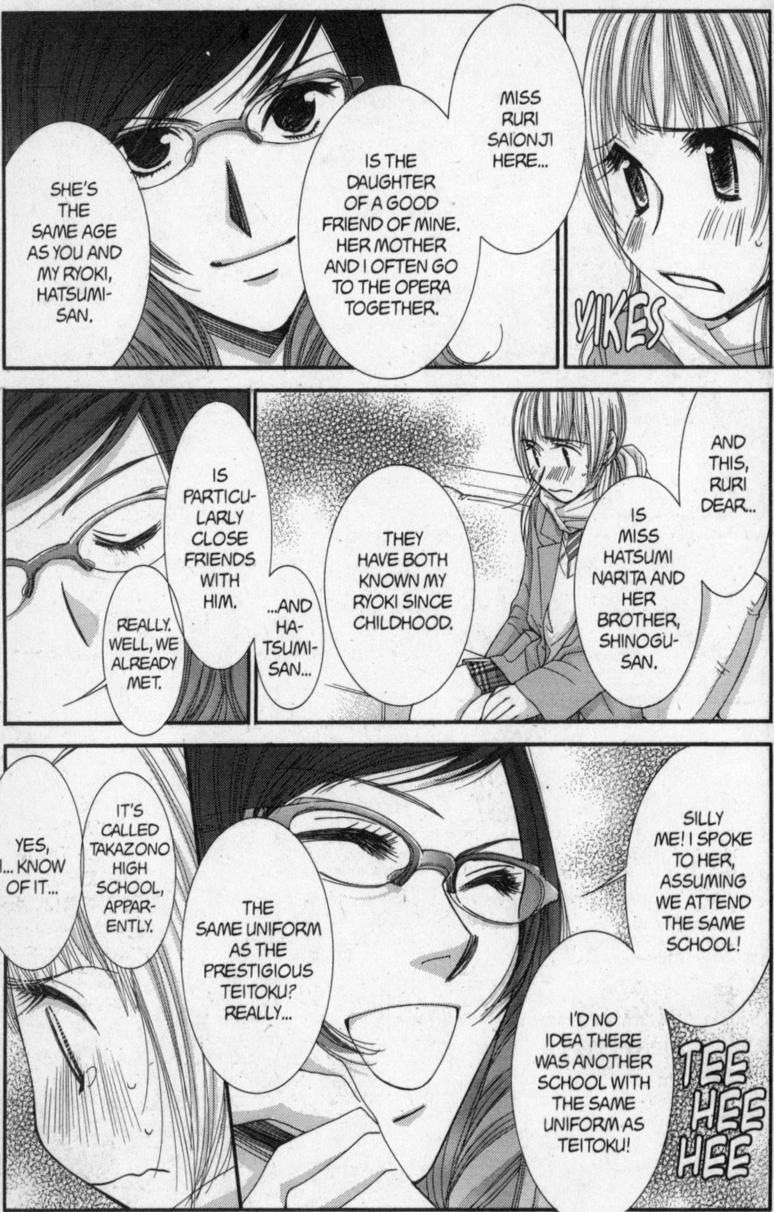
MISS RURI SAIONJI HERE...
IS THE DAUGHTER OF A GOOD FRIEND OF MINE. HER MOTHER AND I OFTEN GO TO THE OPERA TOGETHER.
SHE'S THE SAME AGE AS YOU AND MY RYOKI, HATSUMI-SAN.
YIKES
AND THIS, RURI DEAR...
IS MISS HATSUMI NARITA AND HER BROTHER, SHINOGU-SAN.
THEY HAVE BOTH KNOWN MY RYOKI SINCE CHILDHOOD.
...AND HA-TSUMI-SAN...
IS PARTICU-LARLY CLOSE FRIENDS WITH HIM.
REALLY. WELL, WE ALREADY MET.
SILLY ME! I SPOKE TO HER, ASSUMING WE ATTEND THE SAME SCHOOL!
I'D NO IDEA THERE WAS ANOTHER SCHOOL WITH THE SAME UNIFORM AS TEITOKU!
TEE HEE HEE
THE SAME UNIFORM AS THE PRESTIGIOUS TEITOKU? REALLY...
IT'S CALLED TAKAZONO HIGH SCHOOL, APPAR-ENTLY.
YES, I... KNOW OF IT...

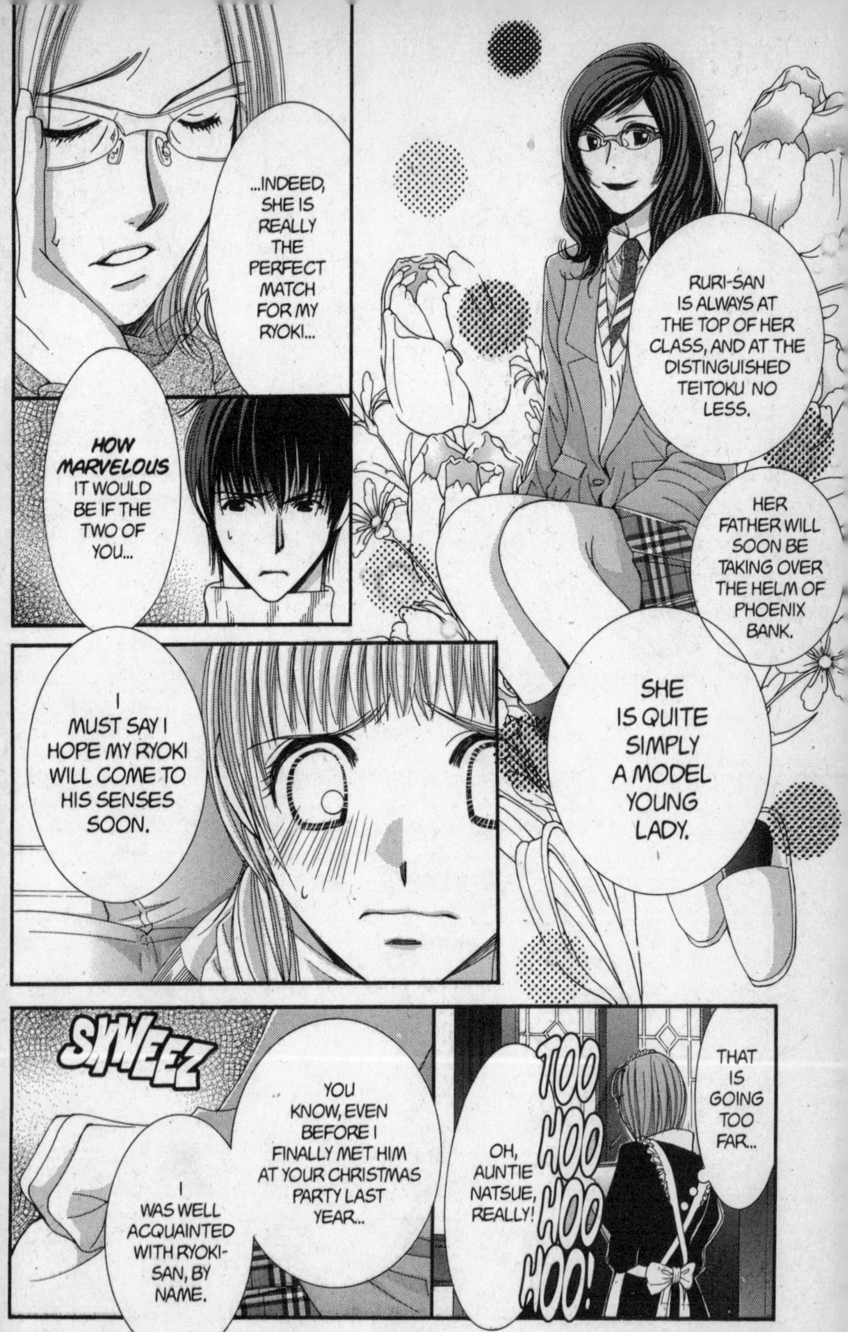
RURI-SAN IS ALWAYS AT THE TOP OF HER CLASS, AND AT THE DISTINGUISHED TEITOKU NO LESS.
HER FATHER WILL SOON BE TAKING OVER THE HELM OF PHOENIX BANK.
SHE IS QUITE SIMPLY A MODEL YOUNG LADY.
...INDEED, SHE IS REALLY THE PERFECT MATCH FOR MY RYOKI...
HOW MARVELOUS IT WOULD BE IF THE TWO OF YOU...
I MUST SAY I HOPE MY RYOKI WILL COME TO HIS SENSES SOON.
THAT IS GOING TOO FAR...
TOO HOO HOO HOO!
OH, AUNTIE NATSUE, REALLY!
SKWEEZ
YOU KNOW, EVEN BEFORE I FINALLY MET HIM AT YOUR CHRISTMAS PARTY LAST YEAR...
I WAS WELL ACQUAINTED WITH RYOKI-SAN, BY NAME.

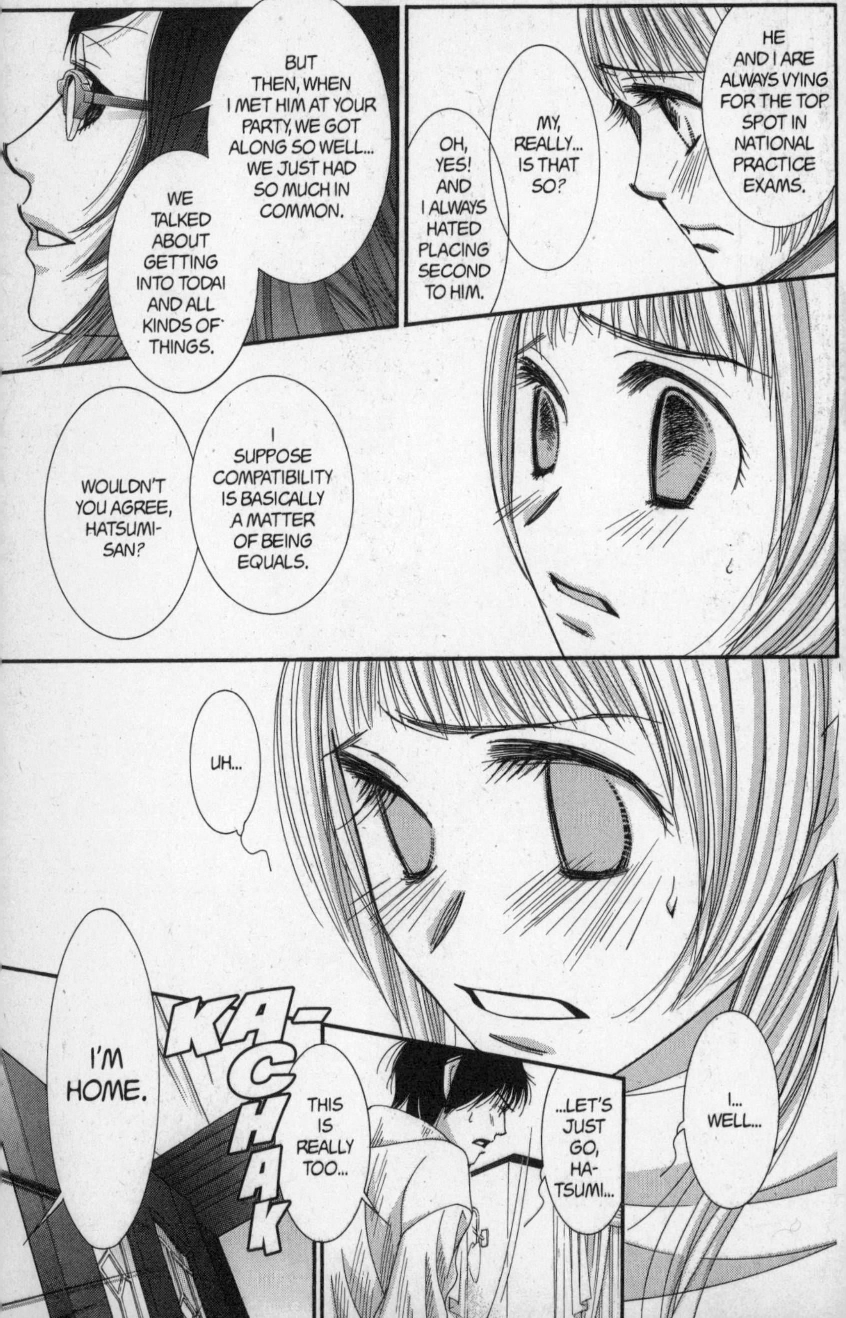
HE AND I ARE ALWAYS VYING FOR THE TOP SPOT IN NATIONAL PRACTICE EXAMS.
MY, REALLY... IS THAT SO?
OH, YES! AND I ALWAYS HATED PLACING SECOND TO HIM.
BUT THEN, WHEN I MET HIM AT YOUR PARTY, WE GOT ALONG SO WELL... WE JUST HAD SO MUCH IN COMMON.
WE TALKED ABOUT GETTING INTO TODAI AND ALL KINDS OF THINGS.
I SUPPOSE COMPATIBILITY IS BASICALLY A MATTER OF BEING EQUALS.
WOULDN'T YOU AGREE, HATSUMI-SAN?
UH...
I... WELL...
...LET'S JUST GO, HA-TSUMI...
THIS IS REALLY TOO...
KA-CHAK
I'M HOME.

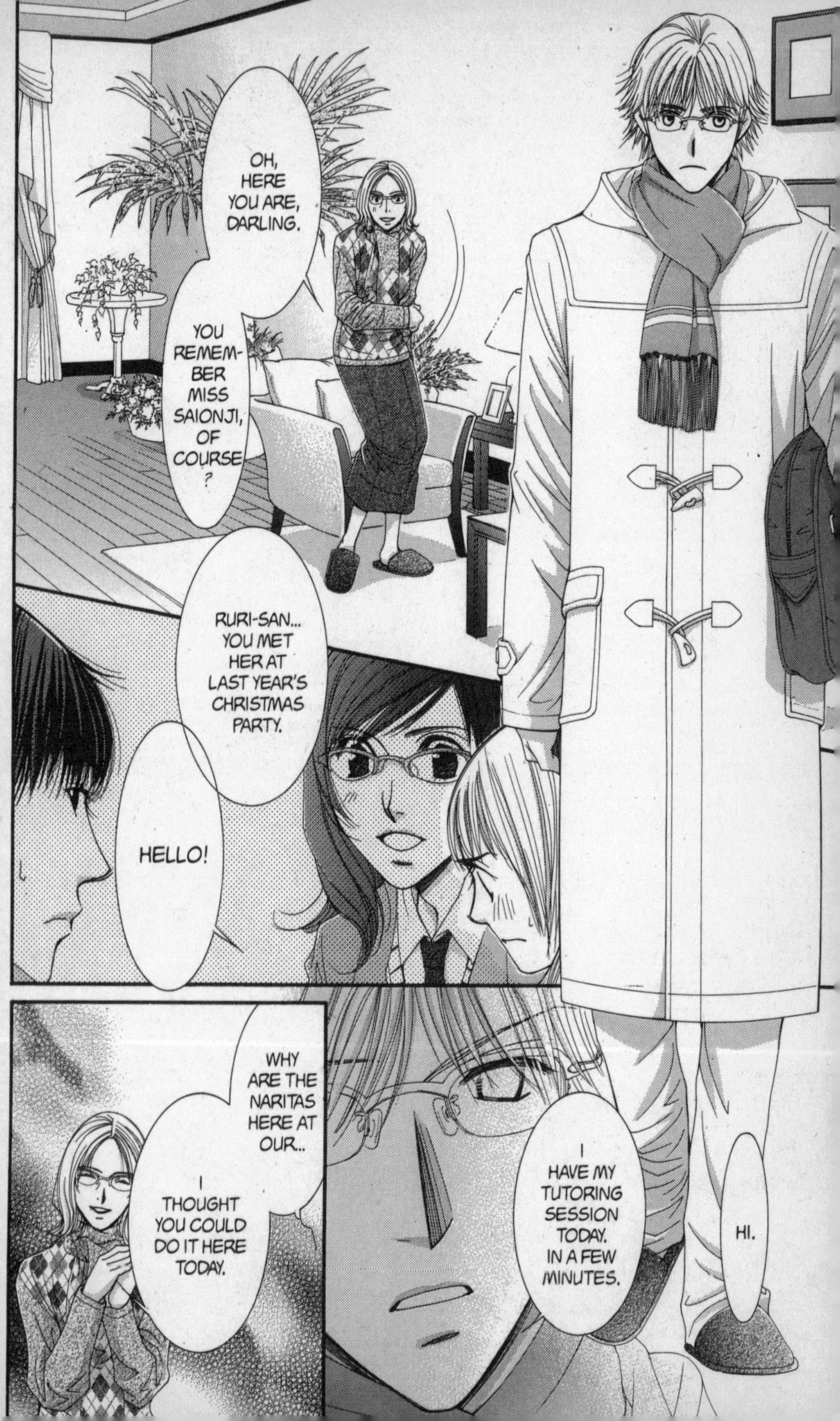
OH, HERE YOU ARE, DARLING.
YOU REMEMBER MISS SAIONJI, OF COURSE?
RURI-SAN... YOU MET HER AT LAST YEAR'S CHRISTMAS PARTY.
HELLO!
HI.
WHY ARE THE NARITAS HERE AT OUR...
I HAVE MY TUTORING SESSION TODAY. IN A FEW MINUTES.
I THOUGHT YOU COULD DO IT HERE TODAY.

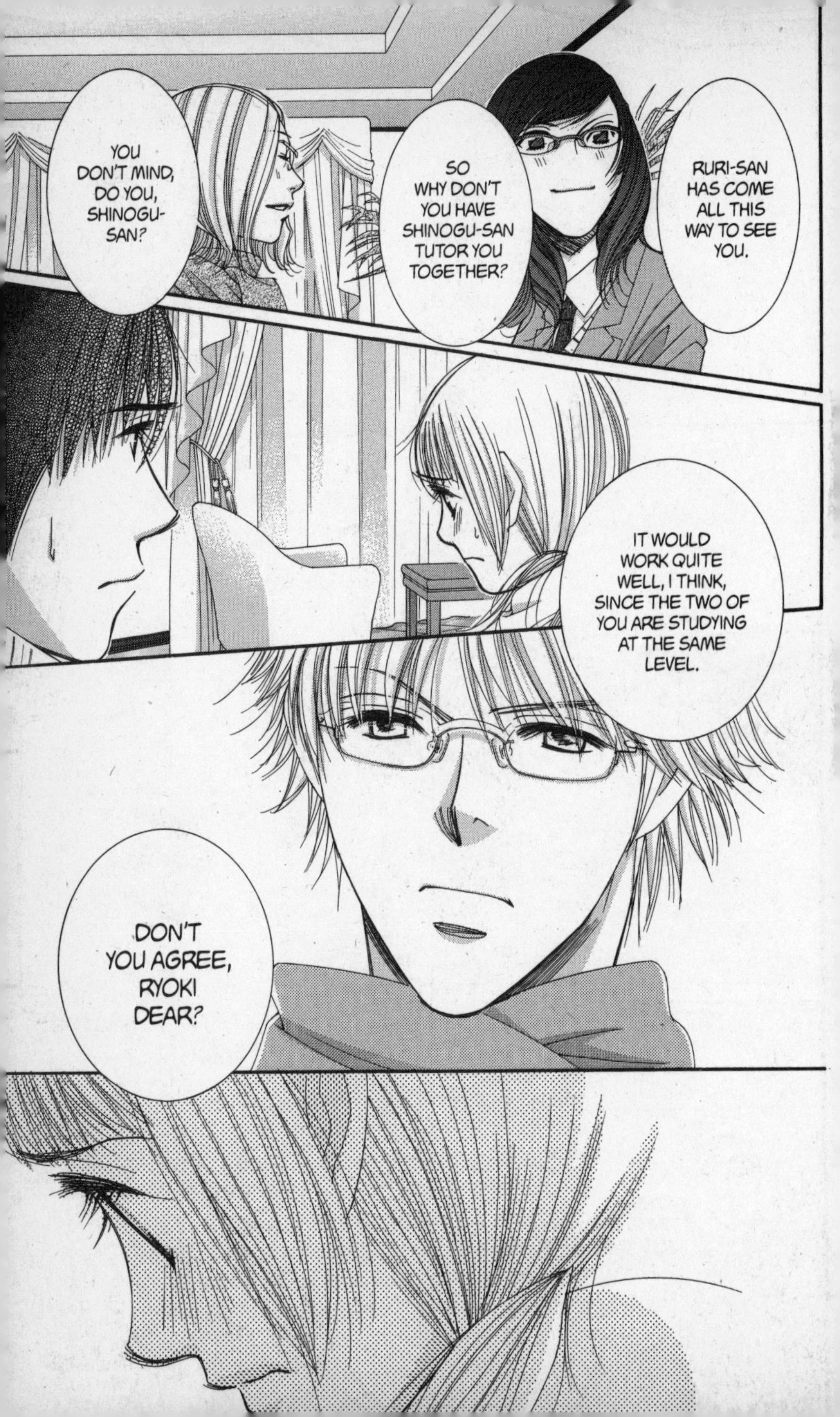
RURI-SAN HAS COME ALL THIS WAY TO SEE YOU.
SO WHY DON'T YOU HAVE SHINOGU-SAN TUTOR YOU TOGETHER?
YOU DON'T MIND, DO YOU, SHINOGU-SAN?
IT WOULD WORK QUITE WELL, I THINK, SINCE THE TWO OF YOU ARE STUDYING AT THE SAME LEVEL.
DON'T YOU AGREE, RYOKI DEAR?

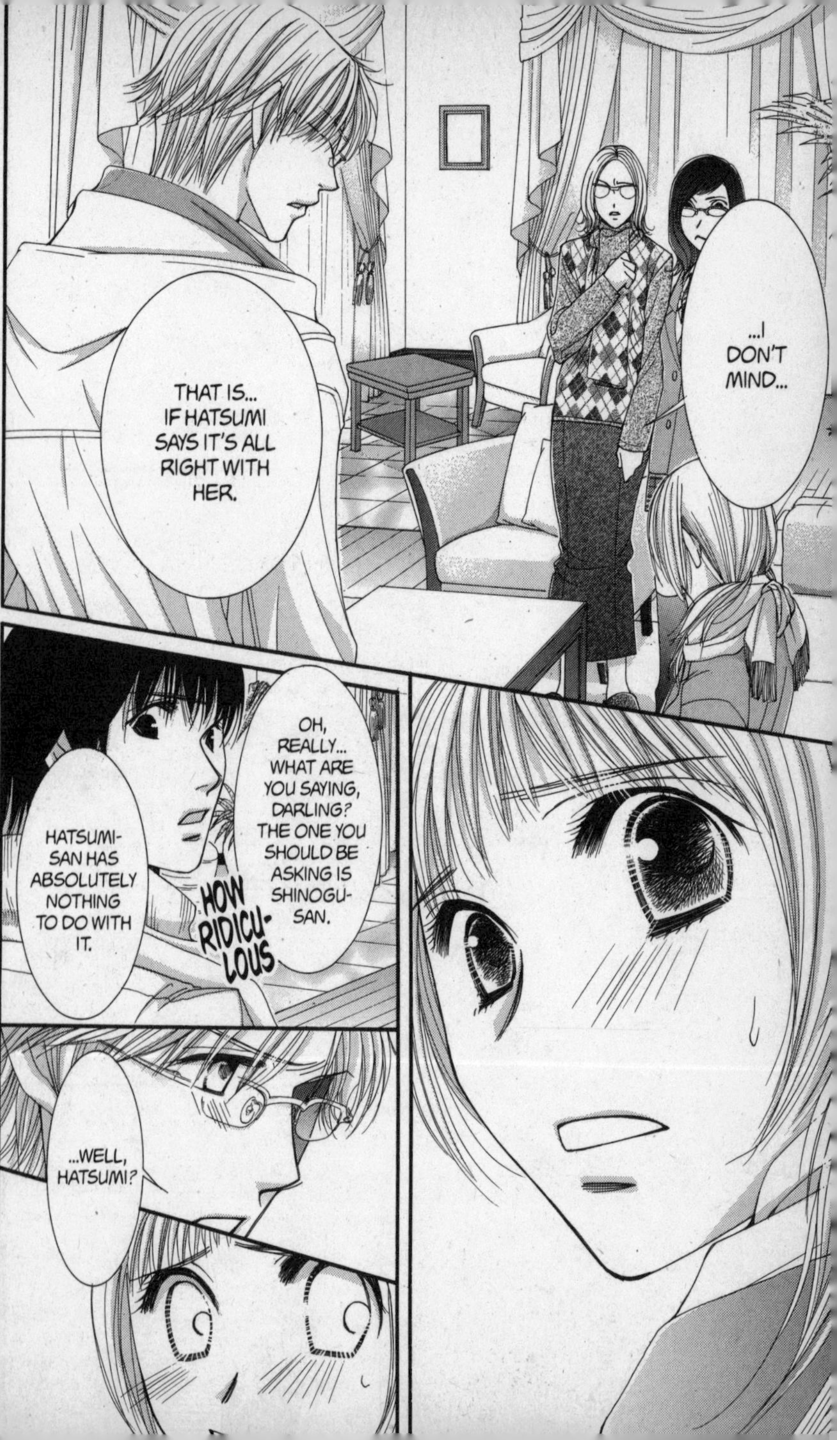
...I DON'T MIND...
THAT IS... IF HATSUMI SAYS IT'S ALL RIGHT WITH HER.
OH, REALLY... WHAT ARE YOU SAYING, DARLING? THE ONE YOU SHOULD BE ASKING IS SHINOGU-SAN.
HOW RIDICU-LOUS
HATSUMI-SAN HAS ABSOLUTELY NOTHING TO DO WITH IT.
...WELL, HATSUMI?

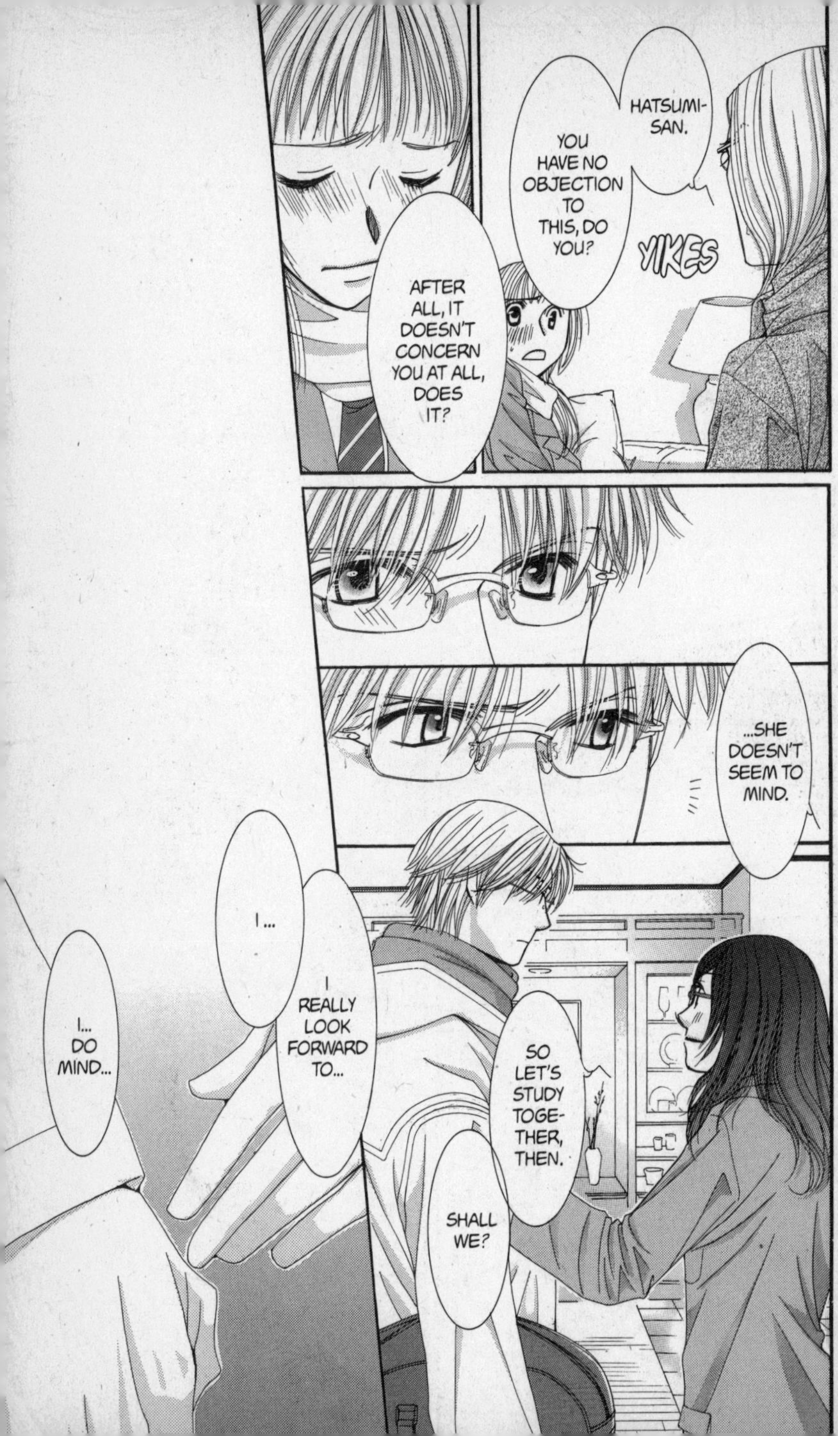
HATSUMI-SAN.
YOU HAVE NO OBJECTION TO THIS, DO YOU?
YIKES
AFTER ALL, IT DOESN'T CONCERN YOU AT ALL, DOES IT?
...SHE DOESN'T SEEM TO MIND.
SO LET'S STUDY TOGE-THER, THEN.
SHALL WE?
I...
I REALLY LOOK FORWARD TO...
I... DO MIND...

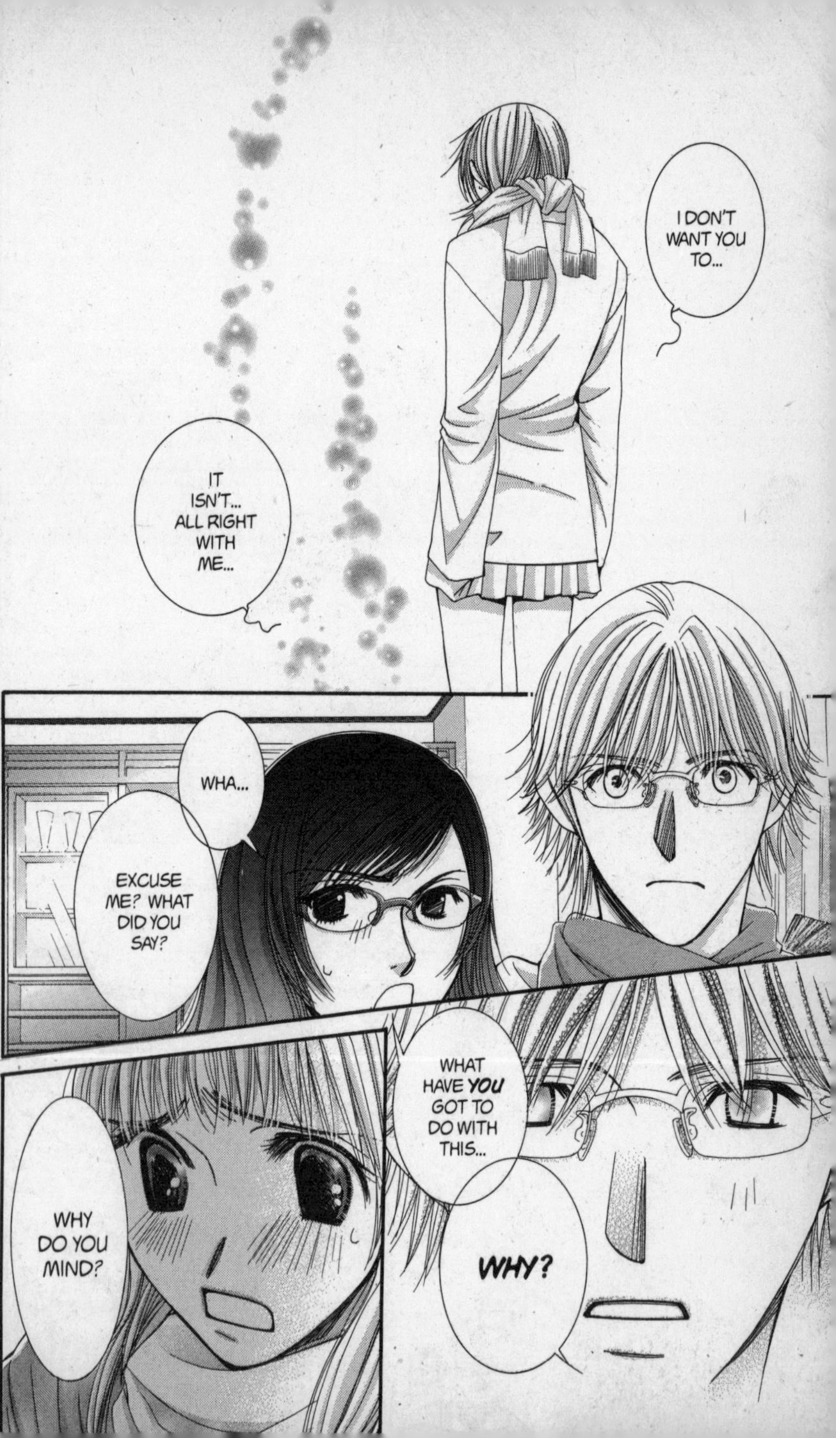
I DON'T WANT YOU TO...
IT ISN'T... ALL RIGHT WITH ME...
WHA...
EXCUSE ME? WHAT DID YOU SAY?
WHAT HAVE ***YOU*** GOT TO DO WITH THIS...
WHY?
WHY DO YOU MIND?

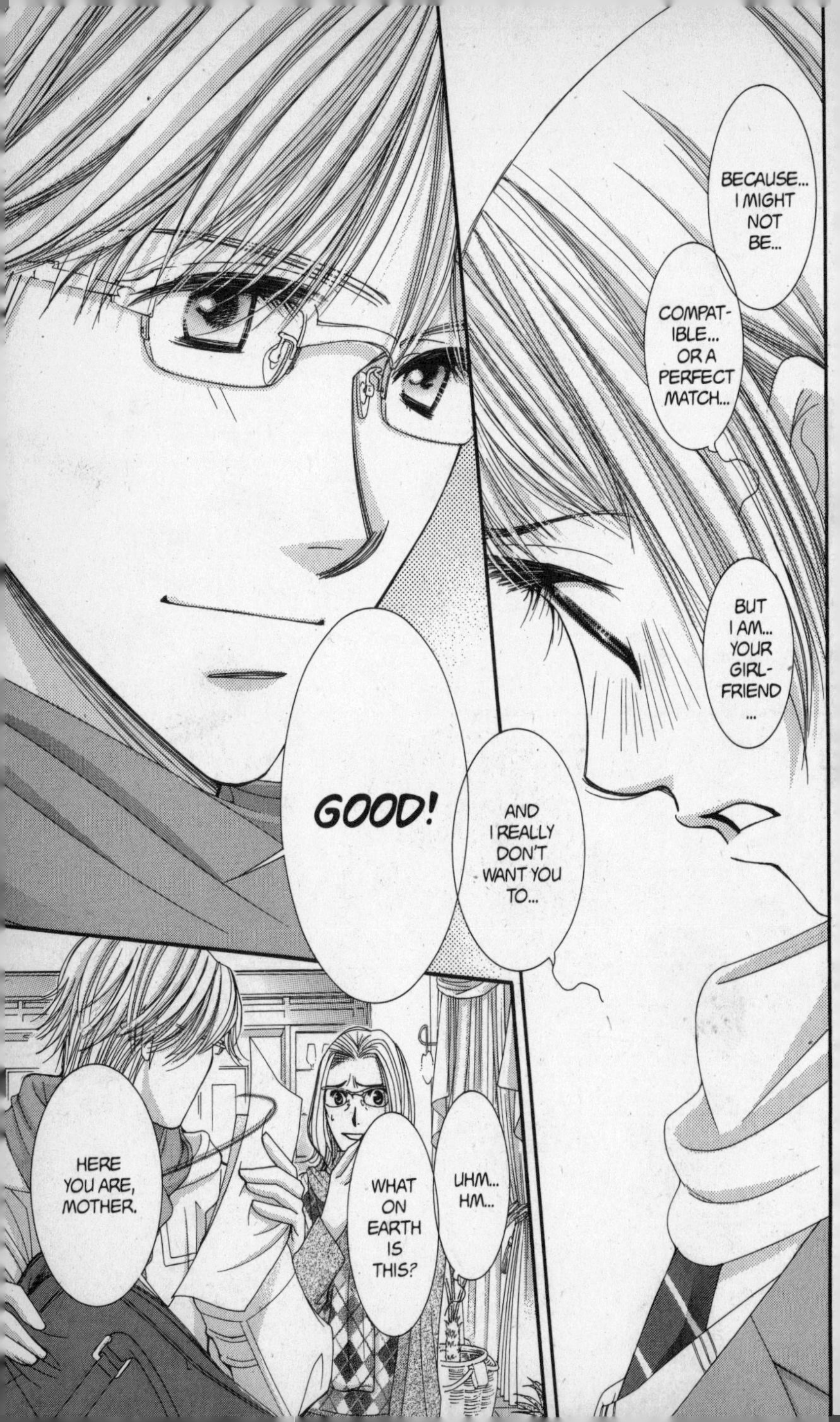
BECAUSE... I MIGHT NOT BE...
COMPAT-IBLE... OR A PERFECT MATCH...
BUT I AM... YOUR GIRL-FRIEND ...
AND I REALLY DON'T WANT YOU TO...
GOOD!
UHM... HM...
WHAT ON EARTH IS THIS?
HERE YOU ARE, MOTHER.

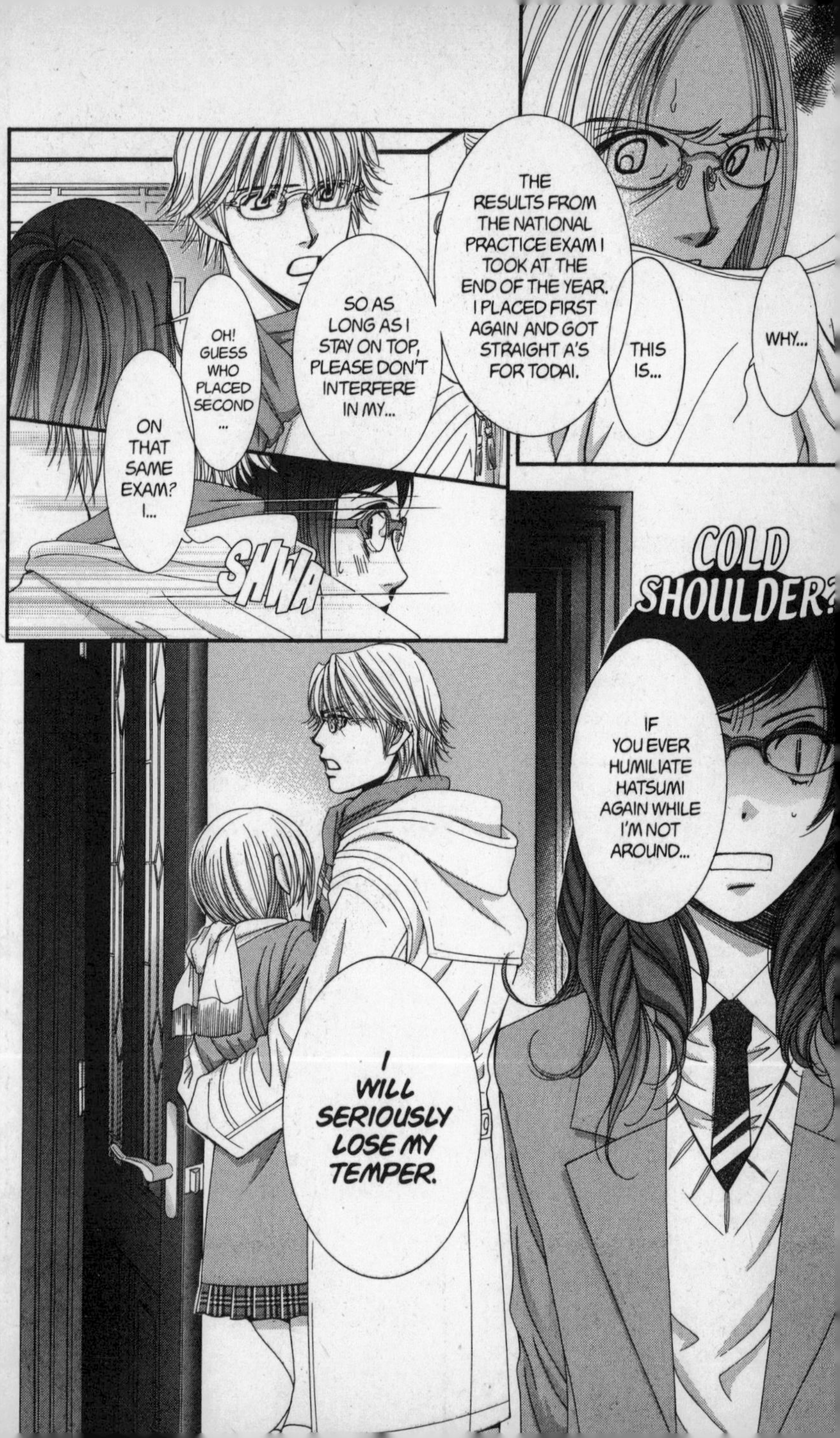
WHY...
THIS IS...
THE RESULTS FROM THE NATIONAL PRACTICE EXAM I TOOK AT THE END OF THE YEAR. I PLACED FIRST AGAIN AND GOT STRAIGHT A'S FOR TODAI.
SO AS LONG AS I STAY ON TOP, PLEASE DON'T INTERFERE IN MY...
OH! GUESS WHO PLACED SECOND ...
ON THAT SAME EXAM? I...
SHWA
COLD SHOULDER?
IF YOU EVER HUMILIATE HATSUMI AGAIN WHILE I'M NOT AROUND...
I WILL SERIOUSLY LOSE MY TEMPER.

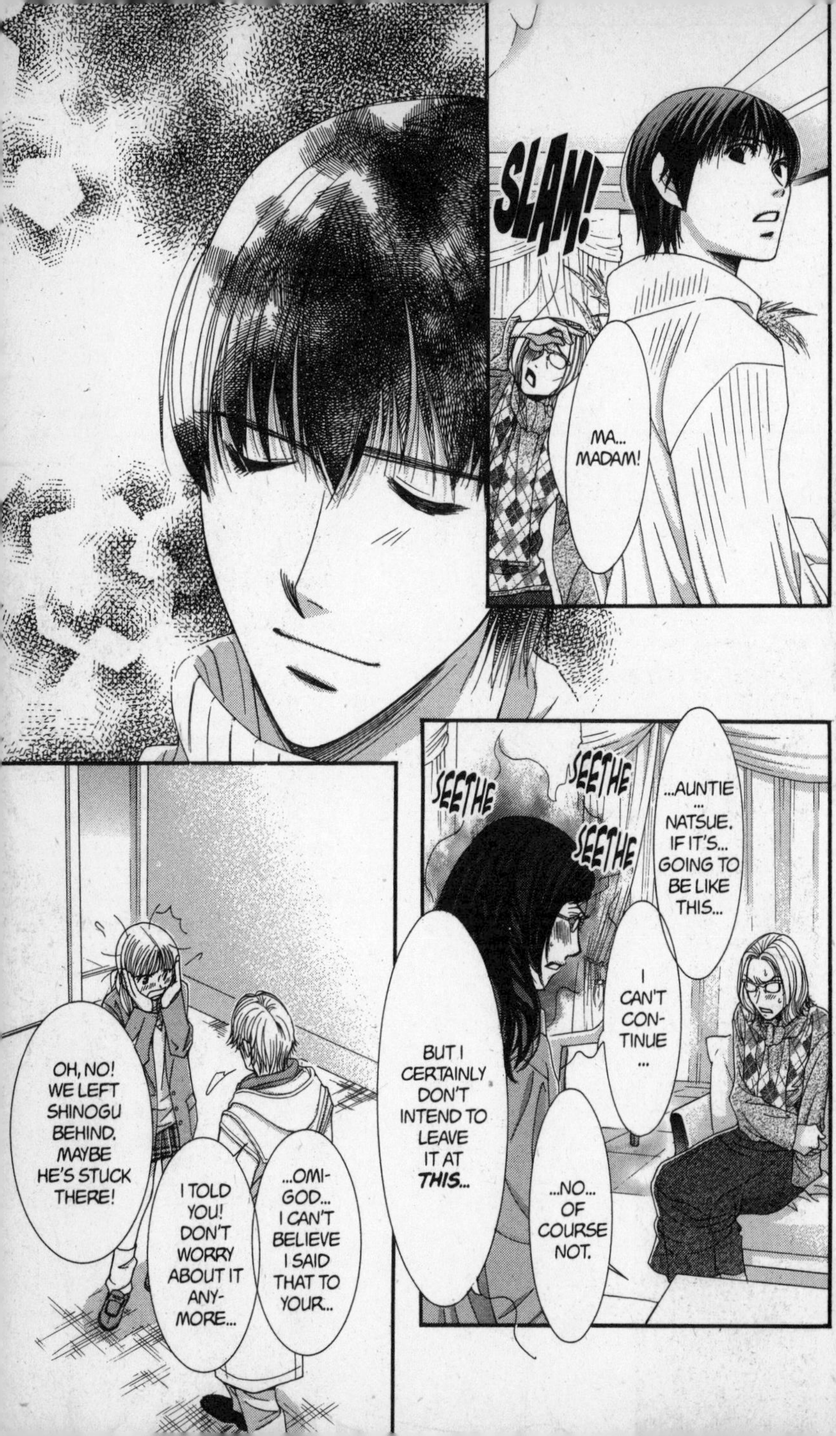
SLAM!
MA... MADAM!
...AUNTIE ... NATSUE. IF IT'S... GOING TO BE LIKE THIS...
SEETHE
SEETHE
SEETHE
I CAN'T CON-TINUE ...
...NO... OF COURSE NOT.
BUT I CERTAINLY DON'T INTEND TO LEAVE IT AT *THIS*...
OH, NO! WE LEFT SHINOGU BEHIND. MAYBE HE'S STUCK THERE!
I TOLD YOU! DON'T WORRY ABOUT IT ANY-MORE...
...OMI-GOD... I CAN'T BELIEVE I SAID THAT TO YOUR...

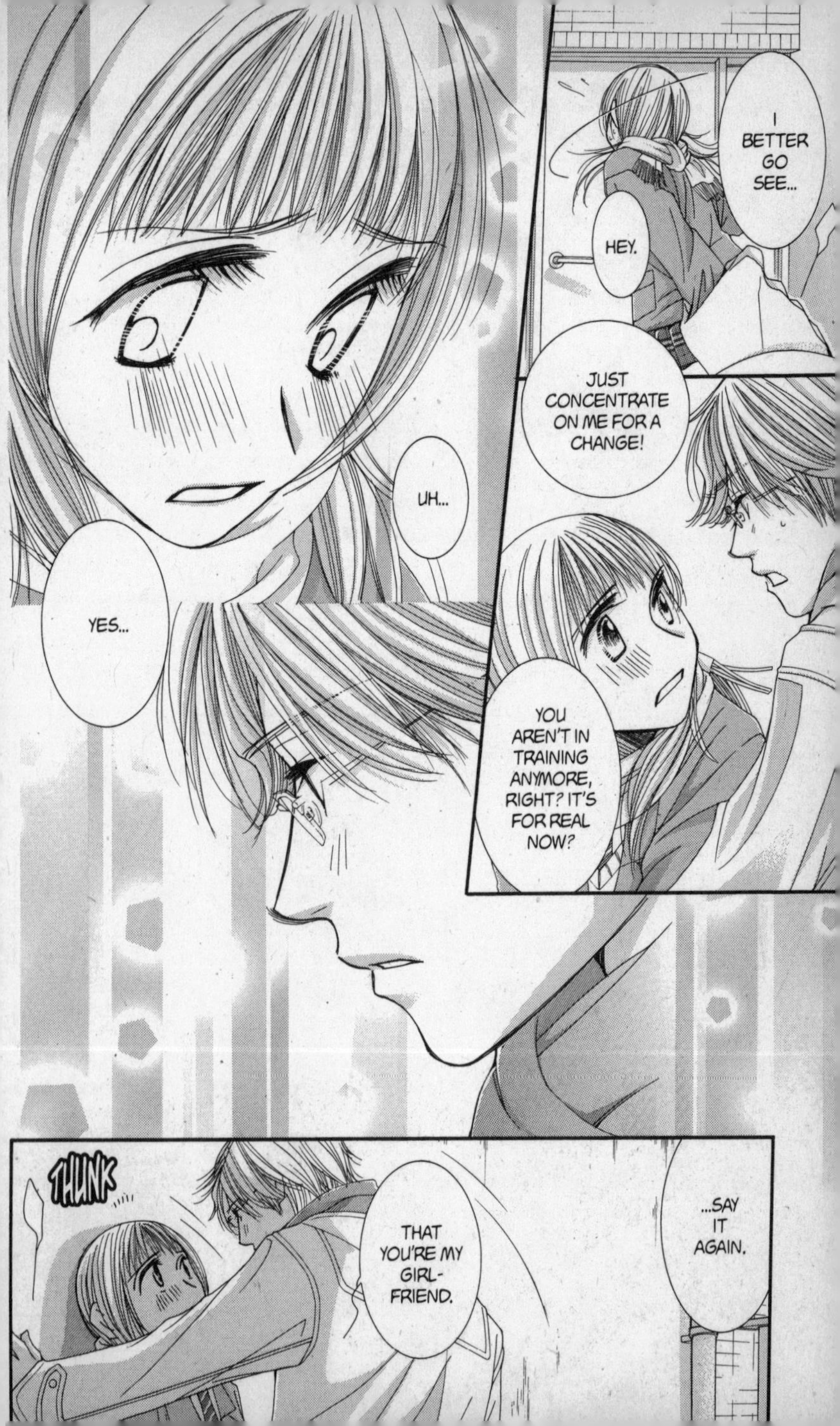

I BETTER GO SEE...
HEY.
JUST CONCENTRATE ON ME FOR A CHANGE!
YOU AREN'T IN TRAINING ANYMORE, RIGHT? IT'S FOR REAL NOW?
UH...
YES...
...SAY IT AGAIN.
THAT YOU'RE MY GIRL-FRIEND.
THUNK

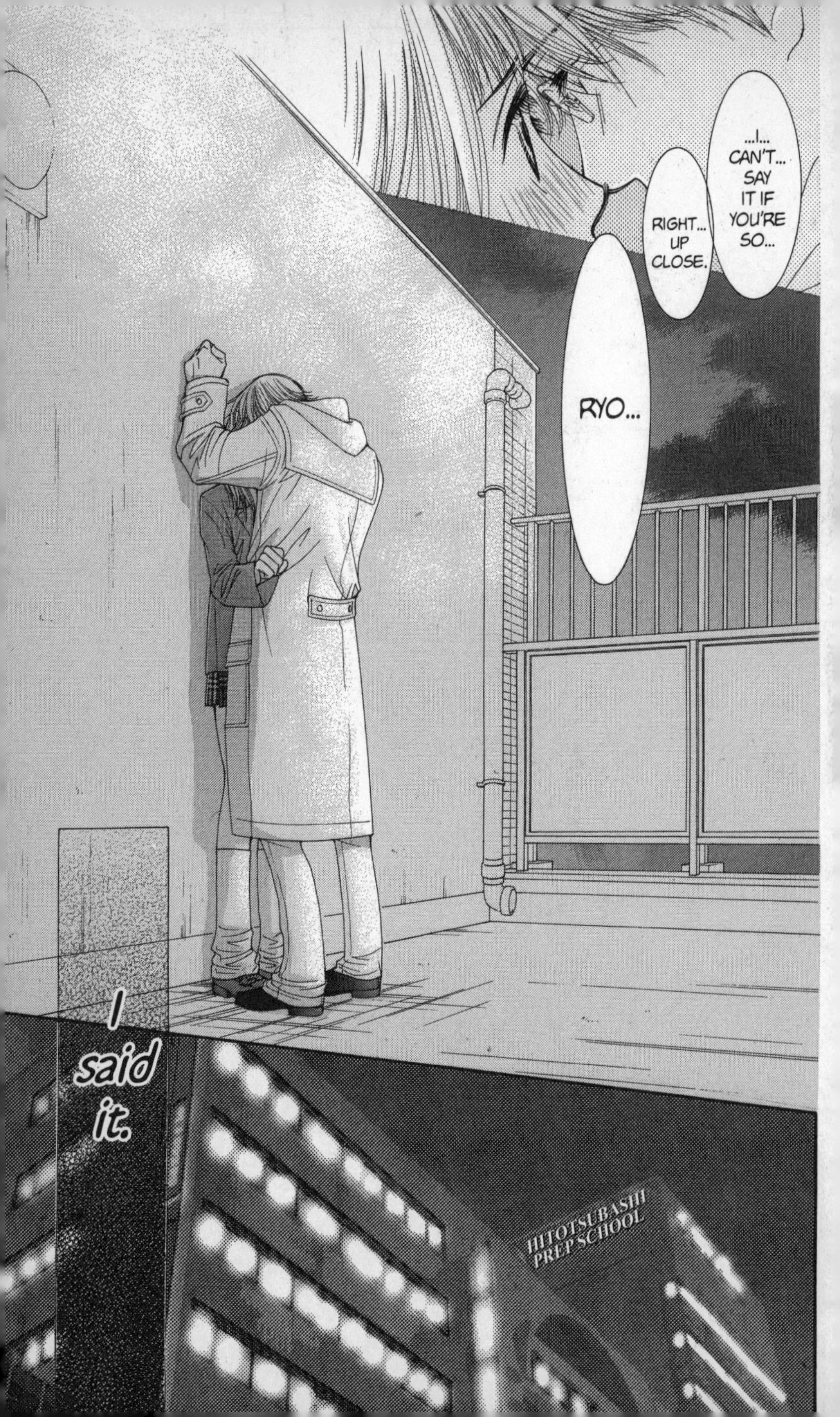
...I... CAN'T... SAY IT IF YOU'RE SO...
RIGHT... UP CLOSE.
RYO...
I said it.
HITOTSUBASHI PREP SCHOOL

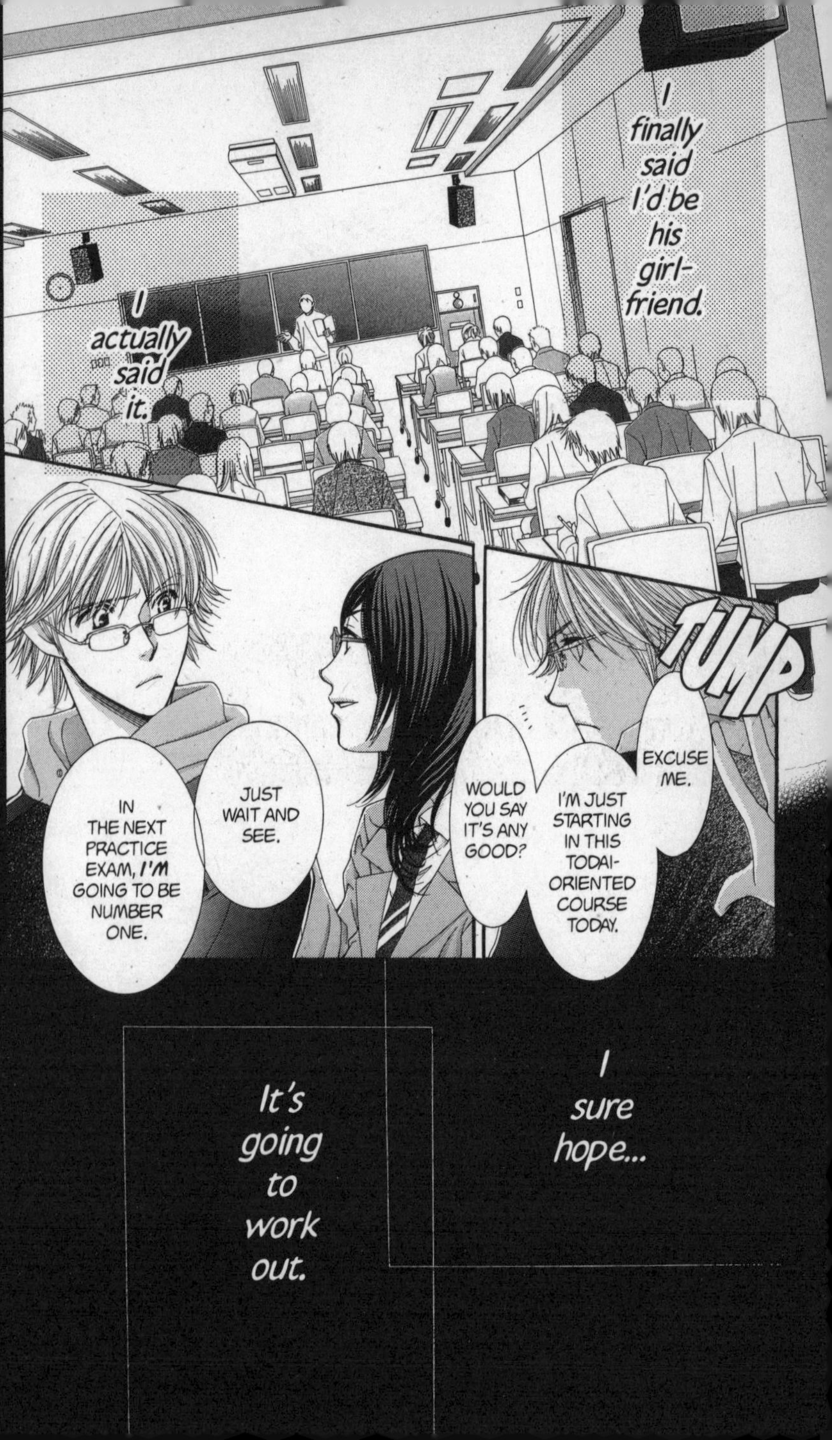
I finally said I'd be his girl-friend.
I actually said it.
TUMP
EXCUSE ME.
I'M JUST STARTING IN THIS TODAI-ORIENTED COURSE TODAY.
WOULD YOU SAY IT'S ANY GOOD?
JUST WAIT AND SEE.
IN THE NEXT PRACTICE EXAM, I'M GOING TO BE NUMBER ONE.
I sure hope...
It's going to work out.

hot gimmick

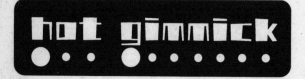

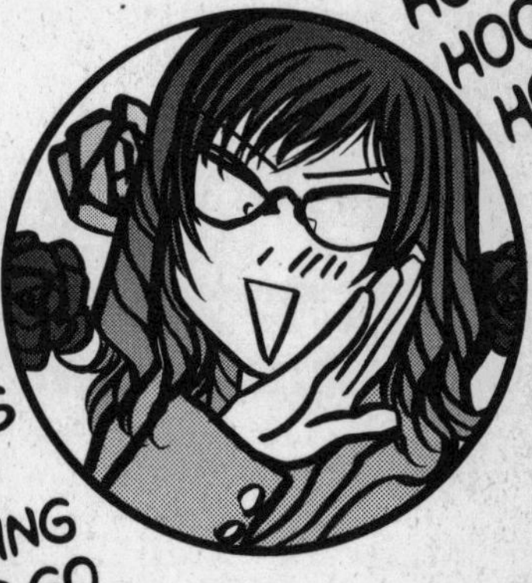
TOO HOO HOO HOO!
SOON ENOUGH HE'LL BE DOWN ON HIS KNEES AND BEGGING ME TO GO OUT WITH HIM!

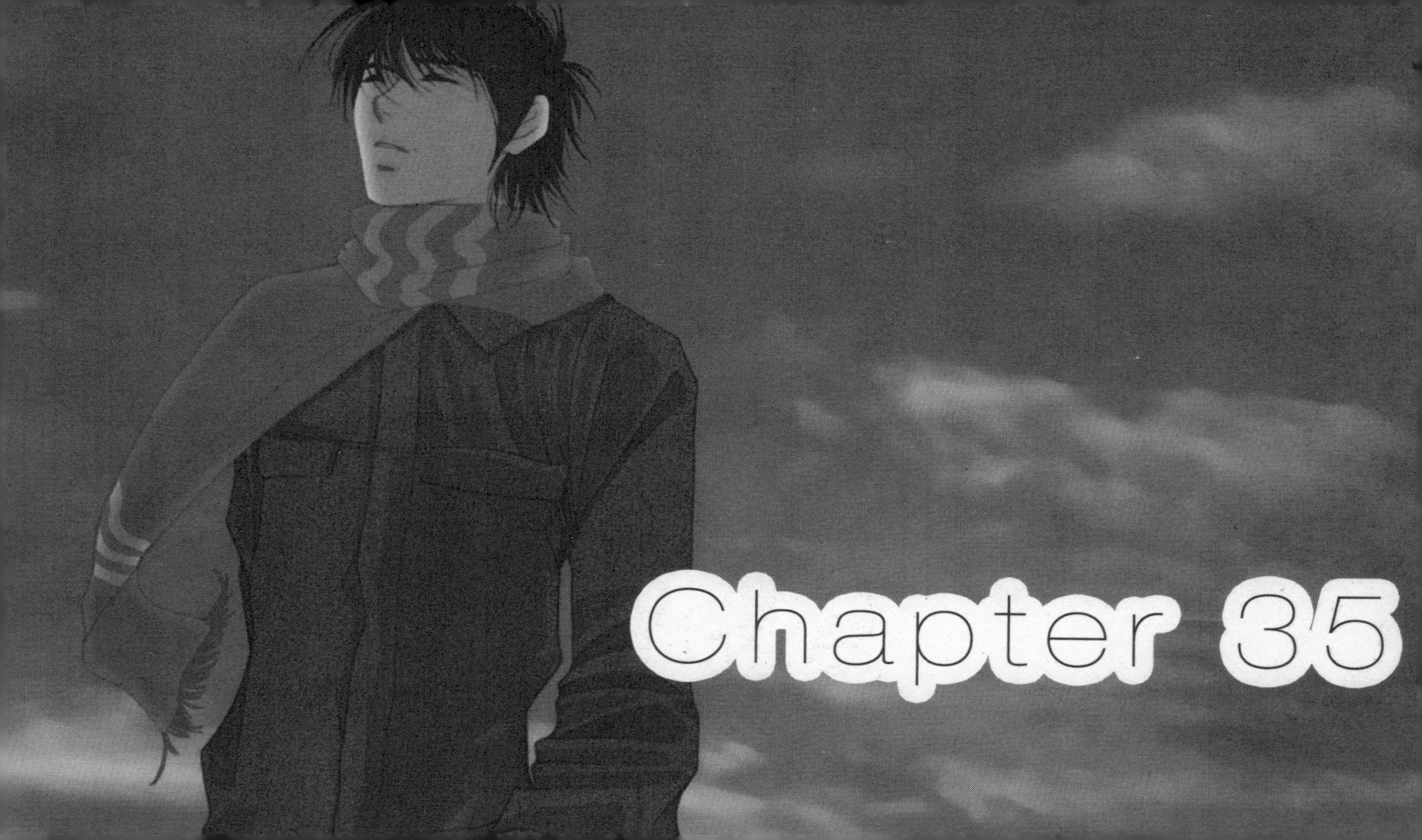
Chapter 35

hot gimmick

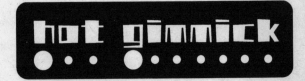

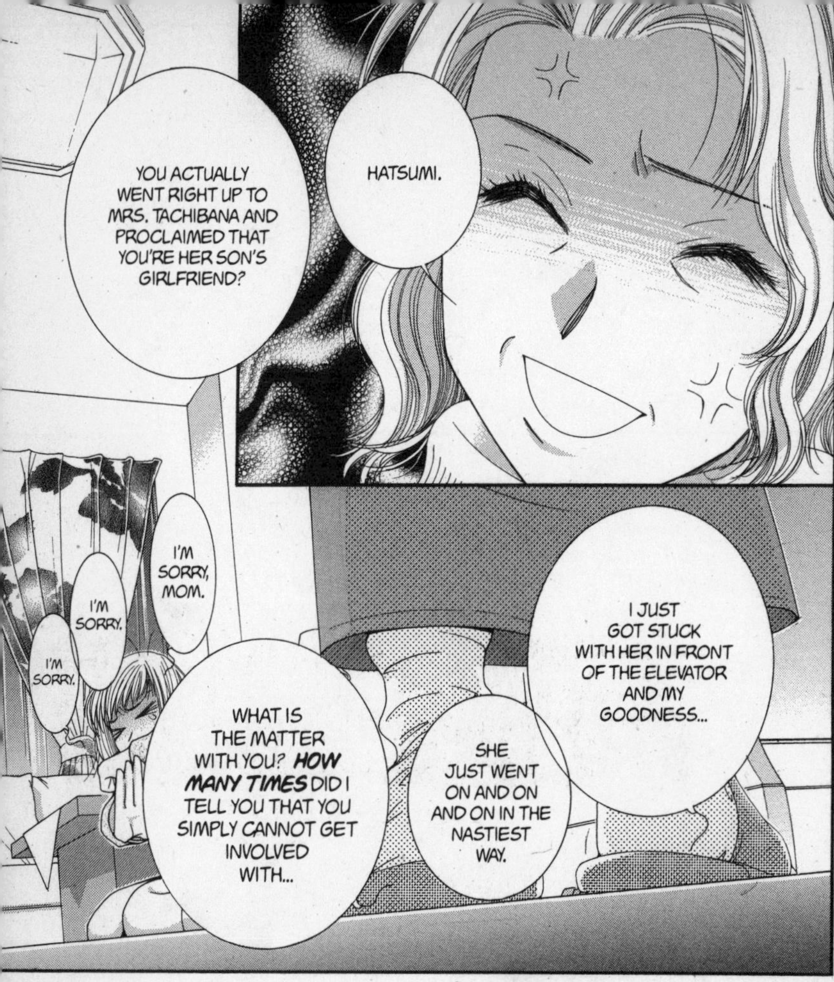
HATSUMI.
YOU ACTUALLY WENT RIGHT UP TO MRS. TACHIBANA AND PROCLAIMED THAT YOU'RE HER SON'S GIRLFRIEND?
I JUST GOT STUCK WITH HER IN FRONT OF THE ELEVATOR AND MY GOODNESS...
SHE JUST WENT ON AND ON AND ON IN THE NASTIEST WAY.
WHAT IS THE MATTER WITH YOU? HOW MANY TIMES DID I TELL YOU THAT YOU SIMPLY CANNOT GET INVOLVED WITH...
I'M SORRY, MOM.
I'M SORRY.
I'M SORRY.

hot gimmick

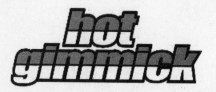

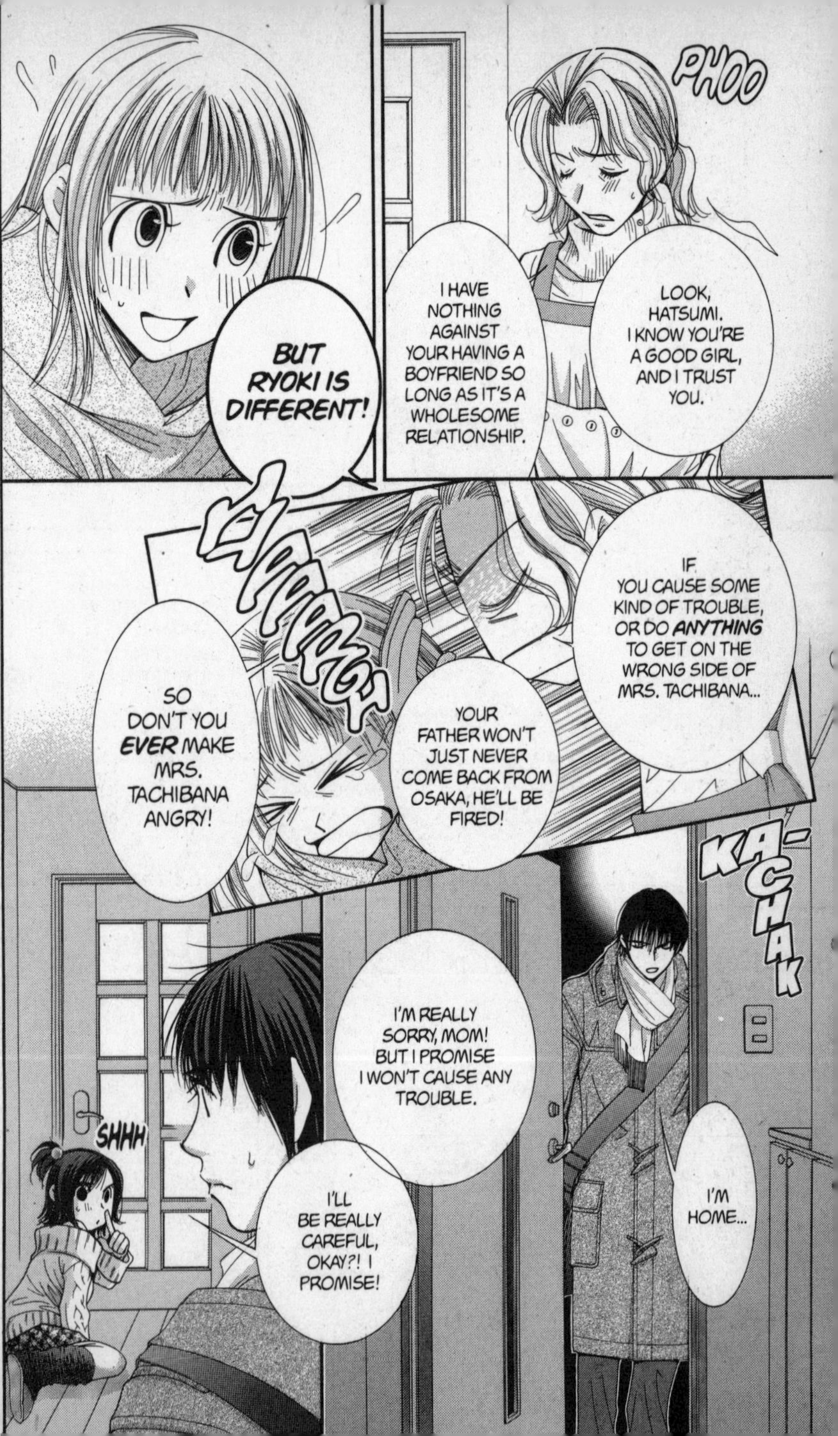
PHOO
LOOK, HATSUMI. I KNOW YOU'RE A GOOD GIRL, AND I TRUST YOU.
I HAVE NOTHING AGAINST YOUR HAVING A BOYFRIEND SO LONG AS IT'S A WHOLESOME RELATIONSHIP.
BUT RYOKI IS DIFFERENT!
IF YOU CAUSE SOME KIND OF TROUBLE, OR DO ANYTHING TO GET ON THE WRONG SIDE OF MRS. TACHIBANA...
YOUR FATHER WON'T JUST NEVER COME BACK FROM OSAKA, HE'LL BE FIRED!
SO DON'T YOU EVER MAKE MRS. TACHIBANA ANGRY!
KA-CHAK
I'M HOME...
I'M REALLY SORRY, MOM! BUT I PROMISE I WON'T CAUSE ANY TROUBLE.
I'LL BE REALLY CAREFUL, OKAY?! I PROMISE!
SHHH

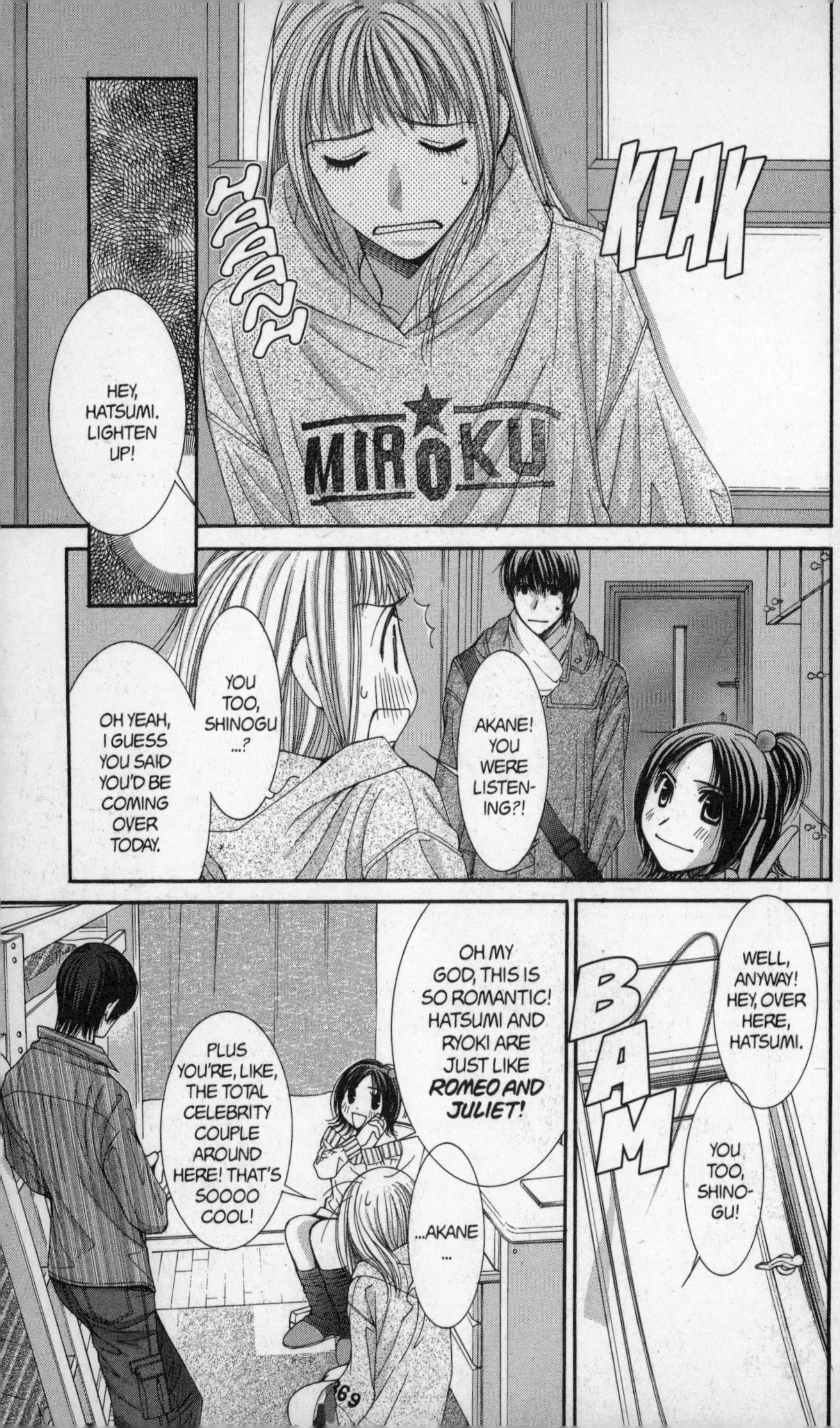
KLAK
HEY, HATSUMI. LIGHTEN UP!
MIROKU
AKANE! YOU WERE LISTENING?!
YOU TOO, SHINOGU ...?
OH YEAH, I GUESS YOU SAID YOU'D BE COMING OVER TODAY.
BAM
WELL, ANYWAY! HEY, OVER HERE, HATSUMI.
YOU TOO, SHINOGU!
OH MY GOD, THIS IS SO ROMANTIC! HATSUMI AND RYOKI ARE JUST LIKE ***ROMEO AND JULIET!***
PLUS YOU'RE, LIKE, THE TOTAL CELEBRITY COUPLE AROUND HERE! THAT'S SOOOO COOL!
...AKANE ...

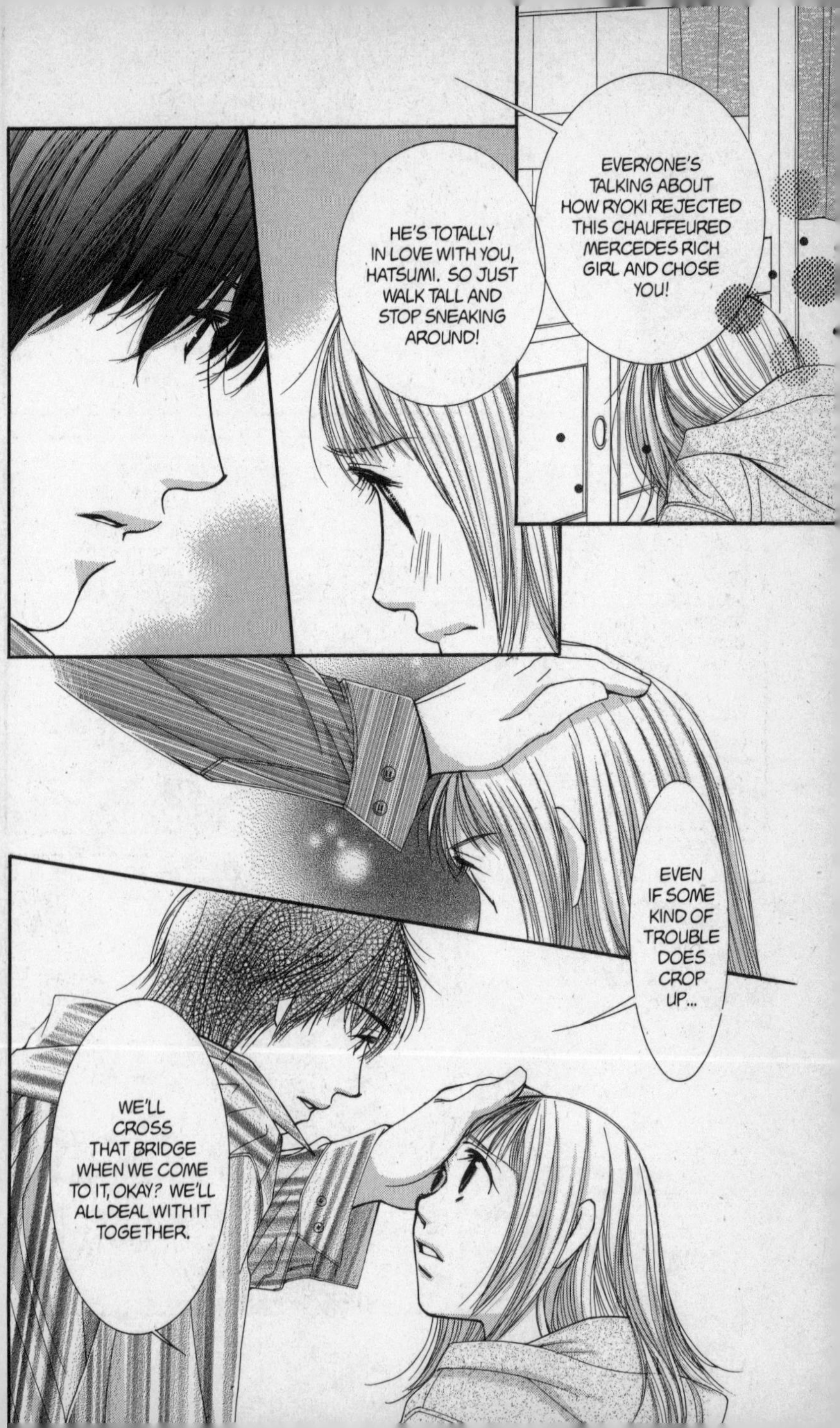
EVERYONE'S TALKING ABOUT HOW RYOKI REJECTED THIS CHAUFFEURED MERCEDES RICH GIRL AND CHOSE YOU!
HE'S TOTALLY IN LOVE WITH YOU, HATSUMI. SO JUST WALK TALL AND STOP SNEAKING AROUND!
EVEN IF SOME KIND OF TROUBLE DOES CROP UP...
WE'LL CROSS THAT BRIDGE WHEN WE COME TO IT, OKAY? WE'LL ALL DEAL WITH IT TOGETHER.

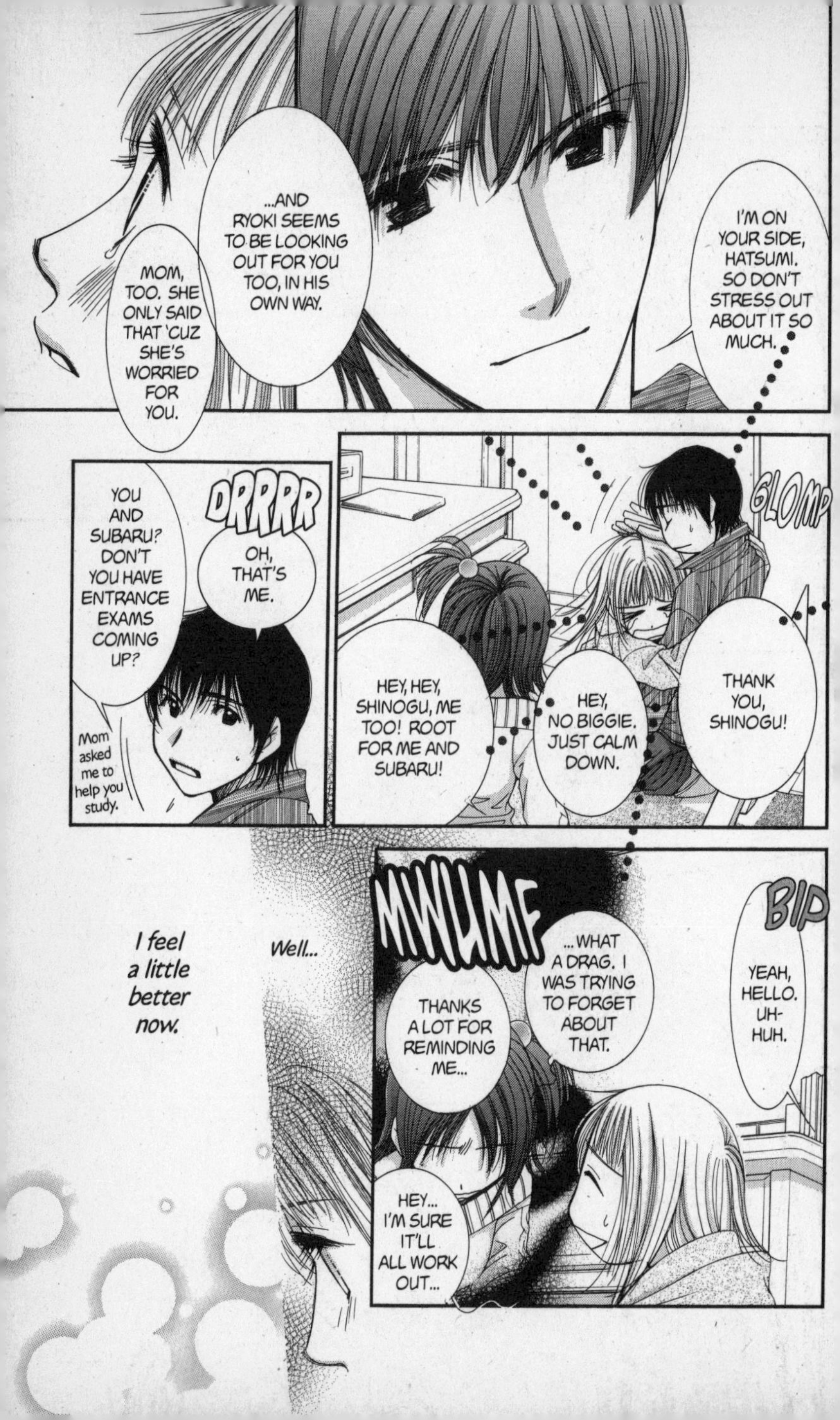
I'M ON YOUR SIDE, HATSUMI. SO DON'T STRESS OUT ABOUT IT SO MUCH.
...AND RYOKI SEEMS TO BE LOOKING OUT FOR YOU TOO, IN HIS OWN WAY.
MOM, TOO. SHE ONLY SAID THAT 'CUZ SHE'S WORRIED FOR YOU.
GLOMP
THANK YOU, SHINOGU!
HEY, NO BIGGIE. JUST CALM DOWN.
HEY, HEY, SHINOGU, ME TOO! ROOT FOR ME AND SUBARU!
DRRRR
OH, THAT'S ME.
YOU AND SUBARU? DON'T YOU HAVE ENTRANCE EXAMS COMING UP?
Mom asked me to help you study.
BIP
YEAH, HELLO. UH-HUH.
...WHAT A DRAG. I WAS TRYING TO FORGET ABOUT THAT.
MWUMF
THANKS A LOT FOR REMINDING ME...
HEY... I'M SURE IT'LL ALL WORK OUT...
Well...
I feel a little better now.

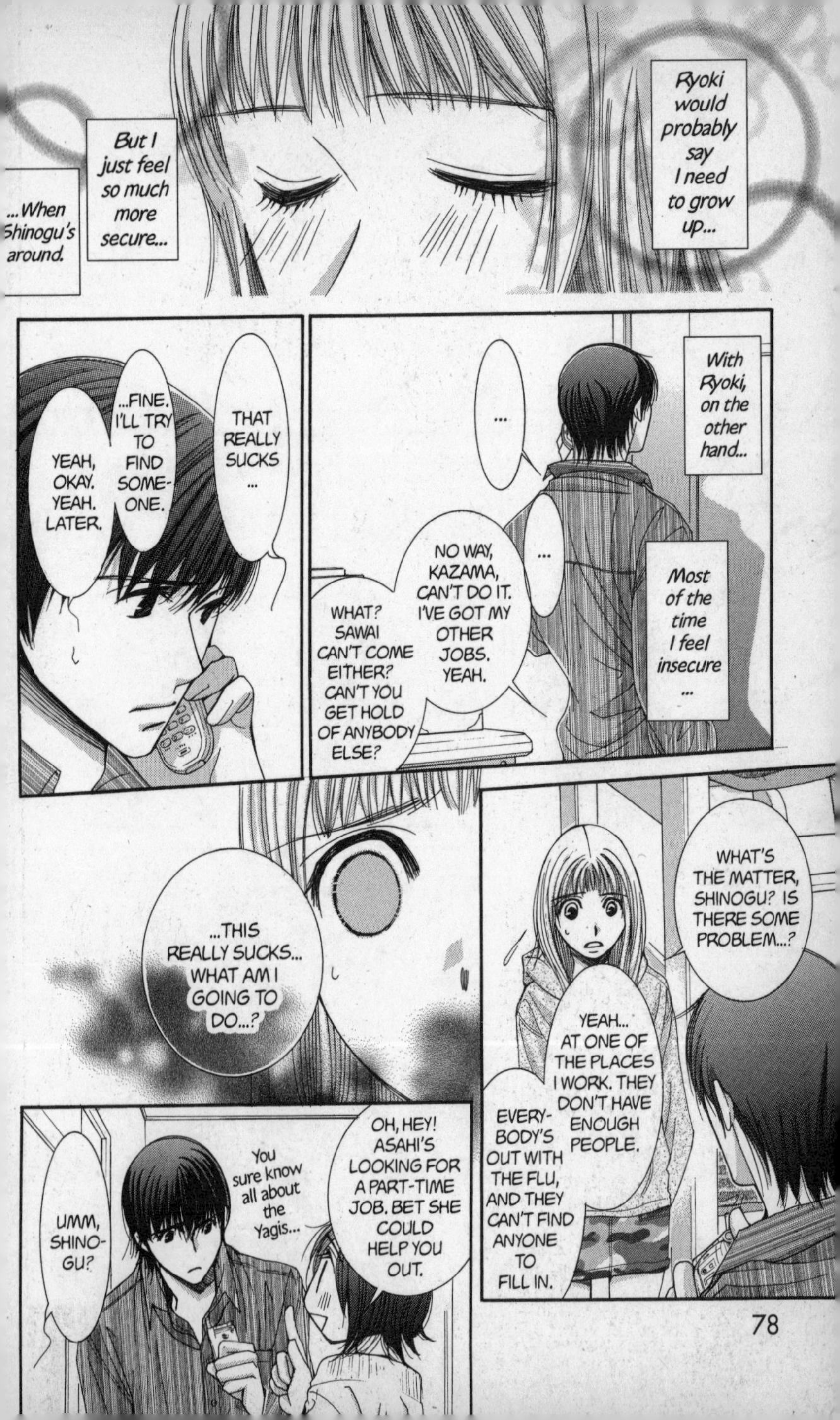
Ryoki would probably say I need to grow up...
But I just feel so much more secure...
...When Shinogu's around.
With Ryoki, on the other hand...
Most of the time I feel insecure ...
...
...
NO WAY, KAZAMA, CAN'T DO IT. I'VE GOT MY OTHER JOBS. YEAH.
WHAT? SAWAI CAN'T COME EITHER? CAN'T YOU GET HOLD OF ANYBODY ELSE?
THAT REALLY SUCKS ...
...FINE. I'LL TRY TO FIND SOME-ONE.
YEAH, OKAY. YEAH. LATER.
WHAT'S THE MATTER, SHINOGU? IS THERE SOME PROBLEM...?
YEAH... AT ONE OF THE PLACES I WORK. THEY DON'T HAVE ENOUGH PEOPLE.
EVERY-BODY'S OUT WITH THE FLU, AND THEY CAN'T FIND ANYONE TO FILL IN.
...THIS REALLY SUCKS... WHAT AM I GOING TO DO...?
OH, HEY! ASAHI'S LOOKING FOR A PART-TIME JOB. BET SHE COULD HELP YOU OUT.
You sure know all about the Yagis...
UMM, SHINO-GU?

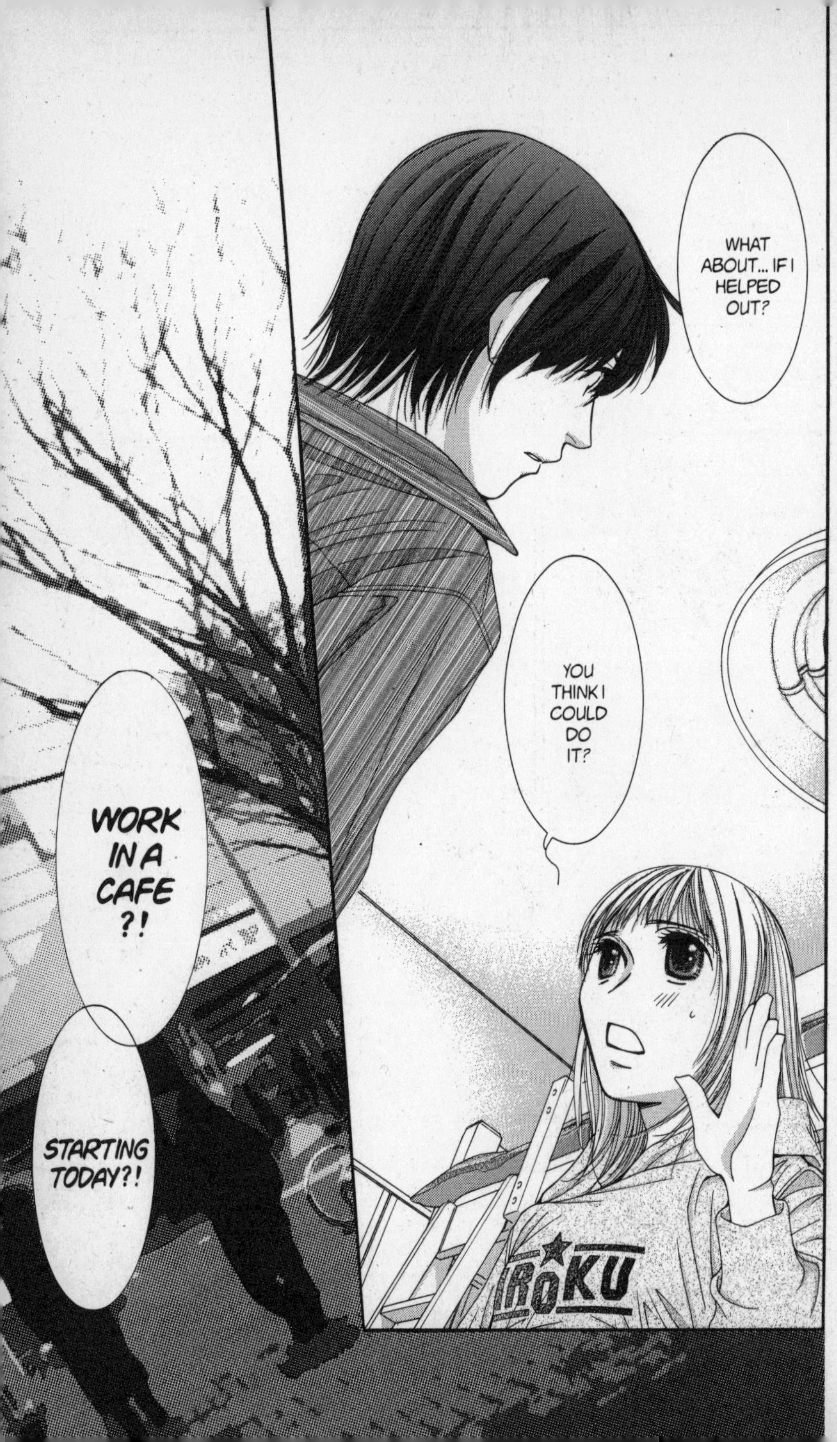
WHAT ABOUT... IF I HELPED OUT?
YOU THINK I COULD DO IT?
WORK IN A CAFE?!
STARTING TODAY?!

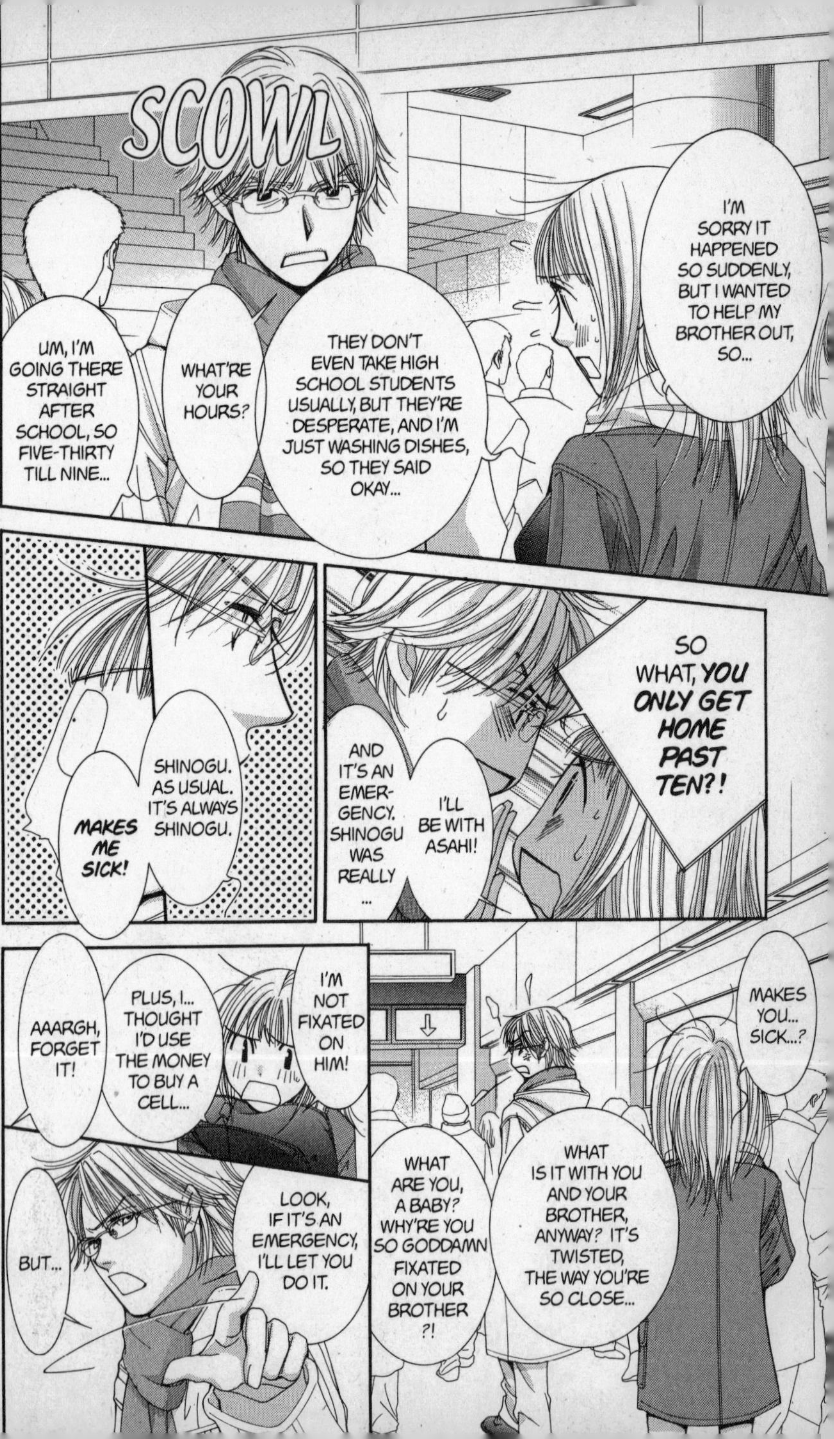
I'M SORRY IT HAPPENED SO SUDDENLY, BUT I WANTED TO HELP MY BROTHER OUT, SO...
SCOWL
THEY DON'T EVEN TAKE HIGH SCHOOL STUDENTS USUALLY, BUT THEY'RE DESPERATE, AND I'M JUST WASHING DISHES, SO THEY SAID OKAY...
WHAT'RE YOUR HOURS?
UM, I'M GOING THERE STRAIGHT AFTER SCHOOL, SO FIVE-THIRTY TILL NINE...
SO WHAT, YOU ONLY GET HOME PAST TEN?!
I'LL BE WITH ASAHI!
AND IT'S AN EMERGENCY. SHINOGU WAS REALLY ...
SHINOGU. AS USUAL. IT'S ALWAYS SHINOGU.
MAKES ME SICK!
MAKES YOU... SICK...?
WHAT IS IT WITH YOU AND YOUR BROTHER, ANYWAY? IT'S TWISTED, THE WAY YOU'RE SO CLOSE...
WHAT ARE YOU, A BABY? WHY'RE YOU SO GODDAMN FIXATED ON YOUR BROTHER ?!
I'M NOT FIXATED ON HIM!
PLUS, I... THOUGHT I'D USE THE MONEY TO BUY A CELL...
AAARGH, FORGET IT!
LOOK, IF IT'S AN EMERGENCY, I'LL LET YOU DO IT.
BUT...

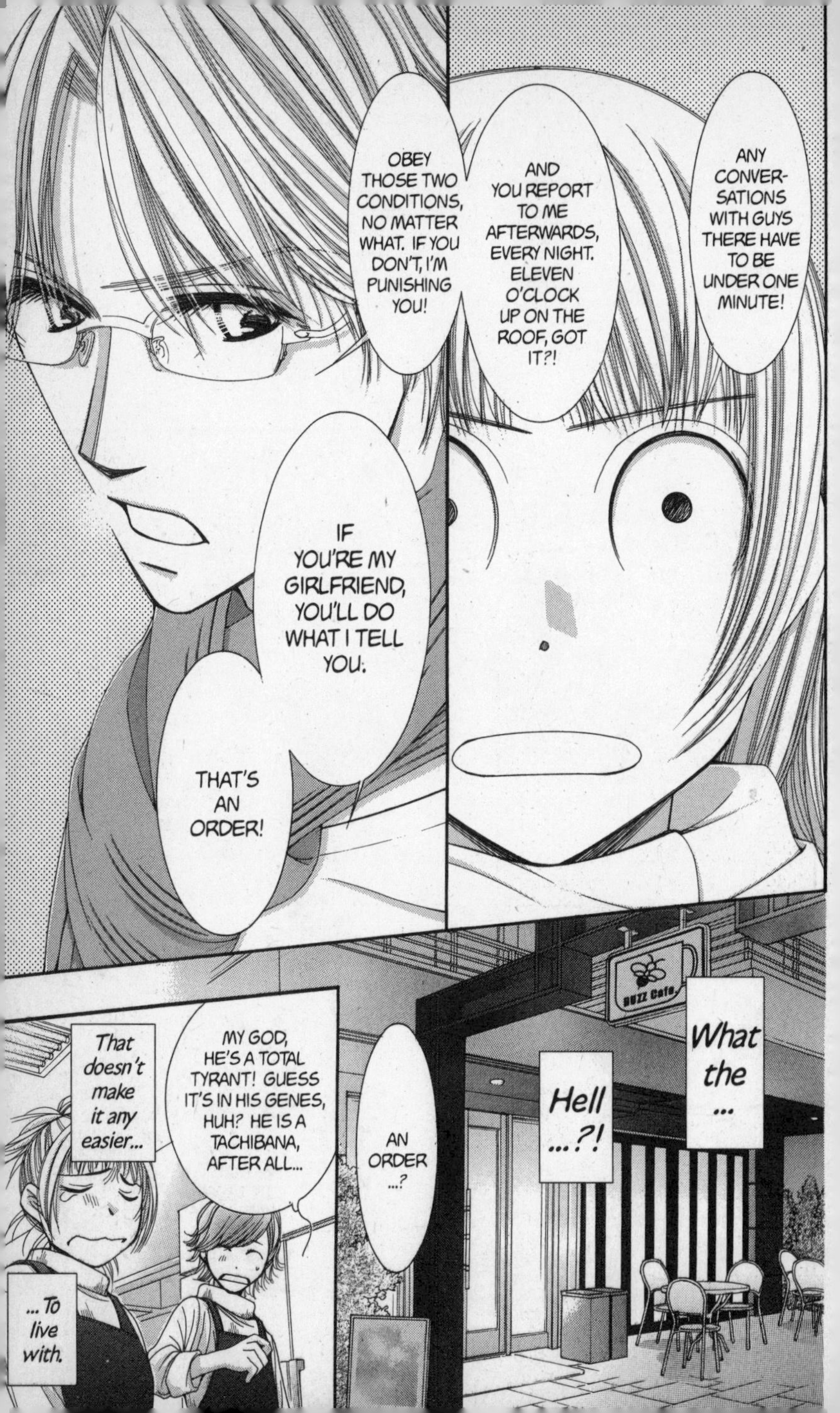
ANY CONVERSATIONS WITH GUYS THERE HAVE TO BE UNDER ONE MINUTE!
AND YOU REPORT TO ME AFTERWARDS, EVERY NIGHT. ELEVEN O'CLOCK UP ON THE ROOF, GOT IT?!
OBEY THOSE TWO CONDITIONS, NO MATTER WHAT. IF YOU DON'T, I'M PUNISHING YOU!
IF YOU'RE MY GIRLFRIEND, YOU'LL DO WHAT I TELL YOU.
THAT'S AN ORDER!
What the ...
Hell ...?!
AN ORDER ...?
MY GOD, HE'S A TOTAL TYRANT! GUESS IT'S IN HIS GENES, HUH? HE IS A TACHIBANA, AFTER ALL...
That doesn't make it any easier...
...To live with.

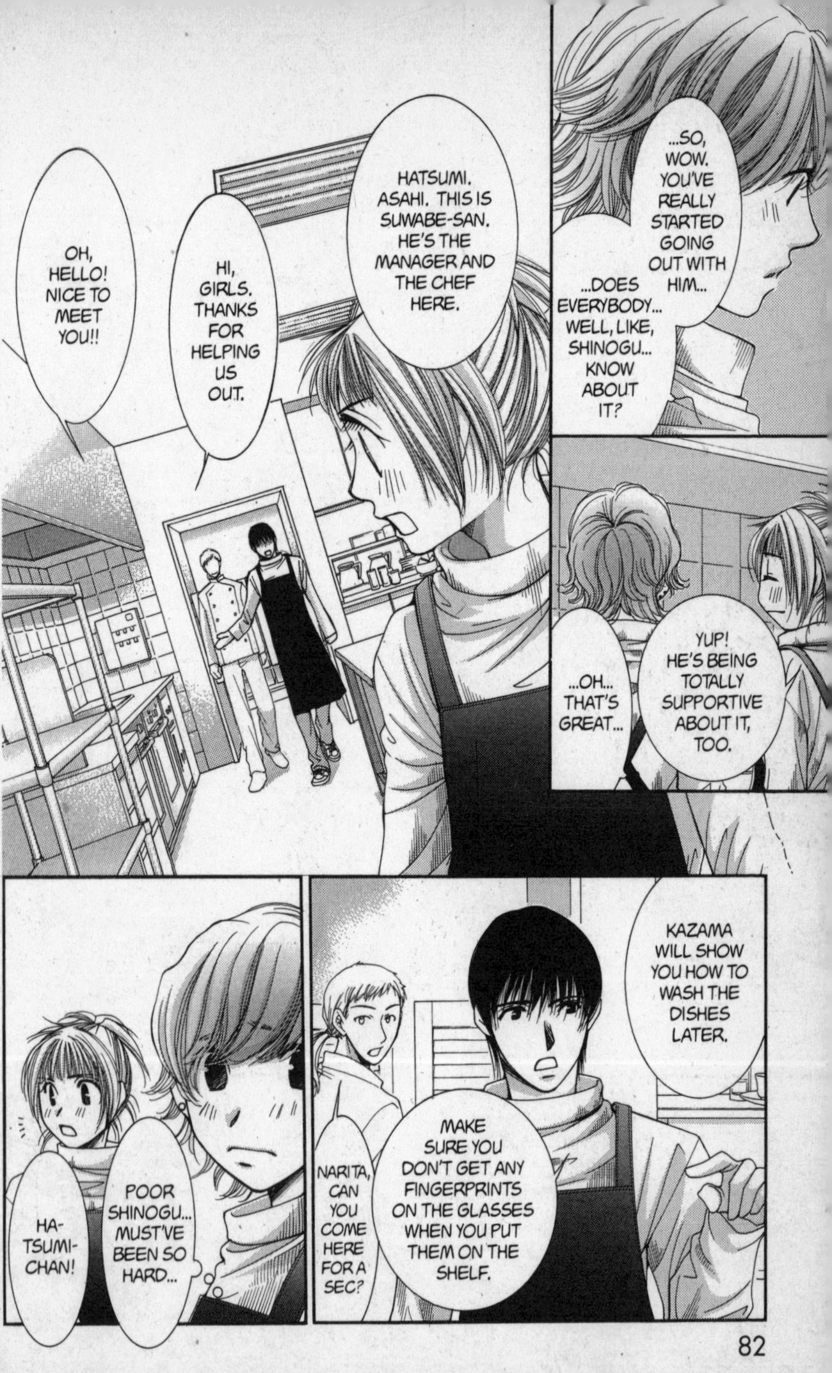
...SO, WOW. YOU'VE REALLY STARTED GOING OUT WITH HIM...
...DOES EVERYBODY... WELL, LIKE, SHINOGU... KNOW ABOUT IT?
YUP! HE'S BEING TOTALLY SUPPORTIVE ABOUT IT, TOO.
...OH... THAT'S GREAT...
HATSUMI. ASAHI. THIS IS SUWABE-SAN. HE'S THE MANAGER AND THE CHEF HERE.
HI, GIRLS. THANKS FOR HELPING US OUT.
OH, HELLO! NICE TO MEET YOU!!
KAZAMA WILL SHOW YOU HOW TO WASH THE DISHES LATER.
MAKE SURE YOU DON'T GET ANY FINGERPRINTS ON THE GLASSES WHEN YOU PUT THEM ON THE SHELF.
NARITA, CAN YOU COME HERE FOR A SEC?
POOR SHINOGU... MUST'VE BEEN SO HARD...
HA-TSUMI-CHAN!

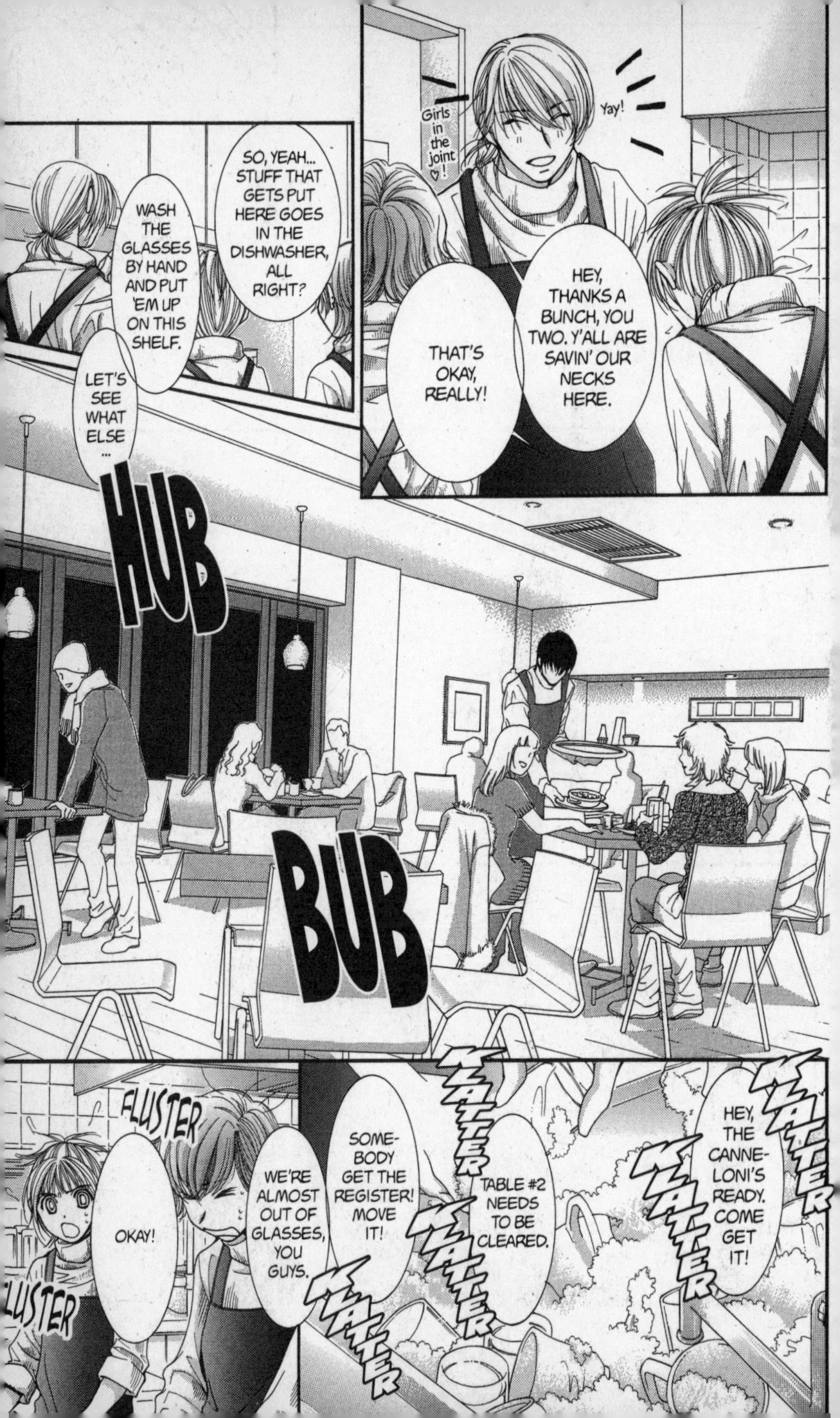
Girls in the joint ♡!
Yay!
HEY, THANKS A BUNCH, YOU TWO. Y'ALL ARE SAVIN' OUR NECKS HERE.
THAT'S OKAY, REALLY!
SO, YEAH... STUFF THAT GETS PUT HERE GOES IN THE DISHWASHER, ALL RIGHT?
WASH THE GLASSES BY HAND AND PUT 'EM UP ON THIS SHELF.
LET'S SEE WHAT ELSE ...
HUB
BUB
KLATTER
HEY, THE CANNE-LONI'S READY. COME GET IT!
KLATTER
TABLE #2 NEEDS TO BE CLEARED.
KLATTER
SOME-BODY GET THE REGISTER! MOVE IT!
KLATTER
WE'RE ALMOST OUT OF GLASSES, YOU GUYS.
FLUSTER
OKAY!
LUSTER

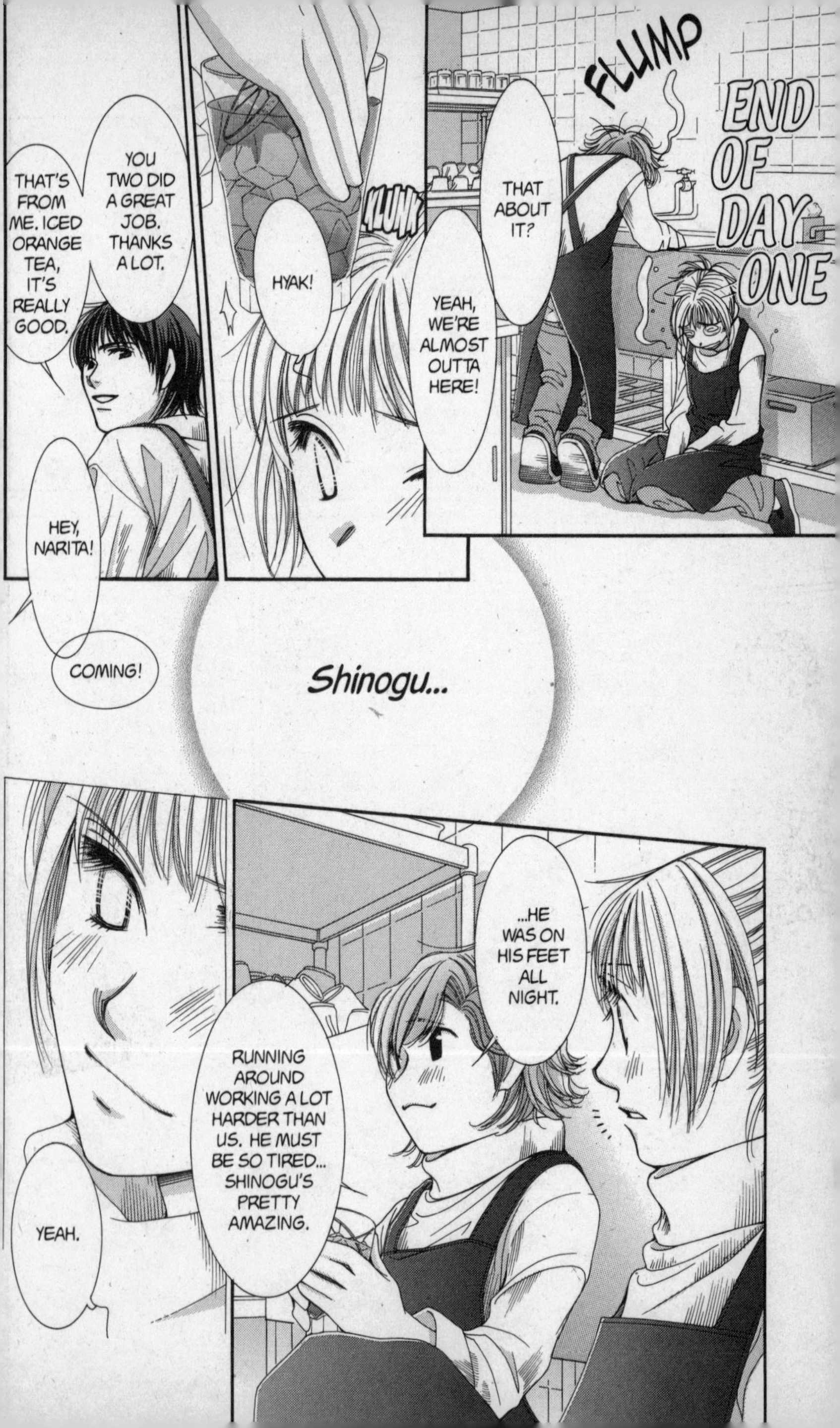
END OF DAY ONE
FLUMP
THAT ABOUT IT?
YEAH, WE'RE ALMOST OUTTA HERE!
KLUNK
HYAK!
YOU TWO DID A GREAT JOB. THANKS A LOT.
THAT'S FROM ME. ICED ORANGE TEA, IT'S REALLY GOOD.
HEY, NARITA!
Shinogu...
COMING!
...HE WAS ON HIS FEET ALL NIGHT.
RUNNING AROUND WORKING A LOT HARDER THAN US. HE MUST BE SO TIRED... SHINOGU'S PRETTY AMAZING.
YEAH.

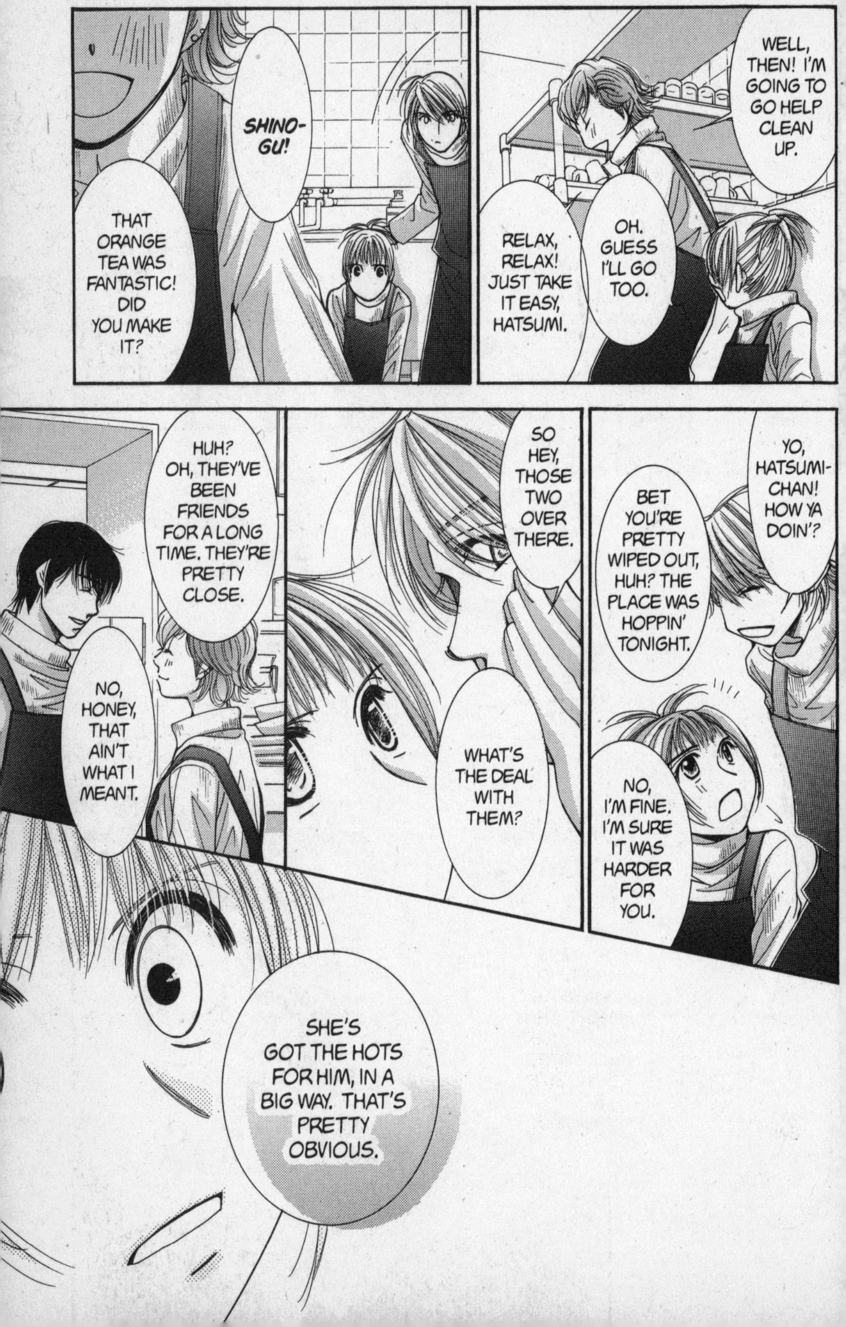
WELL, THEN! I'M GOING TO GO HELP CLEAN UP.
OH. GUESS I'LL GO TOO.
RELAX, RELAX! JUST TAKE IT EASY, HATSUMI.
SHINO-GU!
THAT ORANGE TEA WAS FANTASTIC! DID YOU MAKE IT?
YO, HATSUMI-CHAN! HOW YA DOIN'?
BET YOU'RE PRETTY WIPED OUT, HUH? THE PLACE WAS HOPPIN' TONIGHT.
NO, I'M FINE. I'M SURE IT WAS HARDER FOR YOU.
SO HEY, THOSE TWO OVER THERE.
WHAT'S THE DEAL WITH THEM?
HUH? OH, THEY'VE BEEN FRIENDS FOR A LONG TIME. THEY'RE PRETTY CLOSE.
NO, HONEY, THAT AIN'T WHAT I MEANT.
SHE'S GOT THE HOTS FOR HIM, IN A BIG WAY. THAT'S PRETTY OBVIOUS.

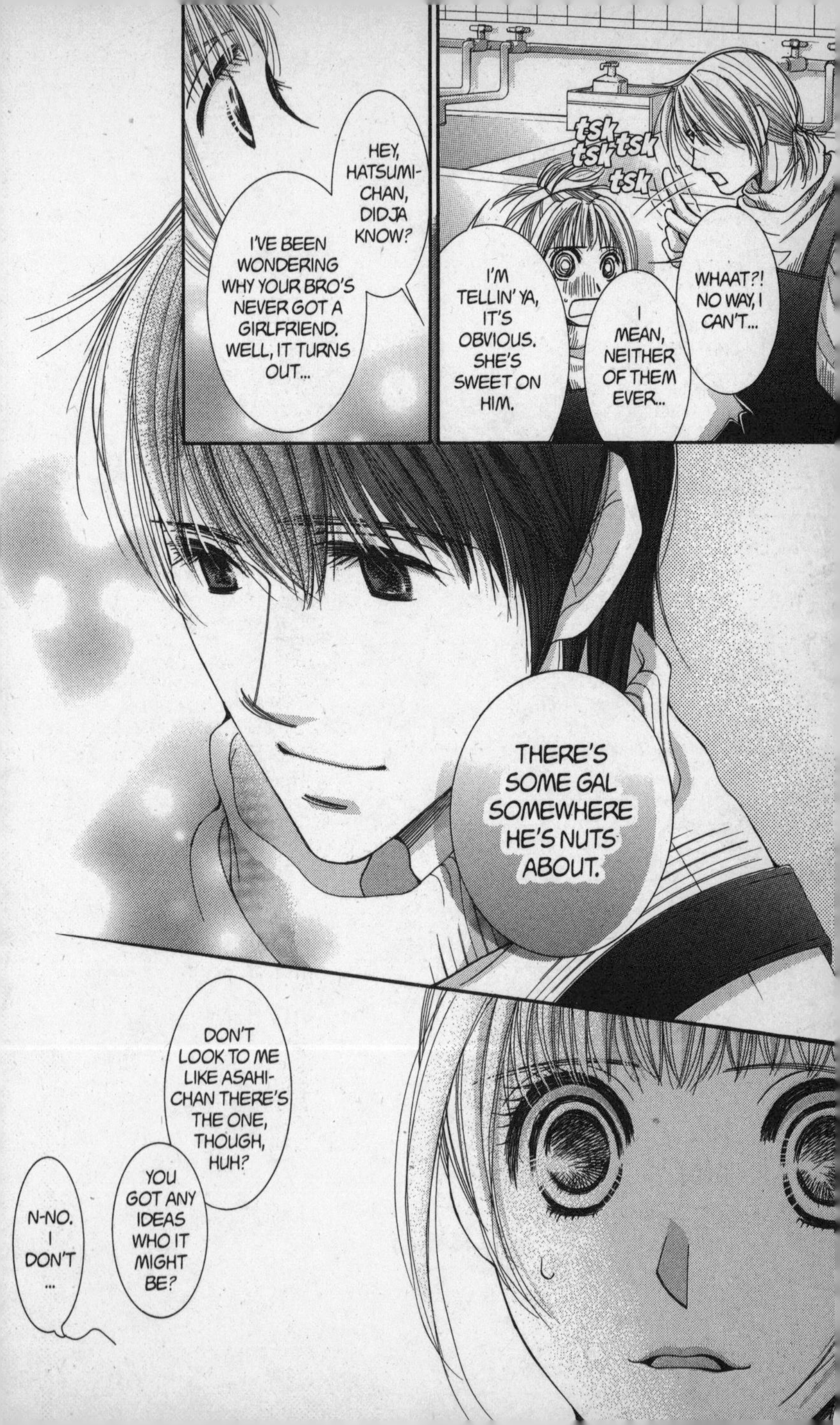
tsk tsk tsk tsk
WHAAT?! NO WAY, I CAN'T...
I MEAN, NEITHER OF THEM EVER...
I'M TELLIN' YA, IT'S OBVIOUS. SHE'S SWEET ON HIM.
HEY, HATSUMI-CHAN, DIDJA KNOW?
I'VE BEEN WONDERING WHY YOUR BRO'S NEVER GOT A GIRLFRIEND. WELL, IT TURNS OUT...
THERE'S SOME GAL SOMEWHERE HE'S NUTS ABOUT.
DON'T LOOK TO ME LIKE ASAHI-CHAN THERE'S THE ONE, THOUGH, HUH?
YOU GOT ANY IDEAS WHO IT MIGHT BE?
N-NO. I DON'T ...

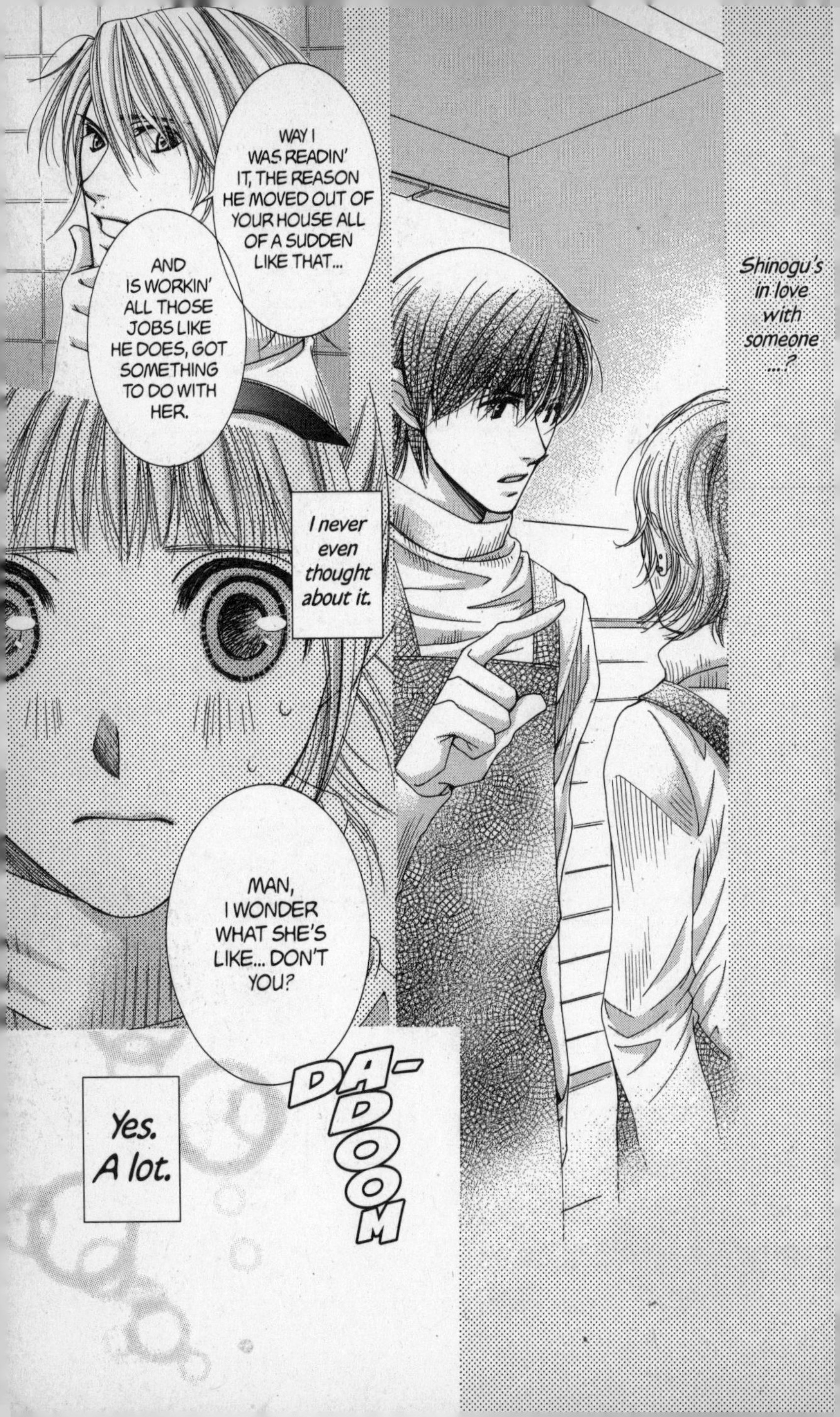
Shinogu's in love with someone ...?
WAY I WAS READIN' IT, THE REASON HE MOVED OUT OF YOUR HOUSE ALL OF A SUDDEN LIKE THAT...
AND IS WORKIN' ALL THOSE JOBS LIKE HE DOES, GOT SOMETHING TO DO WITH HER.
I never even thought about it.
MAN, I WONDER WHAT SHE'S LIKE... DON'T YOU?
DA-DOOOM
Yes. A lot.

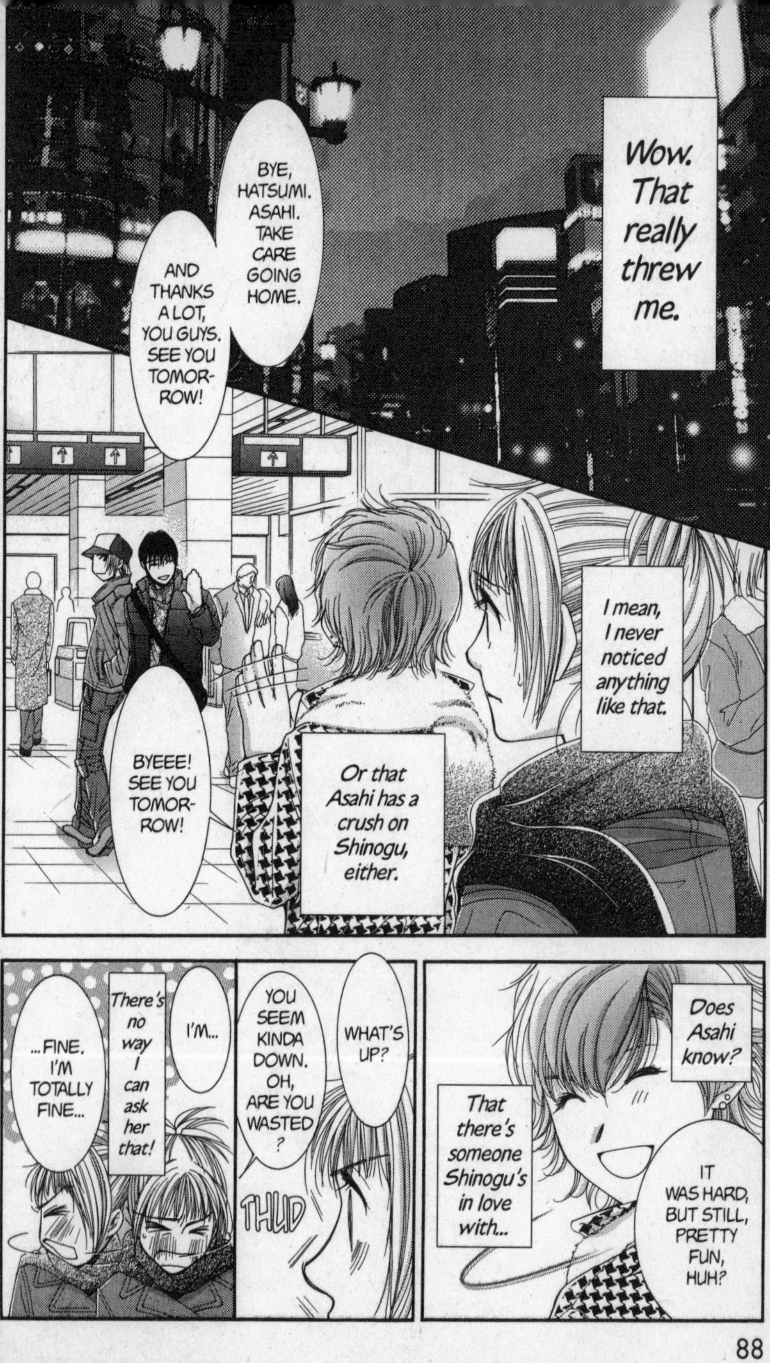
Wow. That really threw me.
BYE, HATSUMI. ASAHI. TAKE CARE GOING HOME.
AND THANKS A LOT, YOU GUYS. SEE YOU TOMOR-ROW!
I mean, I never noticed anything like that.
Or that Asahi has a crush on Shinogu, either.
BYEEE! SEE YOU TOMOR-ROW!
Does Asahi know?
That there's someone Shinogu's in love with...
IT WAS HARD, BUT STILL, PRETTY FUN, HUH?
WHAT'S UP?
YOU SEEM KINDA DOWN. OH, ARE YOU WASTED?
THUD
I'M...
There's no way I can ask her that!
...FINE. I'M TOTALLY FINE...

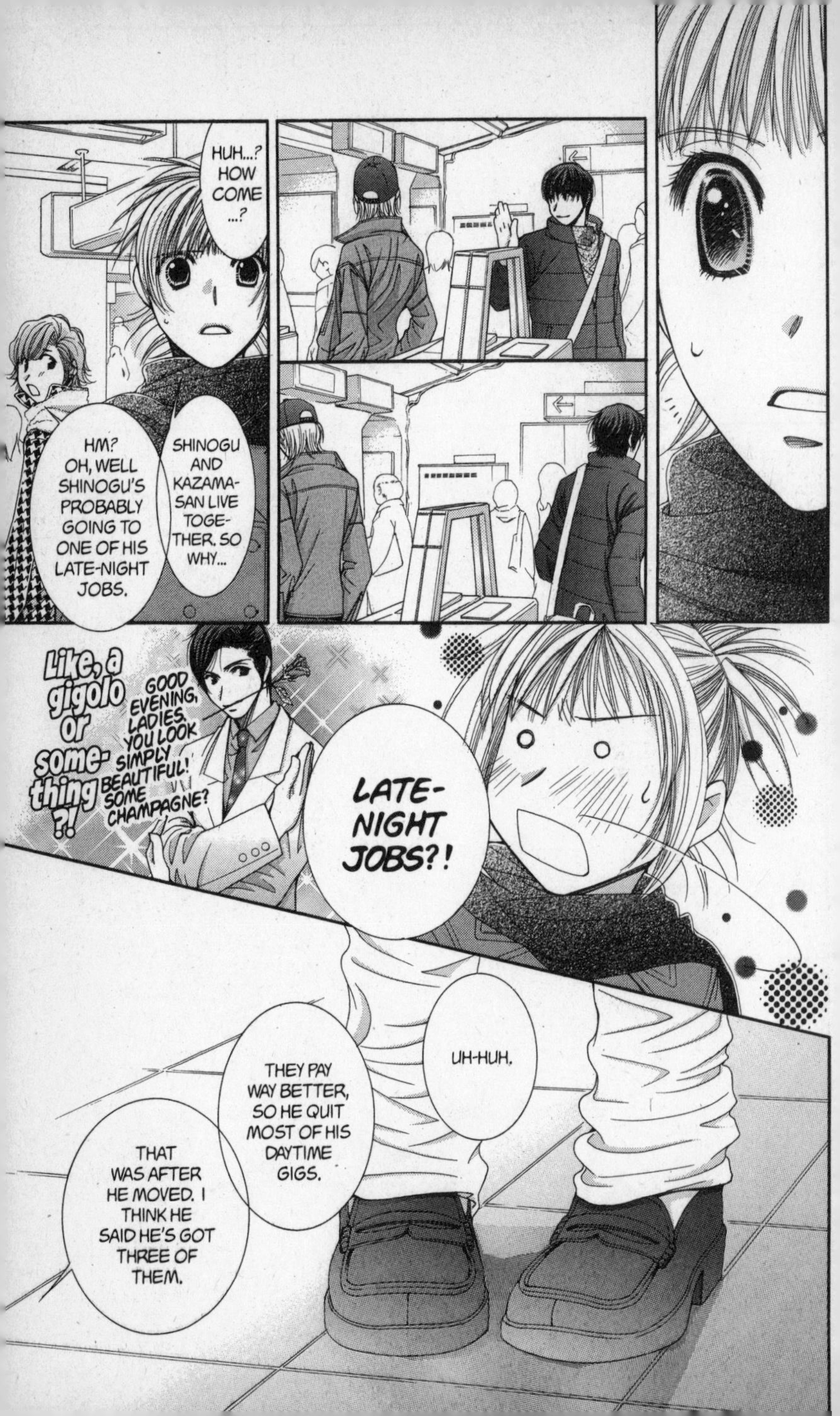
HUH...? HOW COME ...?
SHINOGU AND KAZAMA-SAN LIVE TOGE-THER. SO WHY...
HM? OH, WELL SHINOGU'S PROBABLY GOING TO ONE OF HIS LATE-NIGHT JOBS.
LATE-NIGHT JOBS?!
GOOD EVENING, LADIES. YOU LOOK SIMPLY BEAUTIFUL! SOME CHAMPAGNE?
Like, a gigolo or some-thing?!
UH-HUH.
THEY PAY WAY BETTER, SO HE QUIT MOST OF HIS DAYTIME GIGS.
THAT WAS AFTER HE MOVED. I THINK HE SAID HE'S GOT THREE OF THEM.

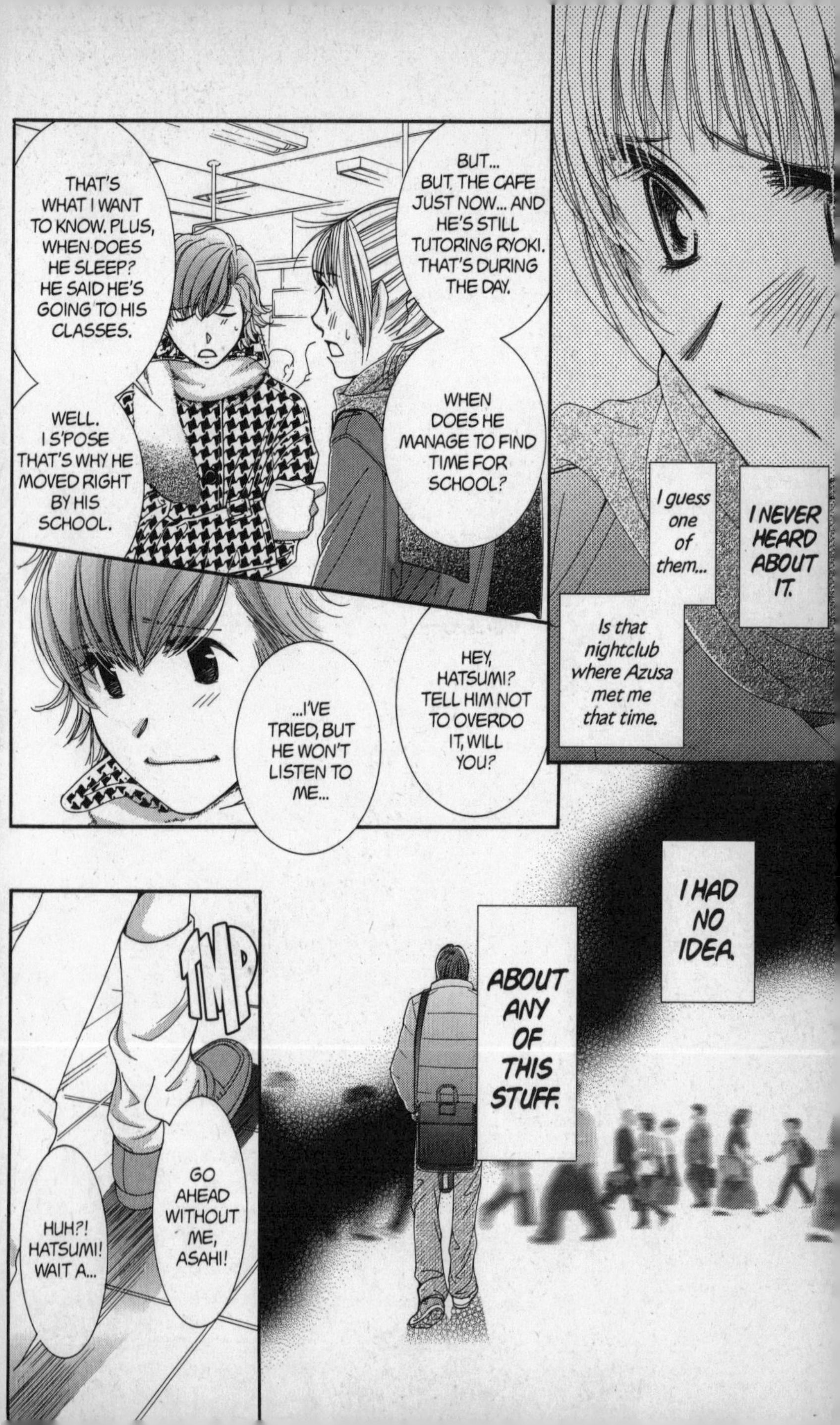
I NEVER HEARD ABOUT IT.
I guess one of them...
Is that nightclub where Azusa met me that time.
BUT... BUT THE CAFE JUST NOW... AND HE'S STILL TUTORING RYOKI. THAT'S DURING THE DAY.
WHEN DOES HE MANAGE TO FIND TIME FOR SCHOOL?
THAT'S WHAT I WANT TO KNOW. PLUS, WHEN DOES HE SLEEP? HE SAID HE'S GOING TO HIS CLASSES.
WELL. I S'POSE THAT'S WHY HE MOVED RIGHT BY HIS SCHOOL.
HEY, HATSUMI? TELL HIM NOT TO OVERDO IT, WILL YOU?
...I'VE TRIED, BUT HE WON'T LISTEN TO ME...
I HAD NO IDEA.
ABOUT ANY OF THIS STUFF.
TMP
GO AHEAD WITHOUT ME, ASAHI!
HUH?! HATSUMI! WAIT A...

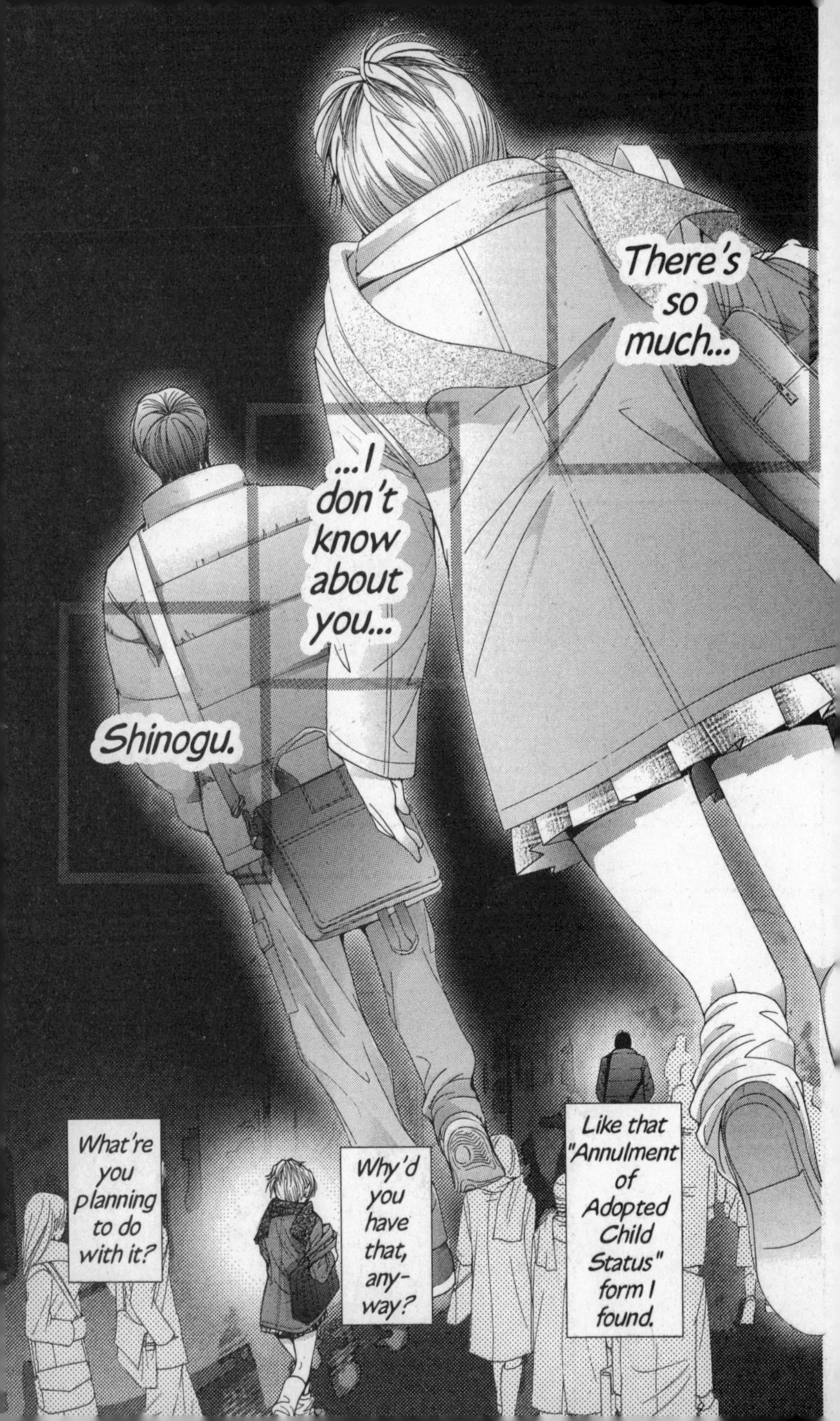
There's so much...
...I don't know about you...
Shinogu.
Like that "Annulment of Adopted Child Status" form I found.
Why'd you have that, anyway?
What're you planning to do with it?

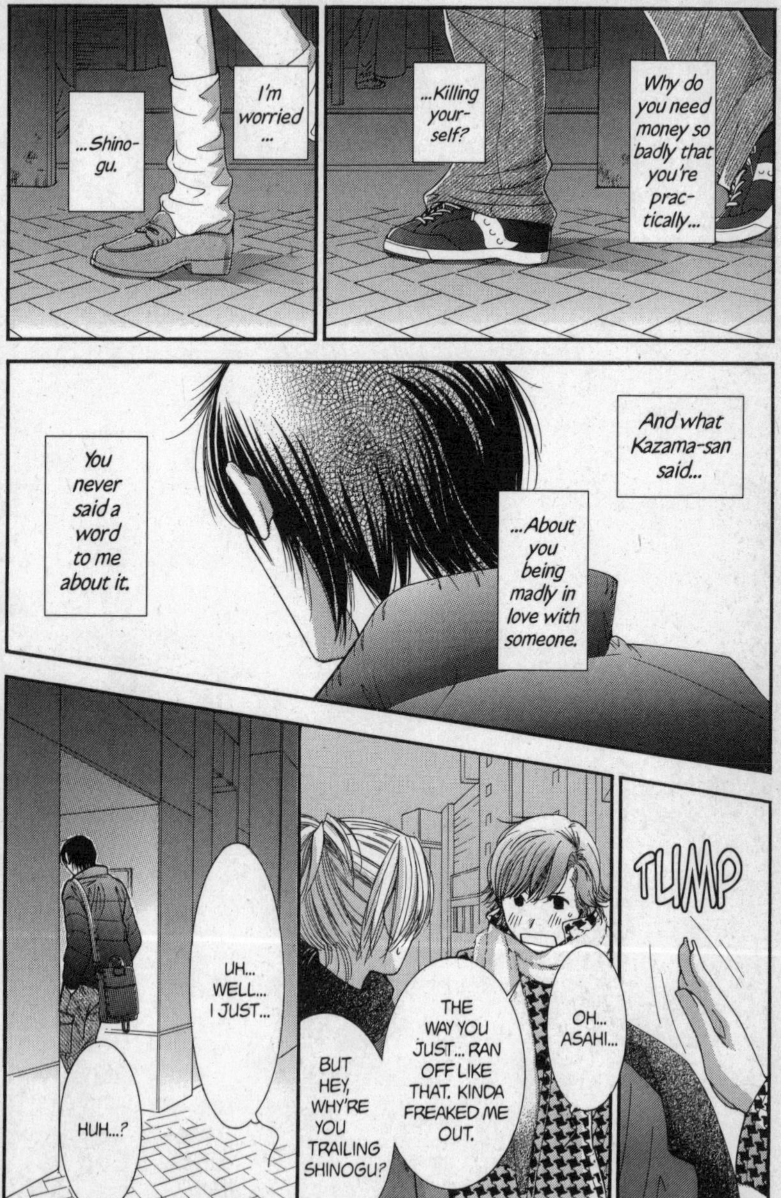

Why do you need money so badly that you're prac-tically...
...Killing your-self?
I'm worried ...
...Shino-gu.
And what Kazama-san said...
...About you being madly in love with someone.
You never said a word to me about it.
TLUMP
OH... ASAHI...
THE WAY YOU JUST... RAN OFF LIKE THAT. KINDA FREAKED ME OUT.
BUT HEY, WHY'RE YOU TRAILING SHINOGU?
UH... WELL... I JUST...
HUH...?

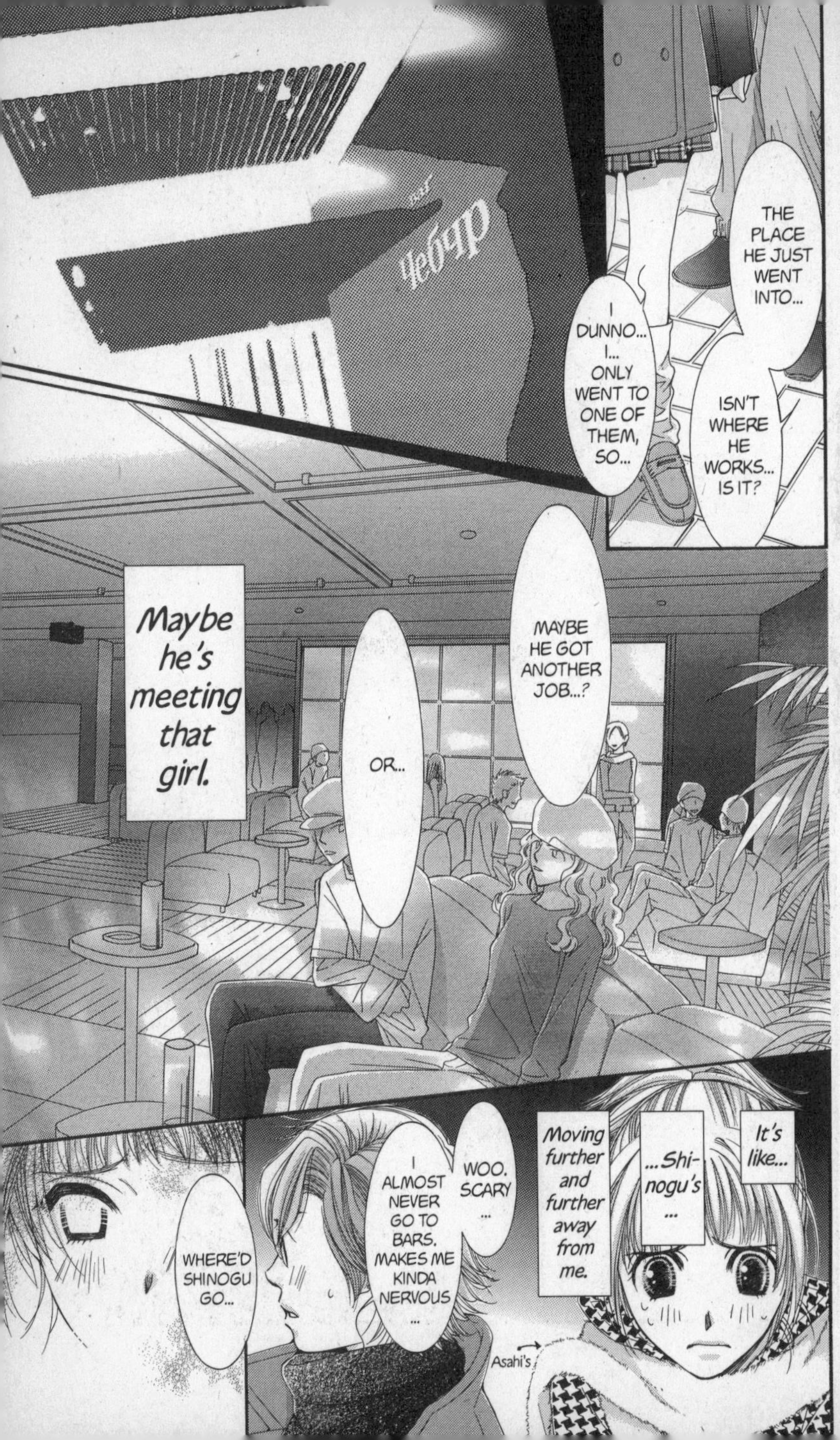
THE PLACE HE JUST WENT INTO...
ISN'T WHERE HE WORKS... IS IT?
I DUNNO... I... ONLY WENT TO ONE OF THEM, SO...
MAYBE HE GOT ANOTHER JOB...?
OR...
Maybe he's meeting that girl.
It's like...
...Shi-nogu's...
Moving further and further away from me.
Asahi's
WOO. SCARY...
I ALMOST NEVER GO TO BARS. MAKES ME KINDA NERVOUS...
WHERE'D SHINOGU GO...

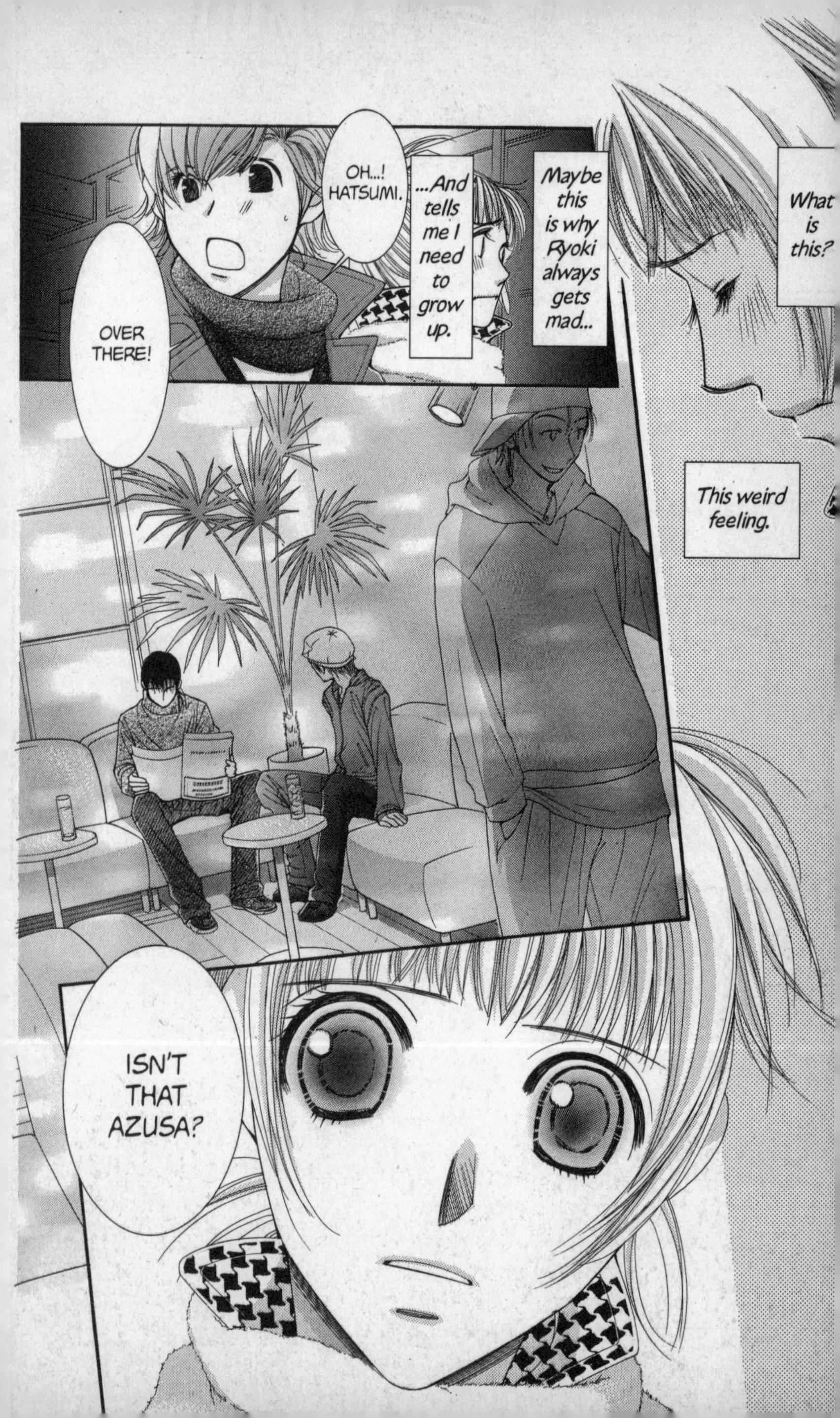

What is this?
This weird feeling.
Maybe this is why Ryoki always gets mad...
...And tells me I need to grow up.
OH...! HATSUMI.
OVER THERE!
ISN'T THAT AZUSA?

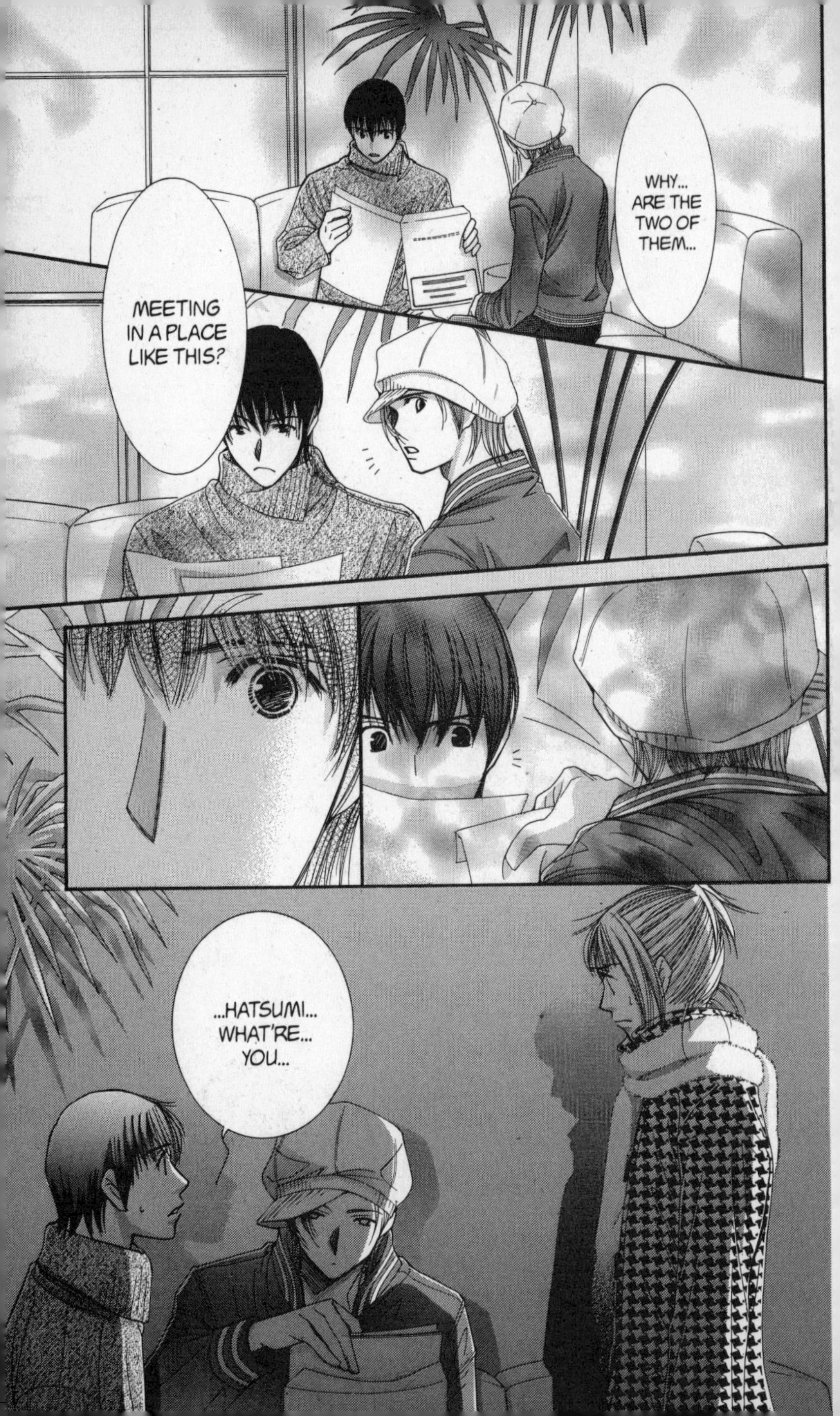
WHY... ARE THE TWO OF THEM...
MEETING IN A PLACE LIKE THIS?
...HATSUMI... WHAT'RE... YOU...

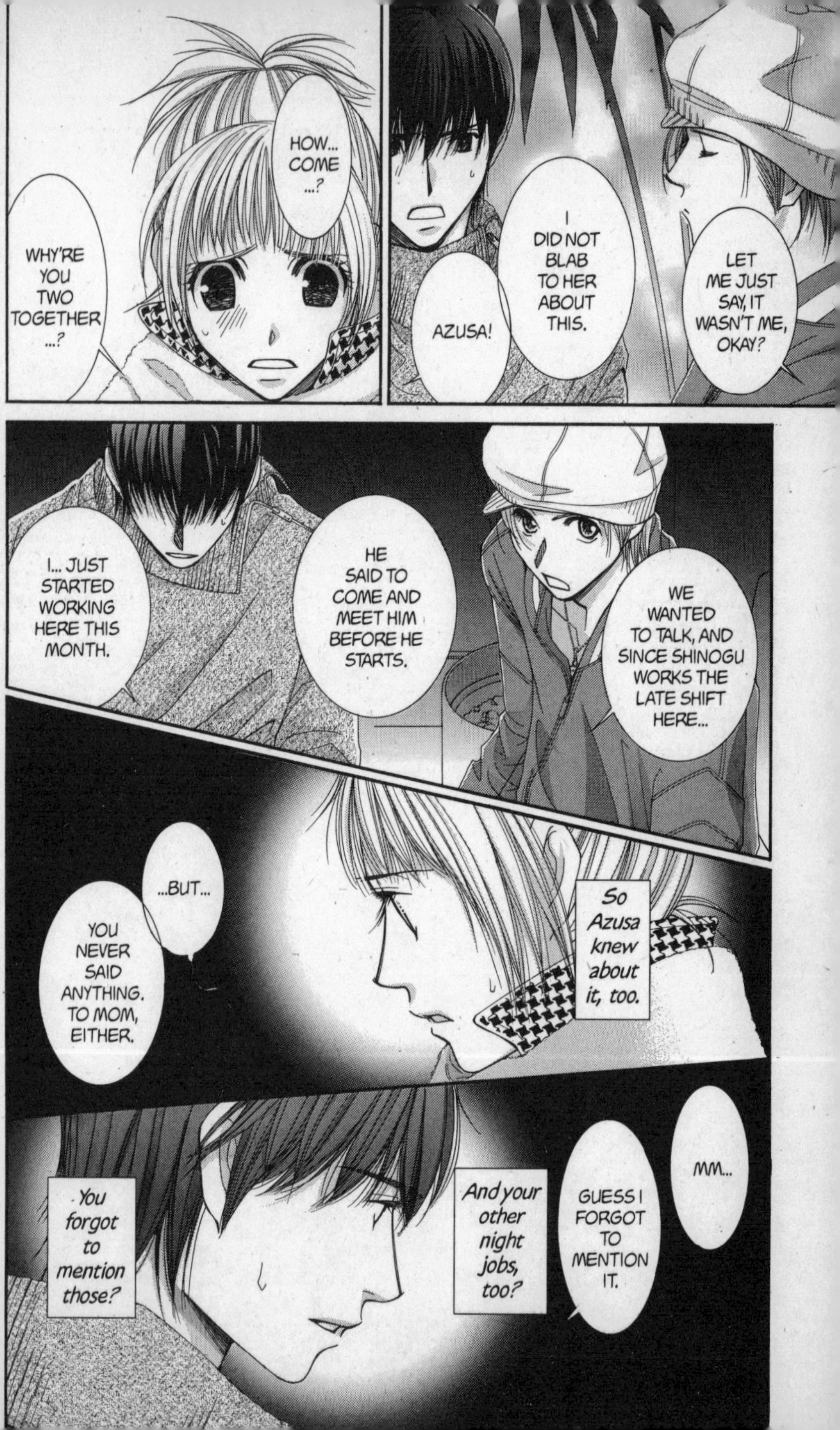
LET ME JUST SAY, IT WASN'T ME, OKAY?
I DID NOT BLAB TO HER ABOUT THIS.
AZUSA!
HOW... COME ...?
WHY'RE YOU TWO TOGETHER ...?
WE WANTED TO TALK, AND SINCE SHINOGU WORKS THE LATE SHIFT HERE...
HE SAID TO COME AND MEET HIM BEFORE HE STARTS.
I... JUST STARTED WORKING HERE THIS MONTH.
So Azusa knew about it, too.
...BUT...
YOU NEVER SAID ANYTHING. TO MOM, EITHER.
MM...
GUESS I FORGOT TO MENTION IT.
And your other night jobs, too?
You forgot to mention those?

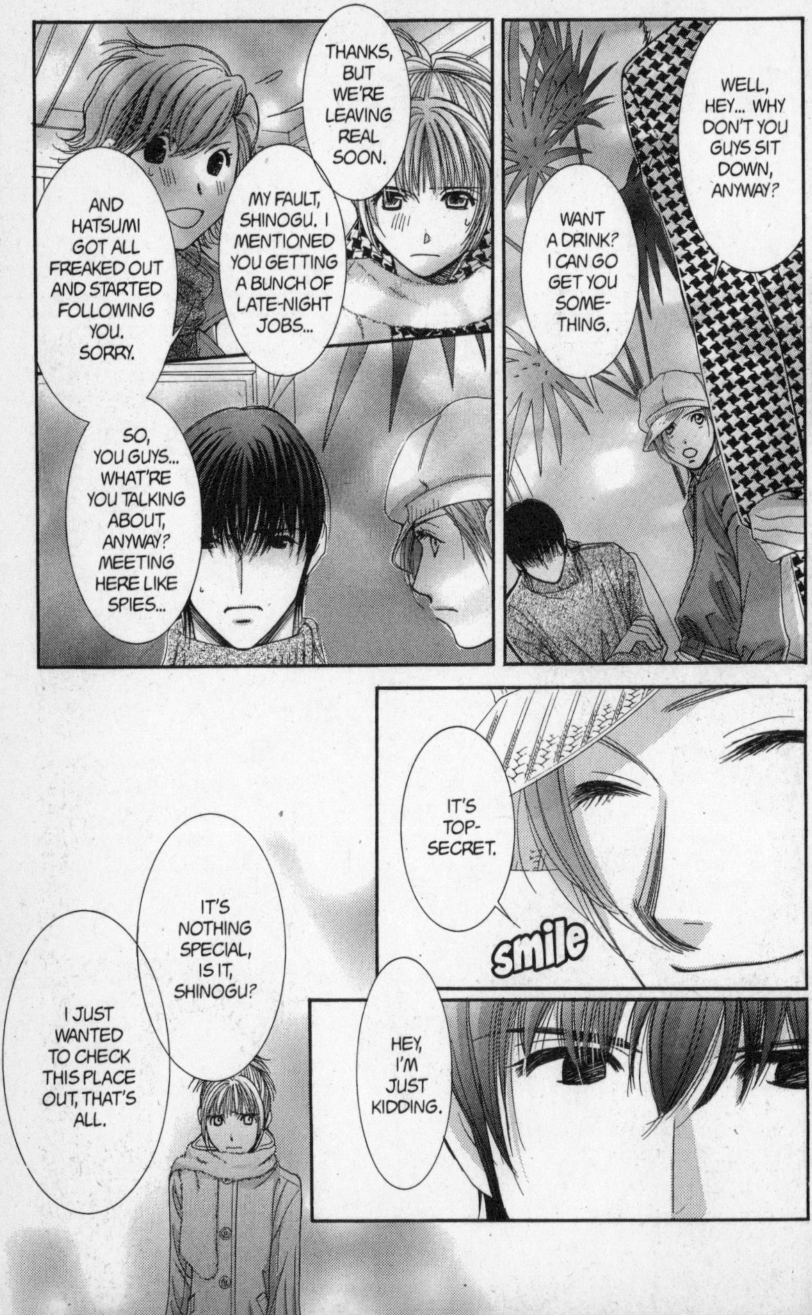
WELL, HEY... WHY DON'T YOU GUYS SIT DOWN, ANYWAY?
WANT A DRINK? I CAN GO GET YOU SOME-THING.
THANKS, BUT WE'RE LEAVING REAL SOON.
MY FAULT, SHINOGU. I MENTIONED YOU GETTING A BUNCH OF LATE-NIGHT JOBS...
AND HATSUMI GOT ALL FREAKED OUT AND STARTED FOLLOWING YOU. SORRY.
SO, YOU GUYS... WHAT'RE YOU TALKING ABOUT, ANYWAY? MEETING HERE LIKE SPIES...
IT'S TOP-SECRET.
smile
HEY, I'M JUST KIDDING.
IT'S NOTHING SPECIAL, IS IT, SHINOGU?
I JUST WANTED TO CHECK THIS PLACE OUT, THAT'S ALL.

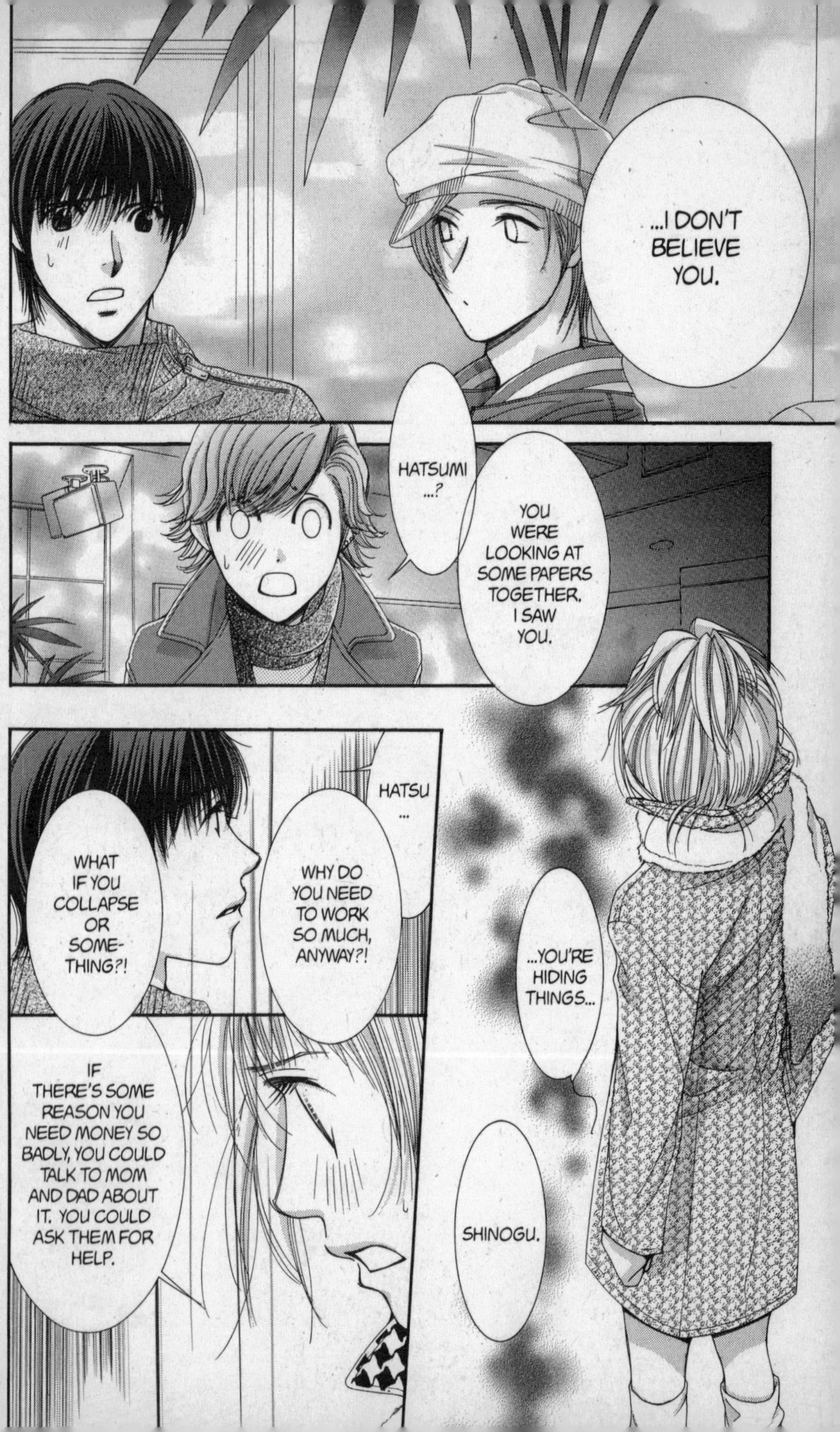
...I DON'T BELIEVE YOU.
HATSUMI ...?
YOU WERE LOOKING AT SOME PAPERS TOGETHER. I SAW YOU.
...YOU'RE HIDING THINGS...
SHINOGU.
HATSU ...
WHY DO YOU NEED TO WORK SO MUCH, ANYWAY?!
WHAT IF YOU COLLAPSE OR SOME-THING?!
IF THERE'S SOME REASON YOU NEED MONEY SO BADLY, YOU COULD TALK TO MOM AND DAD ABOUT IT. YOU COULD ASK THEM FOR HELP.

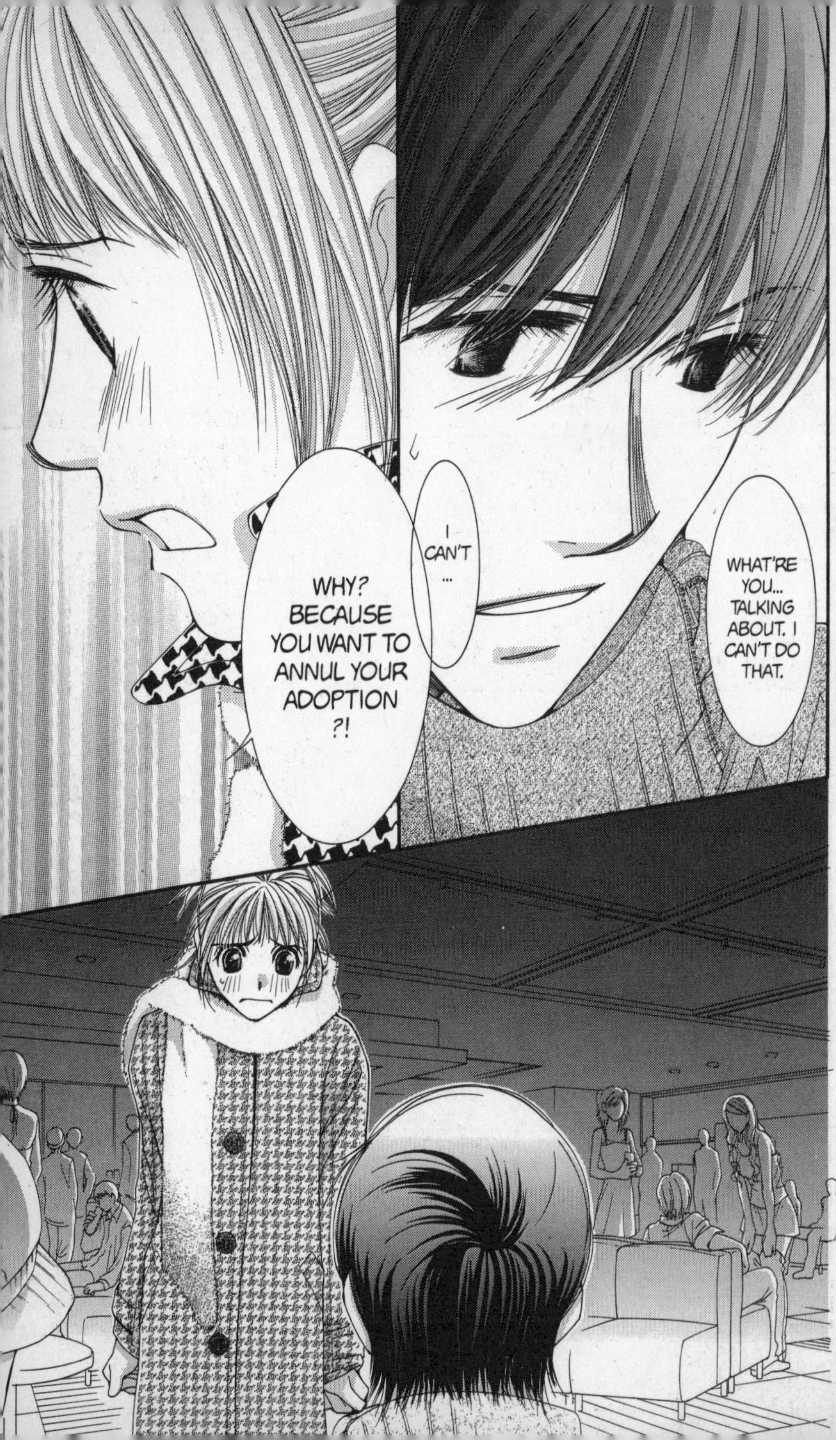
WHAT'RE YOU... TALKING ABOUT. I CAN'T DO THAT.
I CAN'T ...
WHY? BECAUSE YOU WANT TO ANNUL YOUR ADOPTION ?!

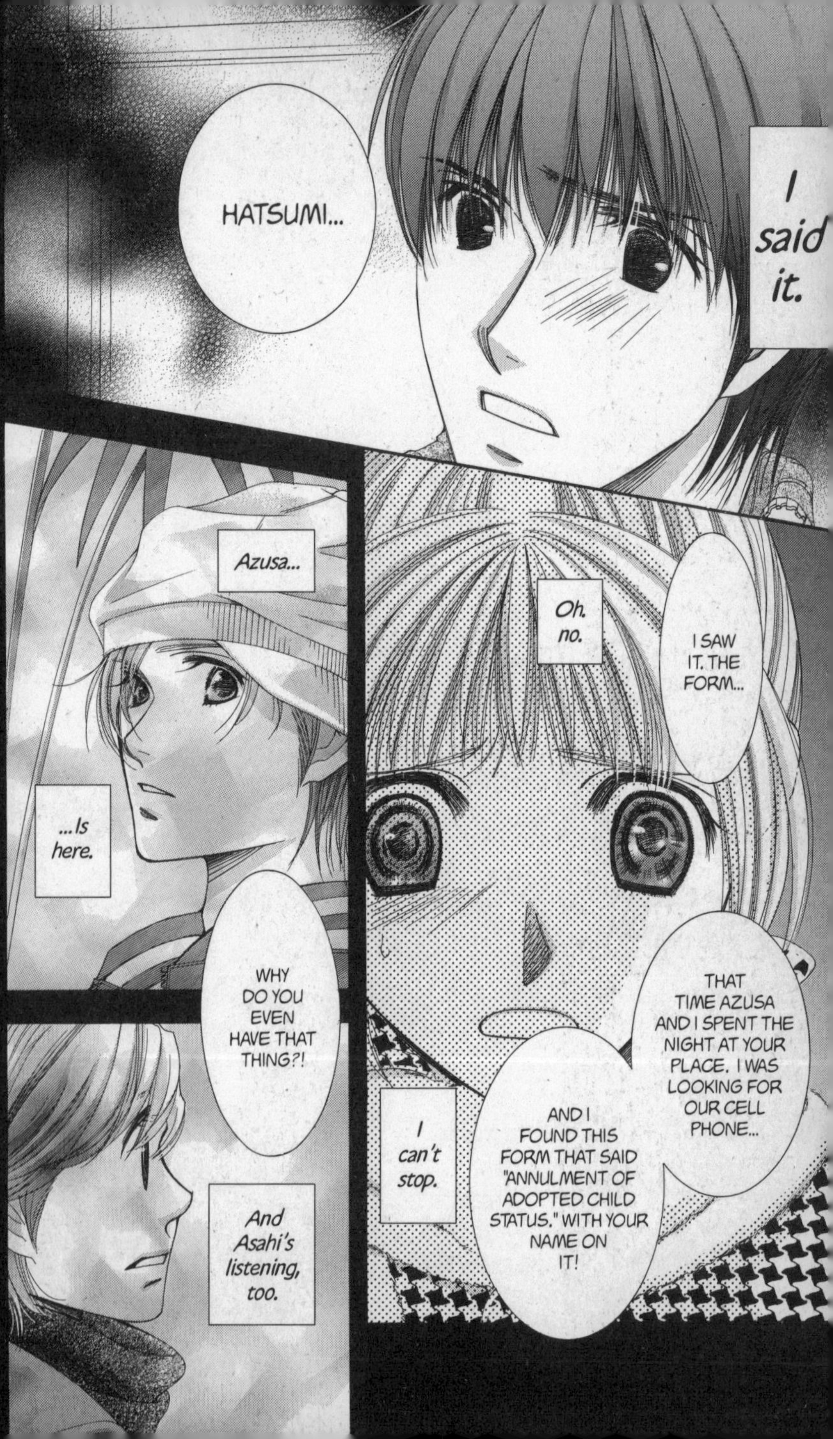
I said it.
HATSUMI...
I SAW IT. THE FORM...
Oh. no.
THAT TIME AZUSA AND I SPENT THE NIGHT AT YOUR PLACE. I WAS LOOKING FOR OUR CELL PHONE...
AND I FOUND THIS FORM THAT SAID "ANNULMENT OF ADOPTED CHILD STATUS." WITH YOUR NAME ON IT!
I can't stop.
Azusa...
...Is here.
WHY DO YOU EVEN HAVE THAT THING?!
And Asahi's listening, too.

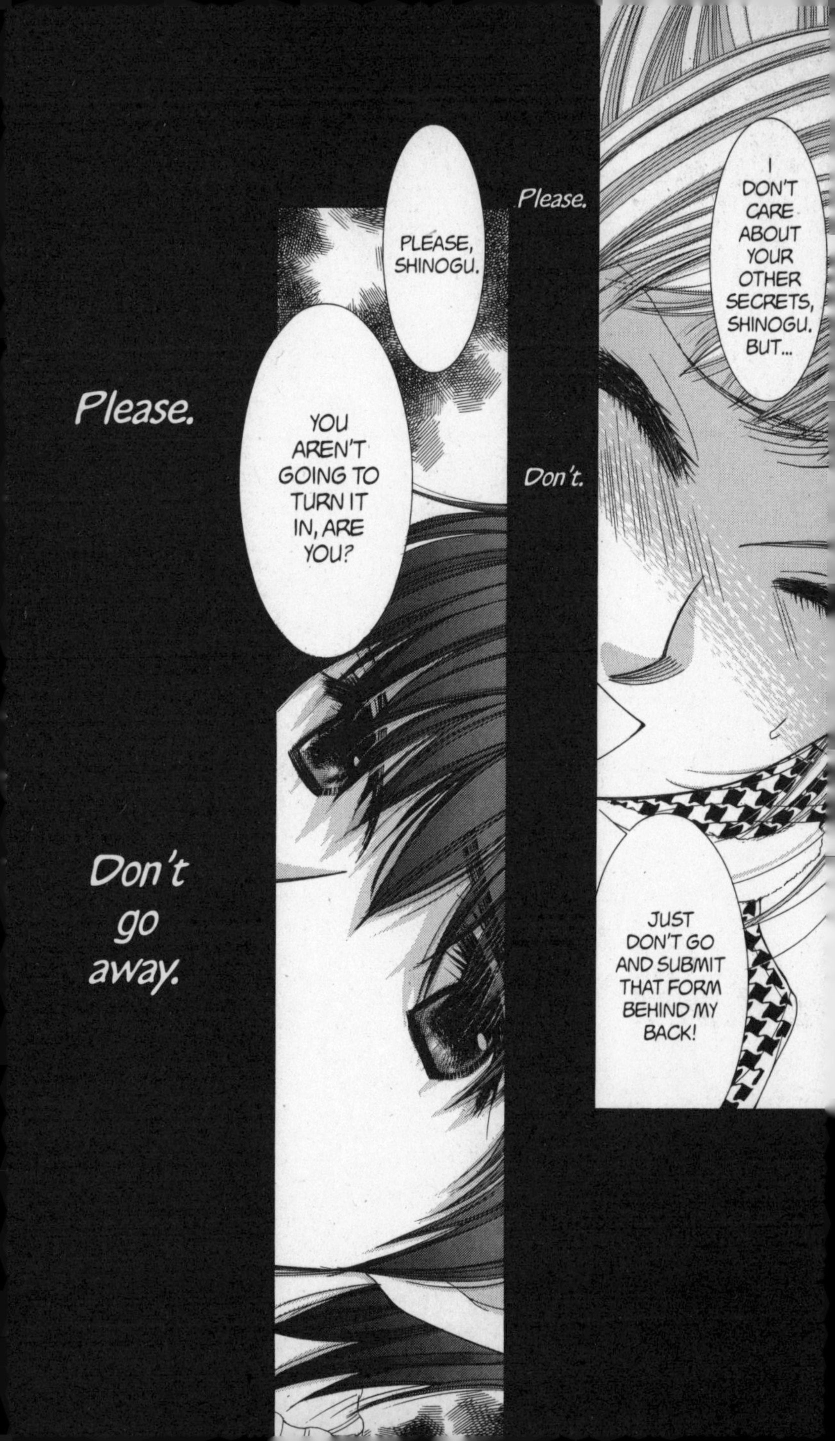
I DON'T CARE ABOUT YOUR OTHER SECRETS, SHINOGU. BUT...
JUST DON'T GO AND SUBMIT THAT FORM BEHIND MY BACK!
Please.
Don't.
PLEASE, SHINOGU.
YOU AREN'T GOING TO TURN IT IN, ARE YOU?
Please.
Don't go away.

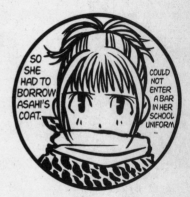

COULD NOT ENTER A BAR IN HER SCHOOL UNIFORM...
SO SHE HAD TO BORROW ASAHI'S COAT.

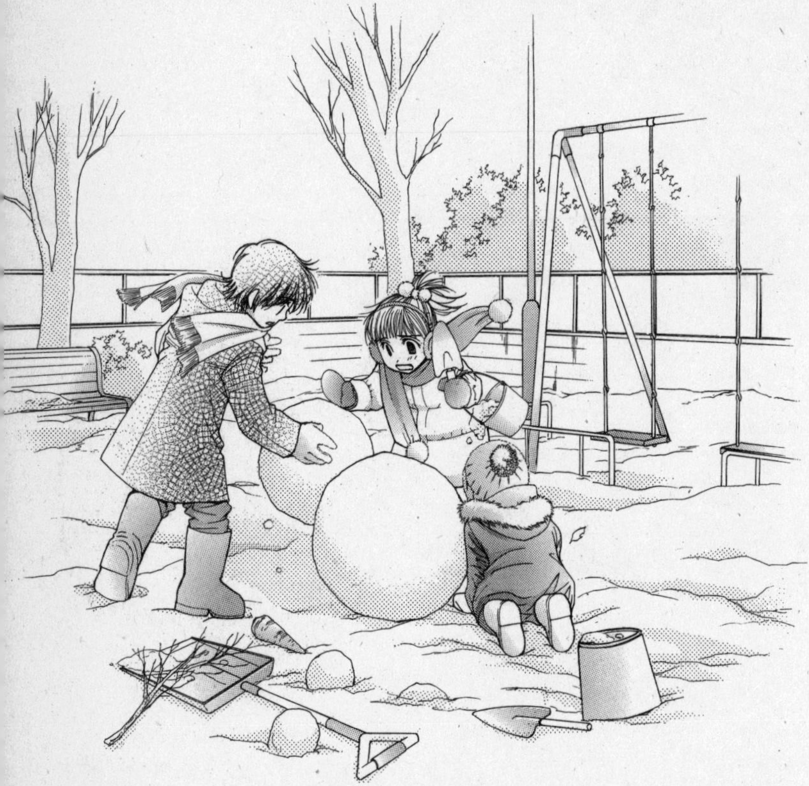

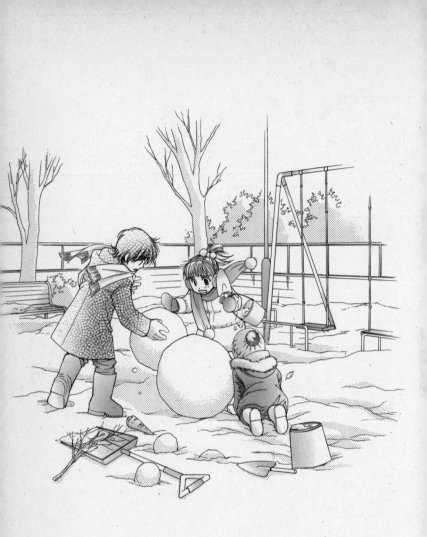

Chapter 36

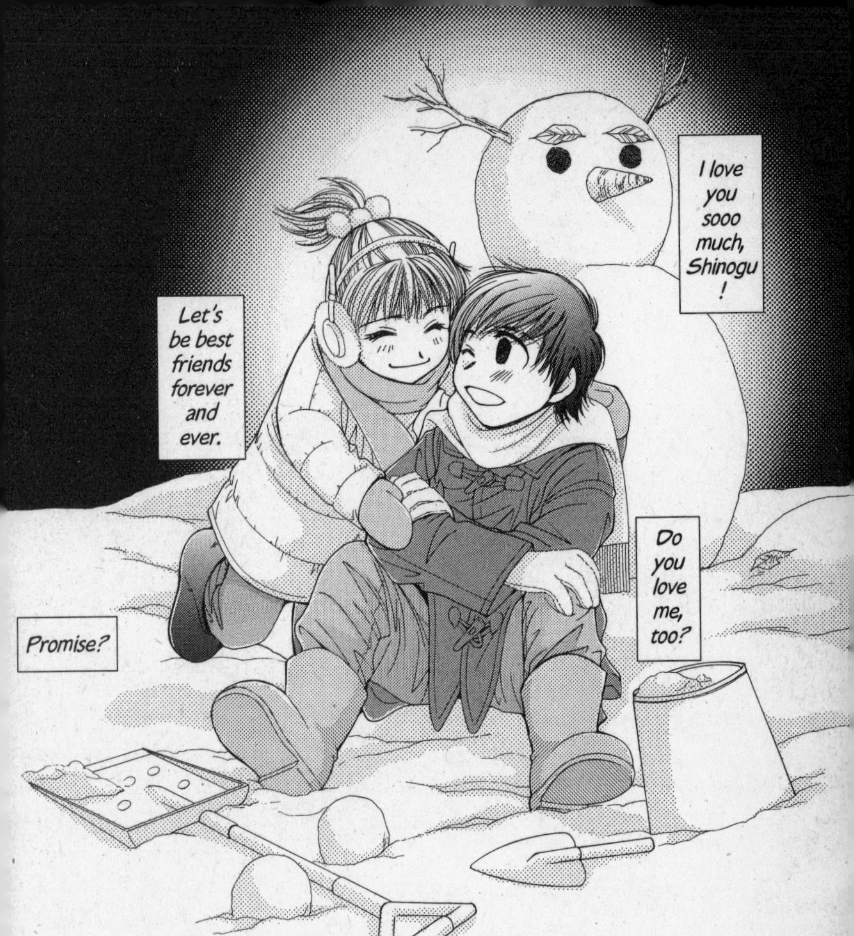
I love you sooo much, Shinogu!
Let's be best friends forever and ever.
Do you love me, too?
Promise?

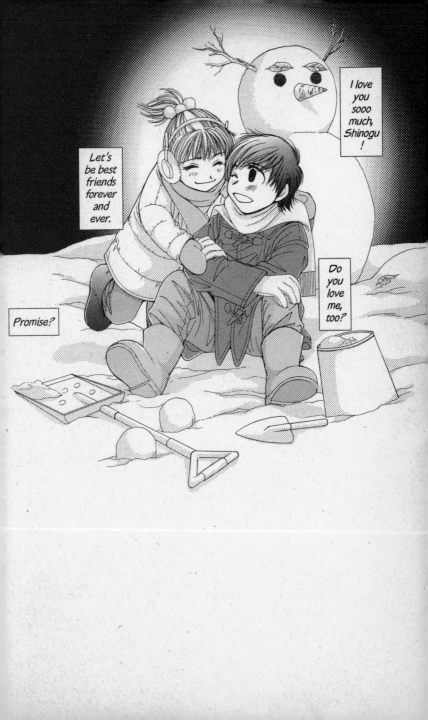

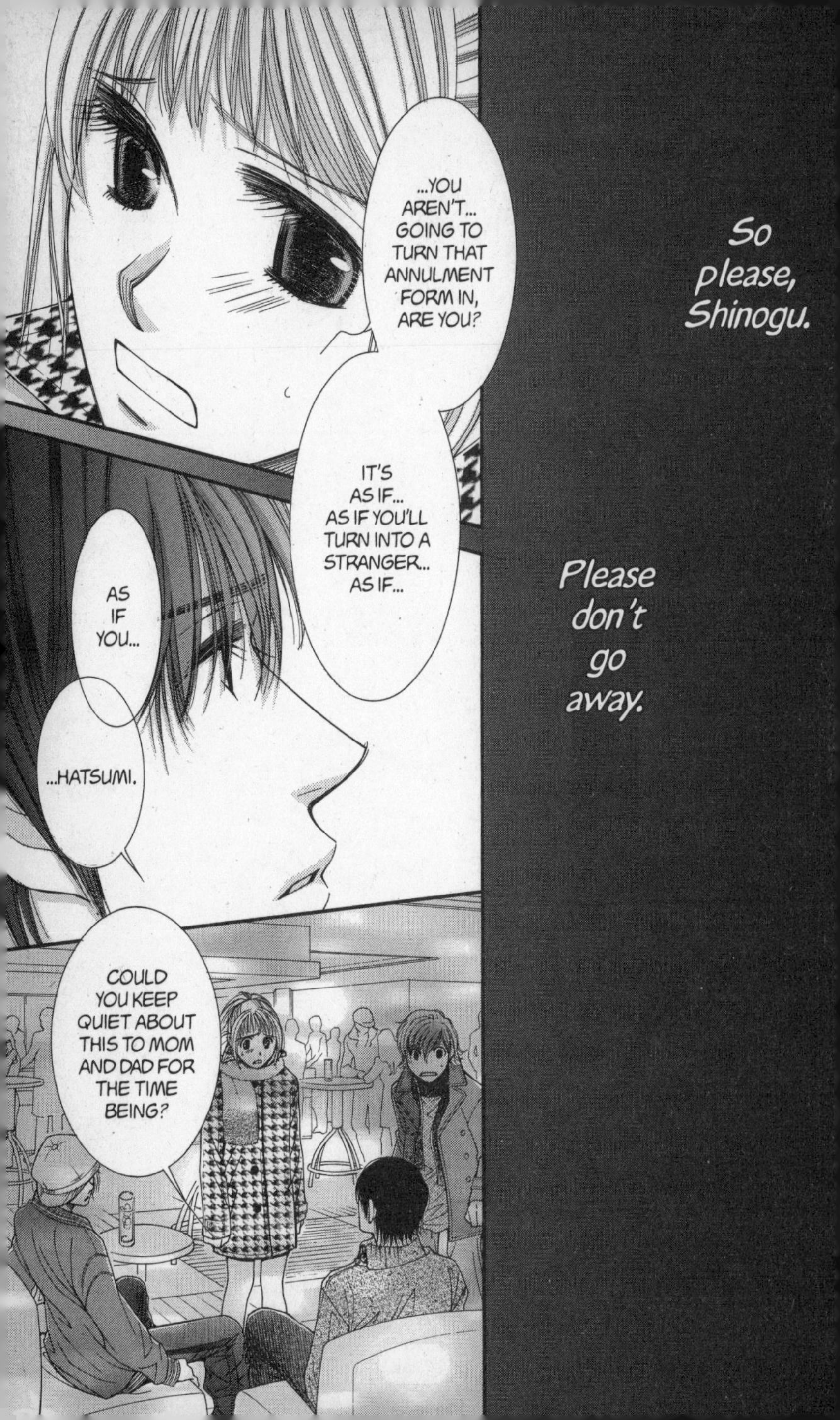
So please, Shinogu.
Please don't go away.
...YOU AREN'T... GOING TO TURN THAT ANNULMENT FORM IN, ARE YOU?
IT'S AS IF... AS IF YOU'LL TURN INTO A STRANGER... AS IF...
AS IF YOU...
...HATSUMI.
COULD YOU KEEP QUIET ABOUT THIS TO MOM AND DAD FOR THE TIME BEING?

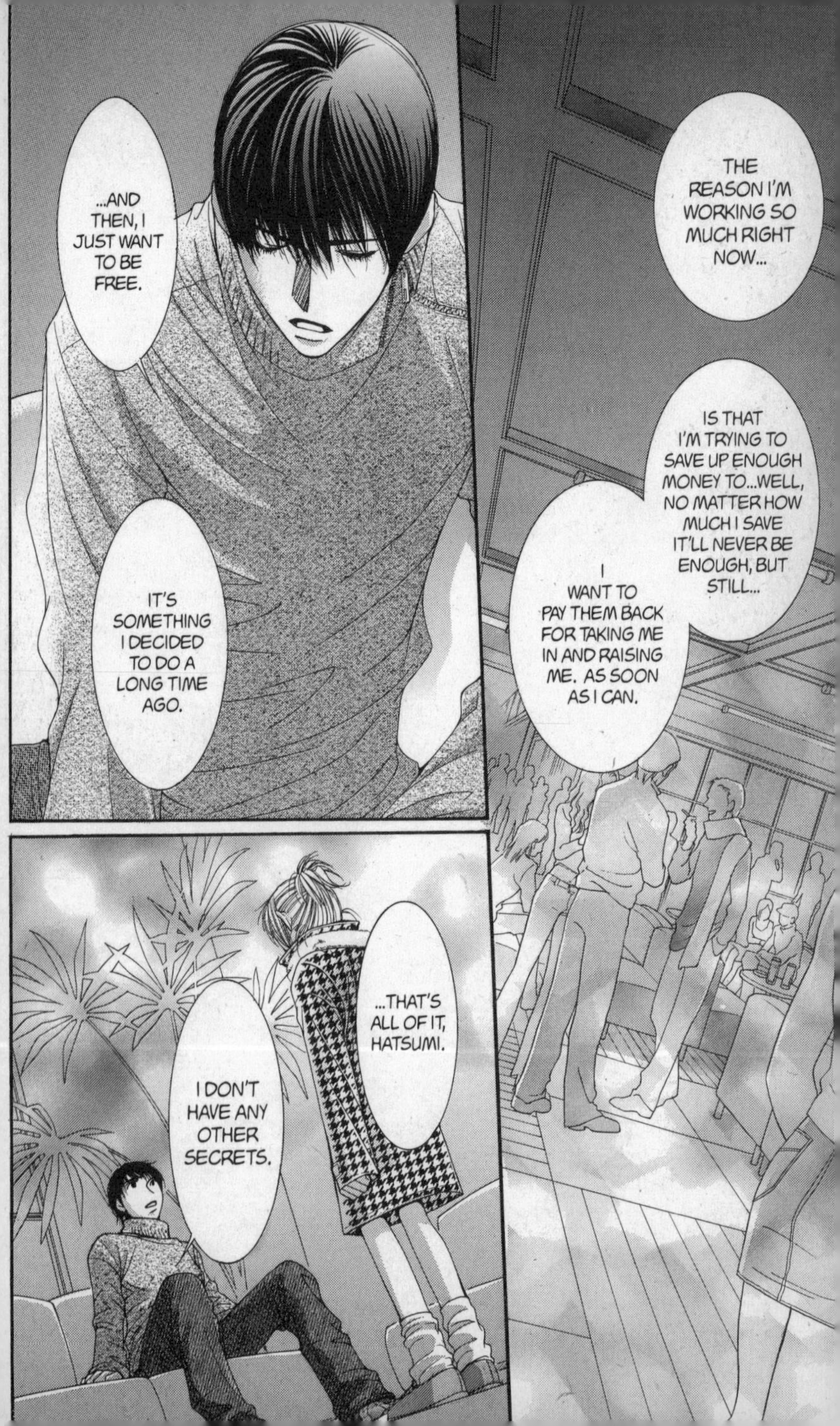
THE REASON I'M WORKING SO MUCH RIGHT NOW...
IS THAT I'M TRYING TO SAVE UP ENOUGH MONEY TO...WELL, NO MATTER HOW MUCH I SAVE IT'LL NEVER BE ENOUGH, BUT STILL...
I WANT TO PAY THEM BACK FOR TAKING ME IN AND RAISING ME. AS SOON AS I CAN.
...AND THEN, I JUST WANT TO BE FREE.
IT'S SOMETHING I DECIDED TO DO A LONG TIME AGO.
...THAT'S ALL OF IT, HATSUMI.
I DON'T HAVE ANY OTHER SECRETS.

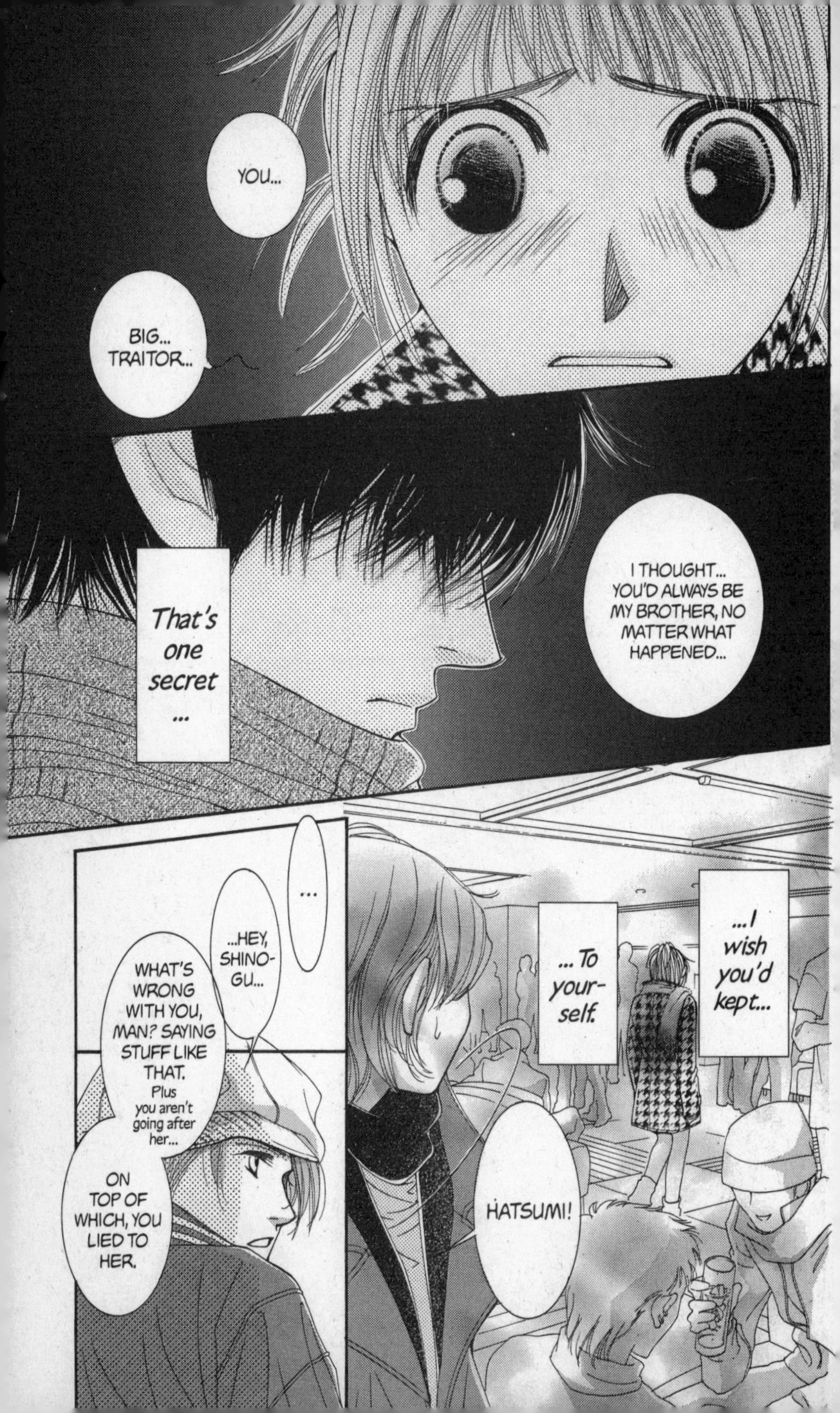
YOU...
BIG... TRAITOR...
I THOUGHT... YOU'D ALWAYS BE MY BROTHER, NO MATTER WHAT HAPPENED...
That's one secret ...
...I wish you'd kept...
... To your-self.
HATSUMI!
...
...HEY, SHINO-GU...
WHAT'S WRONG WITH YOU, MAN? SAYING STUFF LIKE THAT.
Plus you aren't going after her...
ON TOP OF WHICH, YOU LIED TO HER.

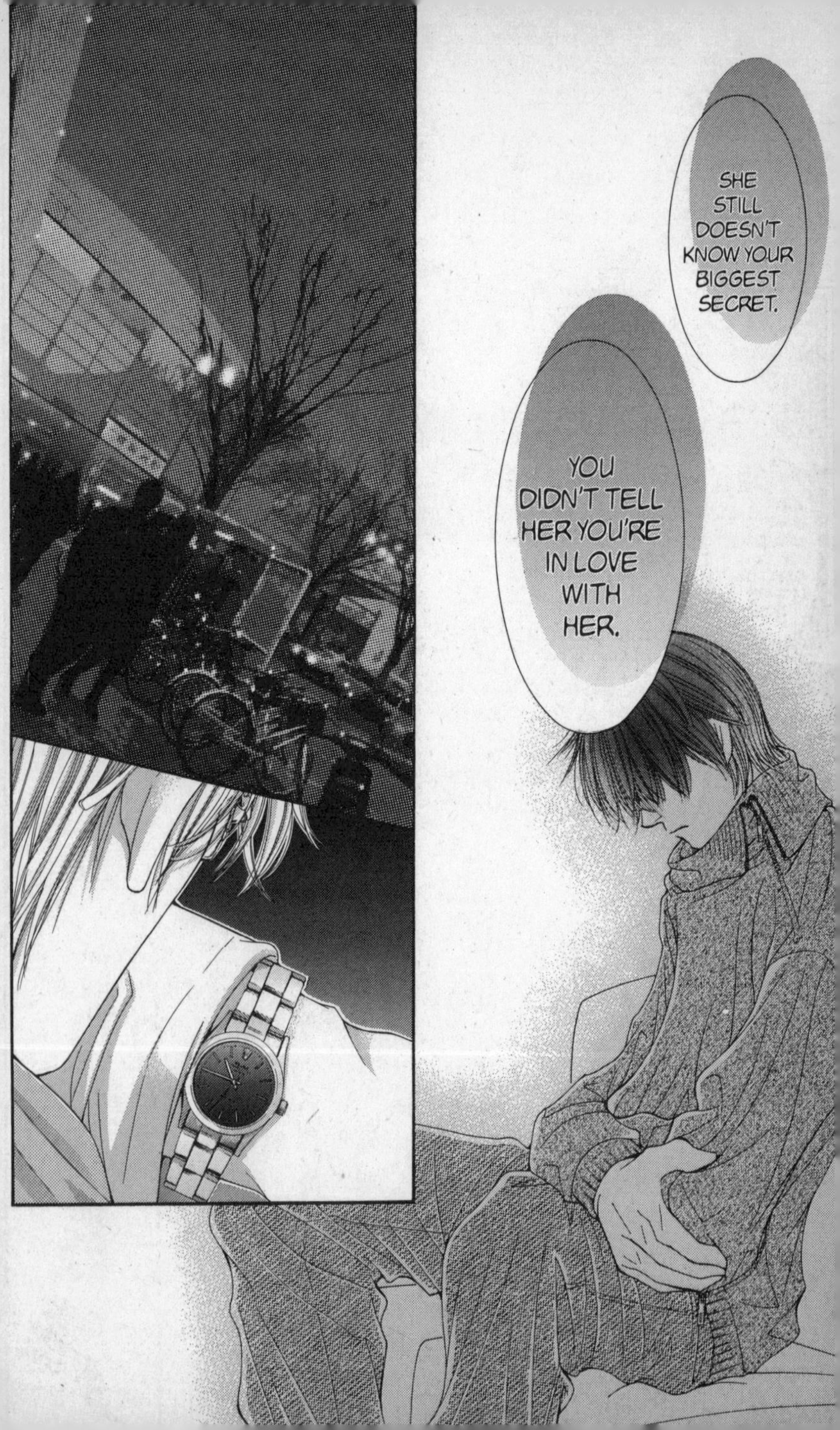
SHE STILL DOESN'T KNOW YOUR BIGGEST SECRET.
YOU DIDN'T TELL HER YOU'RE IN LOVE WITH HER.

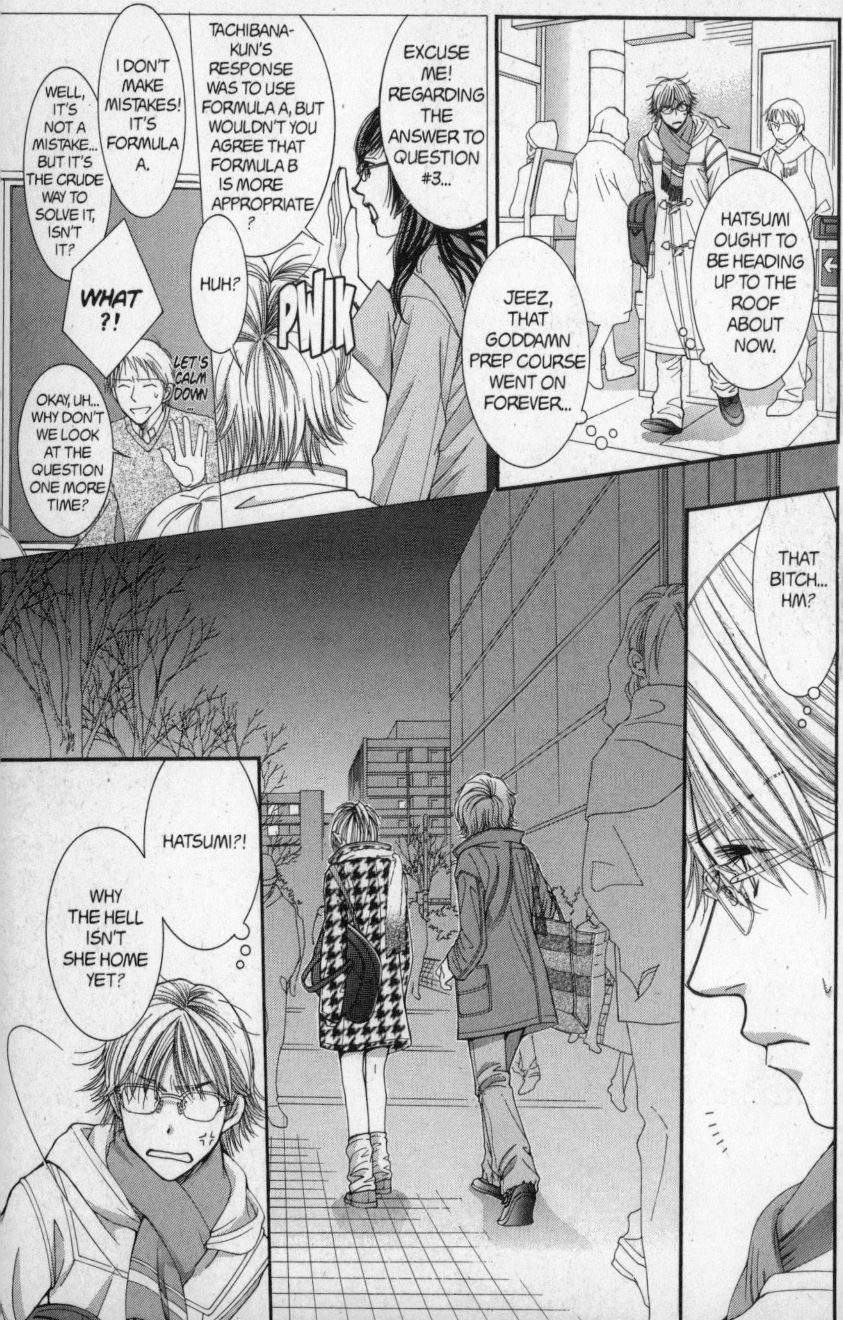
HATSUMI OUGHT TO BE HEADING UP TO THE ROOF ABOUT NOW.
JEEZ, THAT GODDAMN PREP COURSE WENT ON FOREVER...
EXCUSE ME! REGARDING THE ANSWER TO QUESTION #3...
TACHIBANA-KUN'S RESPONSE WAS TO USE FORMULA A, BUT WOULDN'T YOU AGREE THAT FORMULA B IS MORE APPROPRIATE?
PWIK
HUH?
I DON'T MAKE MISTAKES! IT'S FORMULA A.
WELL, IT'S NOT A MISTAKE... BUT IT'S THE CRUDE WAY TO SOLVE IT, ISN'T IT?
WHAT?!
LET'S CALM DOWN...
OKAY, UH... WHY DON'T WE LOOK AT THE QUESTION ONE MORE TIME?
THAT BITCH... HM?
HATSUMI?!
WHY THE HELL ISN'T SHE HOME YET?

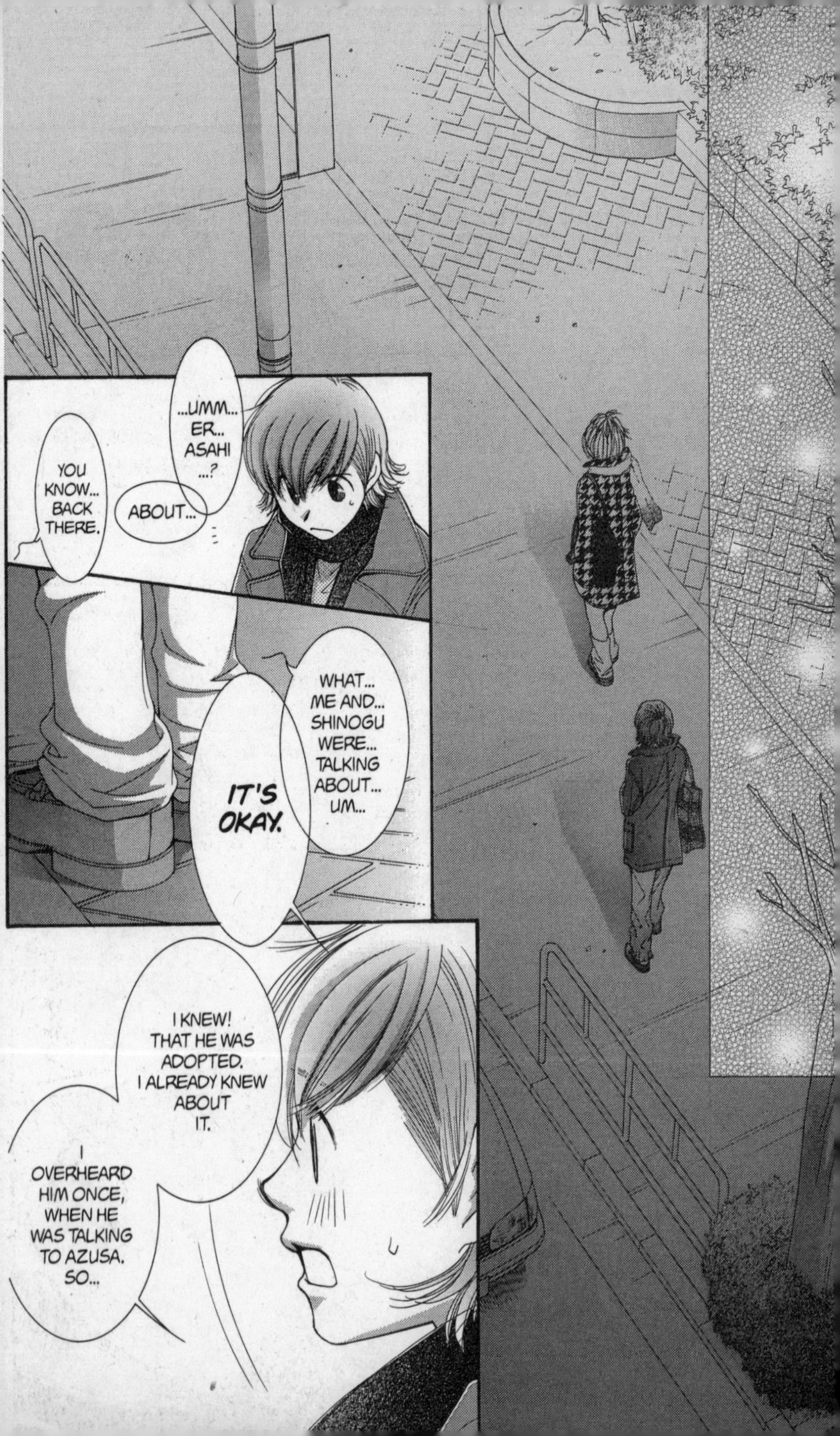
...UMM... ER.. ASAHI ...?
ABOUT...
YOU KNOW... BACK THERE.
WHAT... ME AND... SHINOGU WERE... TALKING ABOUT... UM...
IT'S OKAY.
I KNEW! THAT HE WAS ADOPTED. I ALREADY KNEW ABOUT IT.
I OVERHEARD HIM ONCE, WHEN HE WAS TALKING TO AZUSA. SO...

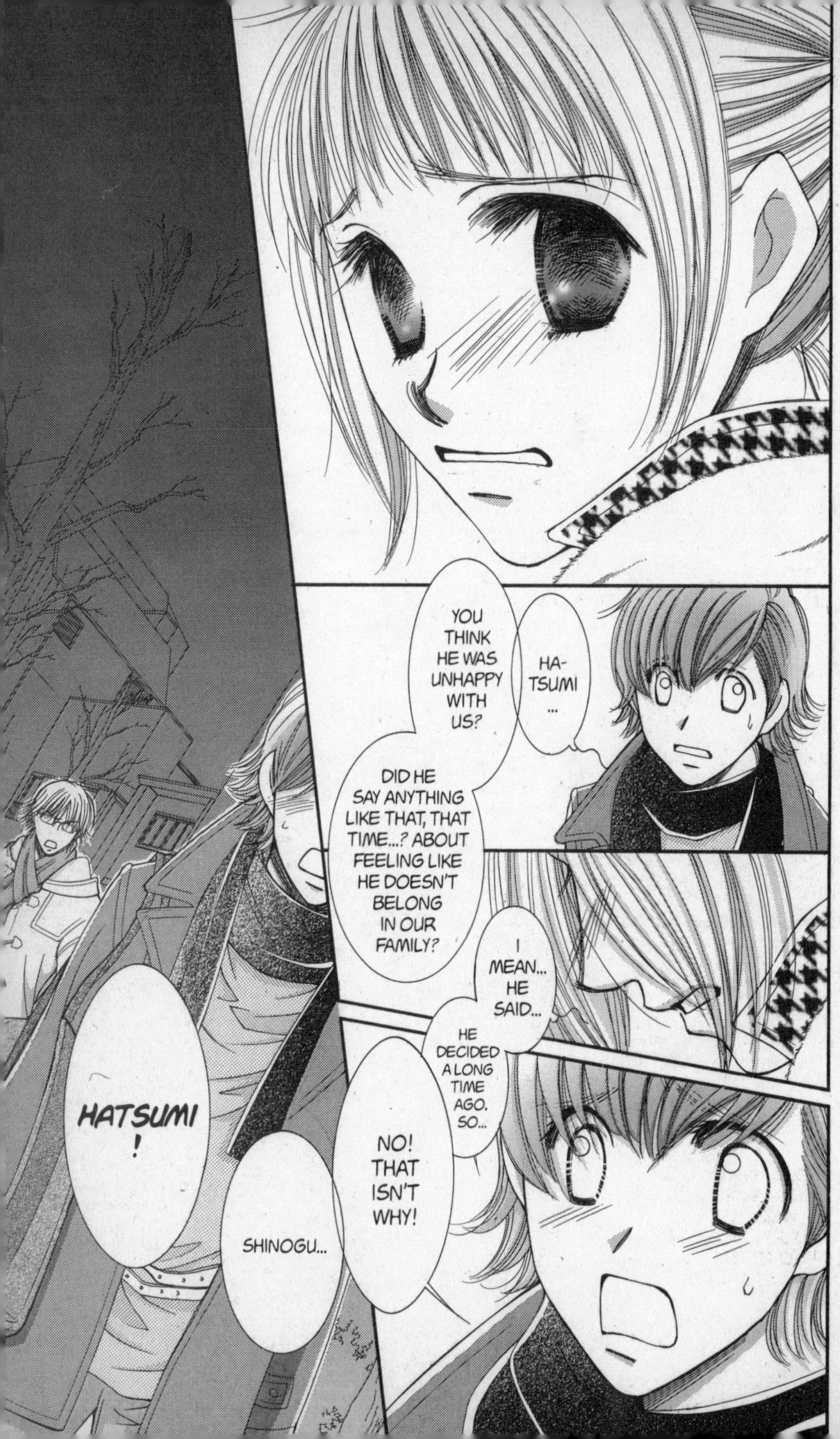
HA-TSUMI...
YOU THINK HE WAS UNHAPPY WITH US?
DID HE SAY ANYTHING LIKE THAT, THAT TIME...? ABOUT FEELING LIKE HE DOESN'T BELONG IN OUR FAMILY?
I MEAN... HE SAID...
HE DECIDED A LONG TIME AGO. SO...
NO! THAT ISN'T WHY!
SHINOGU...
HATSUMI!

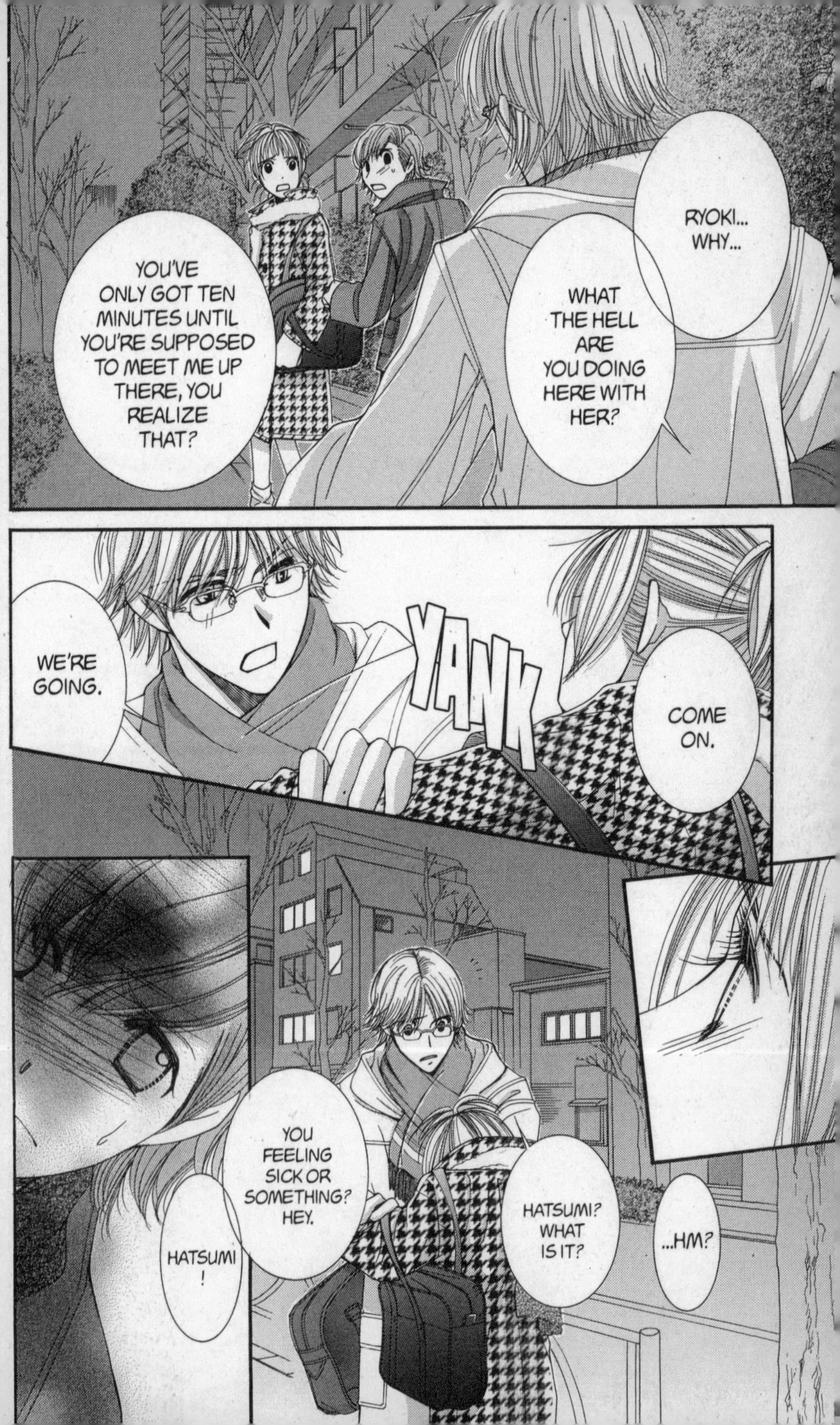
RYOKI... WHY...
WHAT THE HELL ARE YOU DOING HERE WITH HER?
YOU'VE ONLY GOT TEN MINUTES UNTIL YOU'RE SUPPOSED TO MEET ME UP THERE, YOU REALIZE THAT?
COME ON.
YANK
WE'RE GOING.
...HM?
HATSUMI? WHAT IS IT?
YOU FEELING SICK OR SOMETHING? HEY.
HATSUMI!

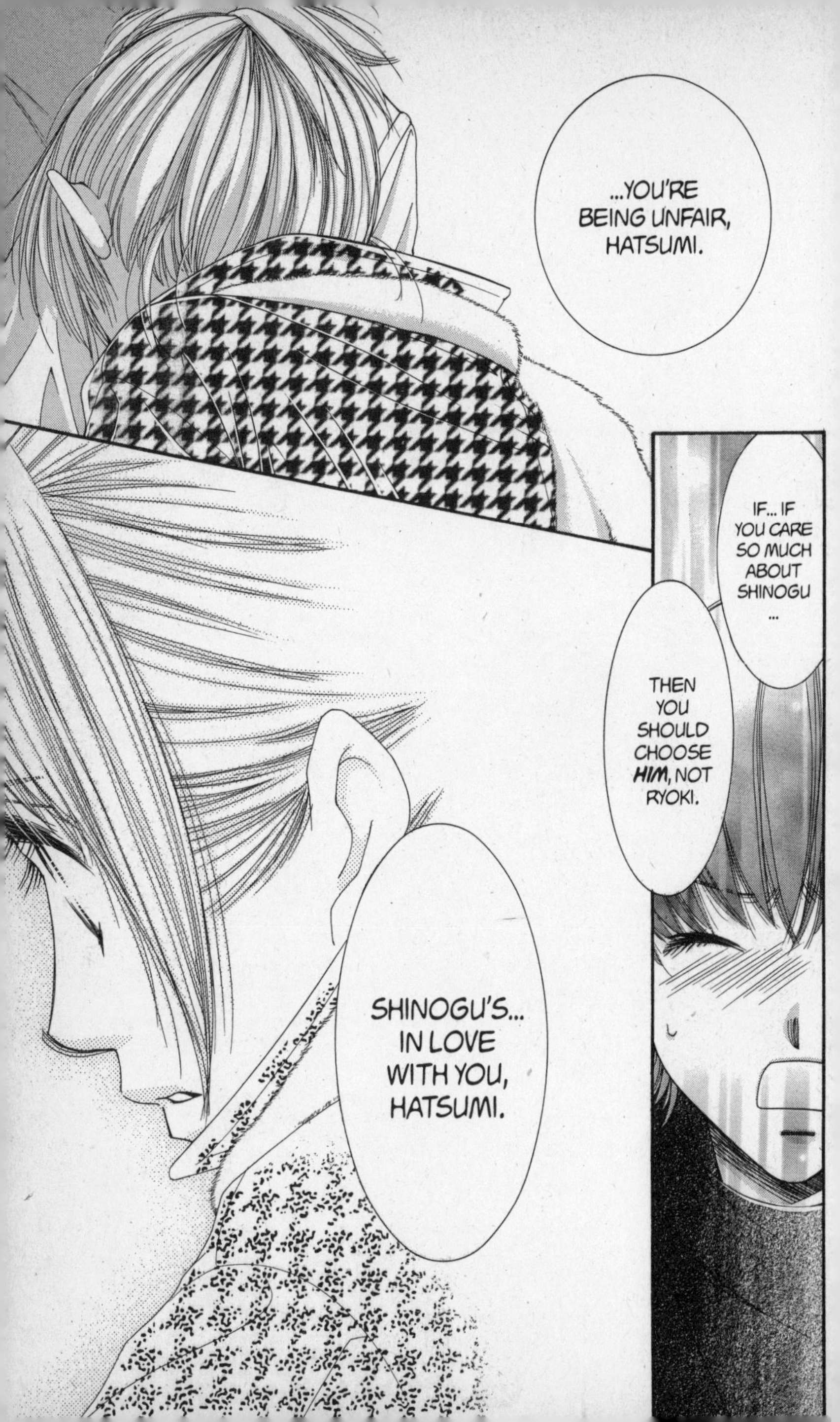
...YOU'RE BEING UNFAIR, HATSUMI.
IF... IF YOU CARE SO MUCH ABOUT SHINOGU ...
THEN YOU SHOULD CHOOSE ***HIM***, NOT RYOKI.
SHINOGU'S... IN LOVE WITH YOU, HATSUMI.

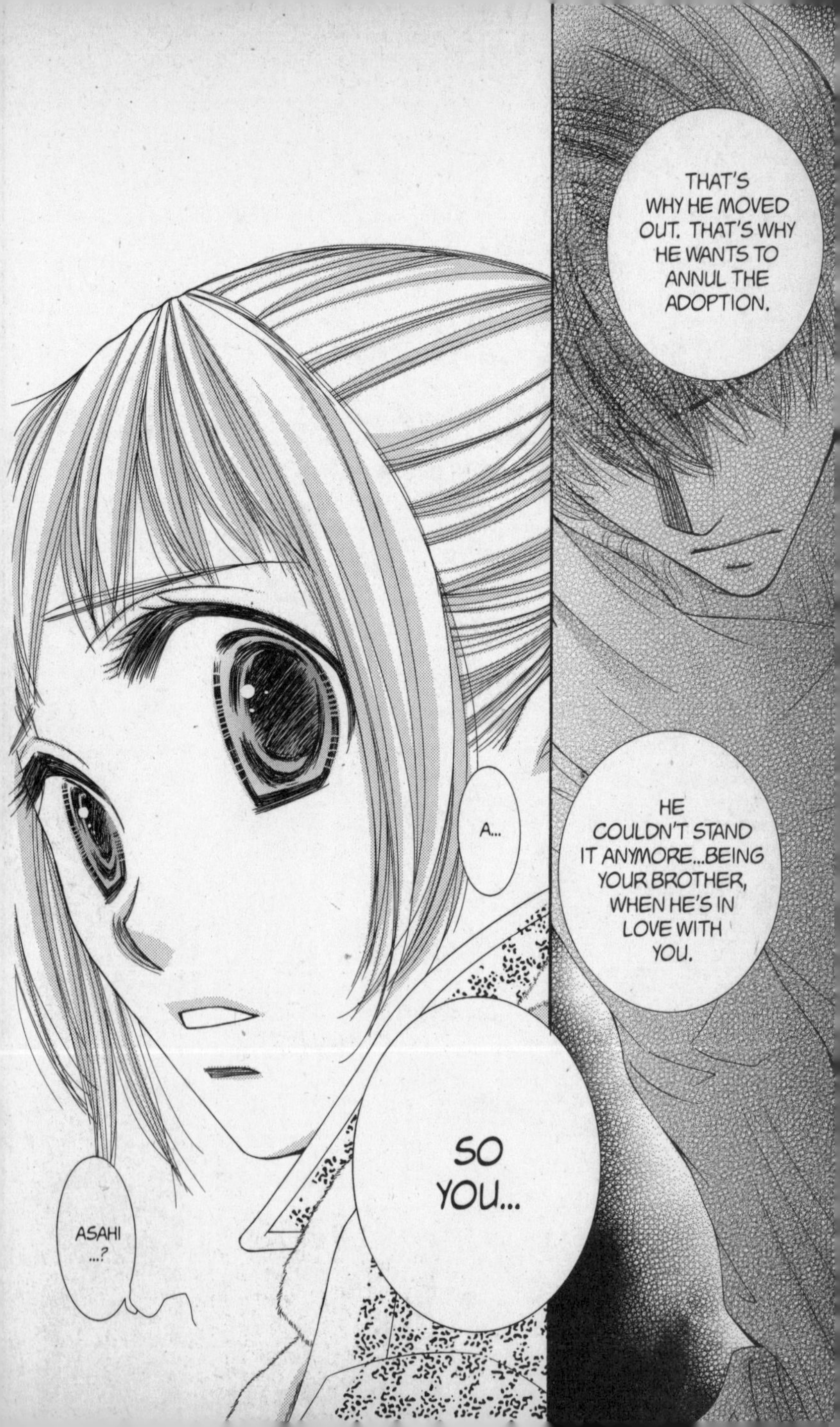
THAT'S WHY HE MOVED OUT. THAT'S WHY HE WANTS TO ANNUL THE ADOPTION.
HE COULDN'T STAND IT ANYMORE...BEING YOUR BROTHER, WHEN HE'S IN LOVE WITH YOU.
SO YOU...
A...
ASAHI ...?

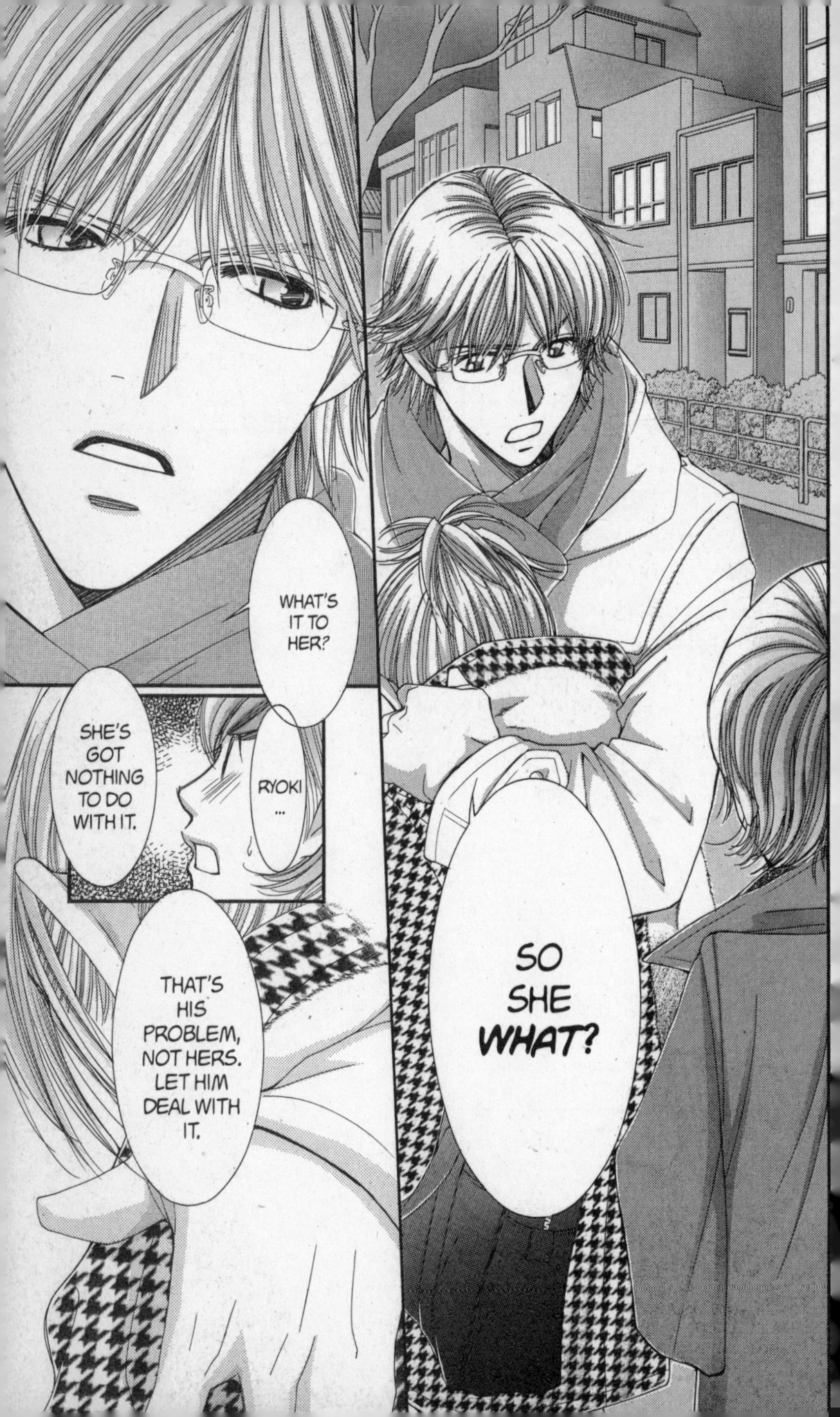
SO SHE WHAT?
WHAT'S IT TO HER?
RYOKI ...
SHE'S GOT NOTHING TO DO WITH IT.
THAT'S HIS PROBLEM, NOT HERS. LET HIM DEAL WITH IT.

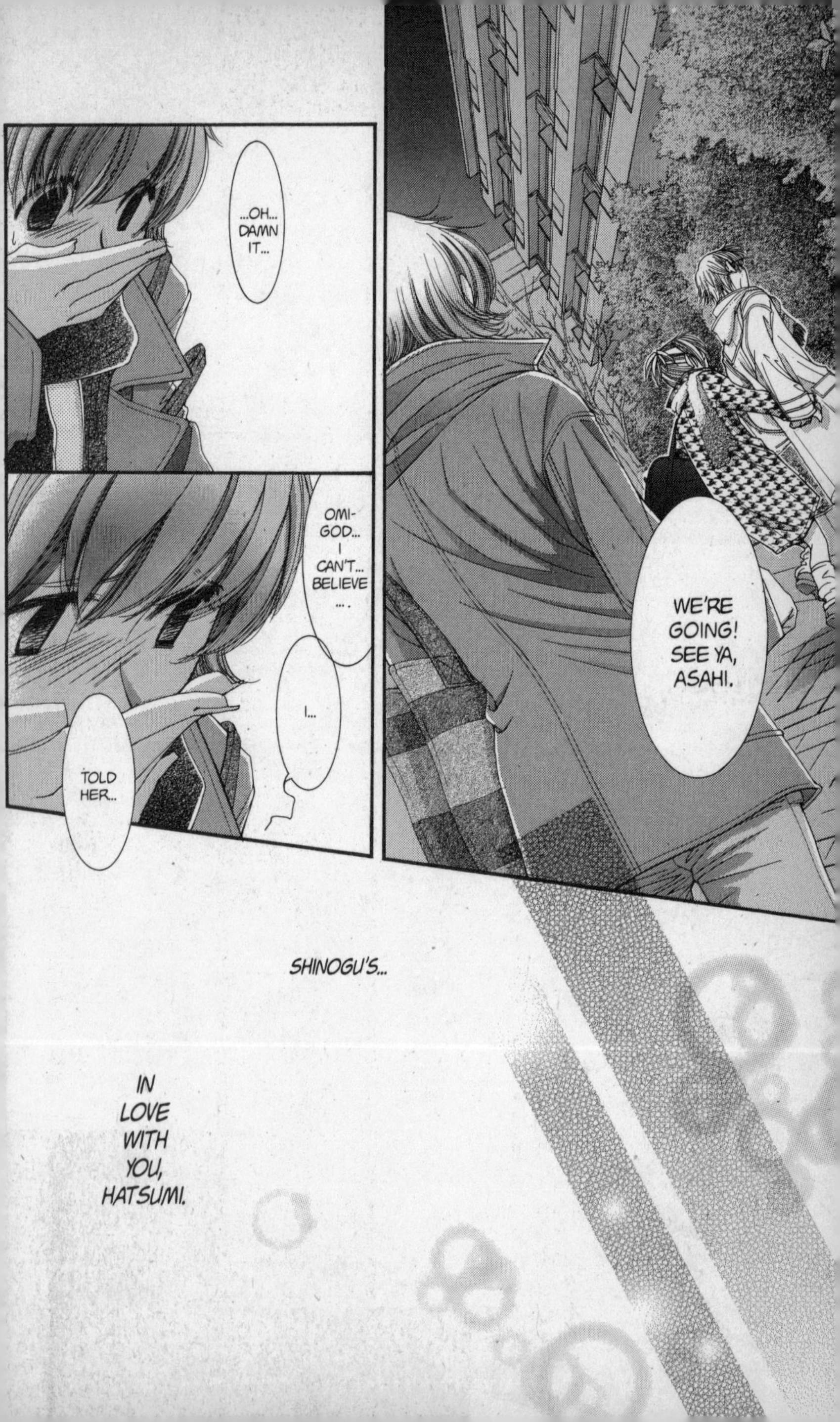
WE'RE GOING! SEE YA, ASAHI.
...OH... DAMN IT...
OMI-GOD... I CAN'T... BELIEVE ... .
I...
TOLD HER...
SHINOGU'S...
IN LOVE WITH YOU, HATSUMI.

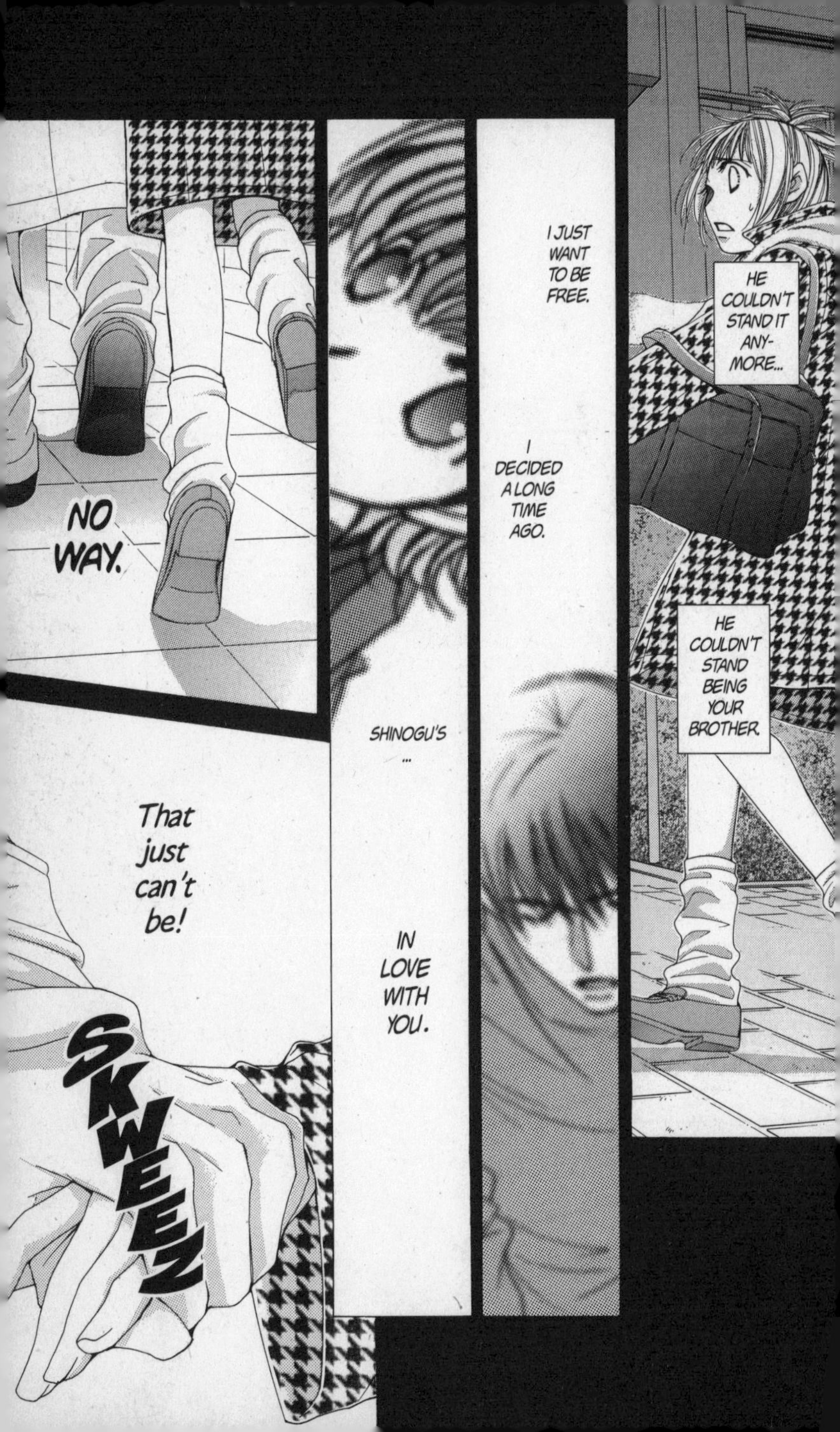

HE COULDN'T STAND IT ANY-MORE...
HE COULDN'T STAND BEING YOUR BROTHER.
I JUST WANT TO BE FREE.
I DECIDED A LONG TIME AGO.
SHINOGU'S...
IN LOVE WITH YOU.
NO WAY.
That just can't be!
SKWEEZ

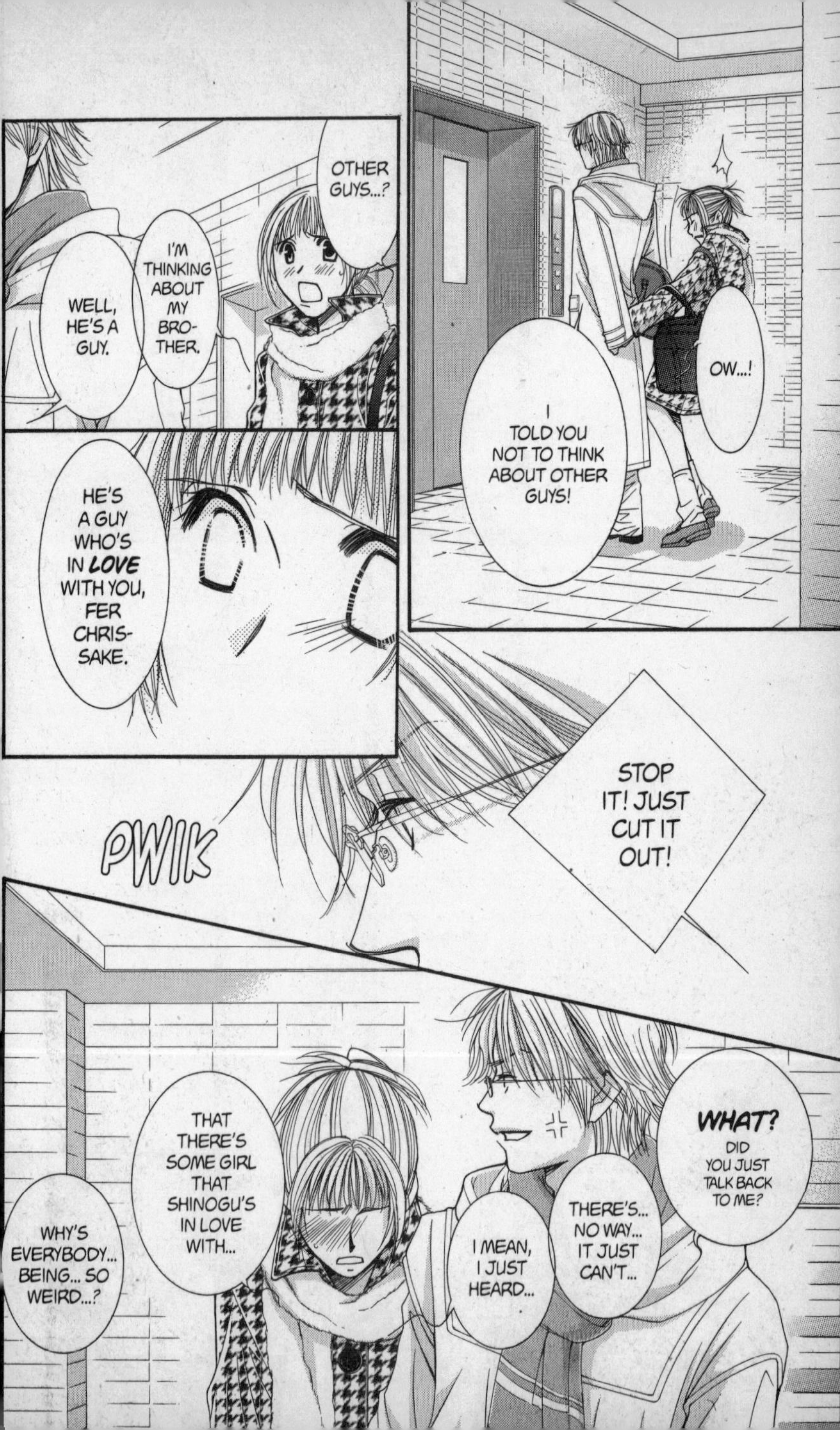
OW...!
I TOLD YOU NOT TO THINK ABOUT OTHER GUYS!
OTHER GUYS...?
I'M THINKING ABOUT MY BROTHER.
WELL, HE'S A GUY.
HE'S A GUY WHO'S IN ***LOVE*** WITH YOU, FER CHRIS-SAKE.
STOP IT! JUST CUT IT OUT!
PWIK
WHAT? DID YOU JUST TALK BACK TO ME?
THERE'S... NO WAY... IT JUST CAN'T...
I MEAN, I JUST HEARD...
THAT THERE'S SOME GIRL THAT SHINOGU'S IN LOVE WITH...
WHY'S EVERYBODY... BEING... SO WEIRD...?

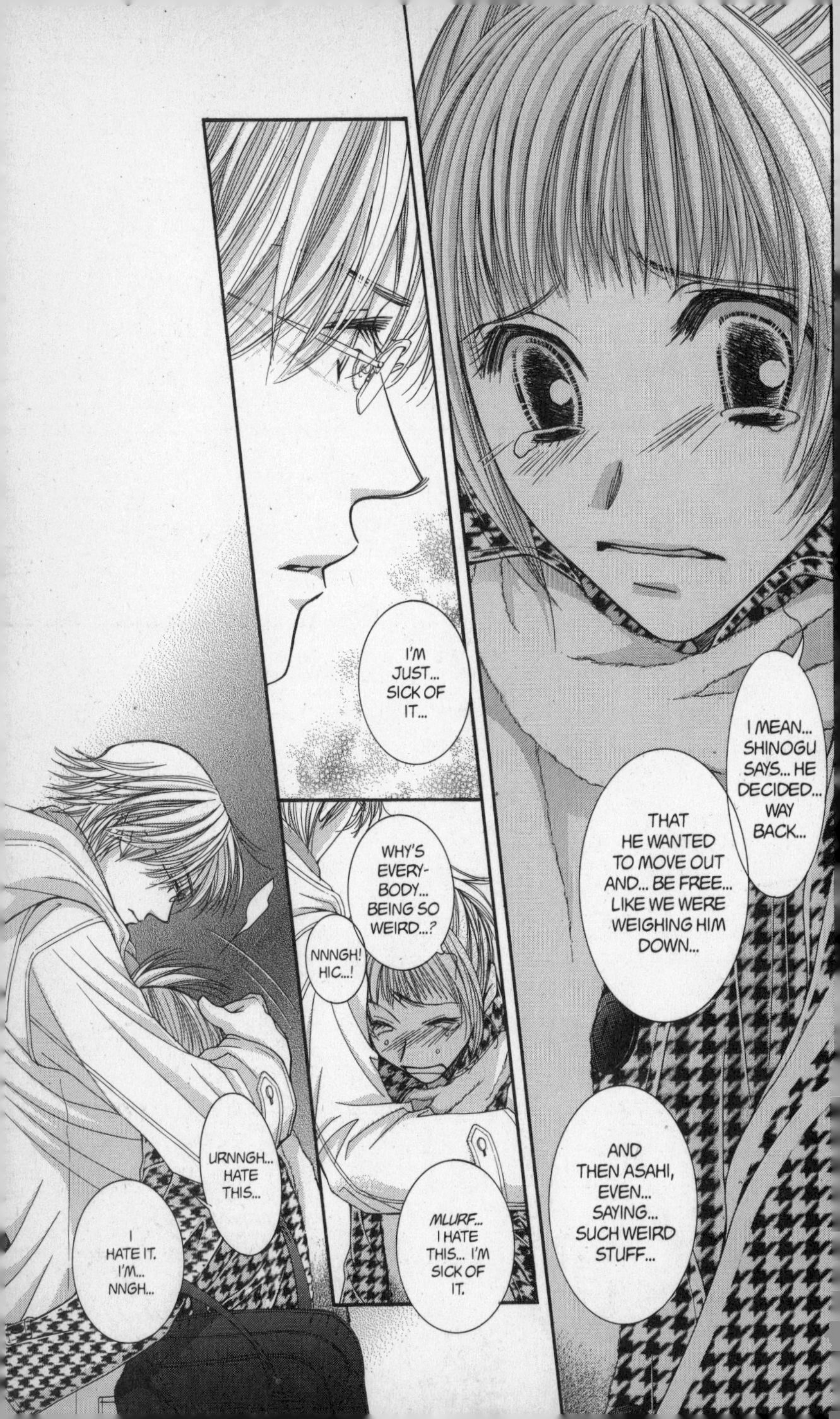
I MEAN... SHINOGU SAYS... HE DECIDED... WAY BACK...
THAT HE WANTED TO MOVE OUT AND... BE FREE... LIKE WE WERE WEIGHING HIM DOWN...
AND THEN ASAHI, EVEN... SAYING... SUCH WEIRD STUFF...
I'M JUST... SICK OF IT...
WHY'S EVERY-BODY... BEING SO WEIRD...?
NNNGH! HIC...!
MLURF... I HATE THIS... I'M SICK OF IT.
URNNGH... HATE THIS...
I HATE IT. I'M... NNGH...

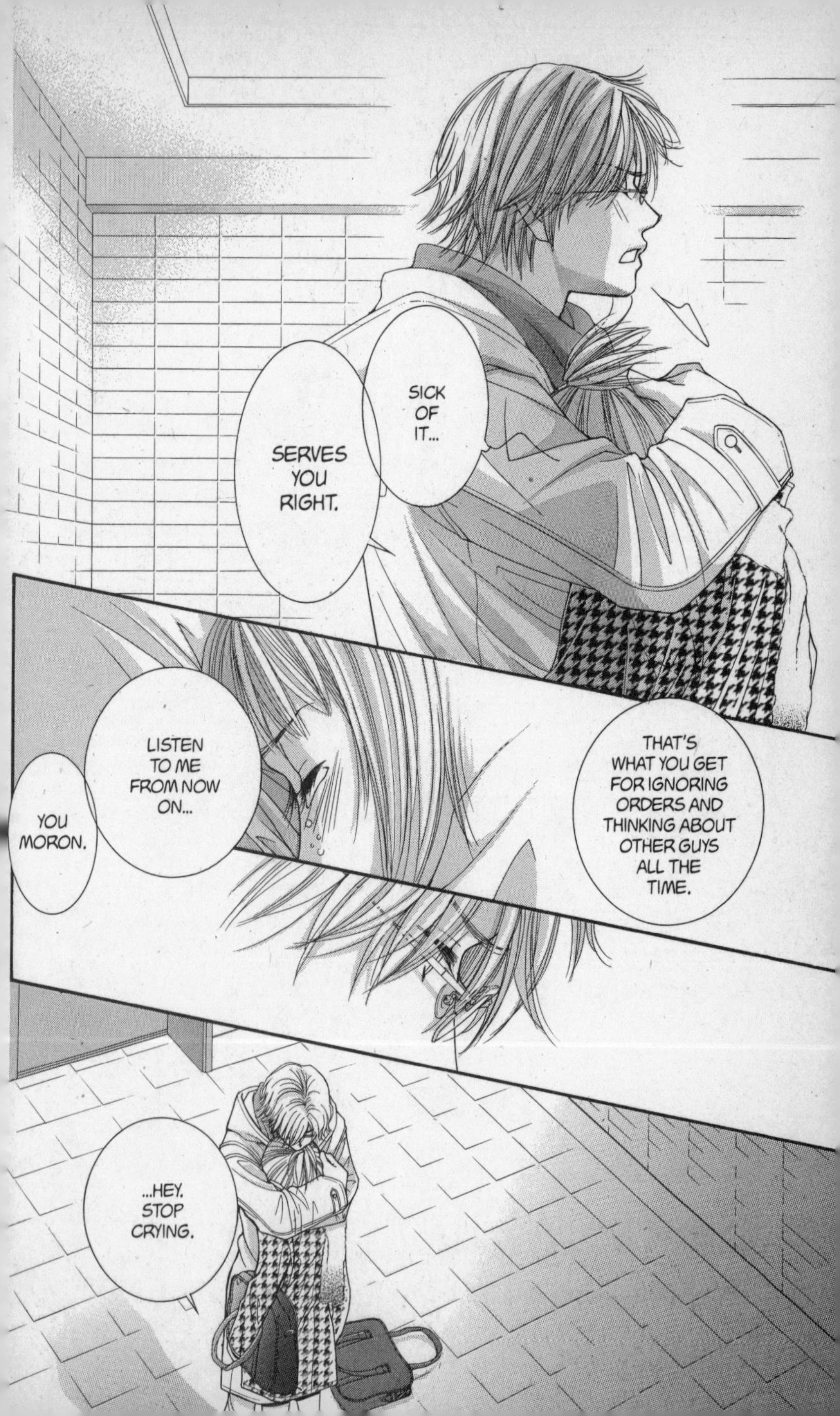
SICK OF IT...
SERVES YOU RIGHT.
THAT'S WHAT YOU GET FOR IGNORING ORDERS AND THINKING ABOUT OTHER GUYS ALL THE TIME.
LISTEN TO ME FROM NOW ON...
YOU MORON.
...HEY. STOP CRYING.

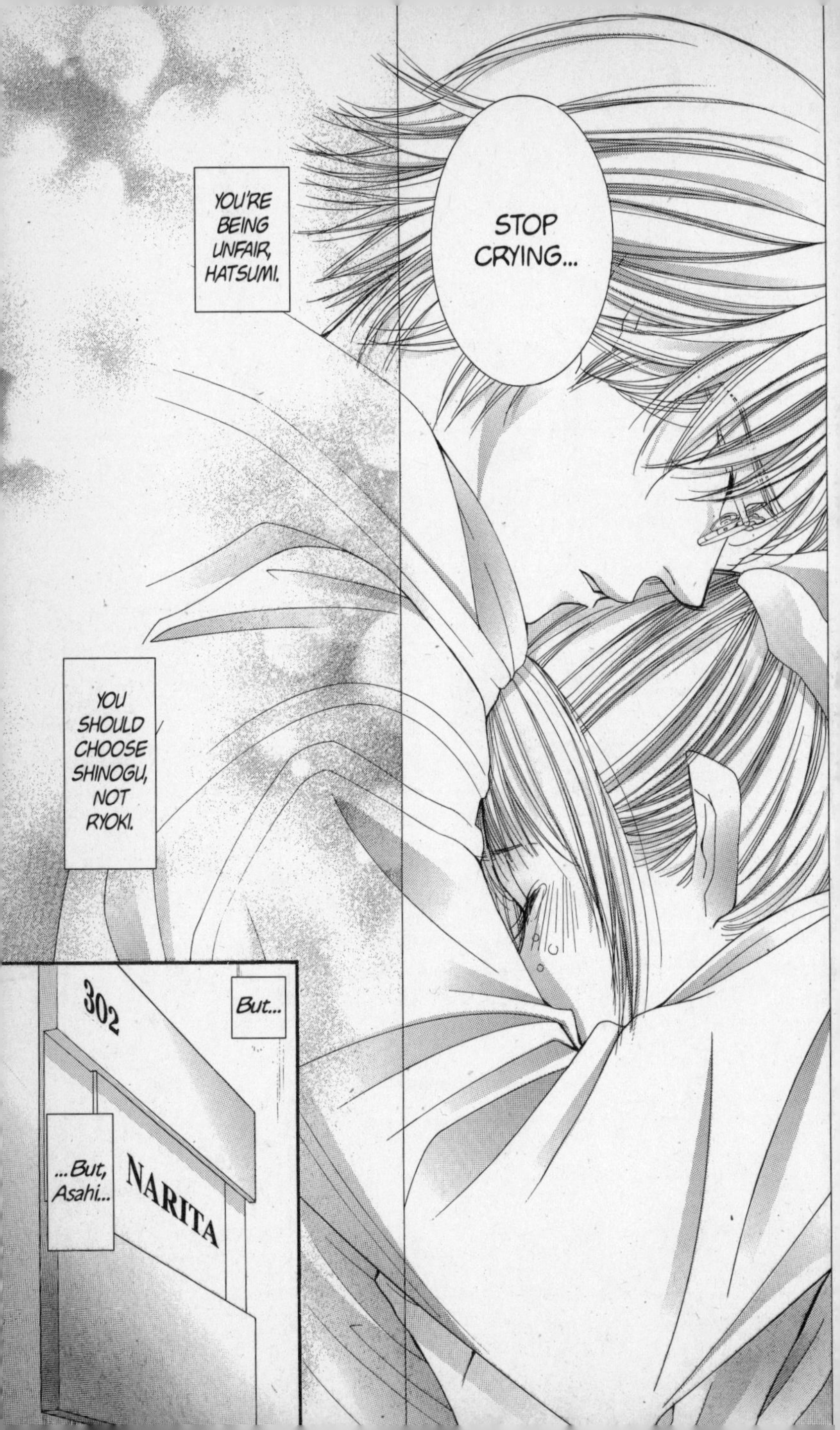
STOP CRYING...
YOU'RE BEING UNFAIR, HATSUMI.
YOU SHOULD CHOOSE SHINOGU, NOT RYOKI.
But...
302
...But, Asahi...
NARITA

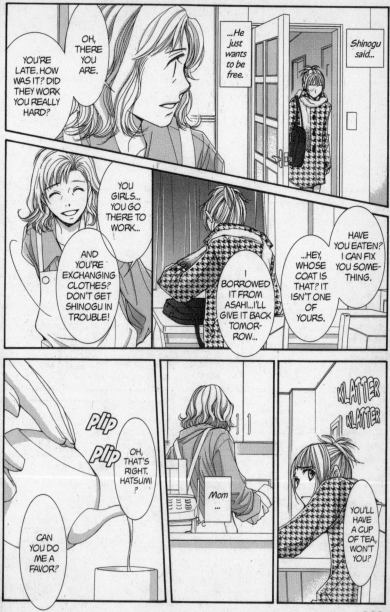

Shinogu said...
...He just wants to be free.
OH, THERE YOU ARE.
YOU'RE LATE. HOW WAS IT? DID THEY WORK YOU REALLY HARD?
HAVE YOU EATEN? I CAN FIX YOU SOME-THING.
...HEY, WHOSE COAT IS THAT? IT ISN'T ONE OF YOURS.
I BORROWED IT FROM ASAHI...I'LL GIVE IT BACK TOMOR-ROW...
YOU GIRLS... YOU GO THERE TO WORK...
AND YOU'RE EXCHANGING CLOTHES? DON'T GET SHINOGU IN TROUBLE!
KLATTER
KLATTER
YOU'LL HAVE A CUP OF TEA, WON'T YOU?
Mom ...
plip
plip
OH, THAT'S RIGHT. HATSUMI?
CAN YOU DO ME A FAVOR?

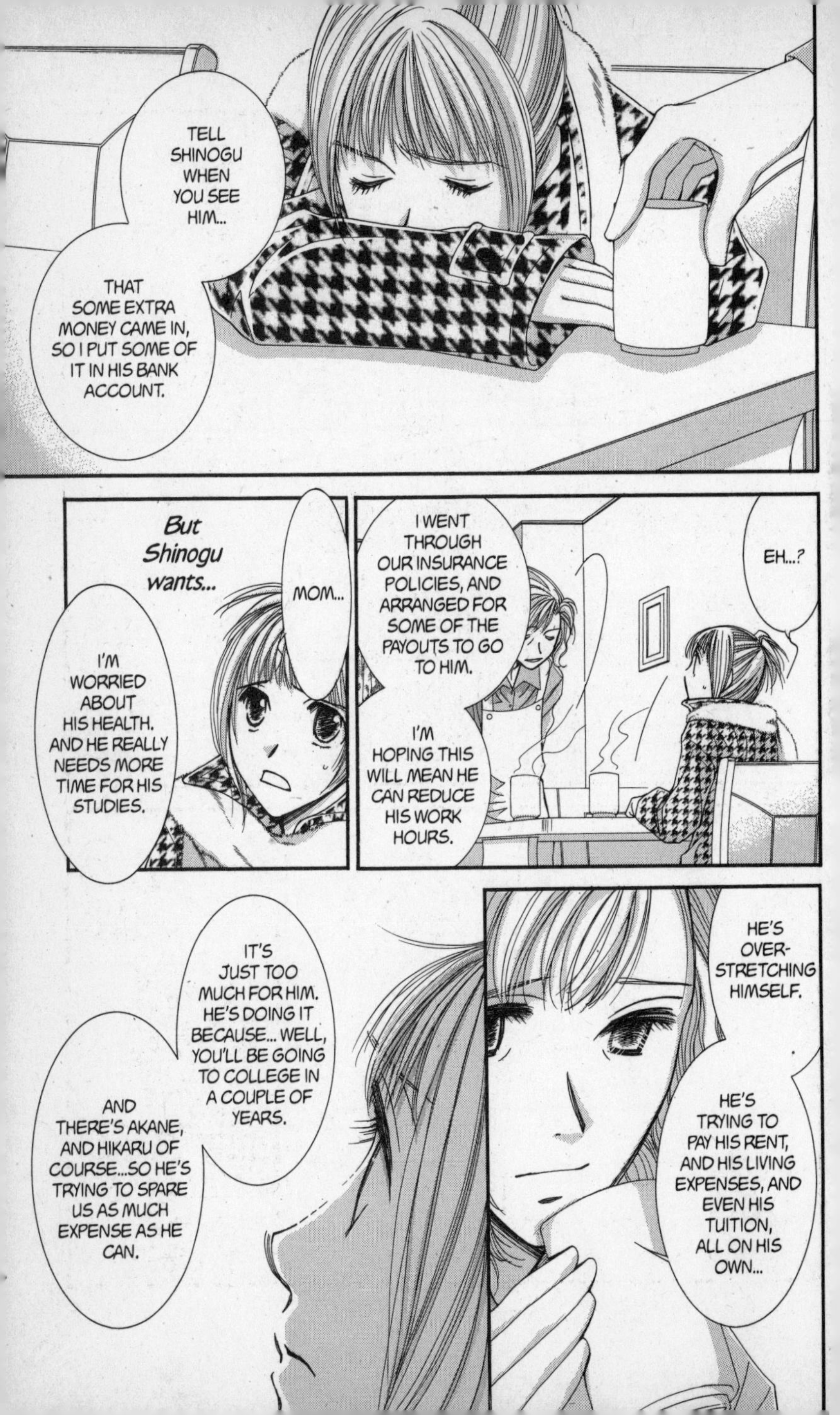
TELL SHINOGU WHEN YOU SEE HIM...
THAT SOME EXTRA MONEY CAME IN, SO I PUT SOME OF IT IN HIS BANK ACCOUNT.
EH...?
I WENT THROUGH OUR INSURANCE POLICIES, AND ARRANGED FOR SOME OF THE PAYOUTS TO GO TO HIM.
I'M HOPING THIS WILL MEAN HE CAN REDUCE HIS WORK HOURS.
MOM...
But Shinogu wants...
I'M WORRIED ABOUT HIS HEALTH. AND HE REALLY NEEDS MORE TIME FOR HIS STUDIES.
HE'S OVER-STRETCHING HIMSELF.
HE'S TRYING TO PAY HIS RENT, AND HIS LIVING EXPENSES, AND EVEN HIS TUITION, ALL ON HIS OWN...
IT'S JUST TOO MUCH FOR HIM. HE'S DOING IT BECAUSE... WELL, YOU'LL BE GOING TO COLLEGE IN A COUPLE OF YEARS.
AND THERE'S AKANE, AND HIKARU OF COURSE...SO HE'S TRYING TO SPARE US AS MUCH EXPENSE AS HE CAN.

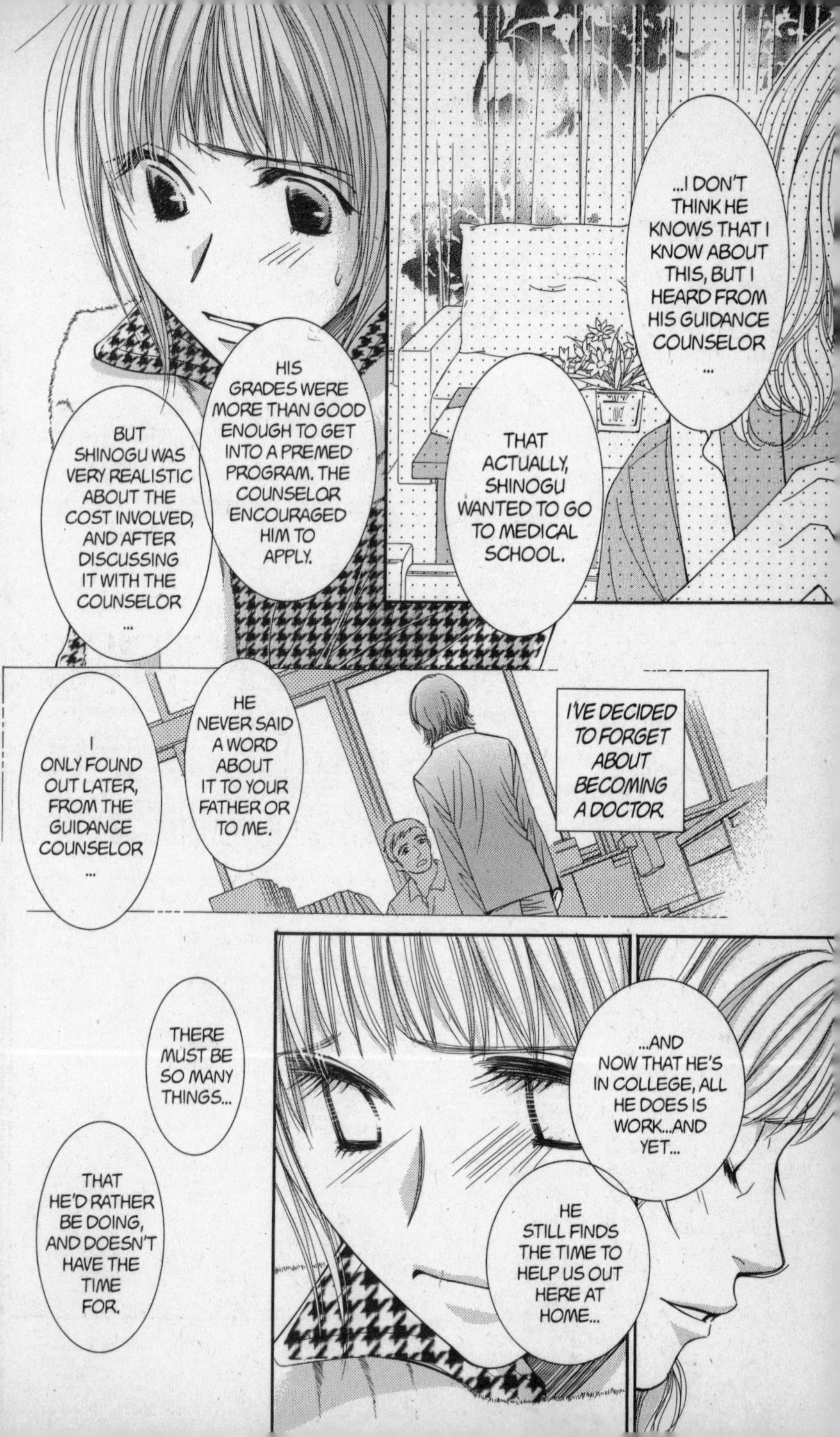
...I DON'T THINK HE KNOWS THAT I KNOW ABOUT THIS, BUT I HEARD FROM HIS GUIDANCE COUNSELOR ...
THAT ACTUALLY, SHINOGU WANTED TO GO TO MEDICAL SCHOOL.
HIS GRADES WERE MORE THAN GOOD ENOUGH TO GET INTO A PREMED PROGRAM. THE COUNSELOR ENCOURAGED HIM TO APPLY.
BUT SHINOGU WAS VERY REALISTIC ABOUT THE COST INVOLVED, AND AFTER DISCUSSING IT WITH THE COUNSELOR ...
I'VE DECIDED TO FORGET ABOUT BECOMING A DOCTOR.
HE NEVER SAID A WORD ABOUT IT TO YOUR FATHER OR TO ME.
I ONLY FOUND OUT LATER, FROM THE GUIDANCE COUNSELOR ...
...AND NOW THAT HE'S IN COLLEGE, ALL HE DOES IS WORK...AND YET...
HE STILL FINDS THE TIME TO HELP US OUT HERE AT HOME...
THERE MUST BE SO MANY THINGS...
THAT HE'D RATHER BE DOING, AND DOESN'T HAVE THE TIME FOR.

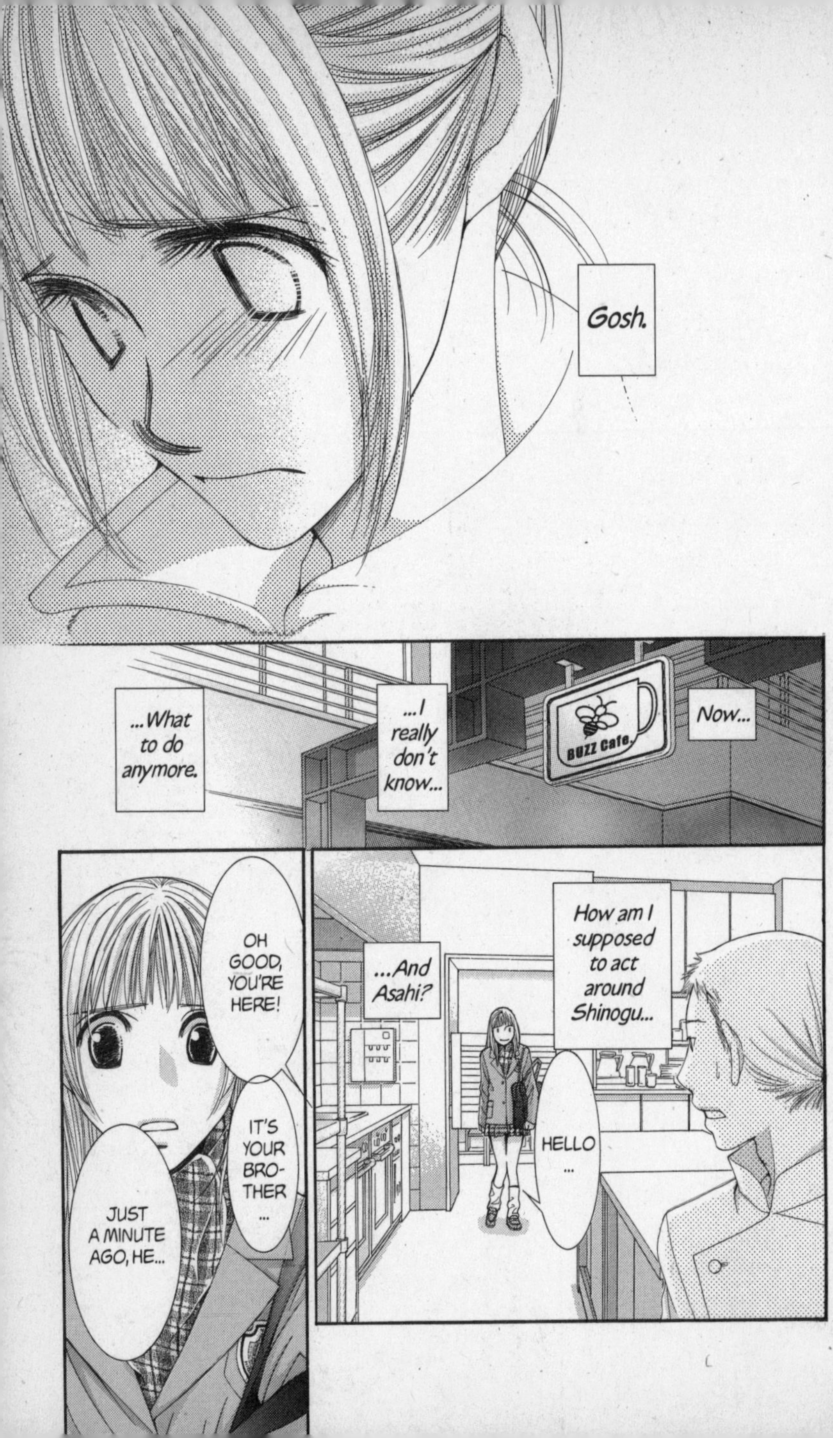
Gosh.
Now...
BUZZ Cafe.
...I really don't know...
...What to do anymore.
How am I supposed to act around Shinogu...
...And Asahi?
HELLO ...
OH GOOD, YOU'RE HERE!
IT'S YOUR BRO-THER ...
JUST A MINUTE AGO, HE...

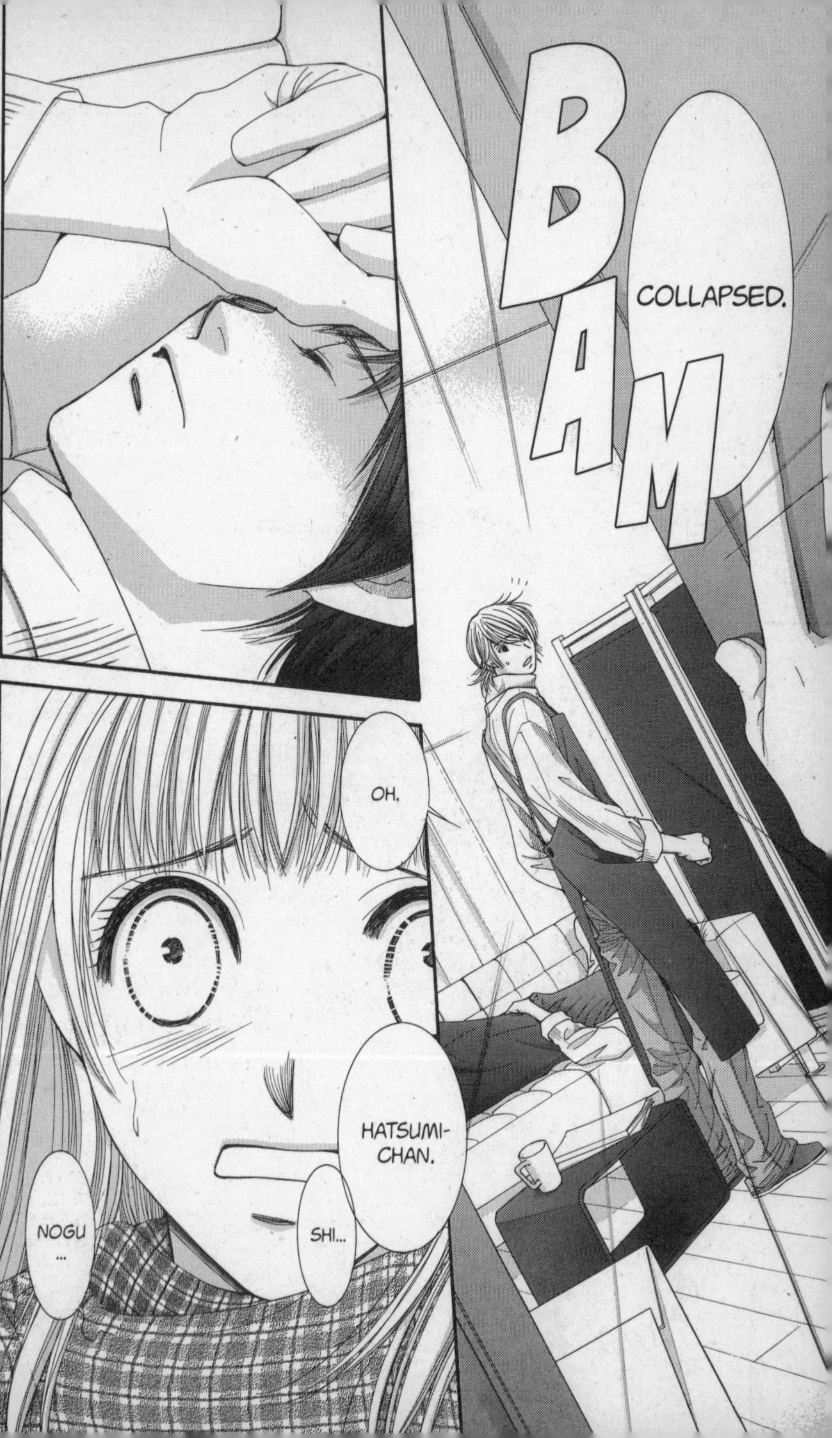
BAM
COLLAPSED.
OH.
HATSUMI-CHAN.
SHI...
NOGU ...

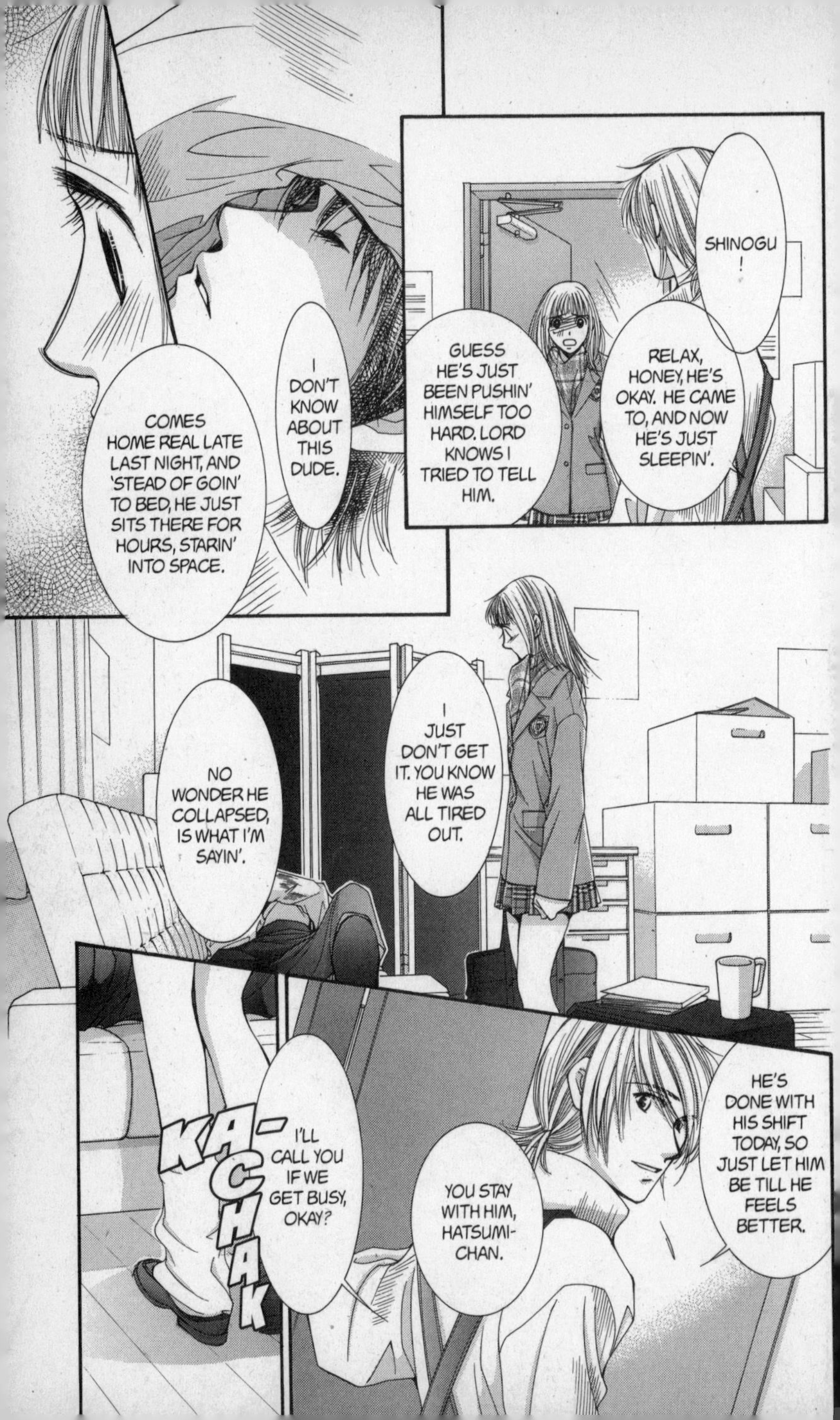
SHINOGU!
RELAX, HONEY, HE'S OKAY. HE CAME TO, AND NOW HE'S JUST SLEEPIN'.
GUESS HE'S JUST BEEN PUSHIN' HIMSELF TOO HARD. LORD KNOWS I TRIED TO TELL HIM.
I DON'T KNOW ABOUT THIS DUDE.
COMES HOME REAL LATE LAST NIGHT, AND 'STEAD OF GOIN' TO BED, HE JUST SITS THERE FOR HOURS, STARIN' INTO SPACE.
I JUST DON'T GET IT. YOU KNOW HE WAS ALL TIRED OUT.
NO WONDER HE COLLAPSED, IS WHAT I'M SAYIN'.
HE'S DONE WITH HIS SHIFT TODAY, SO JUST LET HIM BE TILL HE FEELS BETTER.
YOU STAY WITH HIM, HATSUMI-CHAN.
I'LL CALL YOU IF WE GET BUSY, OKAY?
KA-CHAK

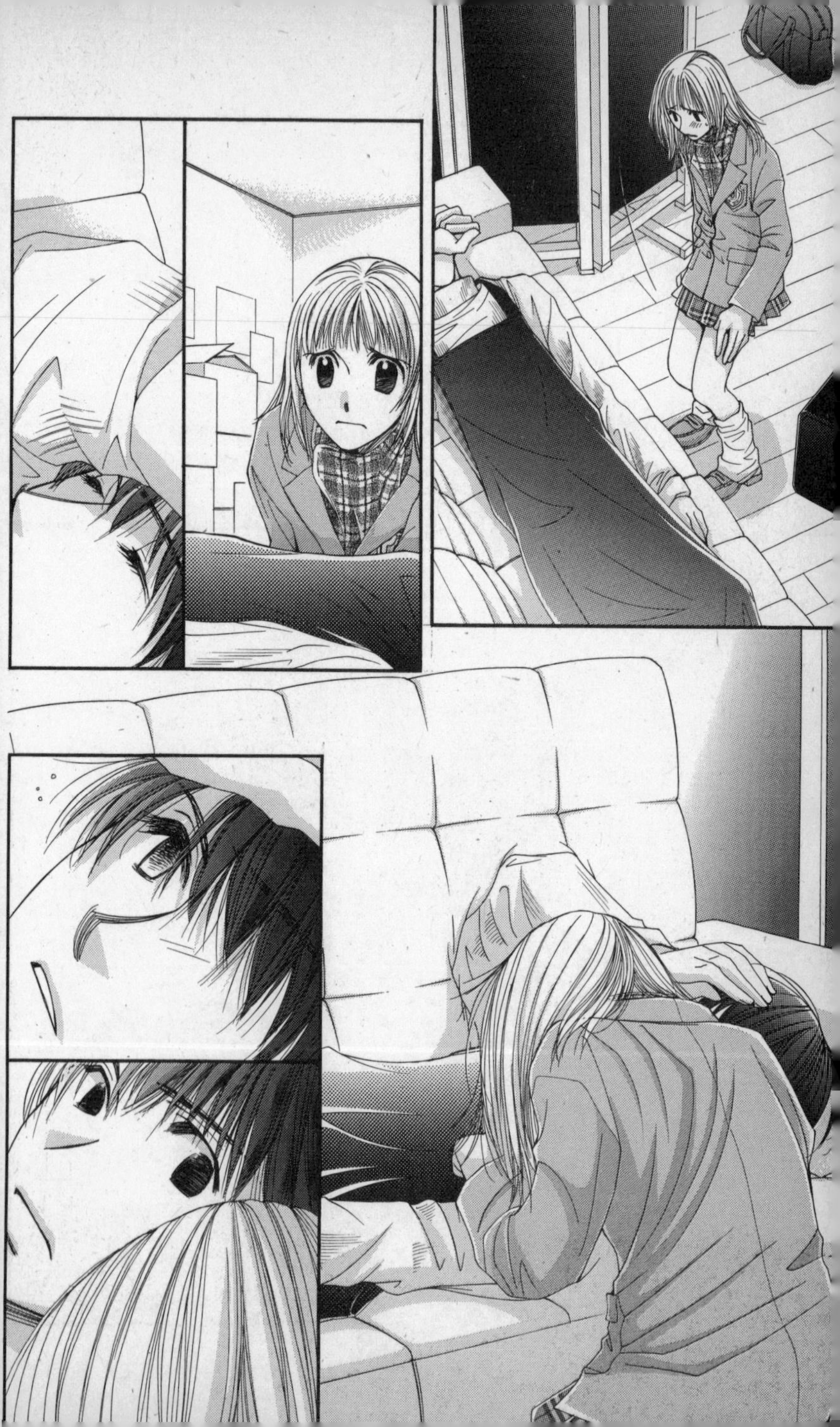

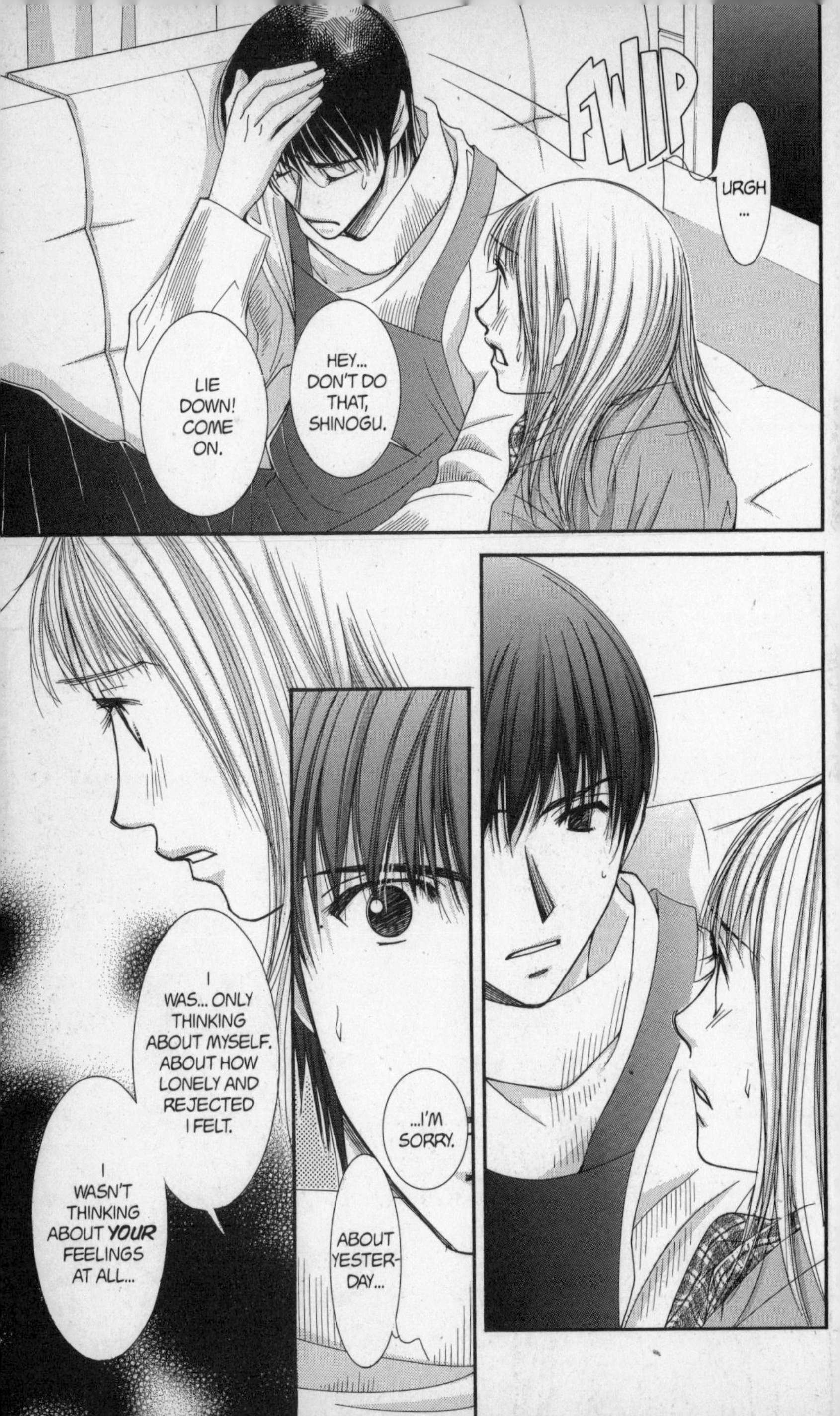
FWIP
URGH...
HEY... DON'T DO THAT, SHINOGU.
LIE DOWN! COME ON.
...I'M SORRY.
ABOUT YESTER-DAY...
I WAS... ONLY THINKING ABOUT MYSELF. ABOUT HOW LONELY AND REJECTED I FELT.
I WASN'T THINKING ABOUT ***YOUR*** FEELINGS AT ALL...

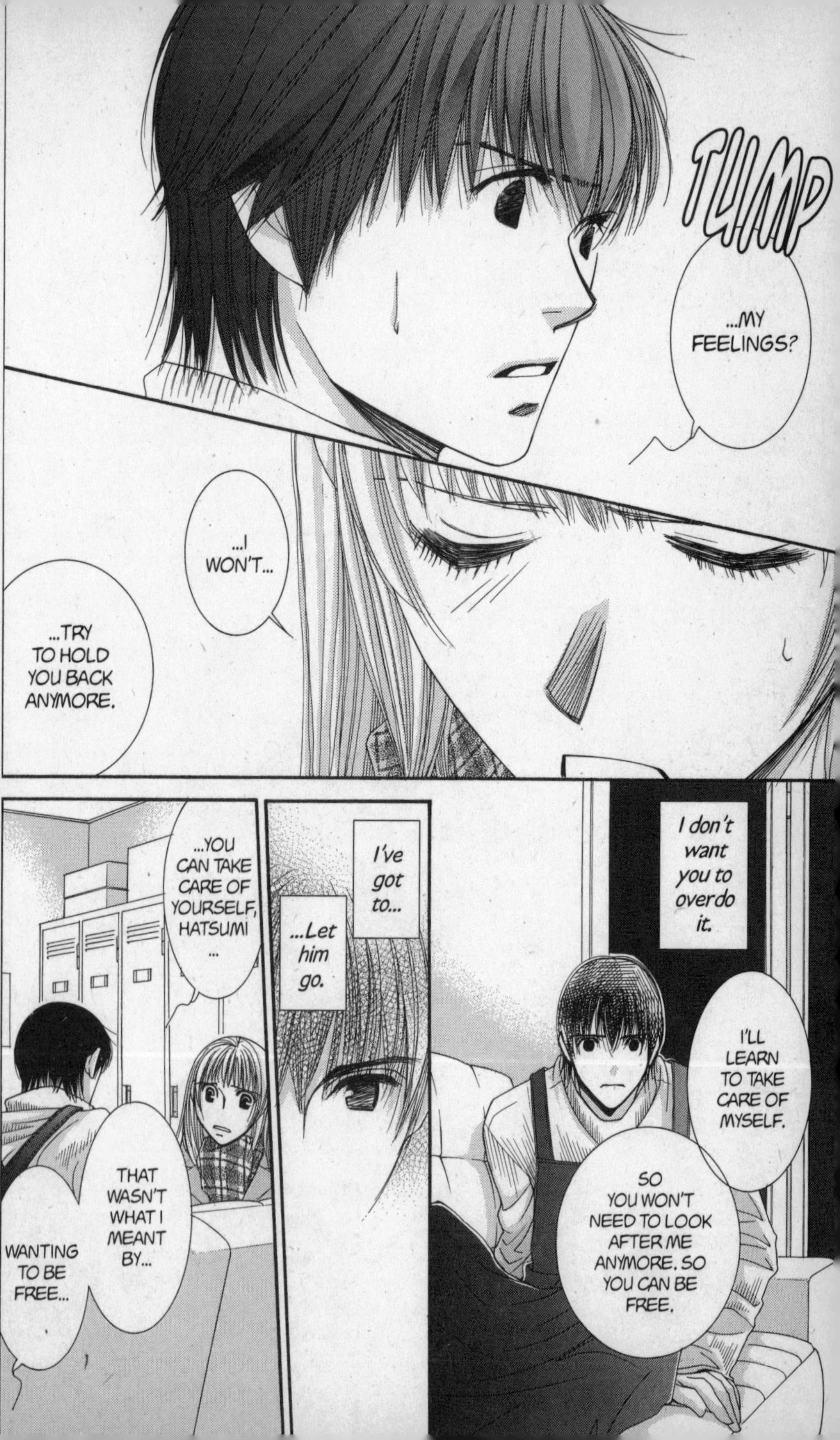
TUMP
...MY FEELINGS?
...I WON'T...
...TRY TO HOLD YOU BACK ANYMORE.
I don't want you to overdo it.
I'LL LEARN TO TAKE CARE OF MYSELF.
SO YOU WON'T NEED TO LOOK AFTER ME ANYMORE. SO YOU CAN BE FREE.
I've got to...
...Let him go.
...YOU CAN TAKE CARE OF YOURSELF, HATSUMI ...
THAT WASN'T WHAT I MEANT BY...
WANTING TO BE FREE...

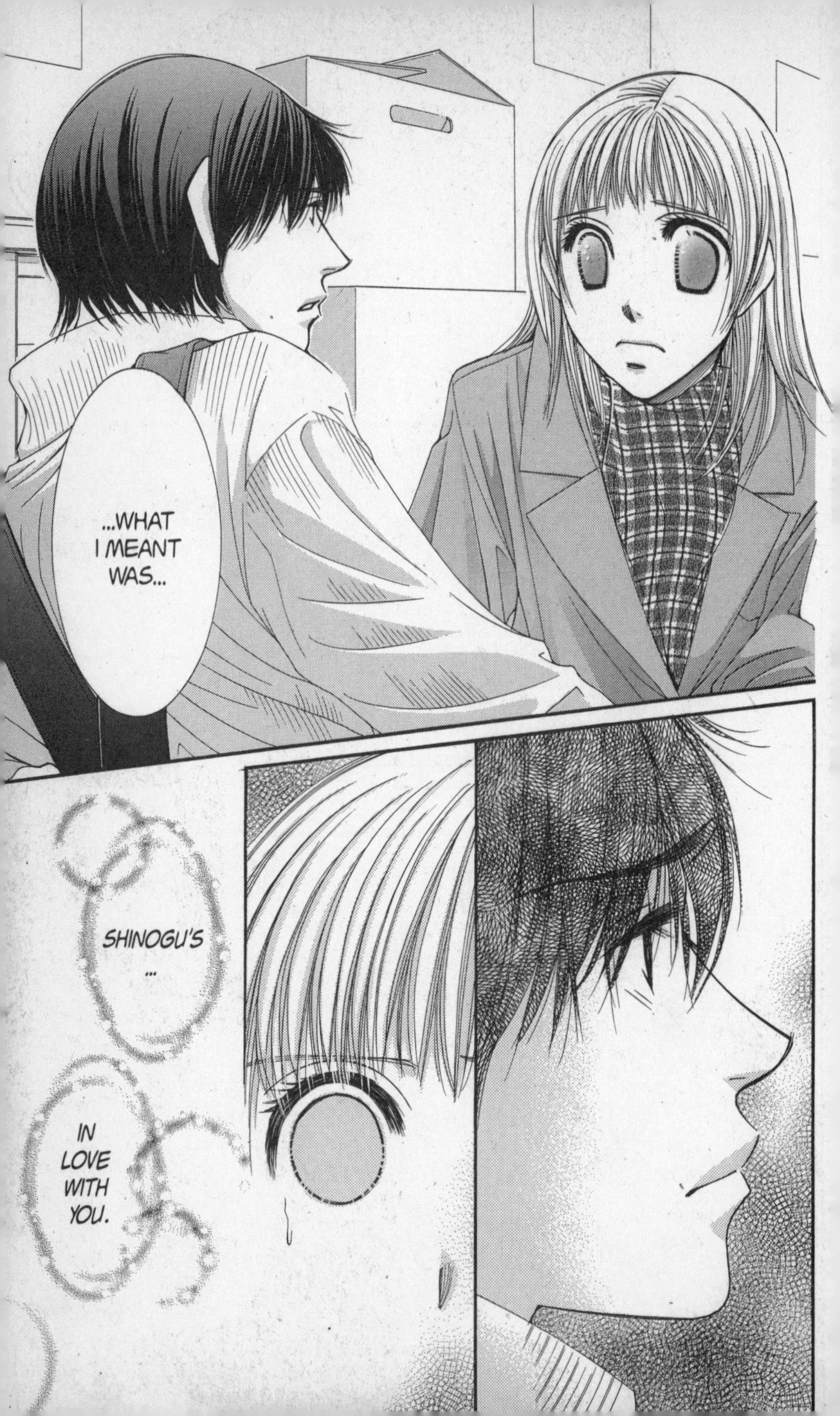
...WHAT I MEANT WAS...
SHINOGU'S ...
IN LOVE WITH YOU.

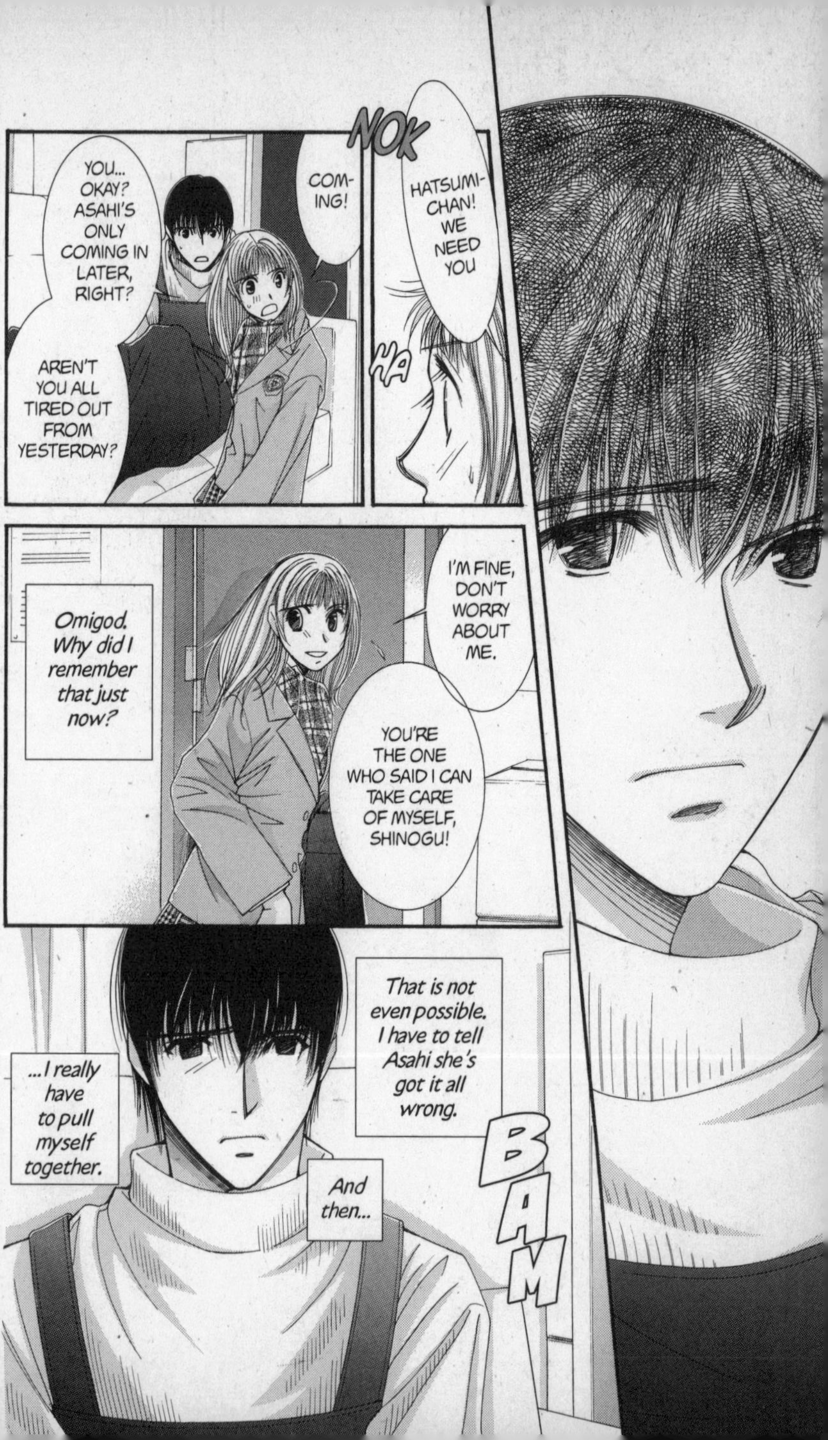
NOK
HATSUMI-CHAN! WE NEED YOU
HA
COM-ING!
YOU... OKAY? ASAHI'S ONLY COMING IN LATER, RIGHT?
AREN'T YOU ALL TIRED OUT FROM YESTERDAY?
I'M FINE, DON'T WORRY ABOUT ME.
YOU'RE THE ONE WHO SAID I CAN TAKE CARE OF MYSELF, SHINOGU!
Omigod. Why did I remember that just now?
That is not even possible. I have to tell Asahi she's got it all wrong.
...I really have to pull myself together.
And then...
BAM

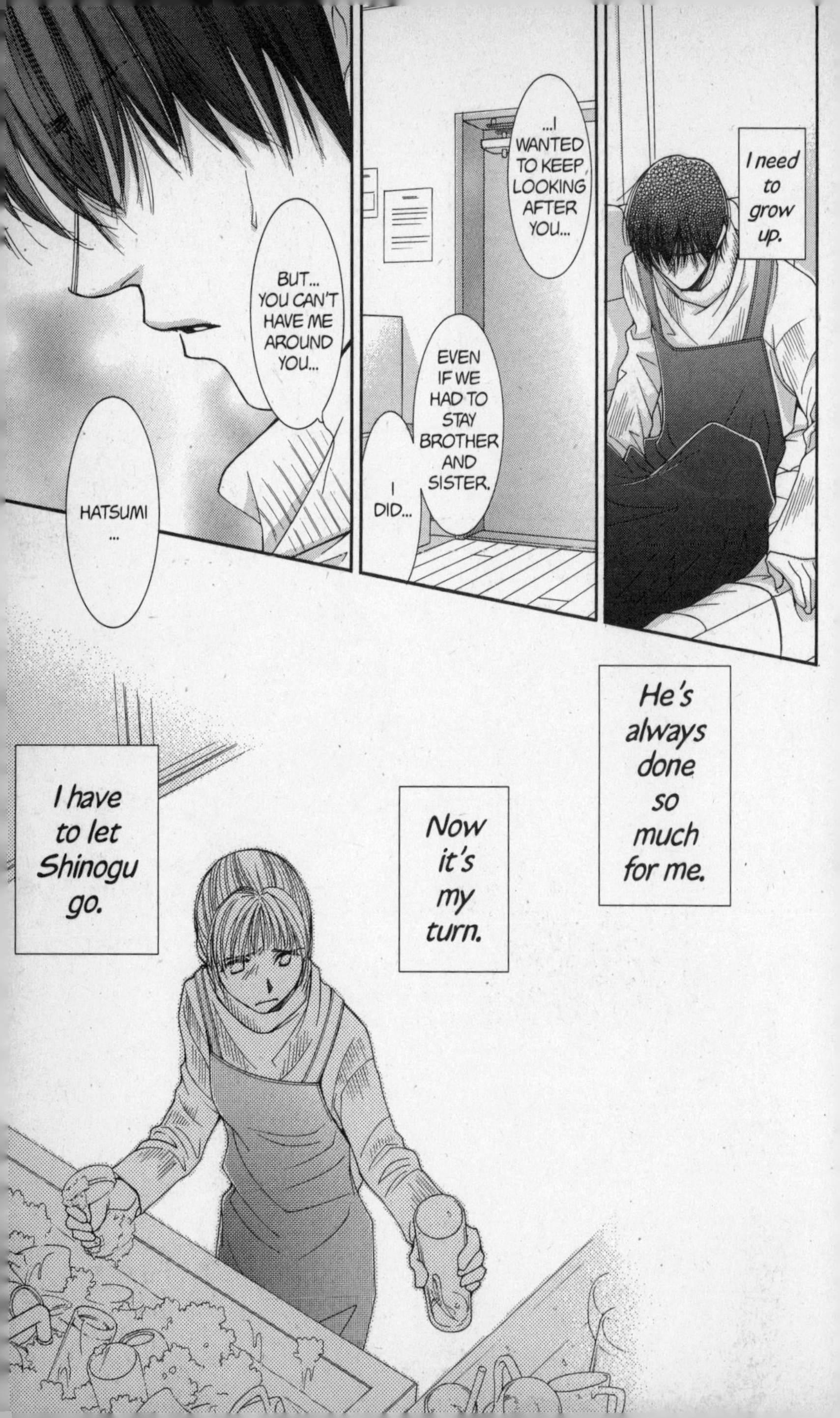
I need to grow up.
...I WANTED TO KEEP LOOKING AFTER YOU...
EVEN IF WE HAD TO STAY BROTHER AND SISTER.
I DID...
BUT... YOU CAN'T HAVE ME AROUND YOU...
HATSUMI ...
He's always done so much for me.
Now it's my turn.
I have to let Shinogu go.

AND NOW, COMING RIGHT UP: A LOOK AT OUR CHILD-HOOD!

NO ROLE THIS TIME.
A.O.

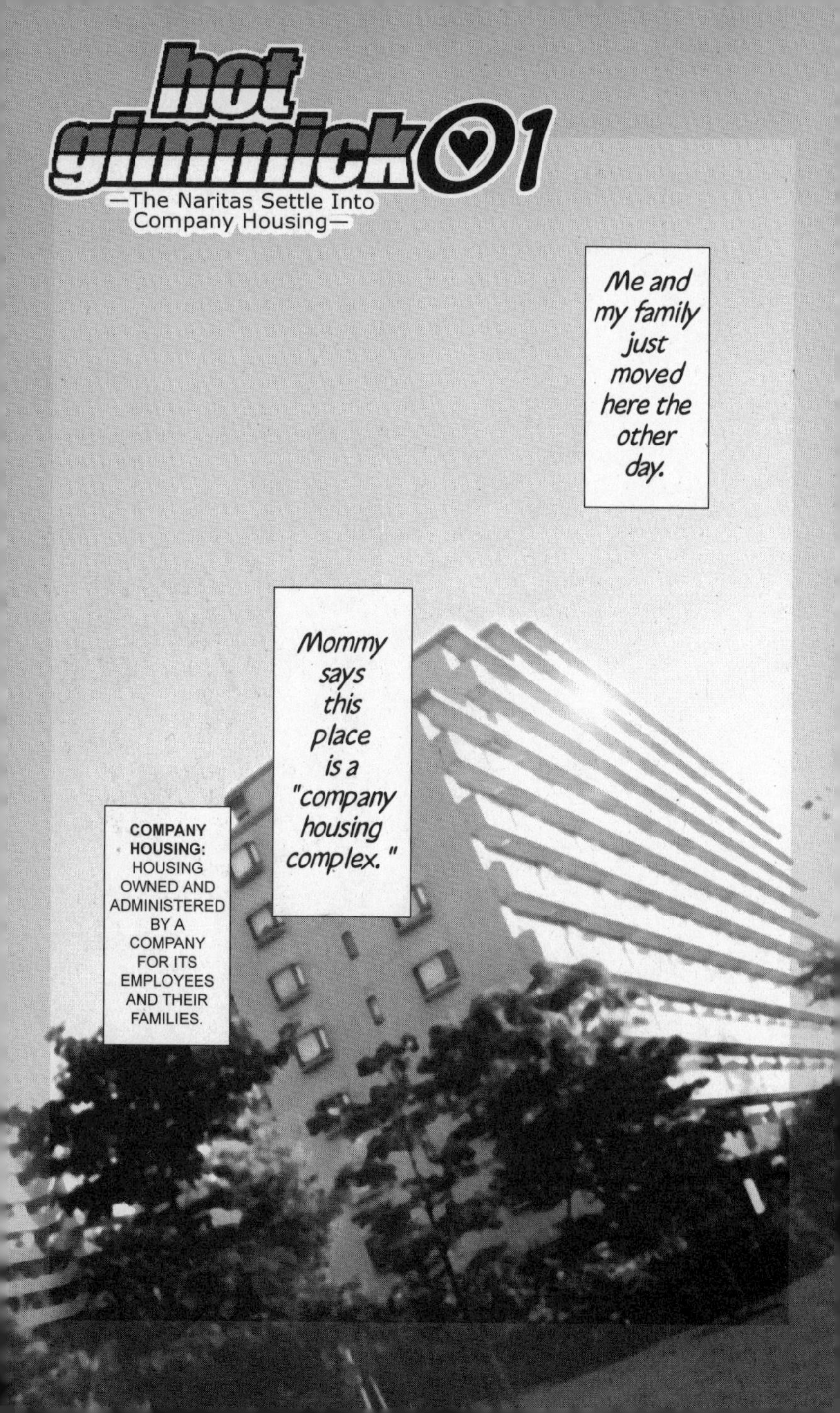
hot gimmick 1
—The Naritas Settle Into Company Housing—
Me and my family just moved here the other day.
Mommy says this place is a "company housing complex."
COMPANY HOUSING: HOUSING OWNED AND ADMINISTERED BY A COMPANY FOR ITS EMPLOYEES AND THEIR FAMILIES.

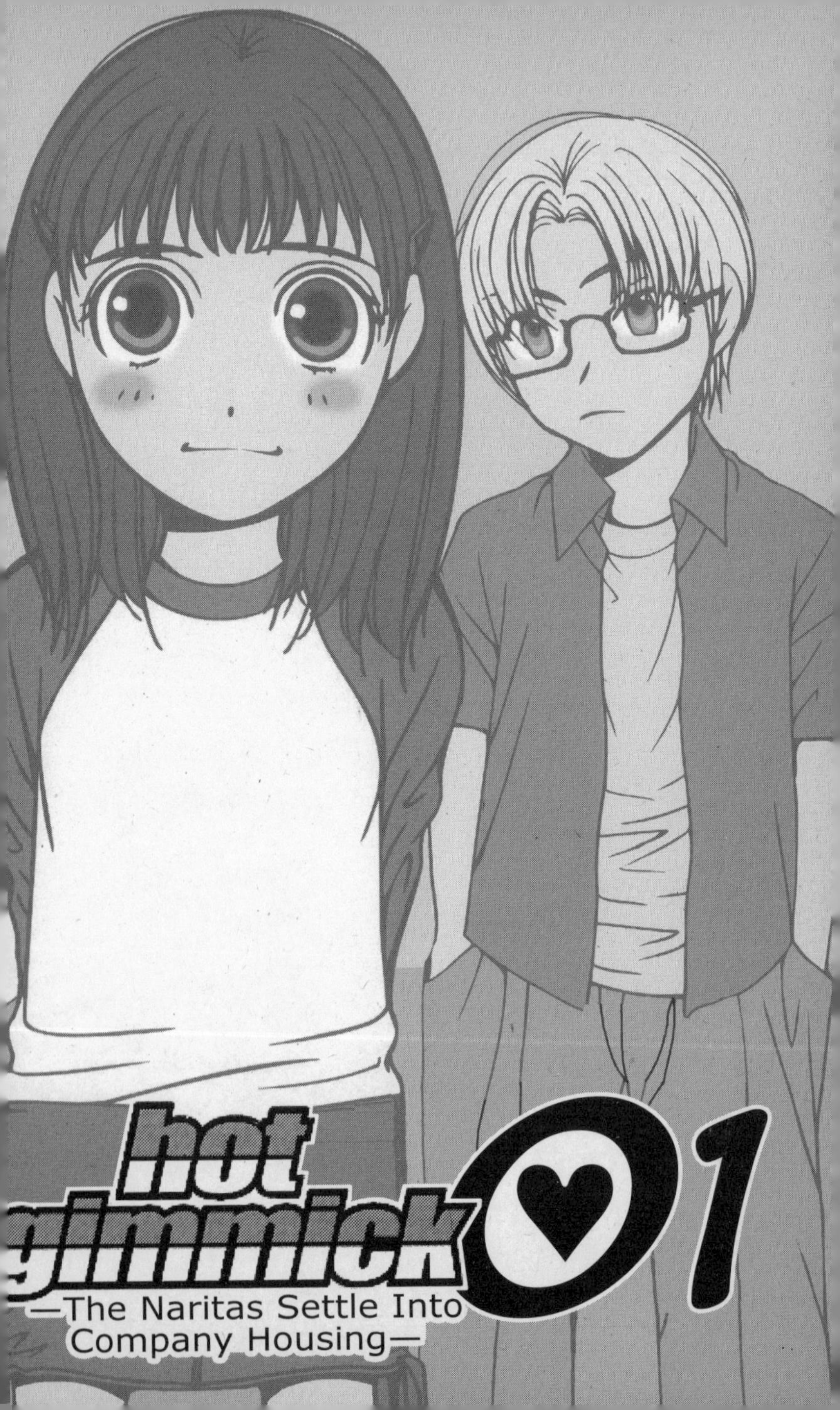
hot gimmick
01
—The Naritas Settle Into Company Housing—

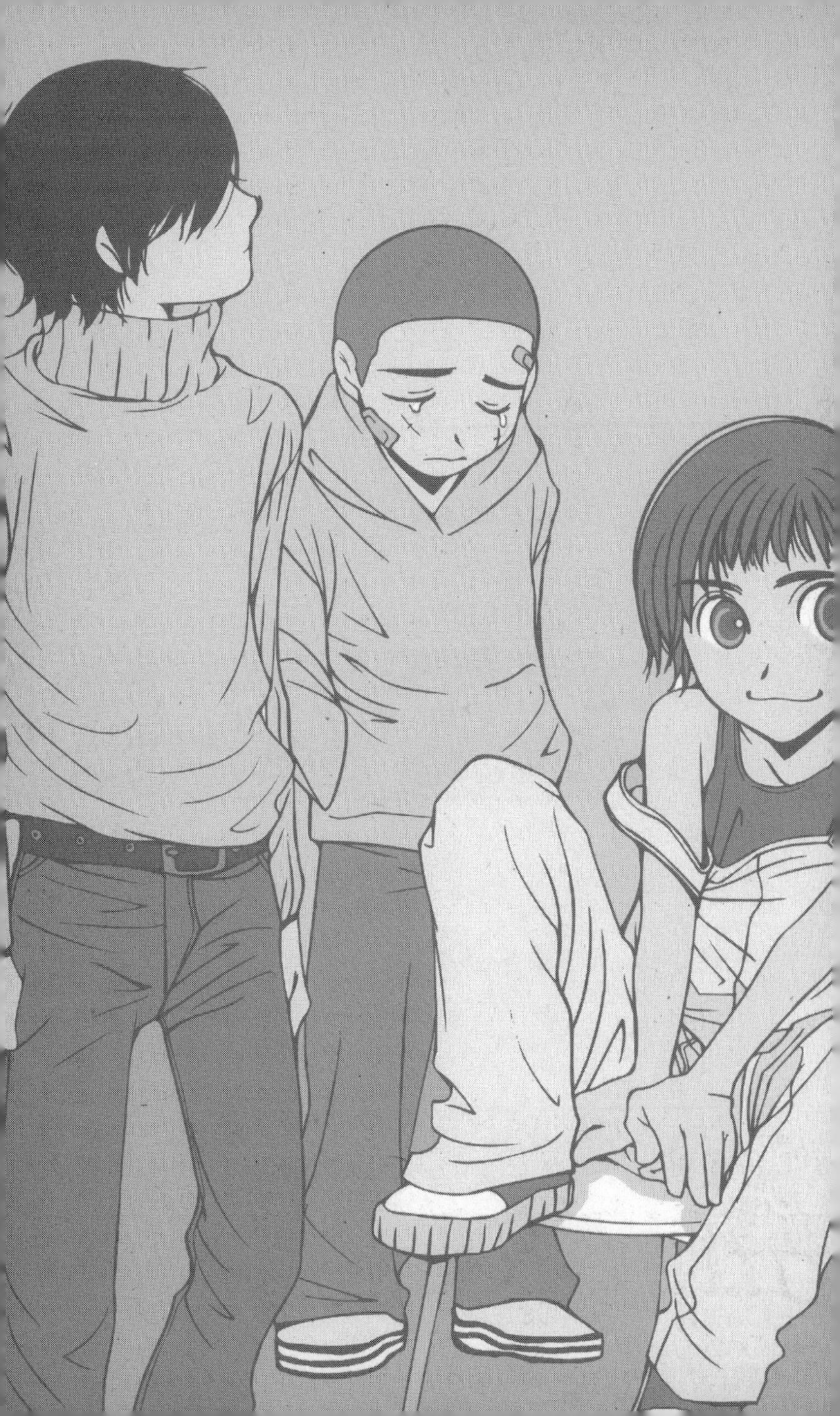

hot gimmick

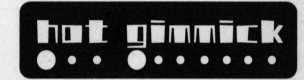

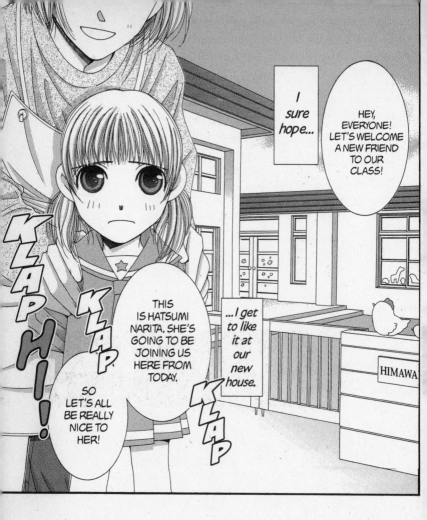

HEY, EVERYONE! LET'S WELCOME A NEW FRIEND TO OUR CLASS!
I sure hope...
...I get to like it at our new house.
HIMAWA
THIS IS HATSUMI NARITA. SHE'S GOING TO BE JOINING US HERE FROM TODAY.
KLAP
KLAP
KLAP
SO LET'S ALL BE REALLY NICE TO HER!
HI!!
KLAP

hot gimmick

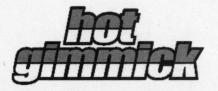

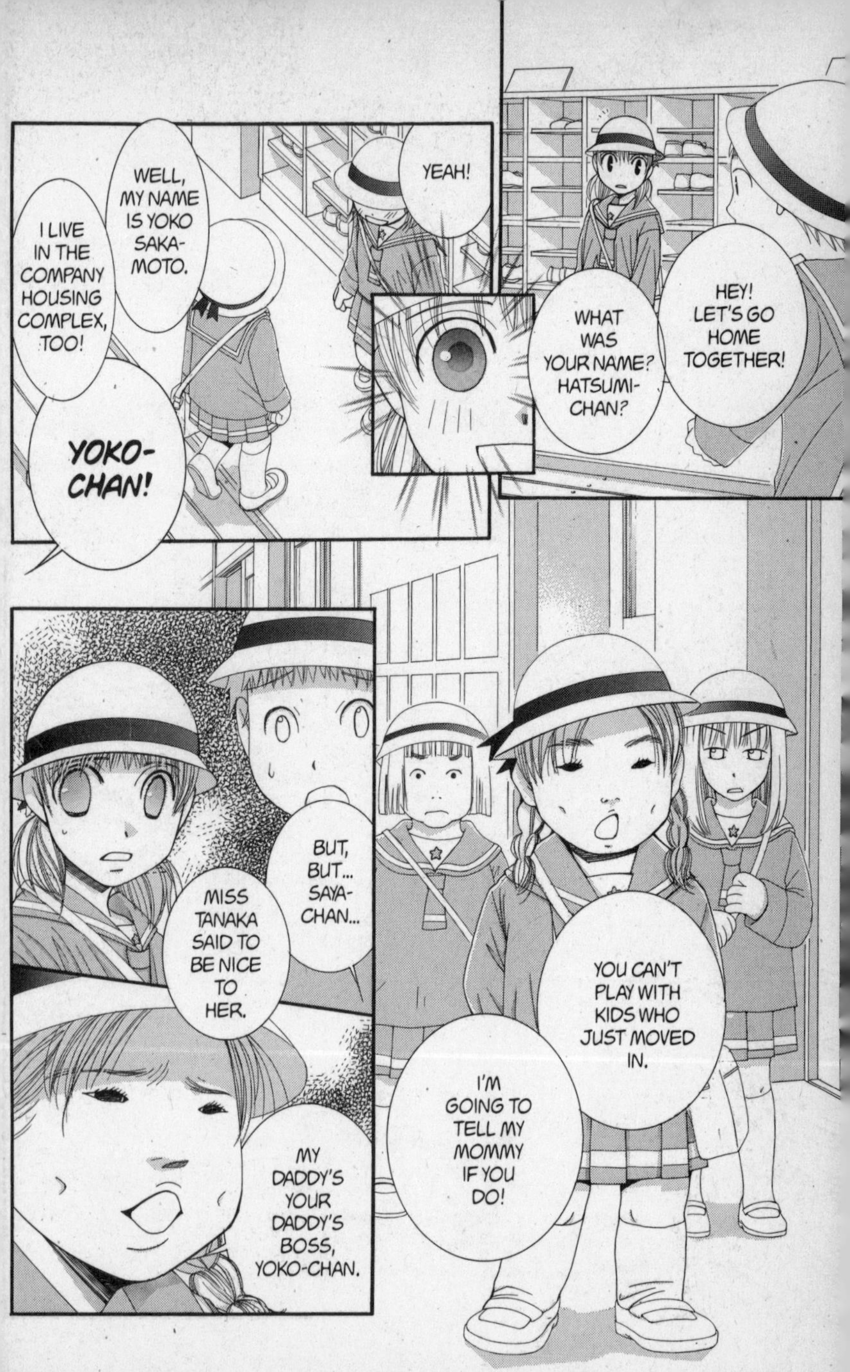
HEY! LET'S GO HOME TOGETHER!
WHAT WAS YOUR NAME? HATSUMI-CHAN?
YEAH!
WELL, MY NAME IS YOKO SAKAMOTO.
I LIVE IN THE COMPANY HOUSING COMPLEX, TOO!
YOKO-CHAN!
YOU CAN'T PLAY WITH KIDS WHO JUST MOVED IN.
I'M GOING TO TELL MY MOMMY IF YOU DO!
BUT, BUT... SAYA-CHAN...
MISS TANAKA SAID TO BE NICE TO HER.
MY DADDY'S YOUR DADDY'S BOSS, YOKO-CHAN.

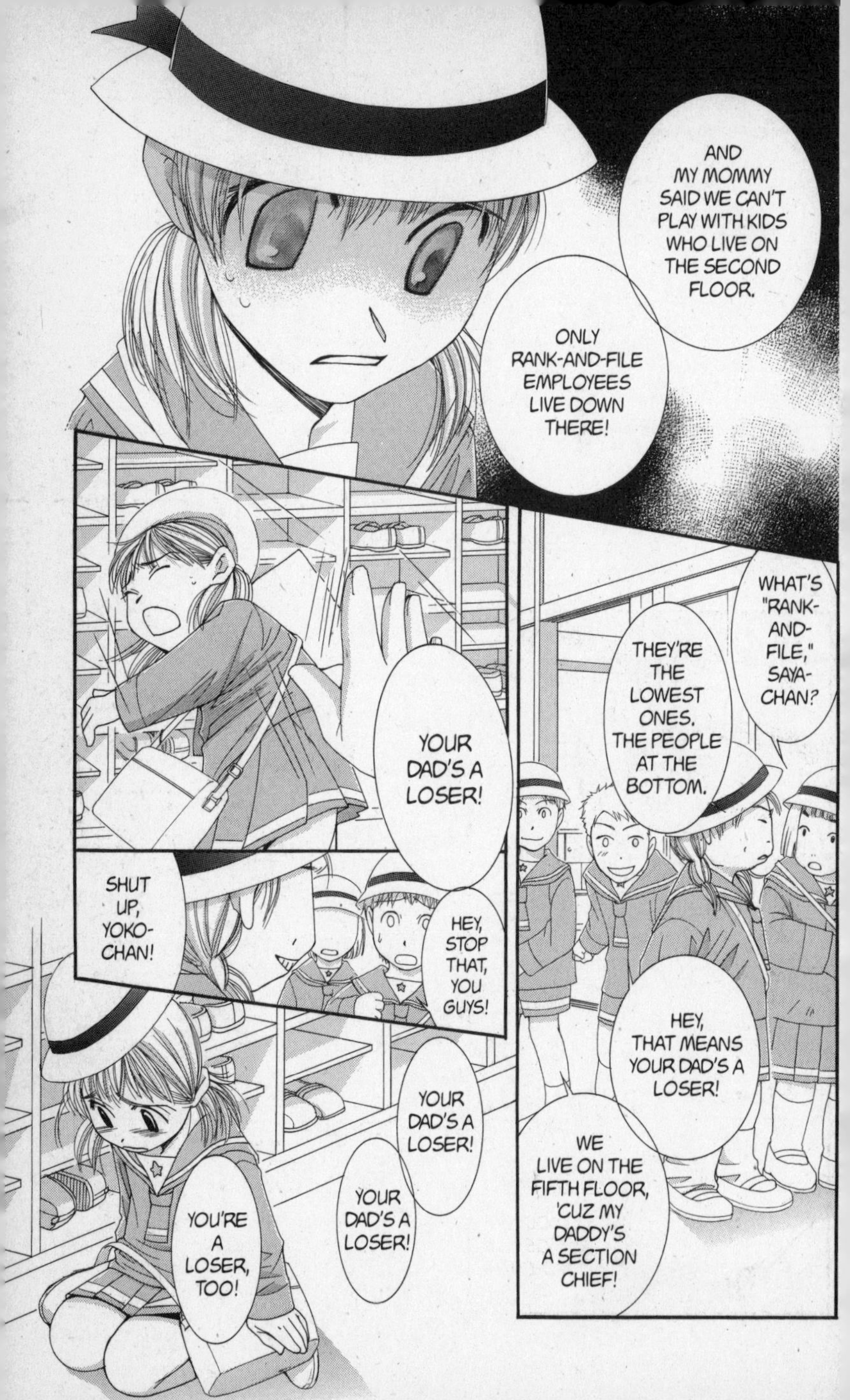
AND MY MOMMY SAID WE CAN'T PLAY WITH KIDS WHO LIVE ON THE SECOND FLOOR.
ONLY RANK-AND-FILE EMPLOYEES LIVE DOWN THERE!
WHAT'S "RANK-AND-FILE," SAYA-CHAN?
THEY'RE THE LOWEST ONES. THE PEOPLE AT THE BOTTOM.
HEY, THAT MEANS YOUR DAD'S A LOSER!
WE LIVE ON THE FIFTH FLOOR, 'CUZ MY DADDY'S A SECTION CHIEF!
YOUR DAD'S A LOSER!
HEY, STOP THAT, YOU GUYS!
SHUT UP, YOKO-CHAN!
YOUR DAD'S A LOSER!
YOUR DAD'S A LOSER!
YOU'RE A LOSER, TOO!

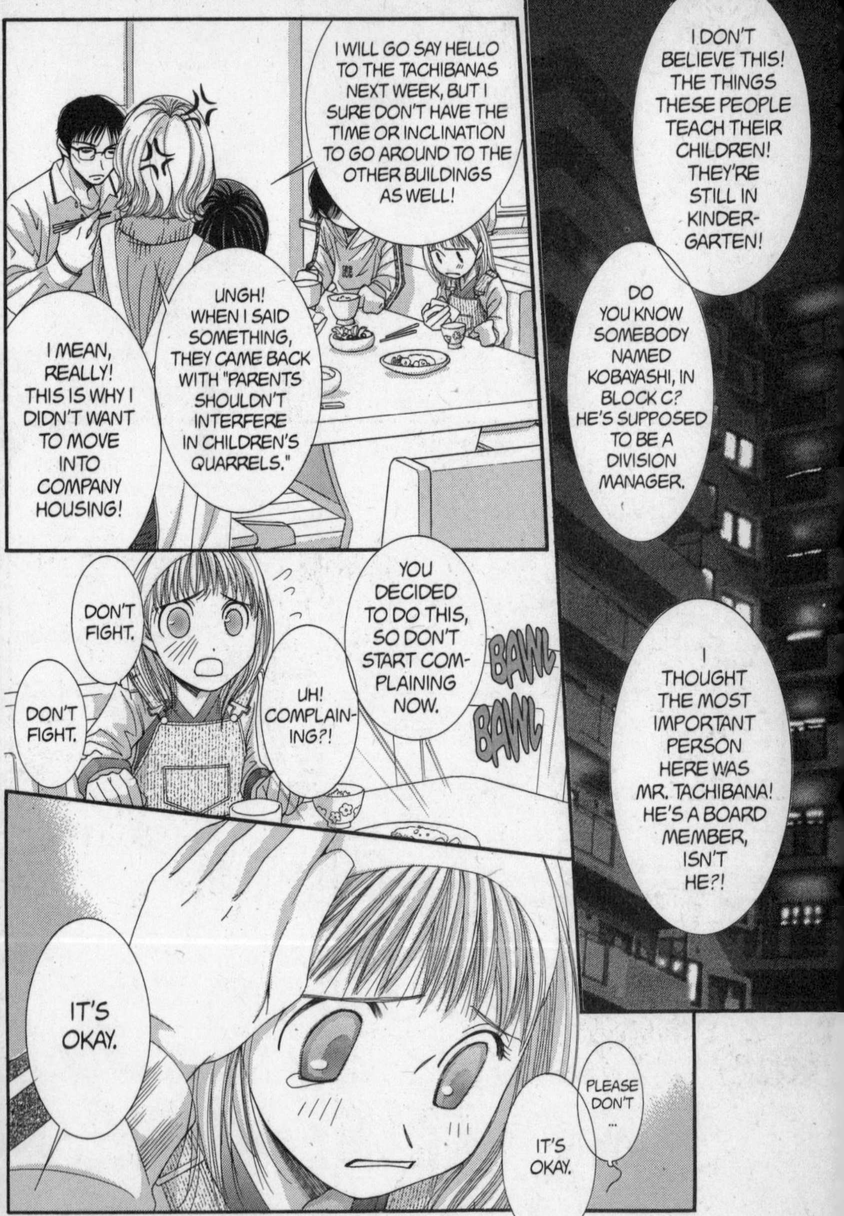
I DON'T BELIEVE THIS! THE THINGS THESE PEOPLE TEACH THEIR CHILDREN! THEY'RE STILL IN KINDER-GARTEN!
DO YOU KNOW SOMEBODY NAMED KOBAYASHI, IN BLOCK C? HE'S SUPPOSED TO BE A DIVISION MANAGER.
I THOUGHT THE MOST IMPORTANT PERSON HERE WAS MR. TACHIBANA! HE'S A BOARD MEMBER, ISN'T HE?!
I WILL GO SAY HELLO TO THE TACHIBANAS NEXT WEEK, BUT I SURE DON'T HAVE THE TIME OR INCLINATION TO GO AROUND TO THE OTHER BUILDINGS AS WELL!
UNGH! WHEN I SAID SOMETHING, THEY CAME BACK WITH "PARENTS SHOULDN'T INTERFERE IN CHILDREN'S QUARRELS."
I MEAN, REALLY! THIS IS WHY I DIDN'T WANT TO MOVE INTO COMPANY HOUSING!
BAWL
BAWL
YOU DECIDED TO DO THIS, SO DON'T START COM-PLAINING NOW.
UH! COMPLAIN-ING?!
DON'T FIGHT.
DON'T FIGHT.
PLEASE DON'T ...
IT'S OKAY.
IT'S OKAY.

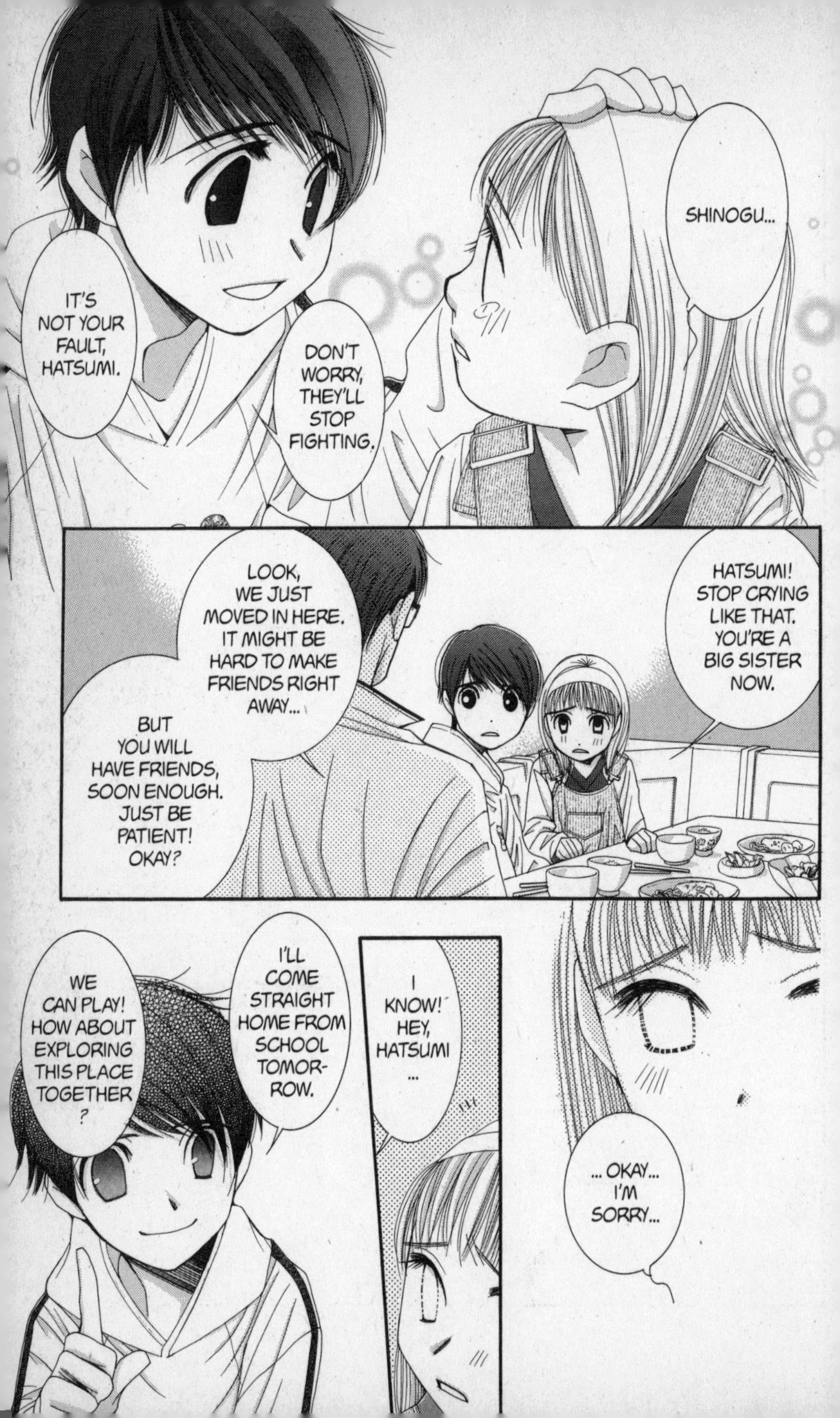
SHINOGU...
DON'T WORRY, THEY'LL STOP FIGHTING.
IT'S NOT YOUR FAULT, HATSUMI.
HATSUMI! STOP CRYING LIKE THAT. YOU'RE A BIG SISTER NOW.
LOOK, WE JUST MOVED IN HERE. IT MIGHT BE HARD TO MAKE FRIENDS RIGHT AWAY...
BUT YOU WILL HAVE FRIENDS, SOON ENOUGH. JUST BE PATIENT! OKAY?
... OKAY... I'M SORRY...
I KNOW! HEY, HATSUMI ...
I'LL COME STRAIGHT HOME FROM SCHOOL TOMOR-ROW.
WE CAN PLAY! HOW ABOUT EXPLORING THIS PLACE TOGETHER ?

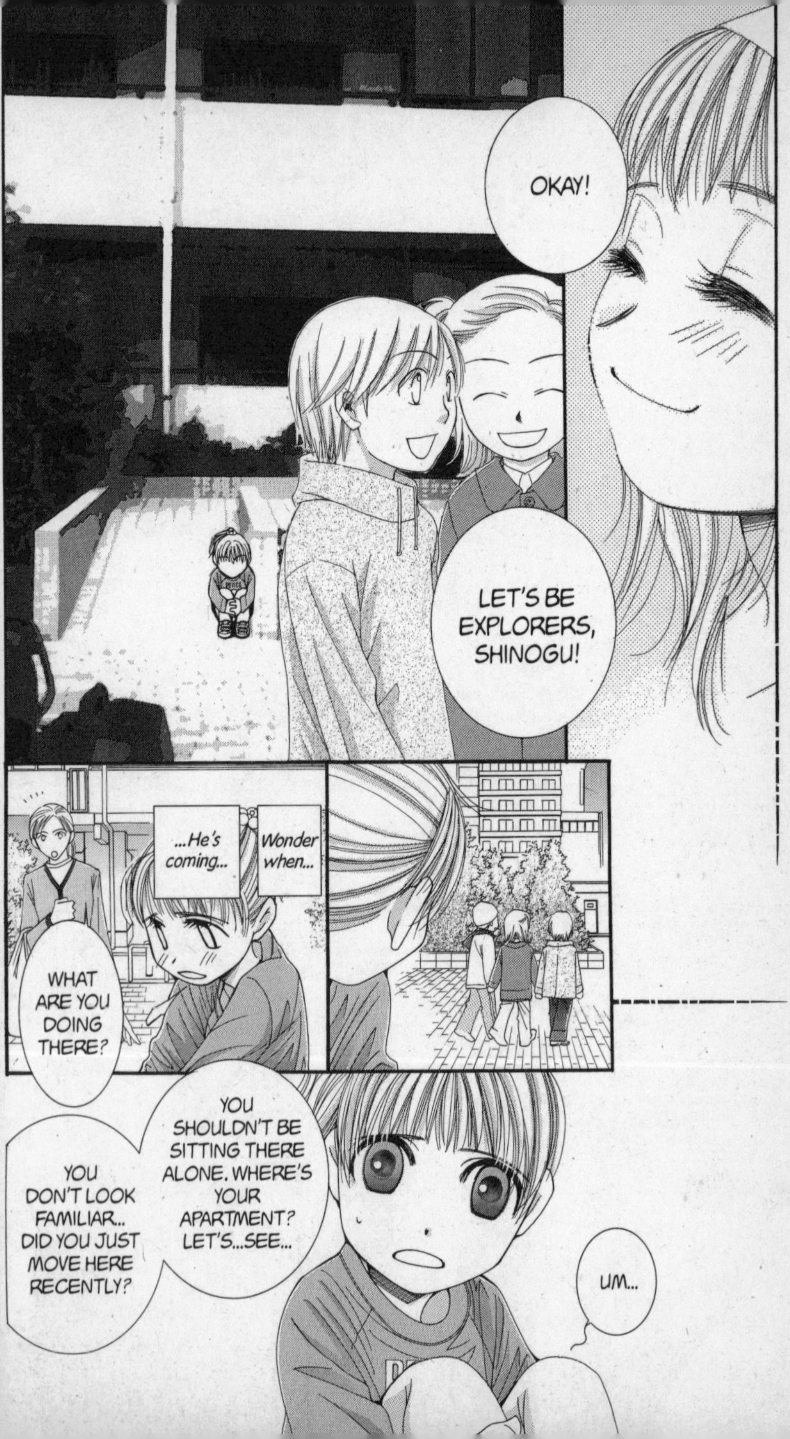
OKAY!
LET'S BE EXPLORERS, SHINOGU!
Wonder when...
...He's coming...
WHAT ARE YOU DOING THERE?
YOU SHOULDN'T BE SITTING THERE ALONE. WHERE'S YOUR APARTMENT? LET'S...SEE...
YOU DON'T LOOK FAMILIAR... DID YOU JUST MOVE HERE RECENTLY?
UM...

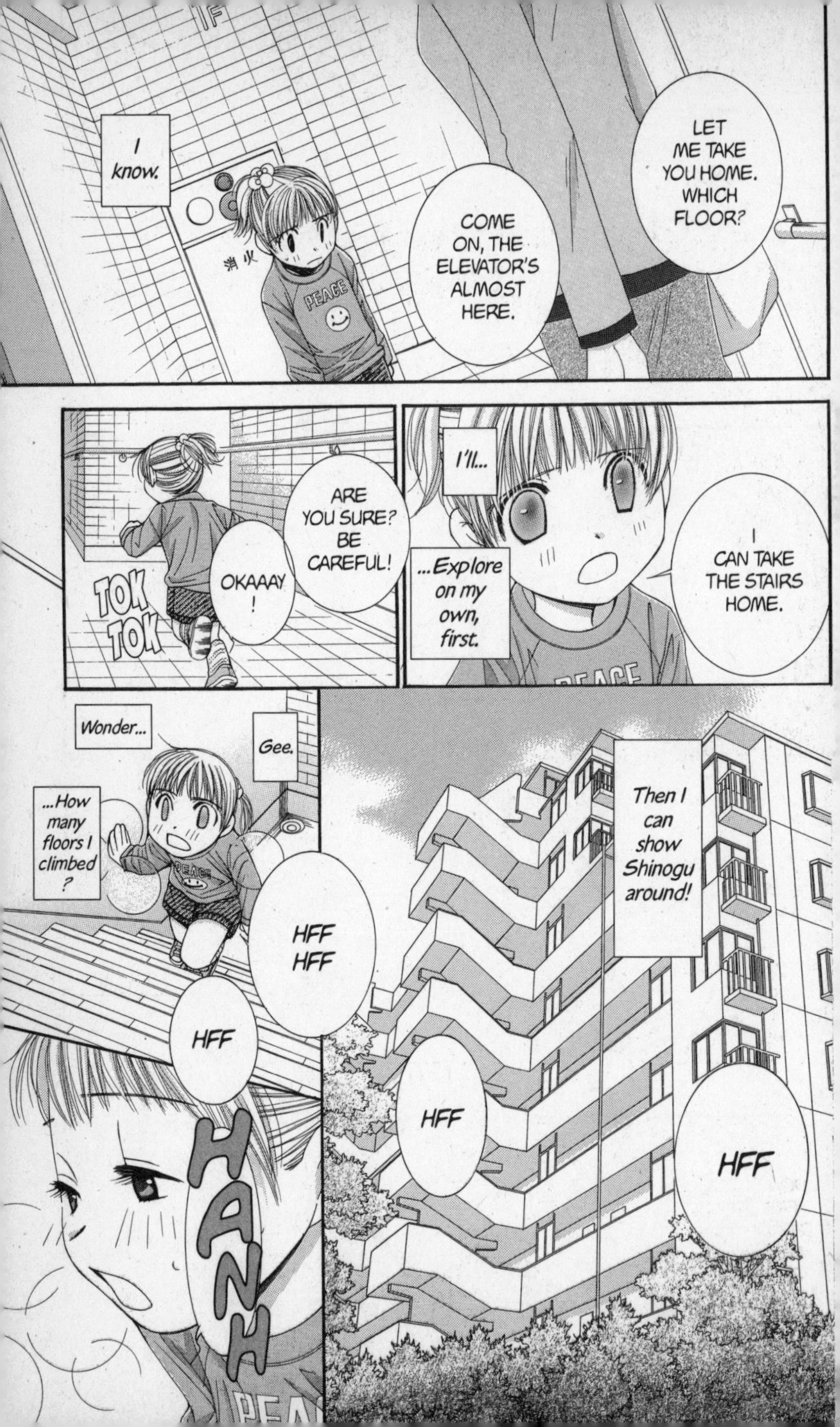

1F
LET ME TAKE YOU HOME. WHICH FLOOR?
COME ON, THE ELEVATOR'S ALMOST HERE.
消火
I know.
I CAN TAKE THE STAIRS HOME.
I'll...
...Explore on my own, first.
ARE YOU SURE? BE CAREFUL!
OKAAAY!
TOK TOK
Then I can show Shinogu around!
HFF
HFF
Gee.
Wonder...
...How many floors I climbed?
HFF HFF
HFF
HANH

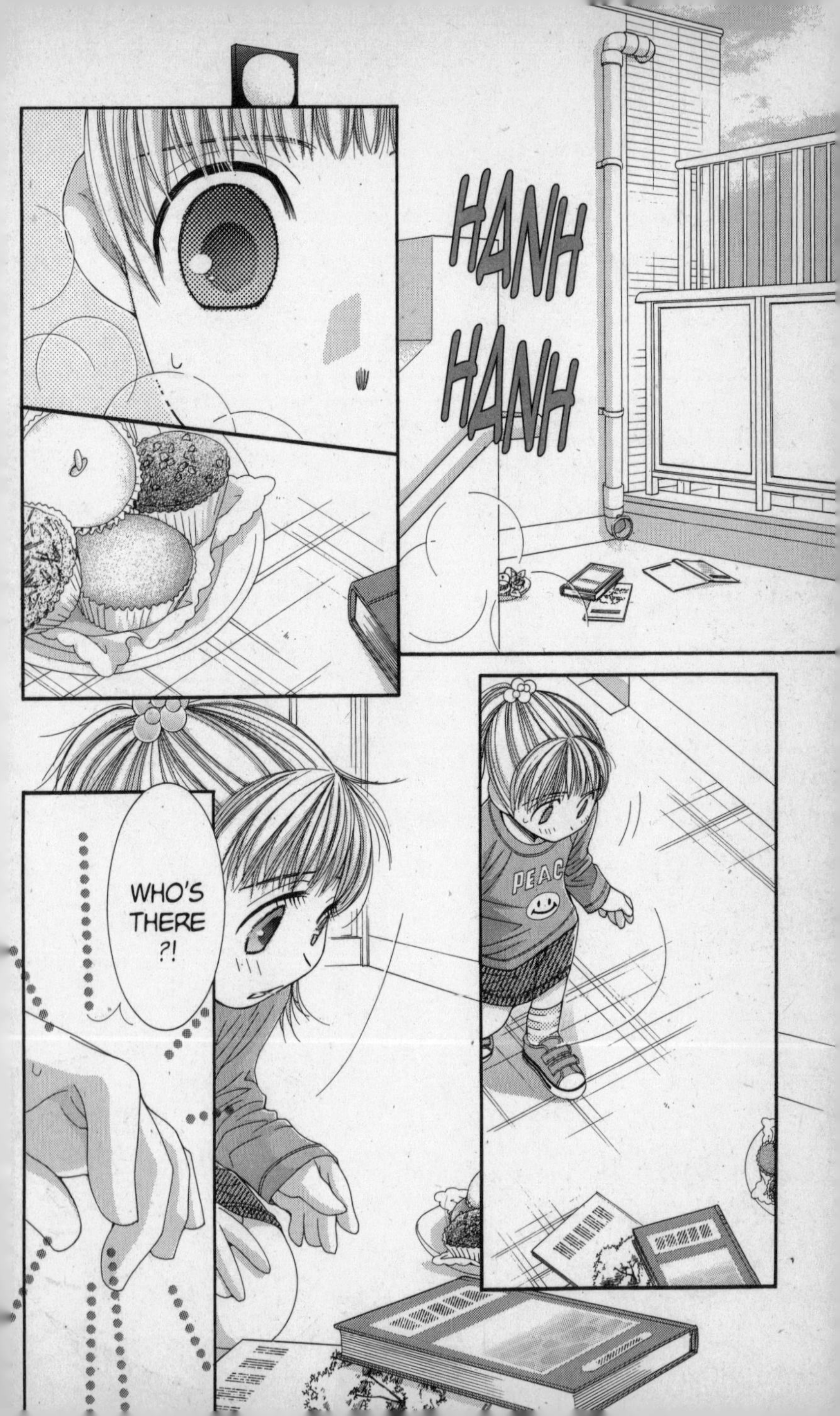
HANH HANH
WHO'S THERE ?!
PEAC

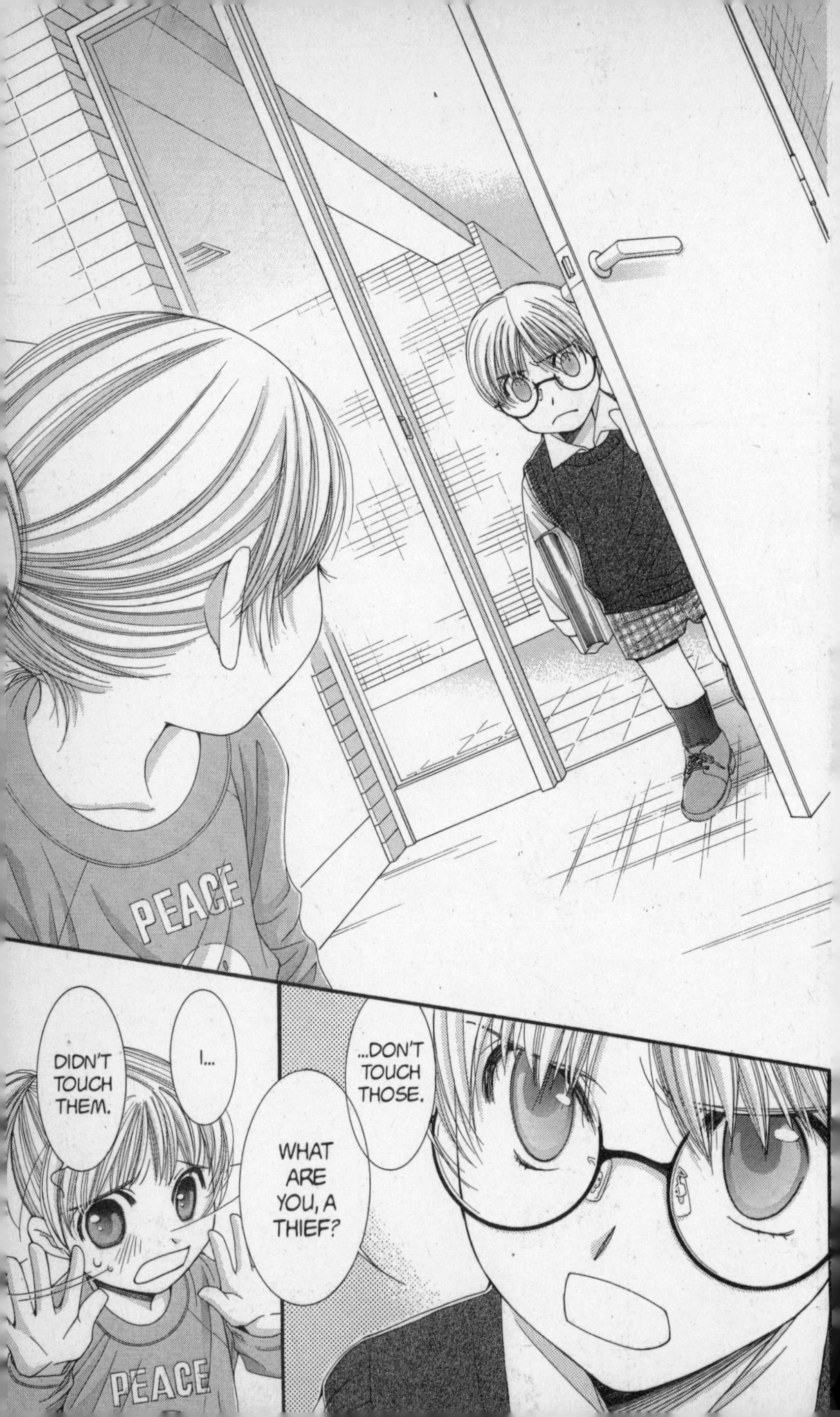
PEACE
...DON'T TOUCH THOSE.
WHAT ARE YOU, A THIEF?
I...
DIDN'T TOUCH THEM.
PEACE

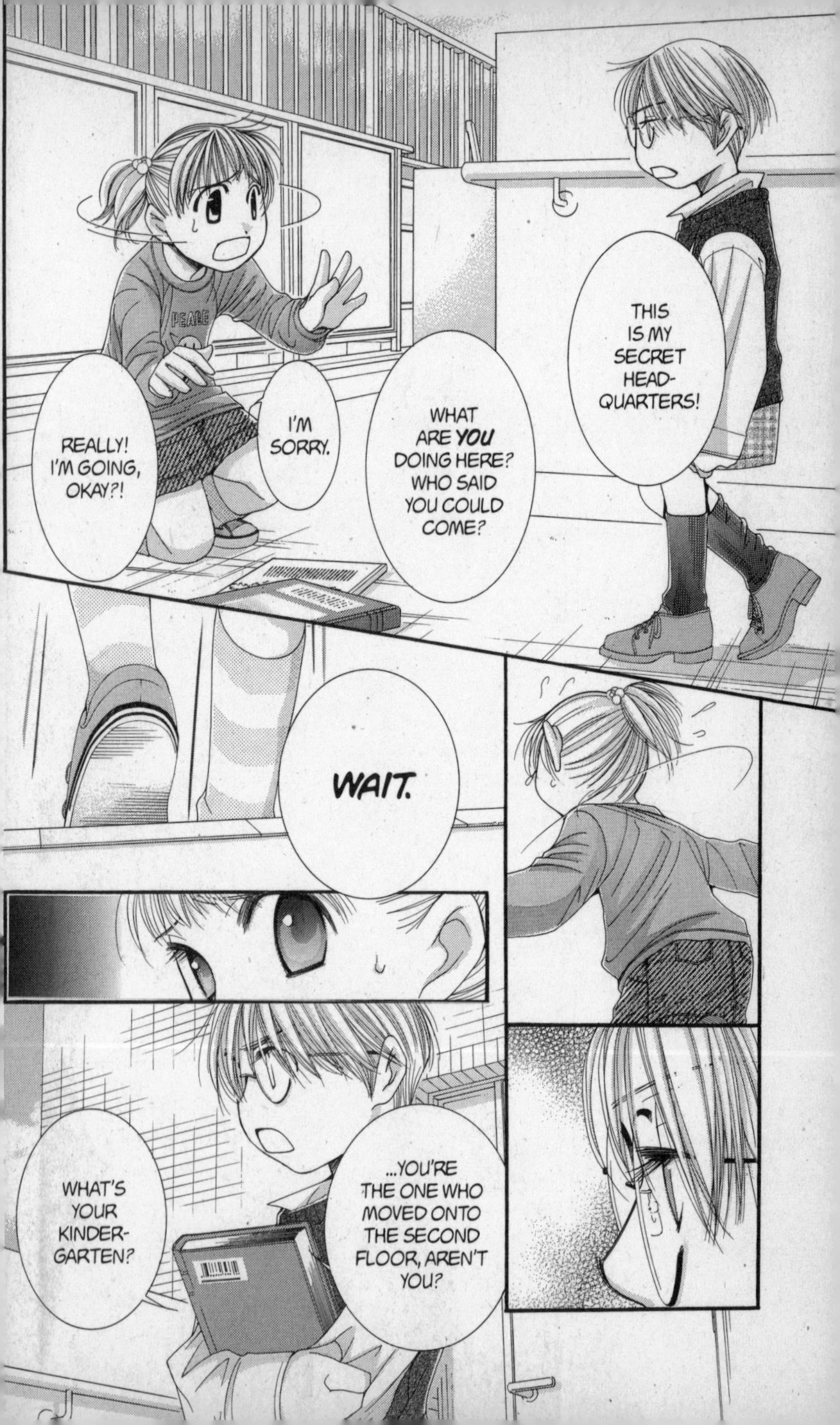
THIS IS MY SECRET HEAD-QUARTERS!
WHAT ARE *YOU* DOING HERE? WHO SAID YOU COULD COME?
I'M SORRY.
REALLY! I'M GOING, OKAY?!
WAIT.
...YOU'RE THE ONE WHO MOVED ONTO THE SECOND FLOOR, AREN'T YOU?
WHAT'S YOUR KINDER-GARTEN?

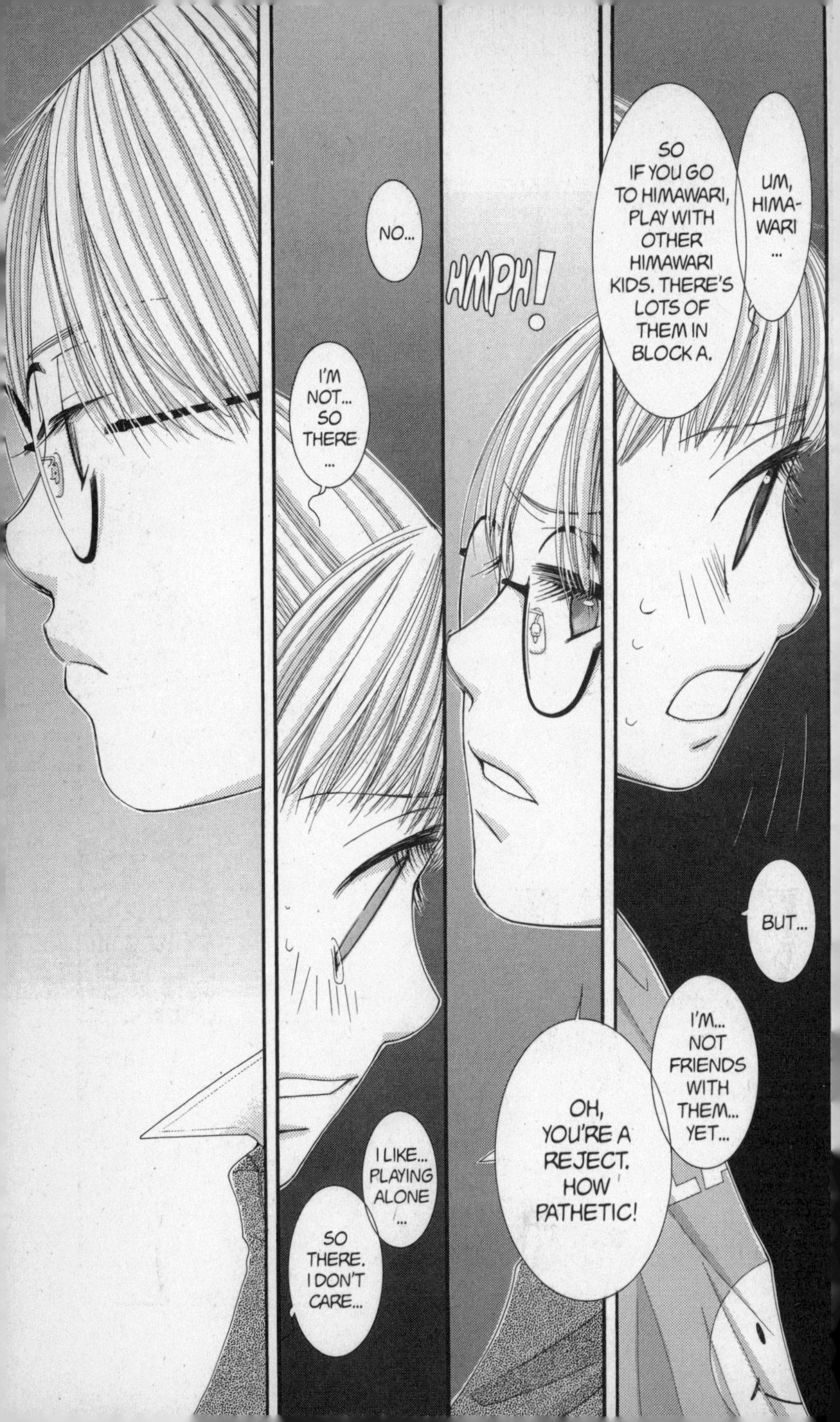
UM, HIMA-WARI...
SO IF YOU GO TO HIMAWARI, PLAY WITH OTHER HIMAWARI KIDS. THERE'S LOTS OF THEM IN BLOCK A.
BUT...
I'M... NOT FRIENDS WITH THEM... YET...
OH, YOU'RE A REJECT. HOW PATHETIC!
HMPH!
NO...
I'M NOT... SO THERE...
I LIKE... PLAYING ALONE...
SO THERE. I DON'T CARE...

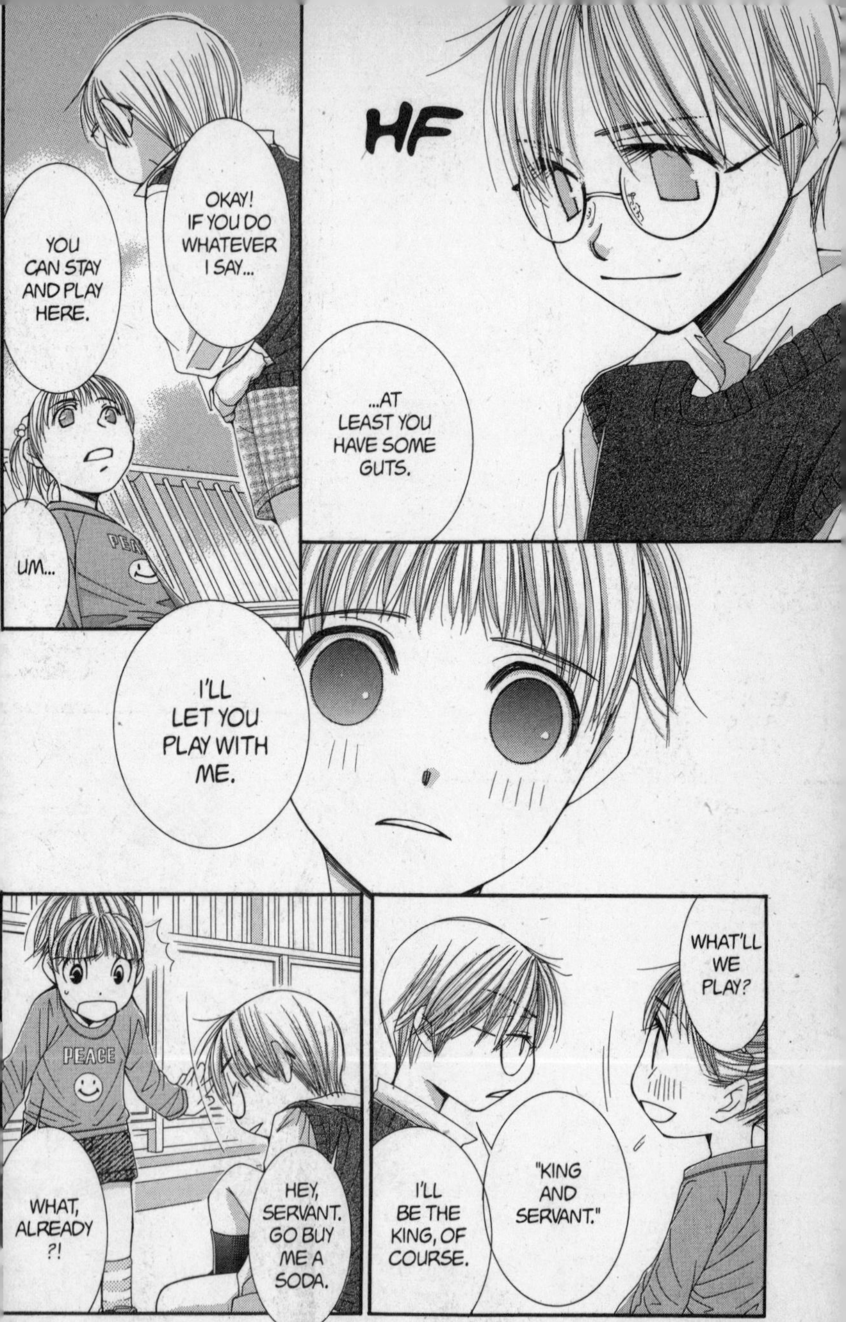
HF
...AT LEAST YOU HAVE SOME GUTS.
OKAY! IF YOU DO WHATEVER I SAY...
YOU CAN STAY AND PLAY HERE.
UM...
I'LL LET YOU PLAY WITH ME.
WHAT'LL WE PLAY?
"KING AND SERVANT."
I'LL BE THE KING, OF COURSE.
HEY, SERVANT. GO BUY ME A SODA.
PEACE
WHAT, ALREADY?!

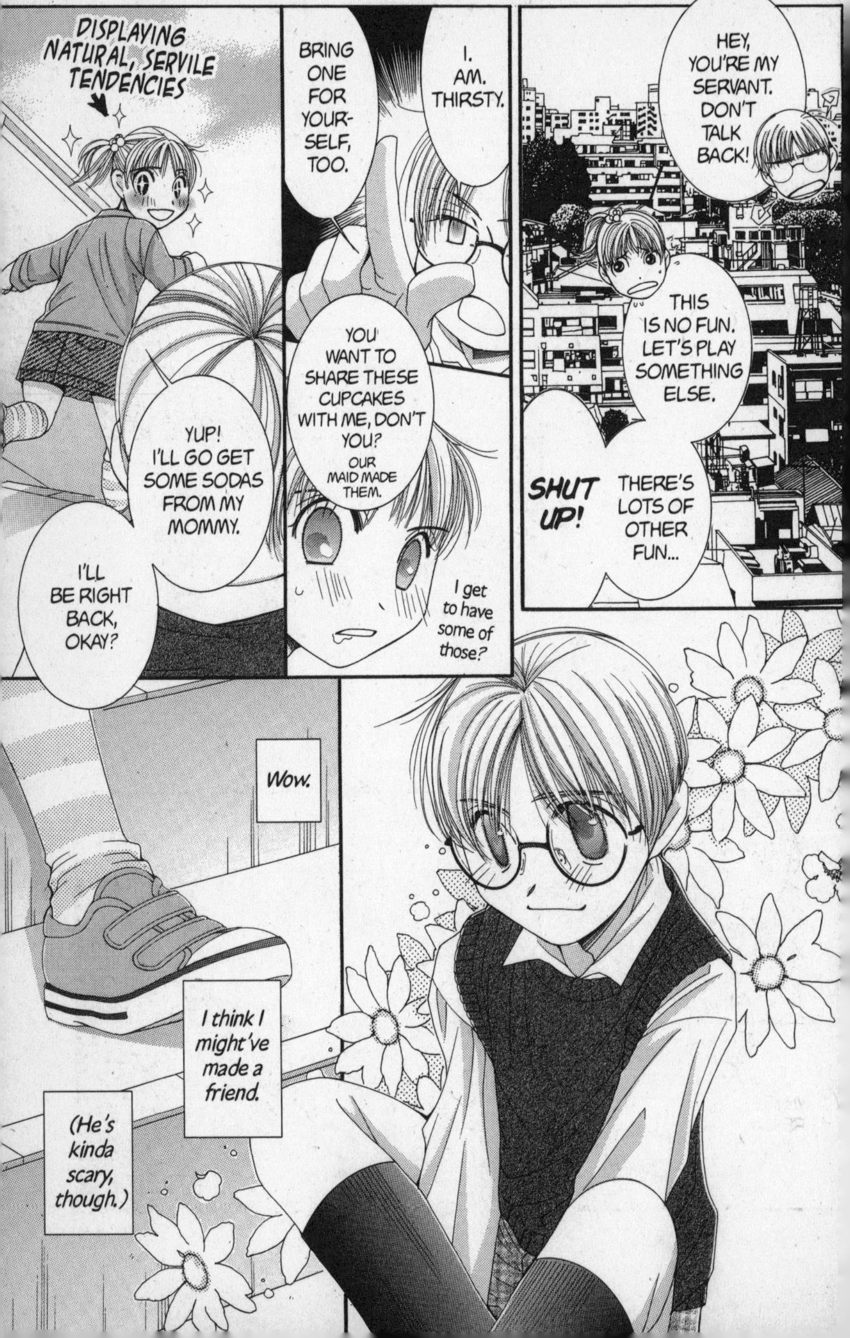
HEY, YOU'RE MY SERVANT. DON'T TALK BACK!
THIS IS NO FUN. LET'S PLAY SOMETHING ELSE.
THERE'S LOTS OF OTHER FUN...
SHUT UP!
I. AM. THIRSTY.
BRING ONE FOR YOUR-SELF, TOO.
YOU WANT TO SHARE THESE CUPCAKES WITH ME, DON'T YOU?
OUR MAID MADE THEM.
I get to have some of those?
DISPLAYING NATURAL, SERVILE TENDENCIES
YUP! I'LL GO GET SOME SODAS FROM MY MOMMY.
I'LL BE RIGHT BACK, OKAY?
Wow.
I think I might've made a friend.
(He's kinda scary, though.)

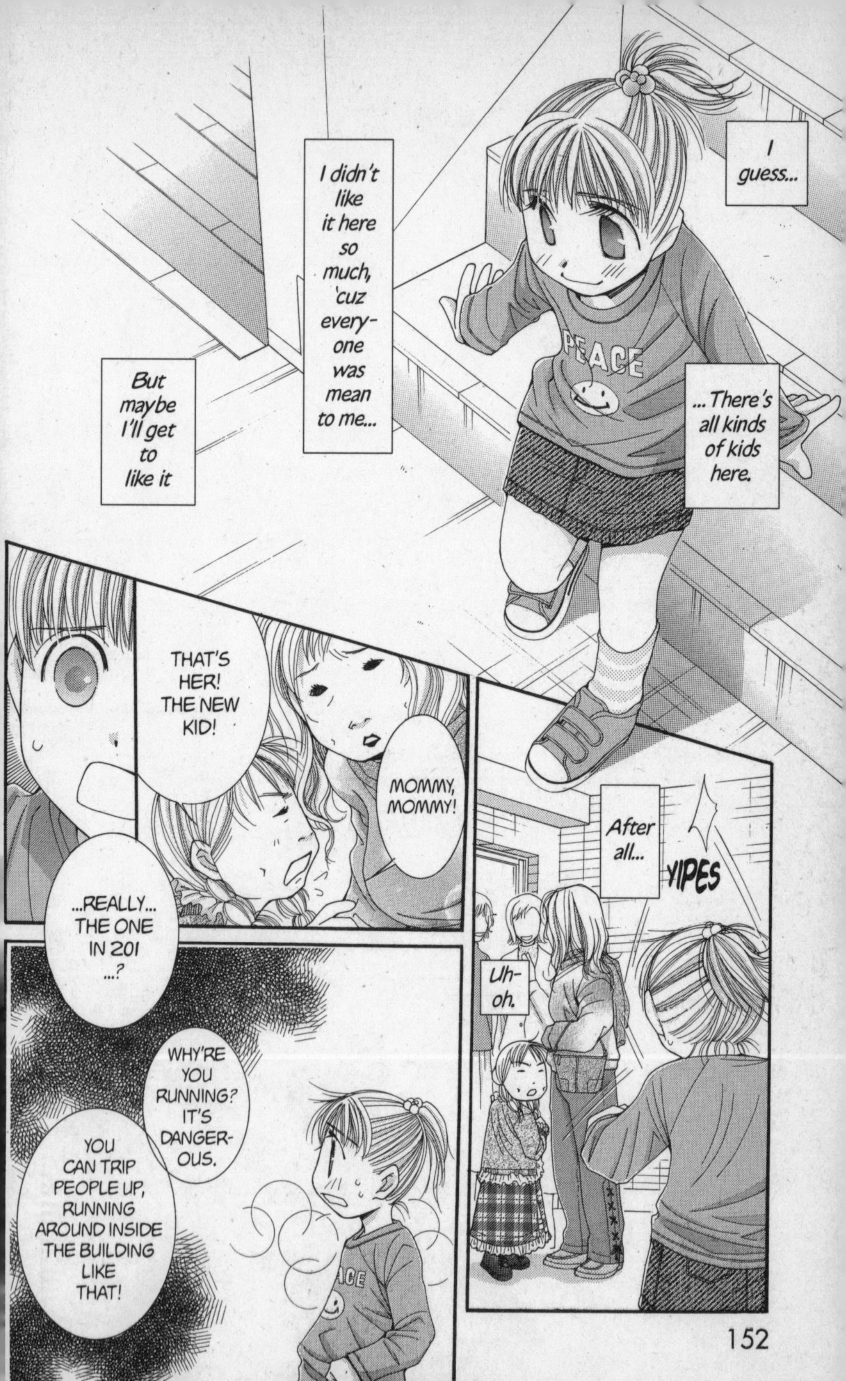

I guess...
...There's all kinds of kids here.
I didn't like it here so much, 'cuz everyone was mean to me...
But maybe I'll get to like it
After all...
YIPES
Uh-oh.
MOMMY, MOMMY!
THAT'S HER! THE NEW KID!
...REALLY... THE ONE IN 201 ...?
WHY'RE YOU RUNNING? IT'S DANGEROUS.
YOU CAN TRIP PEOPLE UP, RUNNING AROUND INSIDE THE BUILDING LIKE THAT!

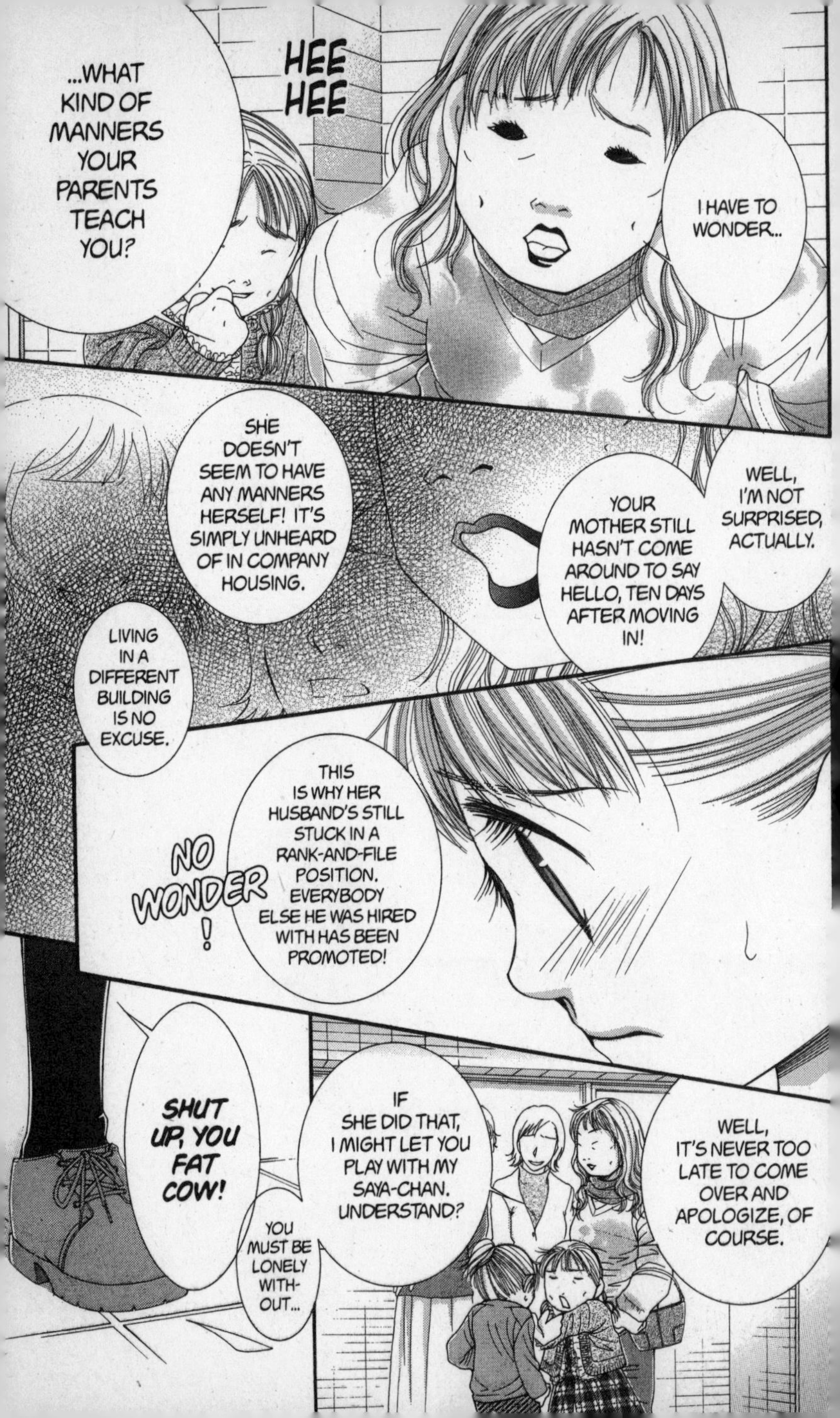
I HAVE TO WONDER...
HEE HEE
...WHAT KIND OF MANNERS YOUR PARENTS TEACH YOU?
WELL, I'M NOT SURPRISED, ACTUALLY.
YOUR MOTHER STILL HASN'T COME AROUND TO SAY HELLO, TEN DAYS AFTER MOVING IN!
SHE DOESN'T SEEM TO HAVE ANY MANNERS HERSELF! IT'S SIMPLY UNHEARD OF IN COMPANY HOUSING.
LIVING IN A DIFFERENT BUILDING IS NO EXCUSE.
THIS IS WHY HER HUSBAND'S STILL STUCK IN A RANK-AND-FILE POSITION. EVERYBODY ELSE HE WAS HIRED WITH HAS BEEN PROMOTED!
NO WONDER!
WELL, IT'S NEVER TOO LATE TO COME OVER AND APOLOGIZE, OF COURSE.
IF SHE DID THAT, I MIGHT LET YOU PLAY WITH MY SAYA-CHAN. UNDERSTAND?
YOU MUST BE LONELY WITH-OUT...
SHUT UP, YOU FAT COW!

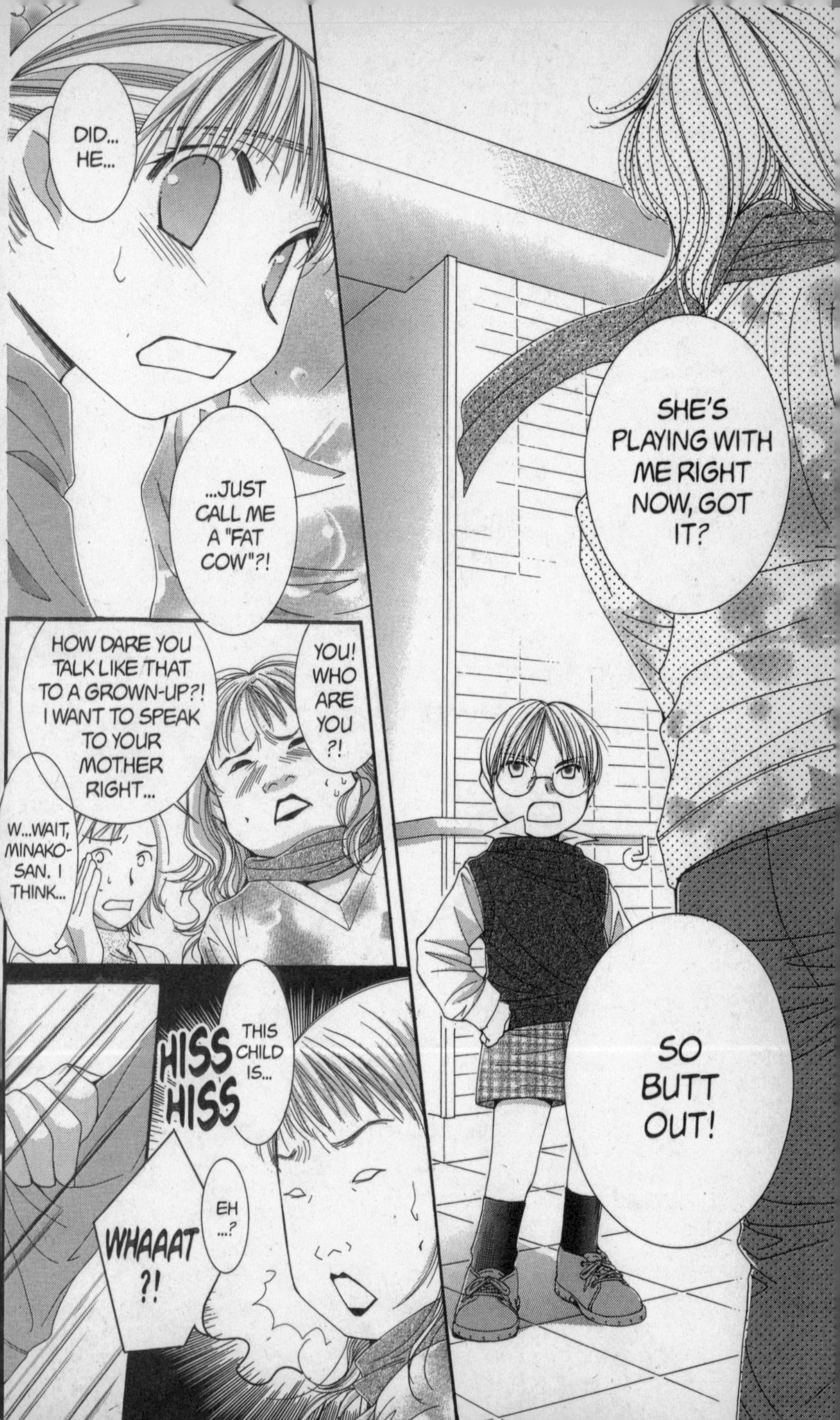
SHE'S PLAYING WITH ME RIGHT NOW, GOT IT?
SO BUTT OUT!
DID... HE...
...JUST CALL ME A "FAT COW"?!
YOU! WHO ARE YOU ?!
HOW DARE YOU TALK LIKE THAT TO A GROWN-UP?! I WANT TO SPEAK TO YOUR MOTHER RIGHT...
W...WAIT, MINAKO-SAN. I THINK...
THIS CHILD IS...
HISS HISS
EH ...?
WHAAAT ?!

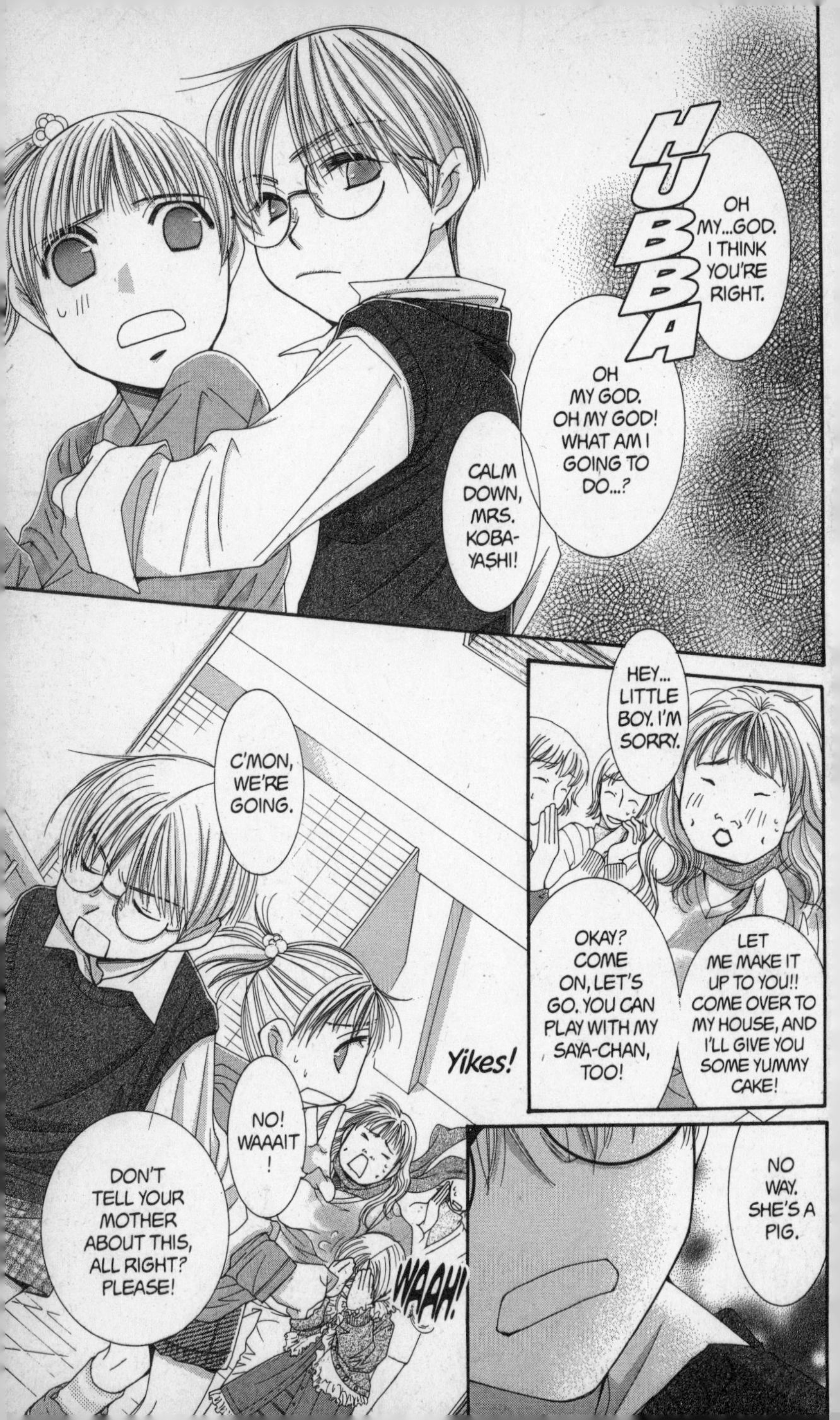
HUBBA
OH MY...GOD. I THINK YOU'RE RIGHT.
OH MY GOD. OH MY GOD! WHAT AM I GOING TO DO...?
CALM DOWN, MRS. KOBA-YASHI!
HEY... LITTLE BOY. I'M SORRY.
LET ME MAKE IT UP TO YOU!! COME OVER TO MY HOUSE, AND I'LL GIVE YOU SOME YUMMY CAKE!
OKAY? COME ON, LET'S GO. YOU CAN PLAY WITH MY SAYA-CHAN, TOO!
NO WAY. SHE'S A PIG.
C'MON, WE'RE GOING.
Yikes!
NO! WAAAIT!
DON'T TELL YOUR MOTHER ABOUT THIS, ALL RIGHT? PLEASE!
WAAH!

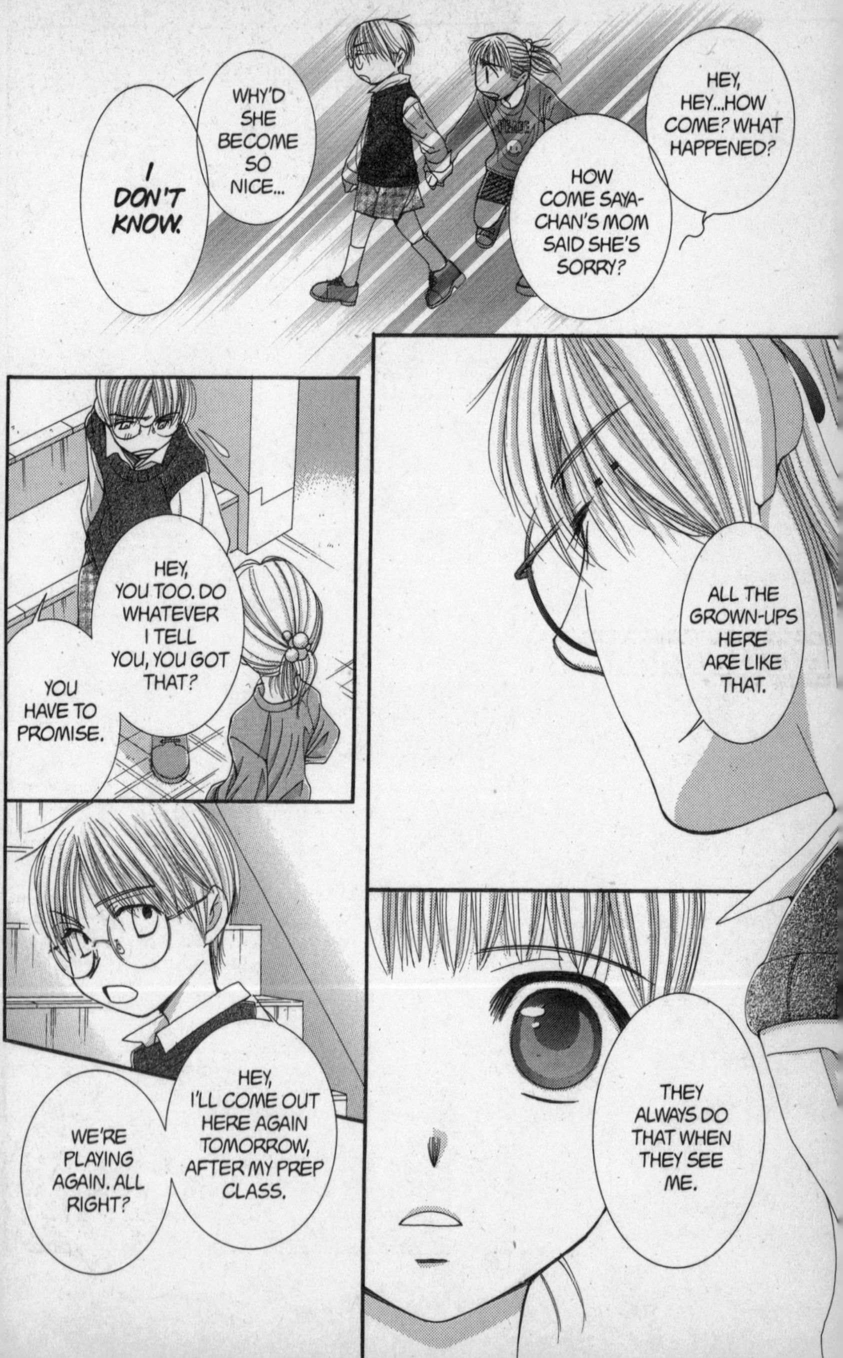
HEY, HEY...HOW COME? WHAT HAPPENED?
HOW COME SAYA-CHAN'S MOM SAID SHE'S SORRY?
WHY'D SHE BECOME SO NICE...
I DON'T KNOW.
ALL THE GROWN-UPS HERE ARE LIKE THAT.
THEY ALWAYS DO THAT WHEN THEY SEE ME.
HEY, YOU TOO. DO WHATEVER I TELL YOU, YOU GOT THAT?
YOU HAVE TO PROMISE.
HEY, I'LL COME OUT HERE AGAIN TOMORROW, AFTER MY PREP CLASS.
WE'RE PLAYING AGAIN. ALL RIGHT?

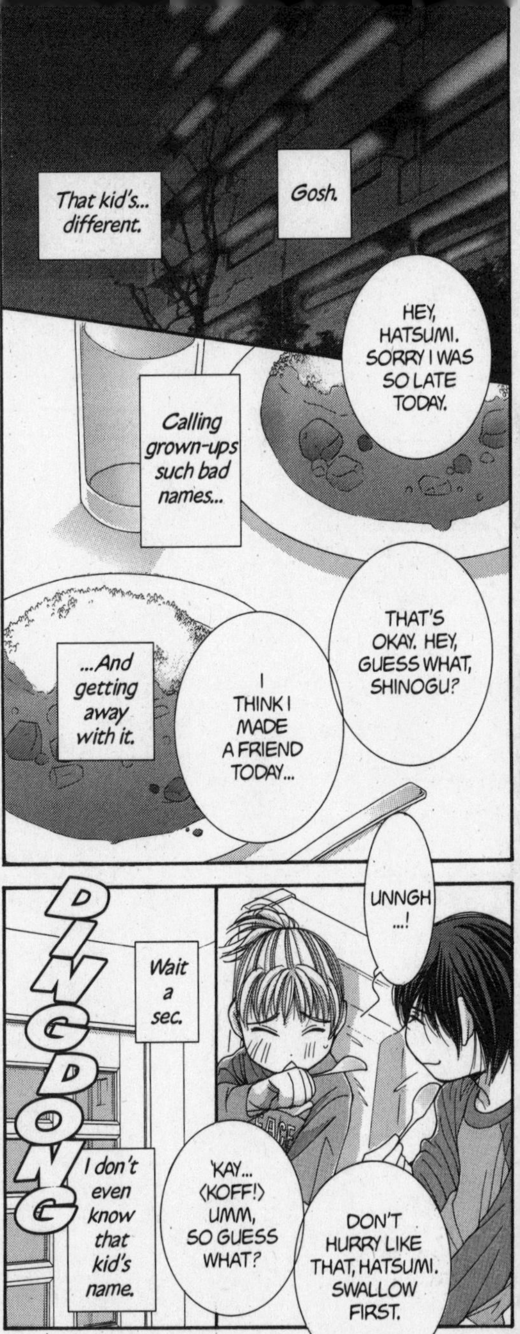
Gosh.
That kid's... different.
HEY, HATSUMI. SORRY I WAS SO LATE TODAY.
Calling grown-ups such bad names...
THAT'S OKAY. HEY, GUESS WHAT, SHINOGU?
I THINK I MADE A FRIEND TODAY...
...And getting away with it.
UNNGH ...!
DON'T HURRY LIKE THAT, HATSUMI. SWALLOW FIRST.
'KAY... ⟨KOFF!⟩ UMM, SO GUESS WHAT?
DING DONG
Wait a sec.
I don't even know that kid's name.

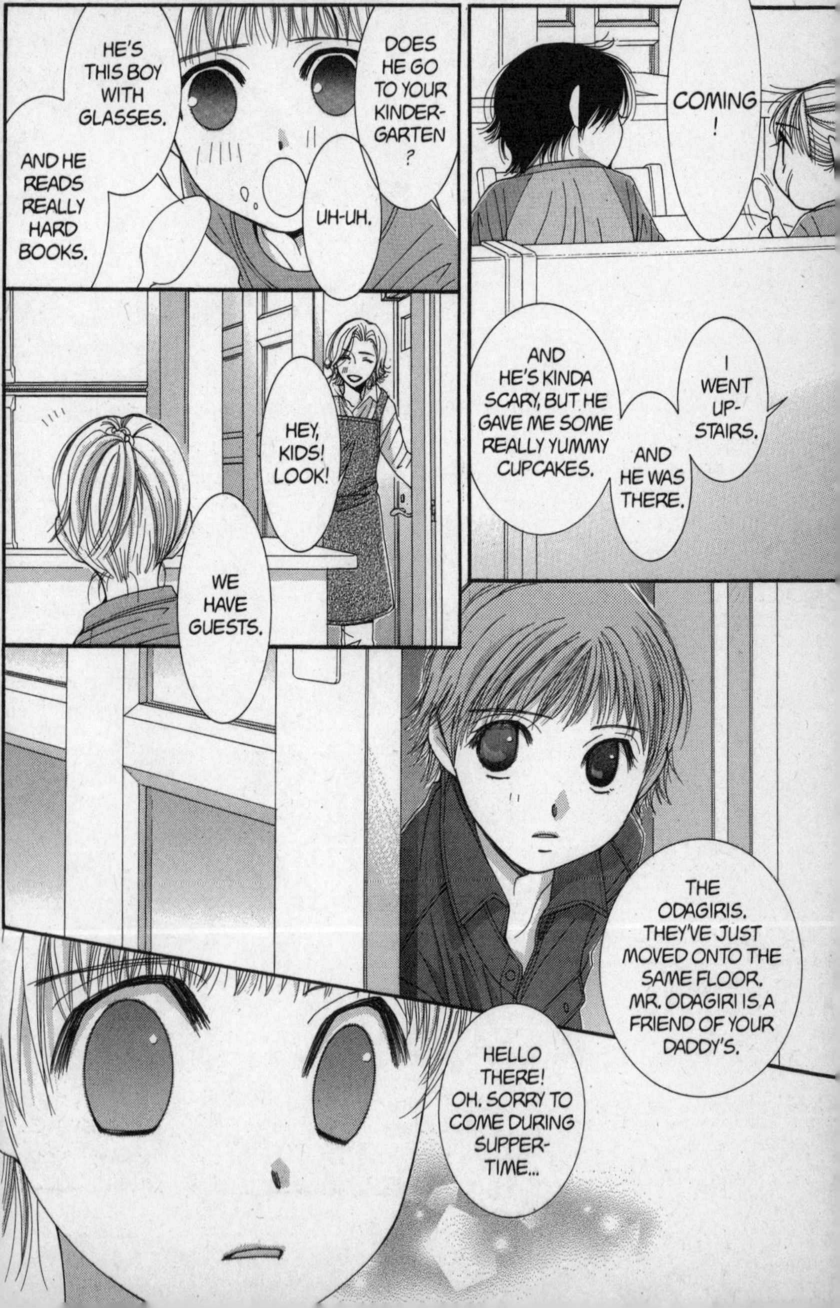
COMING!
DOES HE GO TO YOUR KINDERGARTEN?
UH-UH.
HE'S THIS BOY WITH GLASSES.
AND HE READS REALLY HARD BOOKS.
I WENT UPSTAIRS.
AND HE WAS THERE.
AND HE'S KINDA SCARY, BUT HE GAVE ME SOME REALLY YUMMY CUPCAKES.
HEY, KIDS! LOOK!
WE HAVE GUESTS.
THE ODAGIRIS. THEY'VE JUST MOVED ONTO THE SAME FLOOR. MR. ODAGIRI IS A FRIEND OF YOUR DADDY'S.
HELLO THERE! OH. SORRY TO COME DURING SUPPER-TIME...

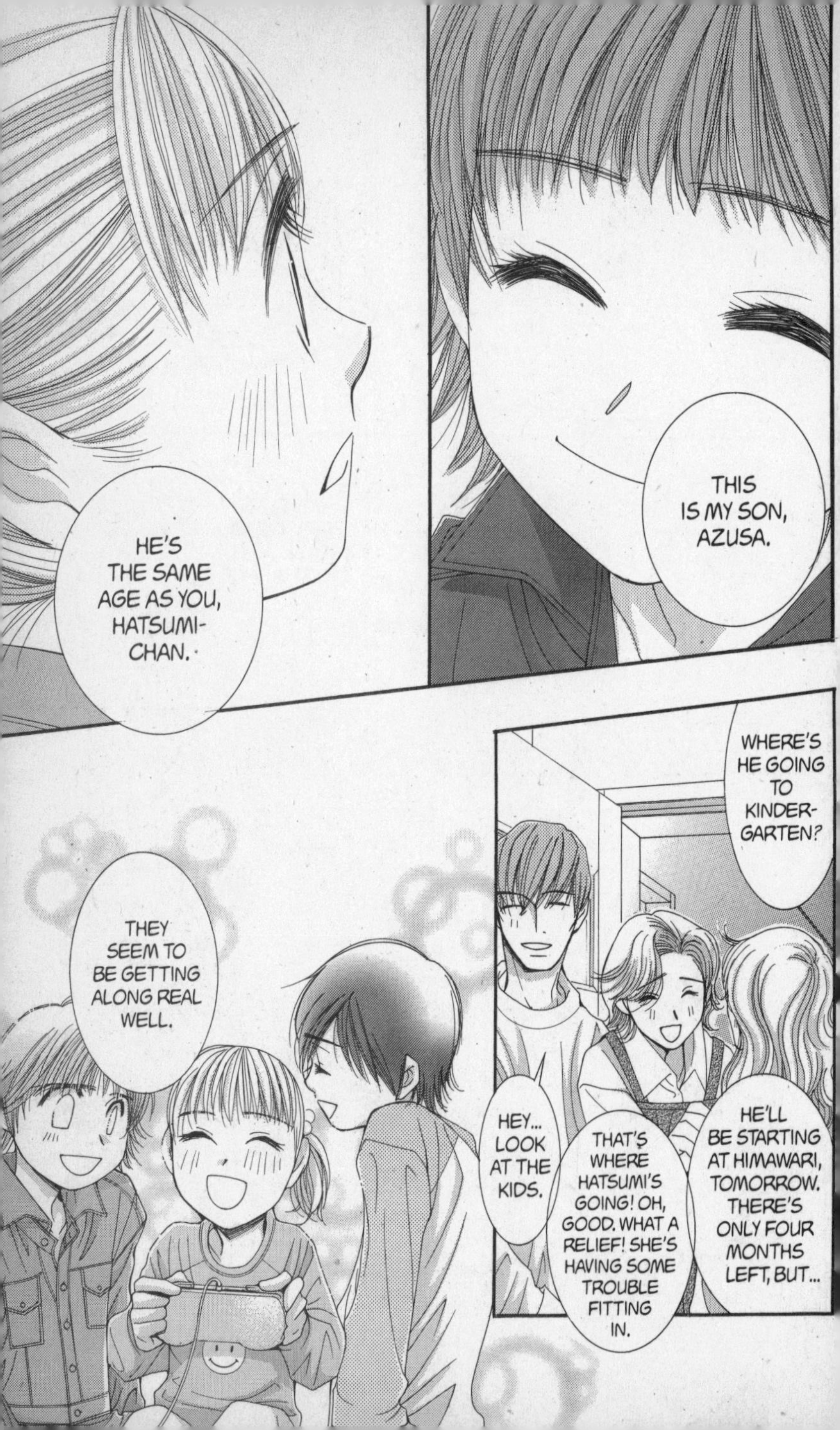
THIS IS MY SON, AZUSA.
HE'S THE SAME AGE AS YOU, HATSUMI-CHAN.
WHERE'S HE GOING TO KINDER-GARTEN?
HE'LL BE STARTING AT HIMAWARI, TOMORROW. THERE'S ONLY FOUR MONTHS LEFT, BUT...
THAT'S WHERE HATSUMI'S GOING! OH, GOOD. WHAT A RELIEF! SHE'S HAVING SOME TROUBLE FITTING IN.
HEY... LOOK AT THE KIDS.
THEY SEEM TO BE GETTING ALONG REAL WELL.

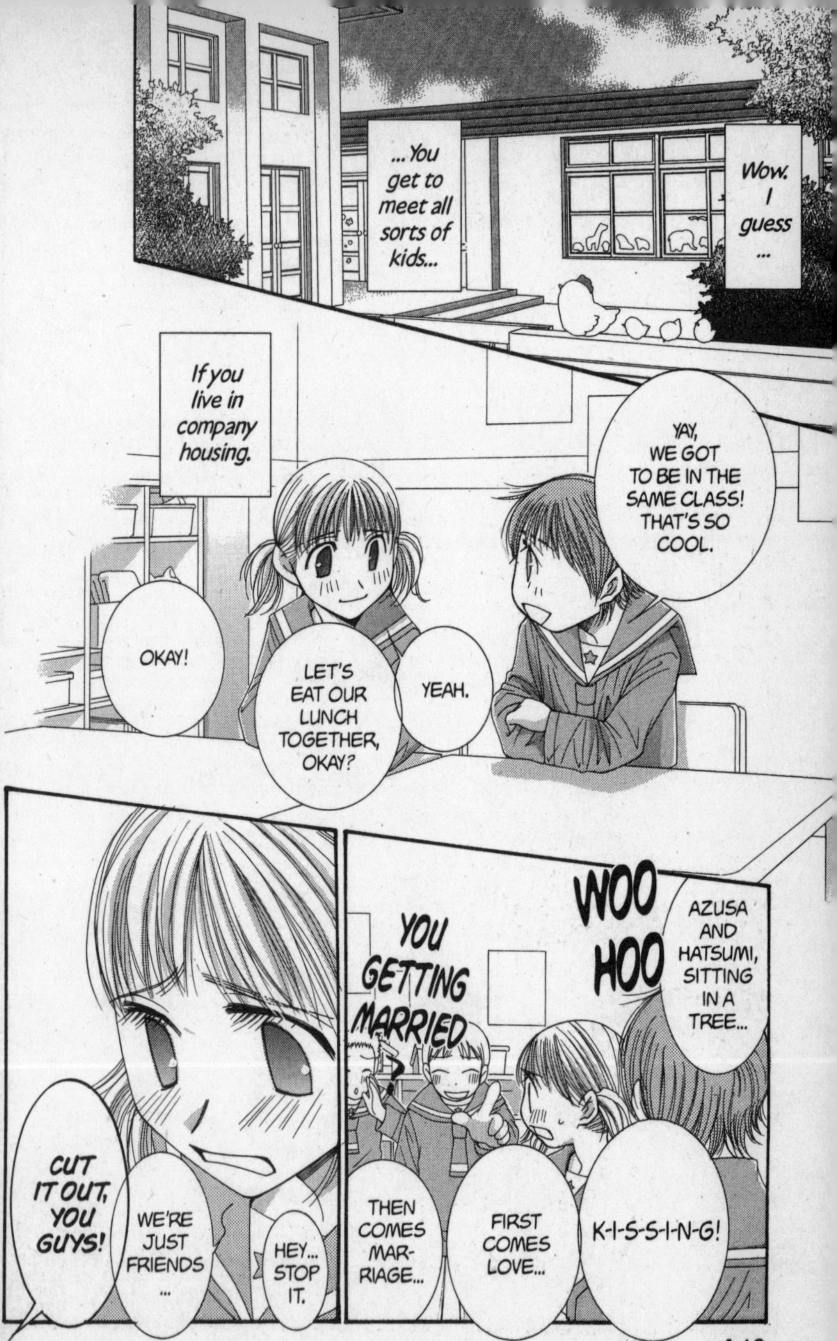
Wow. I guess ...
...You get to meet all sorts of kids...
If you live in company housing.
YAY, WE GOT TO BE IN THE SAME CLASS! THAT'S SO COOL.
YEAH.
LET'S EAT OUR LUNCH TOGETHER, OKAY?
OKAY!
AZUSA AND HATSUMI, SITTING IN A TREE...
WOO HOO
YOU GETTING MARRIED
K-I-S-S-I-N-G!
FIRST COMES LOVE...
THEN COMES MAR-RIAGE...
HEY... STOP IT.
WE'RE JUST FRIENDS ...
CUT IT OUT, YOU GUYS!

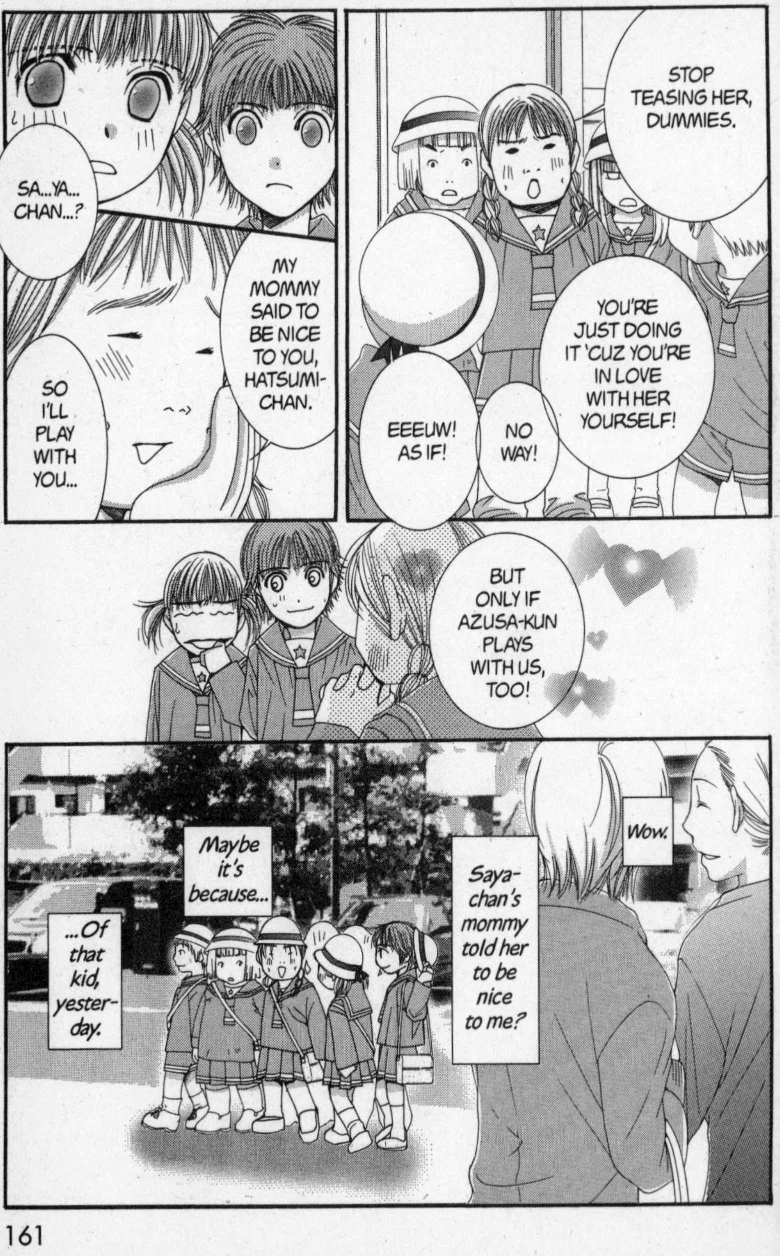
STOP TEASING HER, DUMMIES.
YOU'RE JUST DOING IT 'CUZ YOU'RE IN LOVE WITH HER YOURSELF!
NO WAY!
EEEUW! AS IF!
SA...YA... CHAN...?
MY MOMMY SAID TO BE NICE TO YOU, HATSUMI-CHAN.
SO I'LL PLAY WITH YOU...
BUT ONLY IF AZUSA-KUN PLAYS WITH US, TOO!
Wow.
Saya-chan's mommy told her to be nice to me?
Maybe it's because...
...Of that kid, yester-day.

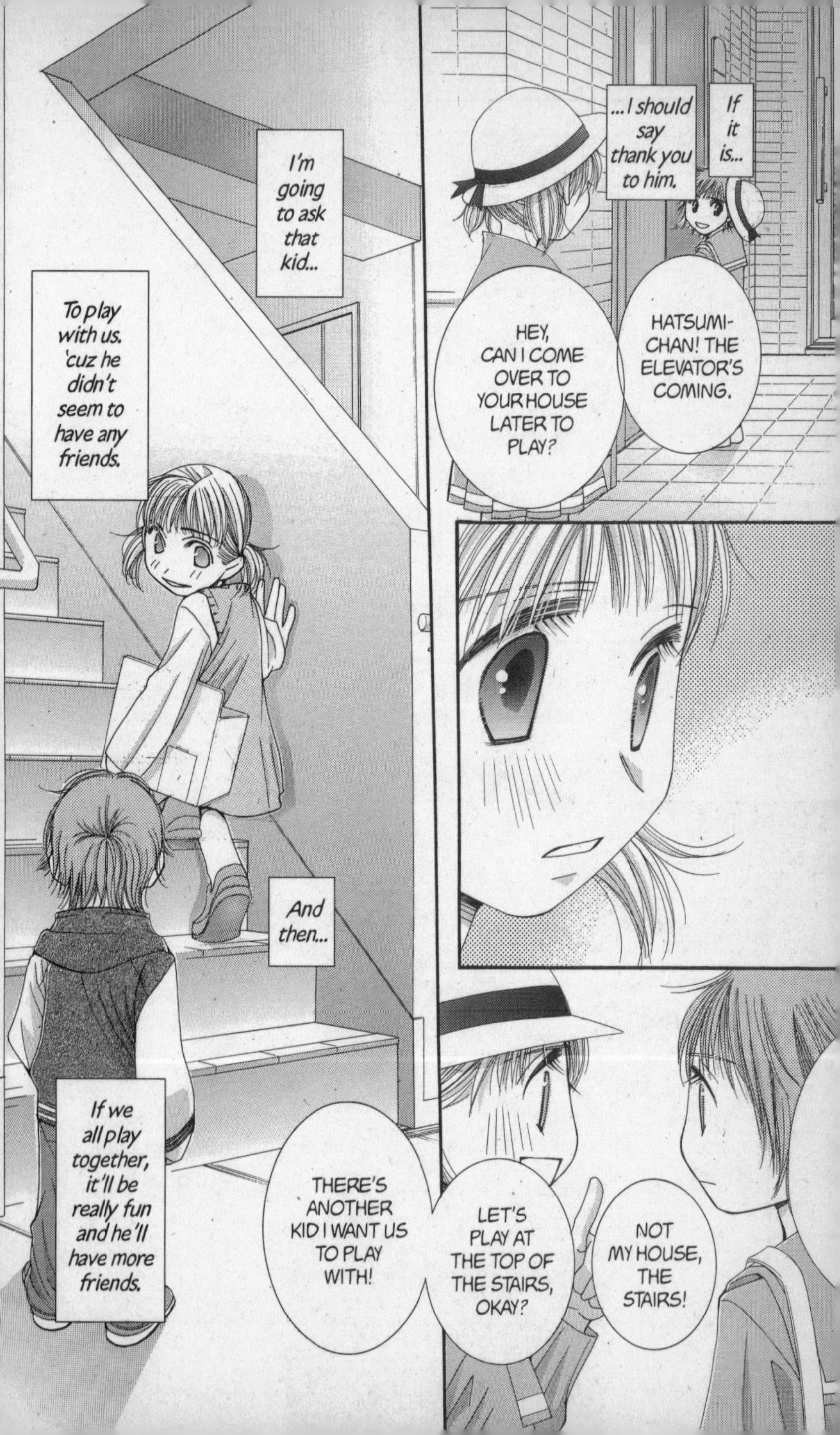
If it is...
...I should say thank you to him.
HATSUMI-CHAN! THE ELEVATOR'S COMING.
HEY, CAN I COME OVER TO YOUR HOUSE LATER TO PLAY?
NOT MY HOUSE, THE STAIRS!
LET'S PLAY AT THE TOP OF THE STAIRS, OKAY?
THERE'S ANOTHER KID I WANT US TO PLAY WITH!
I'm going to ask that kid...
To play with us. 'cuz he didn't seem to have any friends.
And then...
If we all play together, it'll be really fun and he'll have more friends.

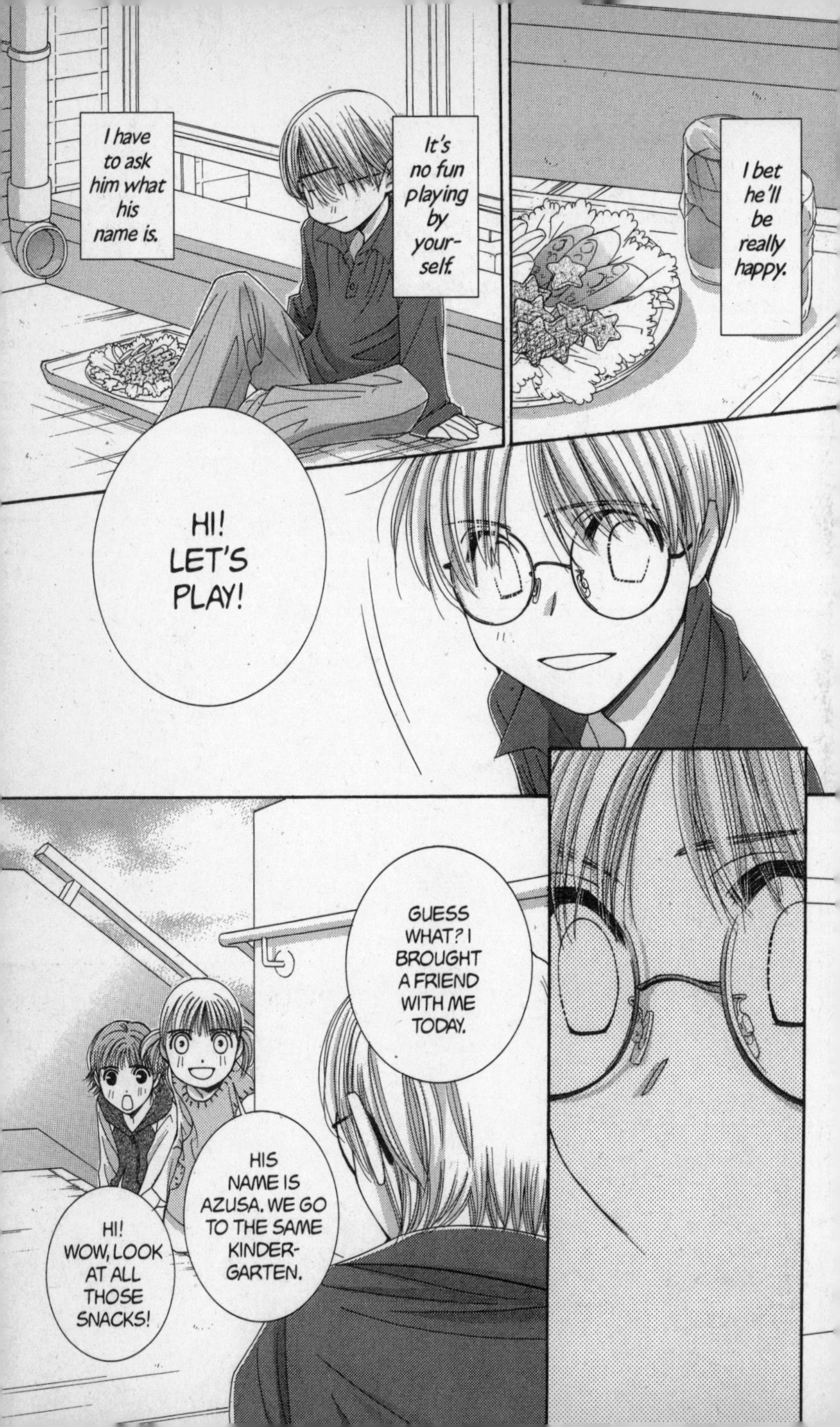
I bet he'll be really happy.
It's no fun playing by yourself.
I have to ask him what his name is.
HI! LET'S PLAY!
GUESS WHAT? I BROUGHT A FRIEND WITH ME TODAY.
HIS NAME IS AZUSA. WE GO TO THE SAME KINDERGARTEN.
HI! WOW, LOOK AT ALL THOSE SNACKS!

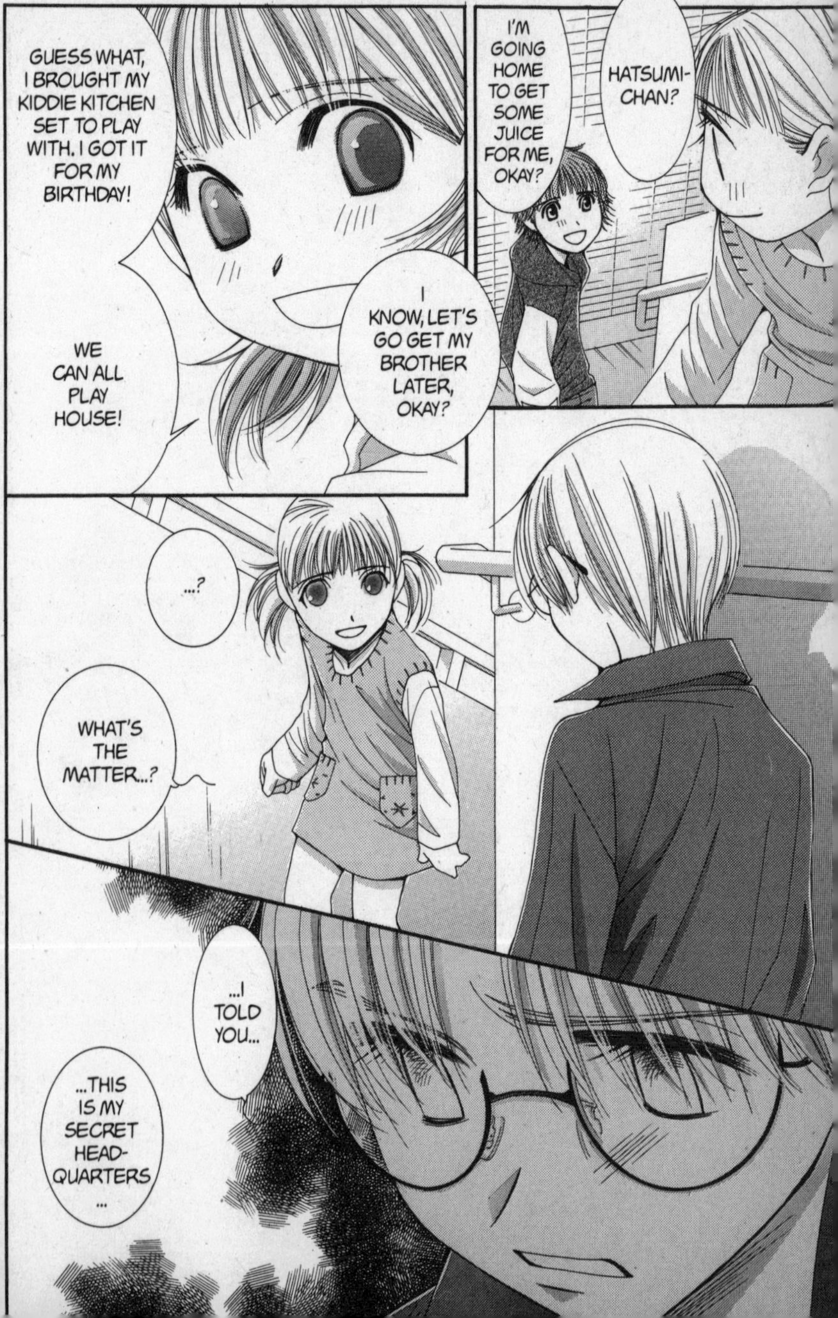
HATSUMI-CHAN?
I'M GOING HOME TO GET SOME JUICE FOR ME, OKAY?
GUESS WHAT, I BROUGHT MY KIDDIE KITCHEN SET TO PLAY WITH. I GOT IT FOR MY BIRTHDAY!
WE CAN ALL PLAY HOUSE!
I KNOW, LET'S GO GET MY BROTHER LATER, OKAY?
...?
WHAT'S THE MATTER...?
...I TOLD YOU...
...THIS IS MY SECRET HEAD-QUARTERS ...

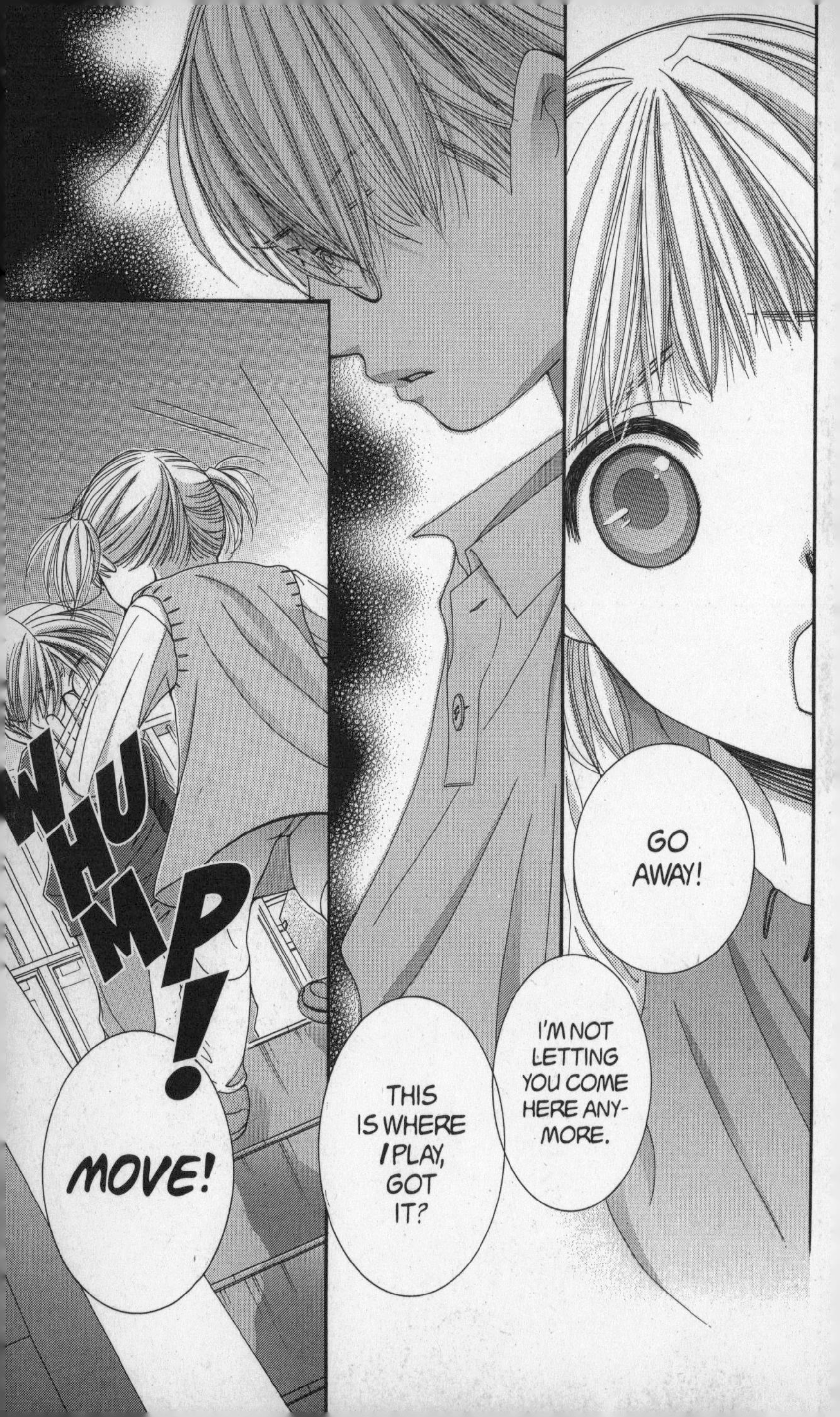
GO AWAY!
I'M NOT LETTING YOU COME HERE ANY-MORE.
THIS IS WHERE *I* PLAY, GOT IT?
WHUMP!
MOVE!

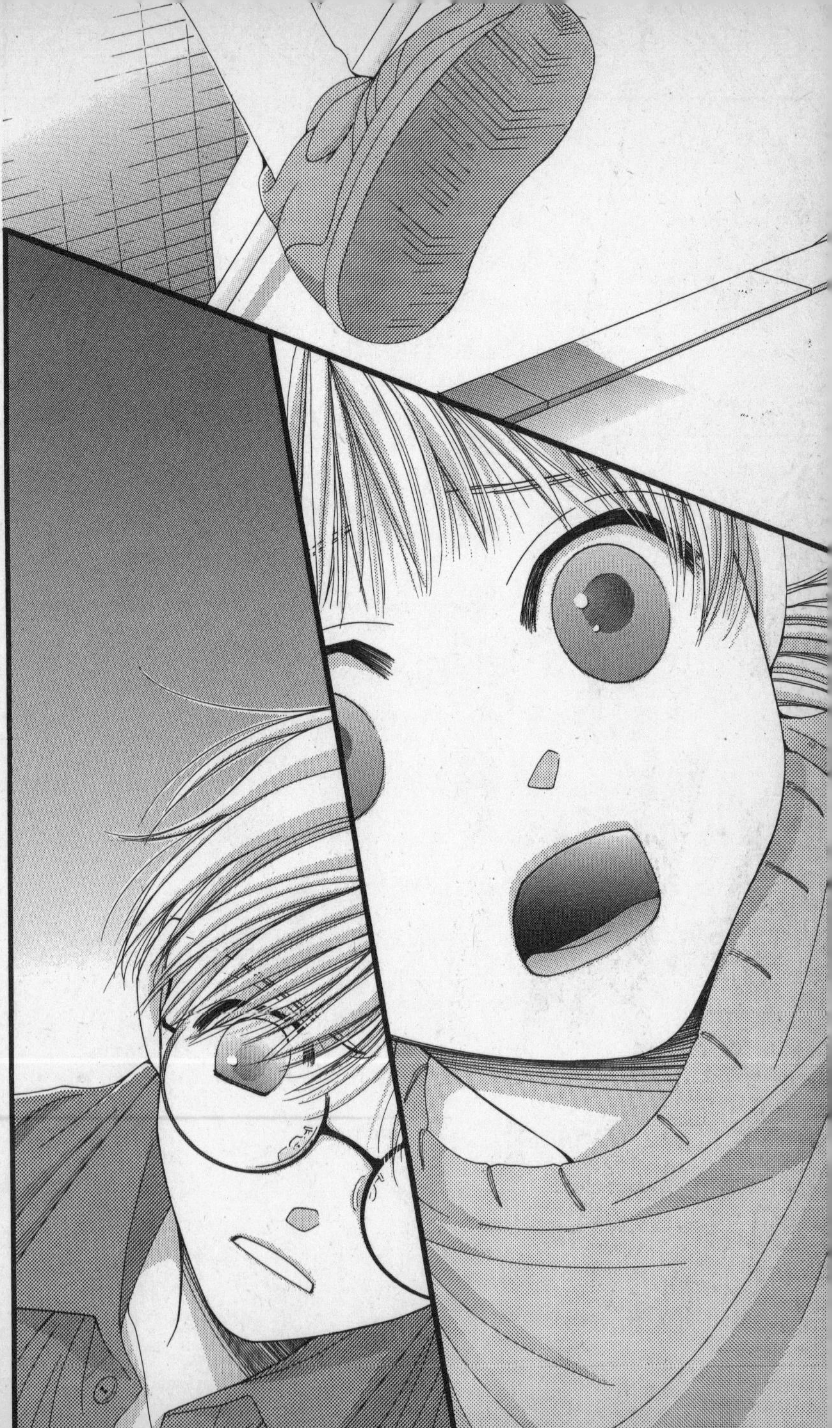

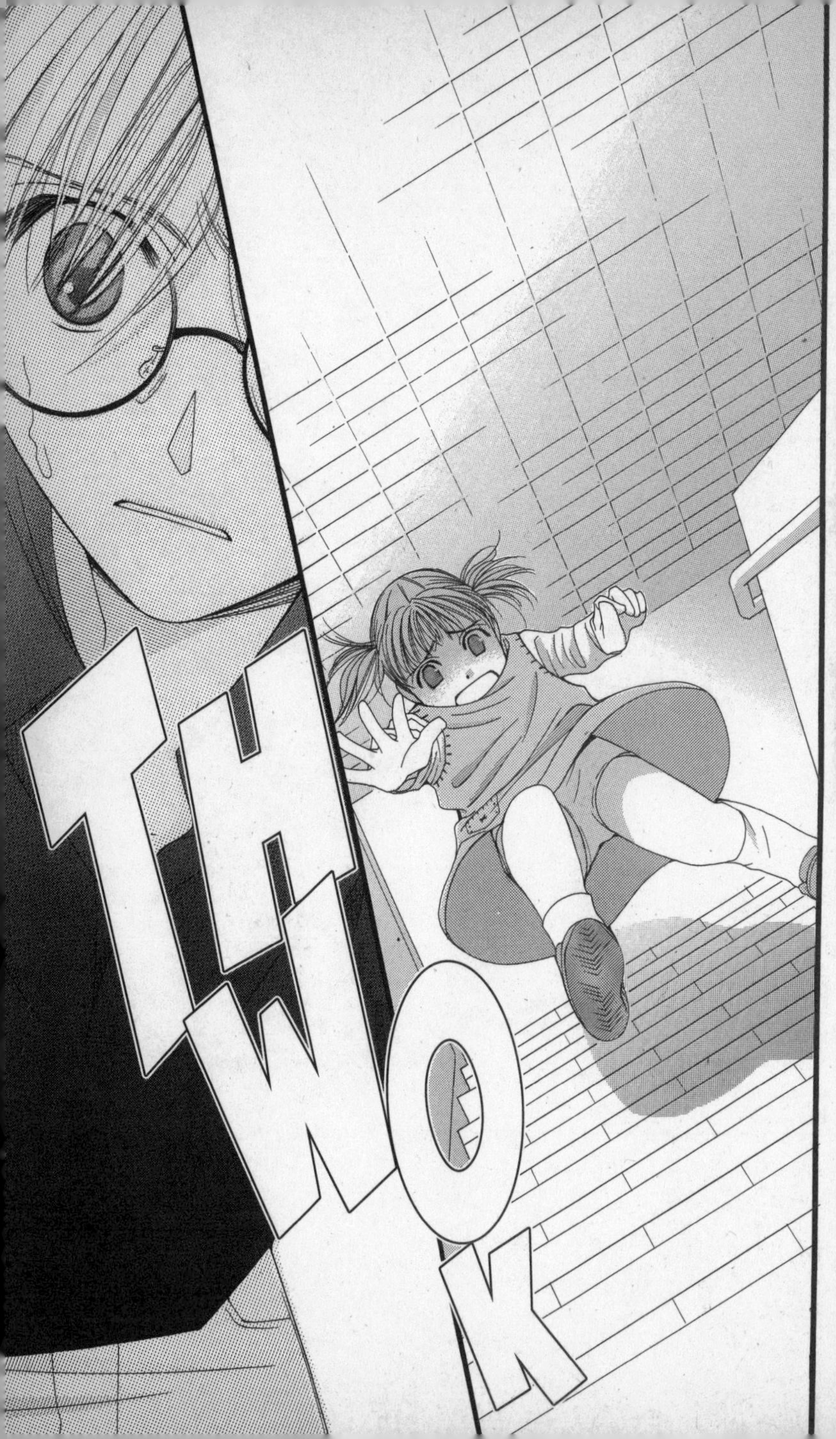
THWOK

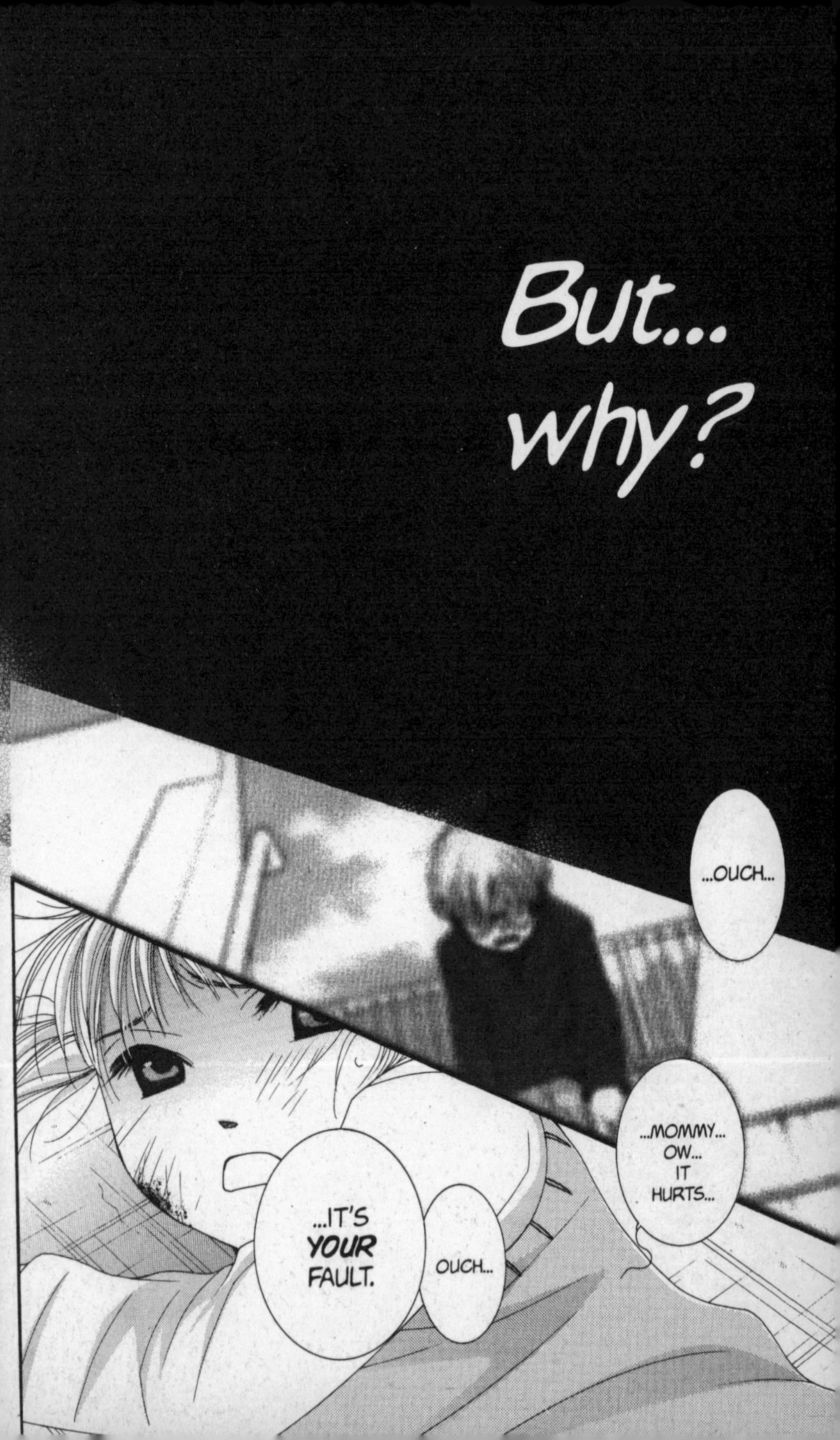
But... why?
...OUCH...
...MOMMY... OW... IT HURTS...
OUCH...
...IT'S ***YOUR*** FAULT.

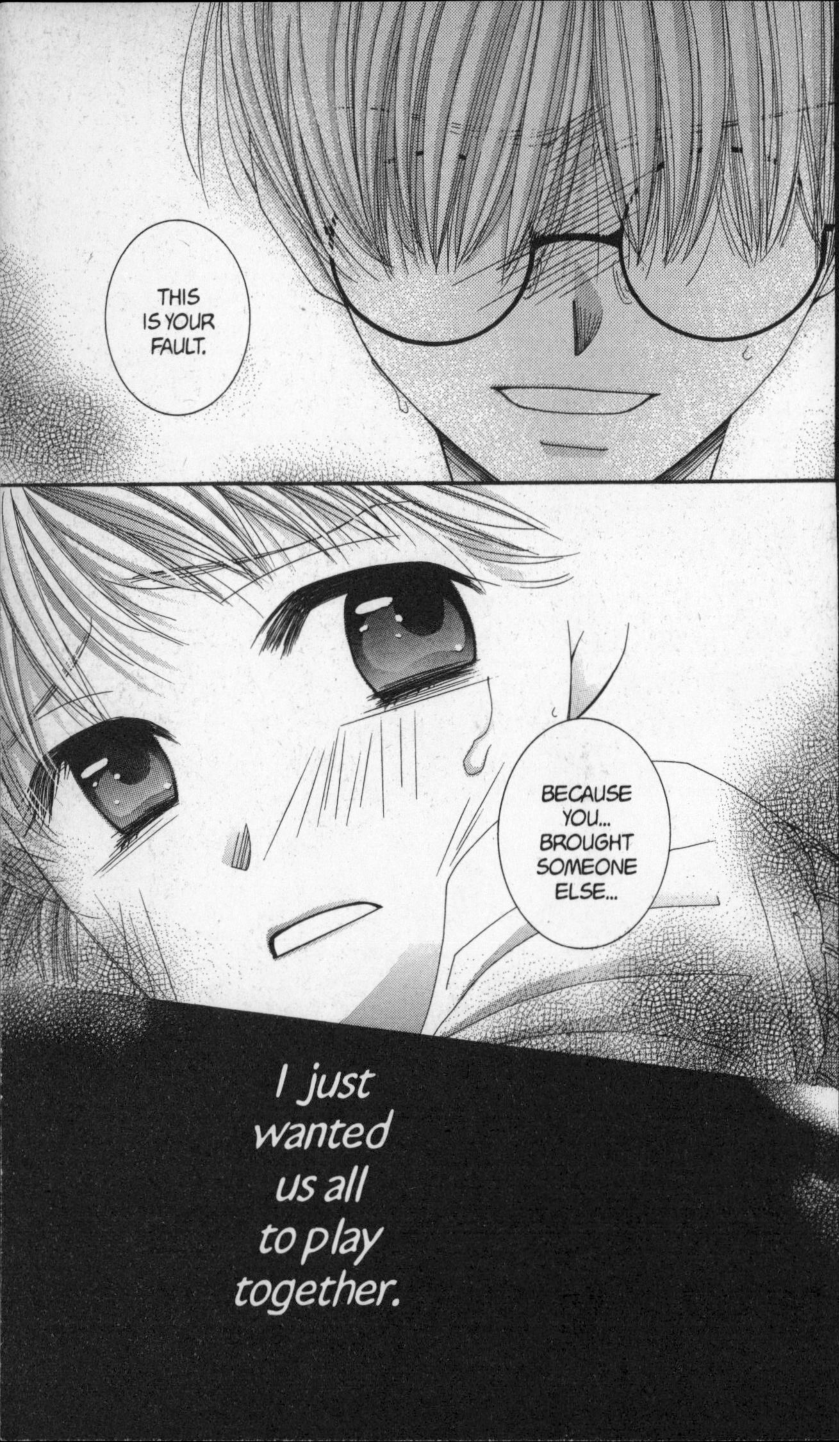
THIS IS YOUR FAULT.
BECAUSE YOU... BROUGHT SOMEONE ELSE...
I just wanted us all to play together.

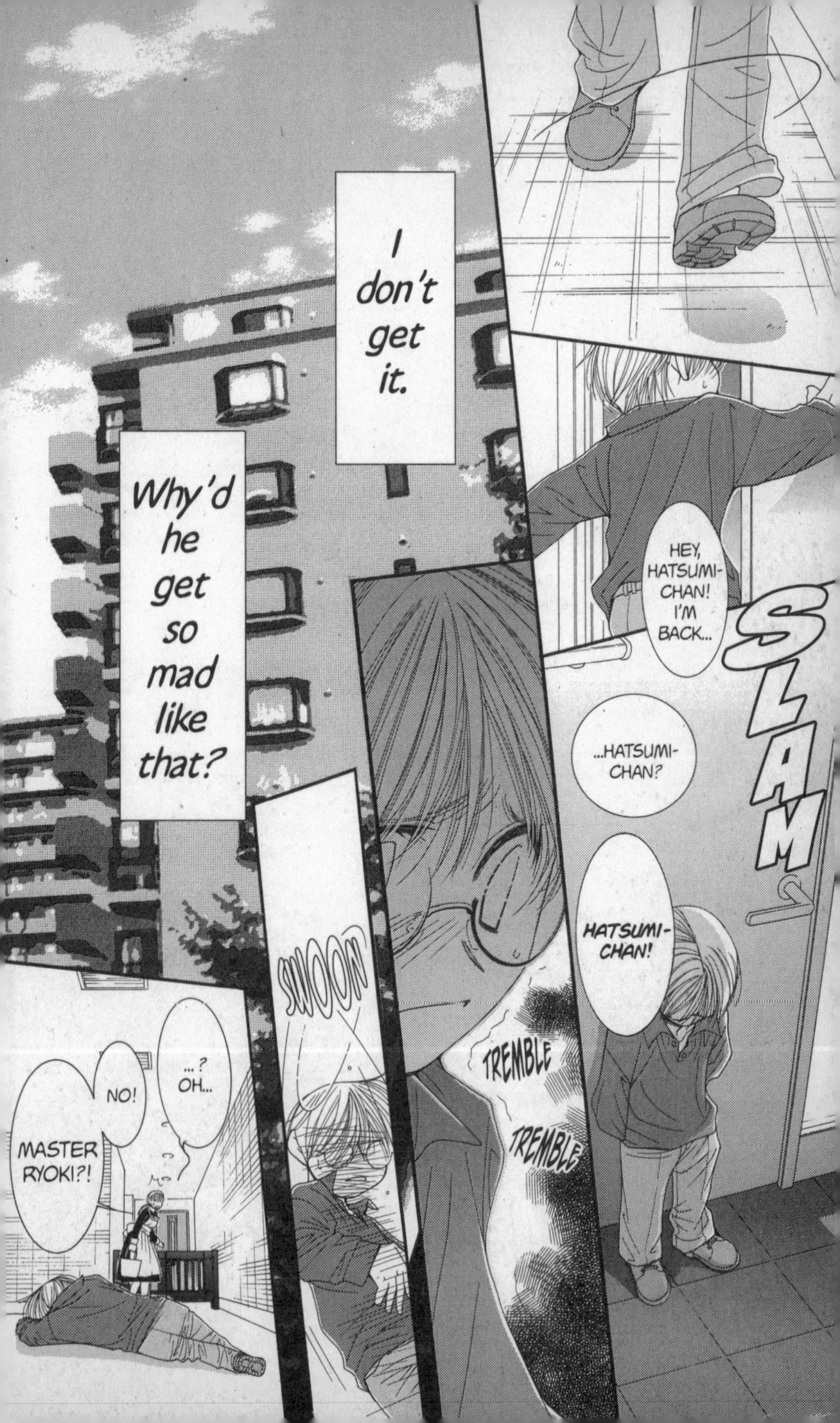
HEY, HATSUMI-CHAN! I'M BACK...
SLAM
...HATSUMI-CHAN?
HATSUMI-CHAN!
I don't get it.
Why'd he get so mad like that?
TREMBLE
TREMBLE
SWOON
...? OH...
NO!
MASTER RYOKI?!

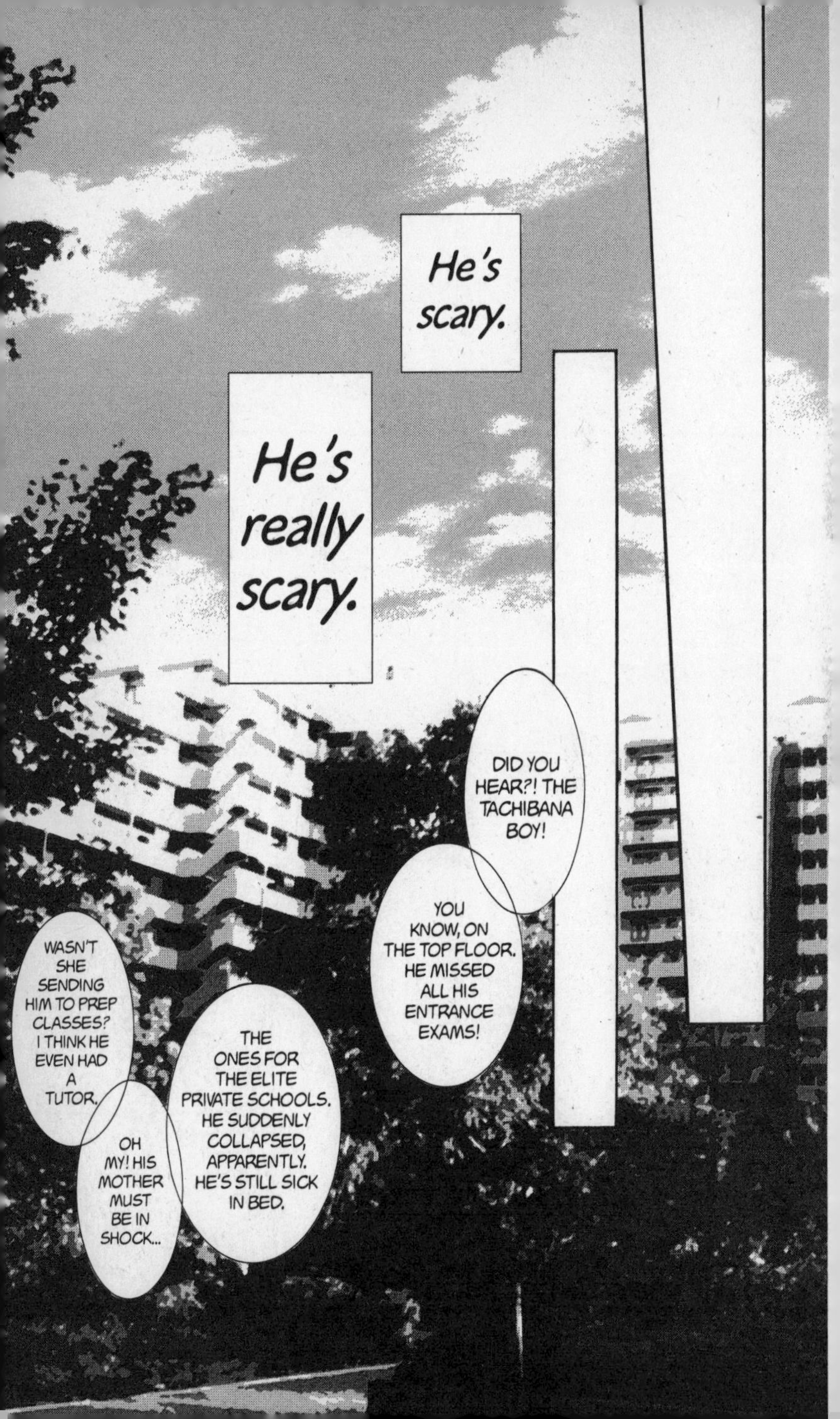
He's scary.
He's really scary.
DID YOU HEAR?! THE TACHIBANA BOY!
YOU KNOW, ON THE TOP FLOOR. HE MISSED ALL HIS ENTRANCE EXAMS!
THE ONES FOR THE ELITE PRIVATE SCHOOLS. HE SUDDENLY COLLAPSED, APPARENTLY. HE'S STILL SICK IN BED.
WASN'T SHE SENDING HIM TO PREP CLASSES? I THINK HE EVEN HAD A TUTOR.
OH MY! HIS MOTHER MUST BE IN SHOCK...

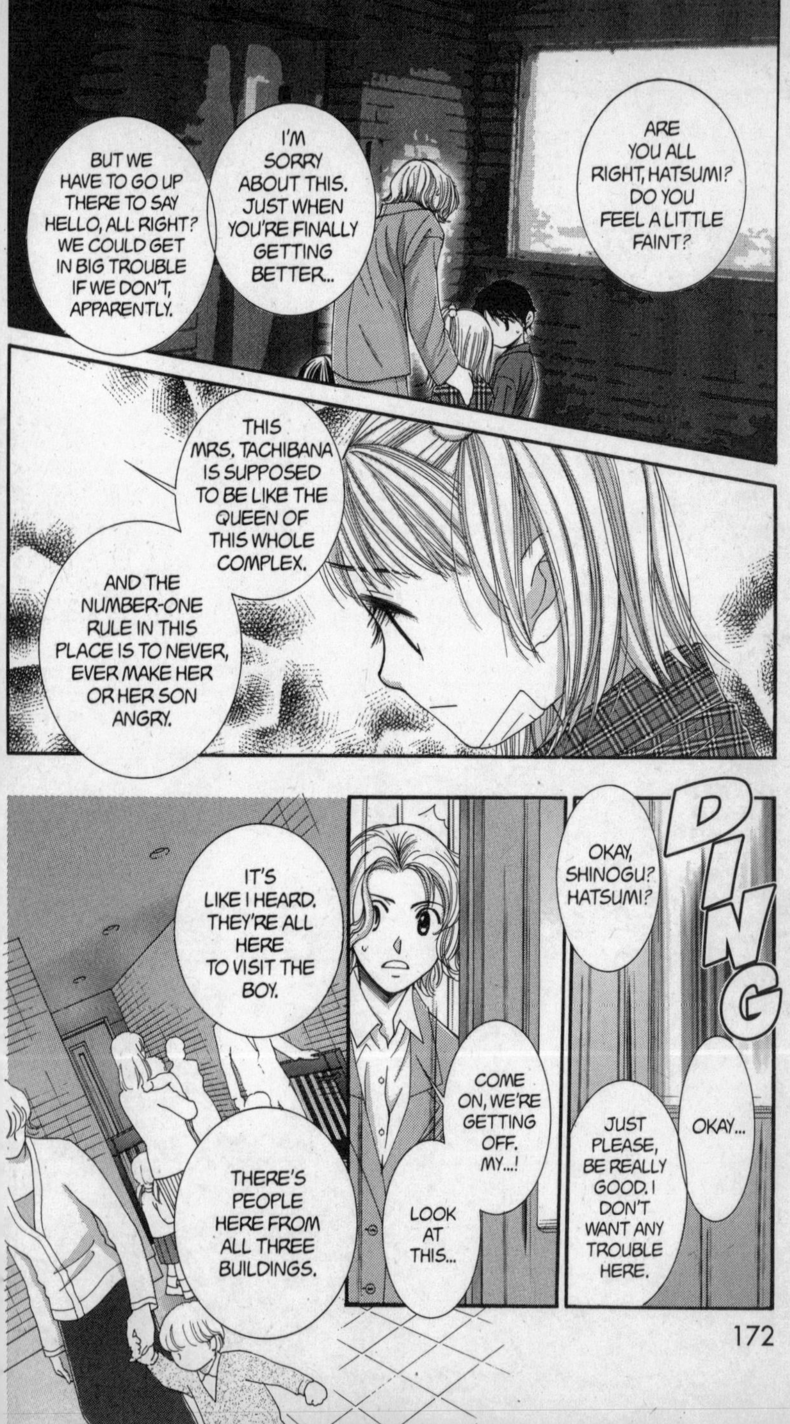
ARE YOU ALL RIGHT, HATSUMI? DO YOU FEEL A LITTLE FAINT?
I'M SORRY ABOUT THIS. JUST WHEN YOU'RE FINALLY GETTING BETTER...
BUT WE HAVE TO GO UP THERE TO SAY HELLO, ALL RIGHT? WE COULD GET IN BIG TROUBLE IF WE DON'T, APPARENTLY.
THIS MRS. TACHIBANA IS SUPPOSED TO BE LIKE THE QUEEN OF THIS WHOLE COMPLEX.
AND THE NUMBER-ONE RULE IN THIS PLACE IS TO NEVER, EVER MAKE HER OR HER SON ANGRY.
DING
OKAY, SHINOGU? HATSUMI?
OKAY...
JUST PLEASE, BE REALLY GOOD. I DON'T WANT ANY TROUBLE HERE.
COME ON, WE'RE GETTING OFF. MY...!
LOOK AT THIS...
IT'S LIKE I HEARD. THEY'RE ALL HERE TO VISIT THE BOY.
THERE'S PEOPLE HERE FROM ALL THREE BUILDINGS.

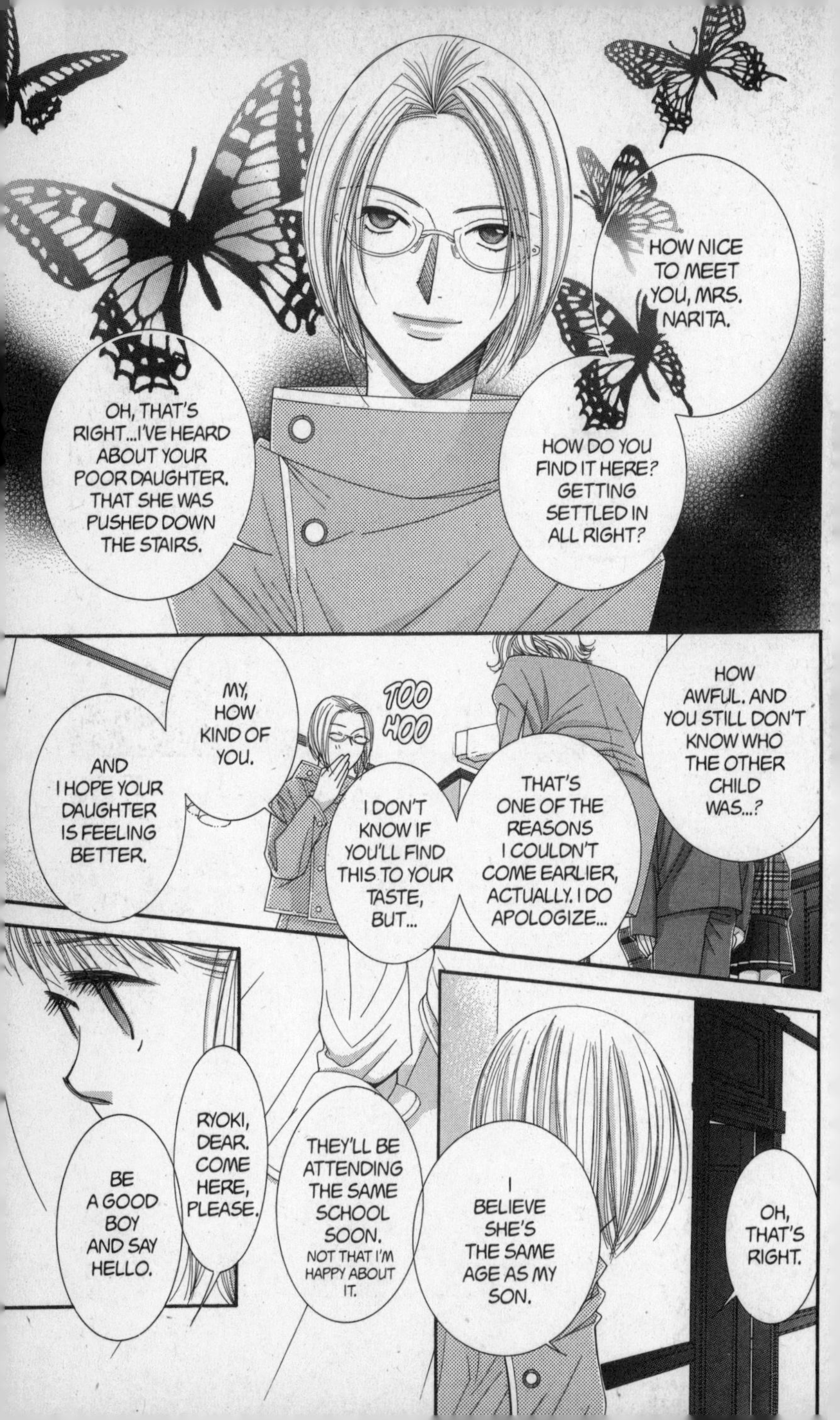
HOW NICE TO MEET YOU, MRS. NARITA.
HOW DO YOU FIND IT HERE? GETTING SETTLED IN ALL RIGHT?
OH, THAT'S RIGHT...I'VE HEARD ABOUT YOUR POOR DAUGHTER. THAT SHE WAS PUSHED DOWN THE STAIRS.
HOW AWFUL. AND YOU STILL DON'T KNOW WHO THE OTHER CHILD WAS...?
THAT'S ONE OF THE REASONS I COULDN'T COME EARLIER, ACTUALLY. I DO APOLOGIZE...
I DON'T KNOW IF YOU'LL FIND THIS TO YOUR TASTE, BUT...
TOO HOO
MY, HOW KIND OF YOU.
AND I HOPE YOUR DAUGHTER IS FEELING BETTER.
OH, THAT'S RIGHT.
I BELIEVE SHE'S THE SAME AGE AS MY SON.
THEY'LL BE ATTENDING THE SAME SCHOOL SOON. NOT THAT I'M HAPPY ABOUT IT.
RYOKI, DEAR. COME HERE, PLEASE.
BE A GOOD BOY AND SAY HELLO.

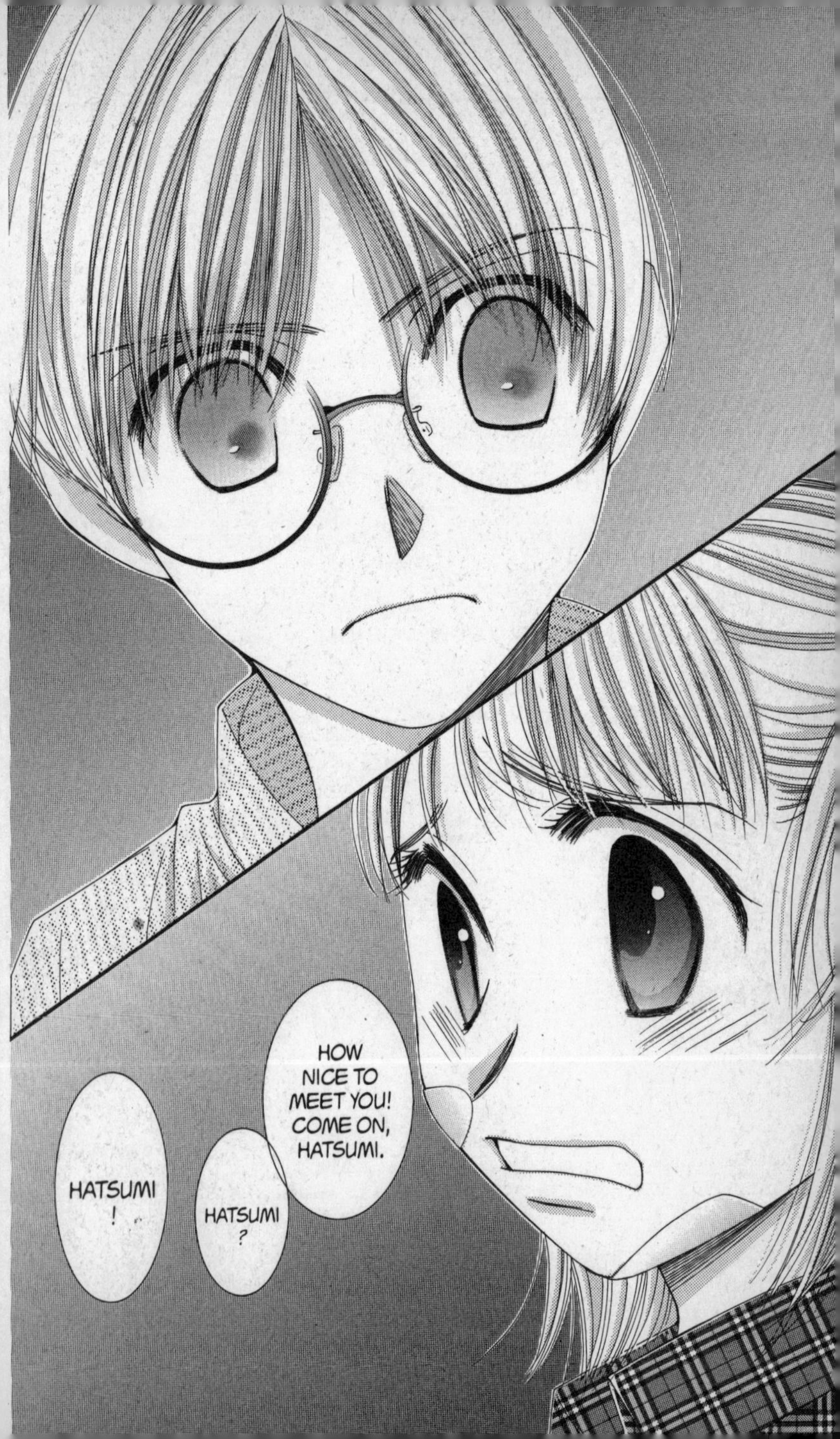
HOW NICE TO MEET YOU! COME ON, HATSUMI.
HATSUMI?
HATSUMI!

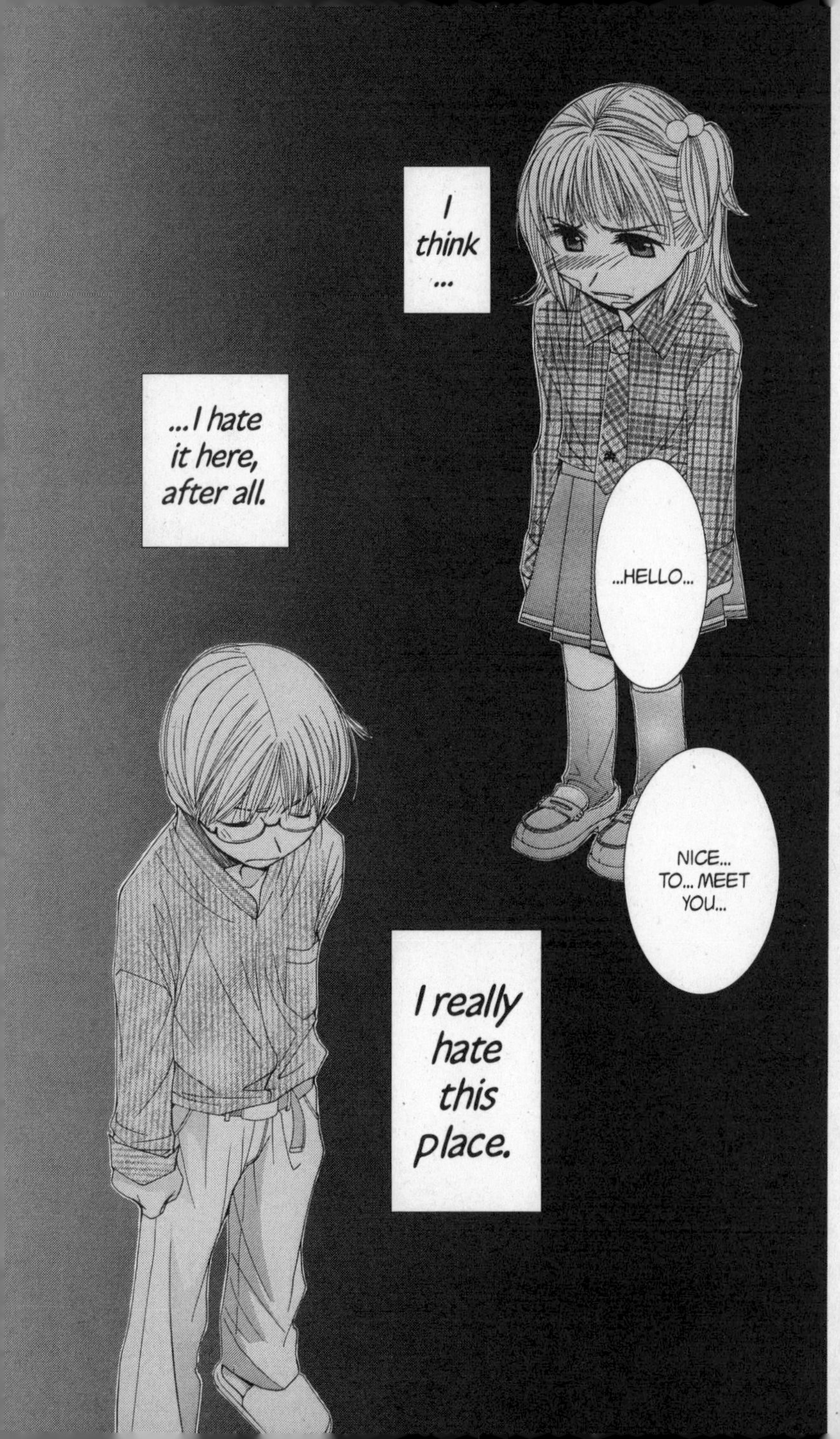
I think...
...I hate it here, after all.
...HELLO...
NICE... TO... MEET YOU...
I really hate this place.

To be continued

EXTRA!! GIMMICK

Thank you for buying Hot Gimmick Vol. 8.
My name is Miki Aihara.
Here, just for you graphic novel readers, is
more of that extra information that's so hard
to put into the actual story.
Read on!

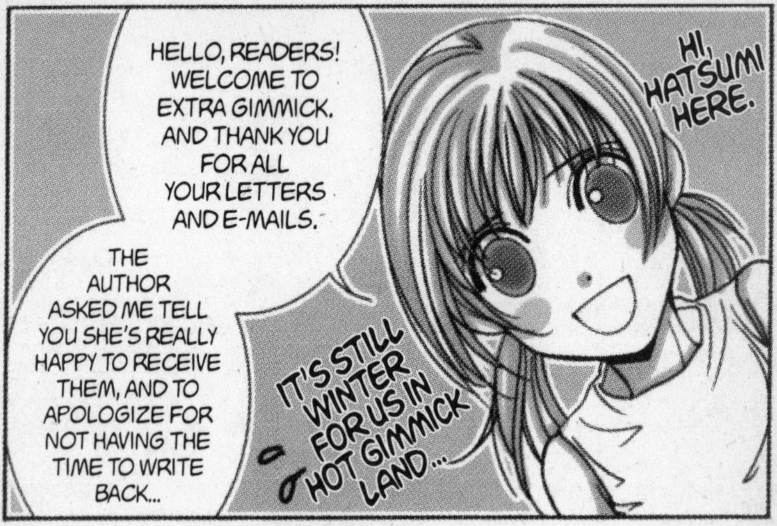
HI, HATSUMI HERE.
HELLO, READERS! WELCOME TO EXTRA GIMMICK. AND THANK YOU FOR ALL YOUR LETTERS AND E-MAILS.
IT'S STILL WINTER FOR US IN HOT GIMMICK LAND...
THE AUTHOR ASKED ME TELL YOU SHE'S REALLY HAPPY TO RECEIVE THEM, AND TO APOLOGIZE FOR NOT HAVING THE TIME TO WRITE BACK...

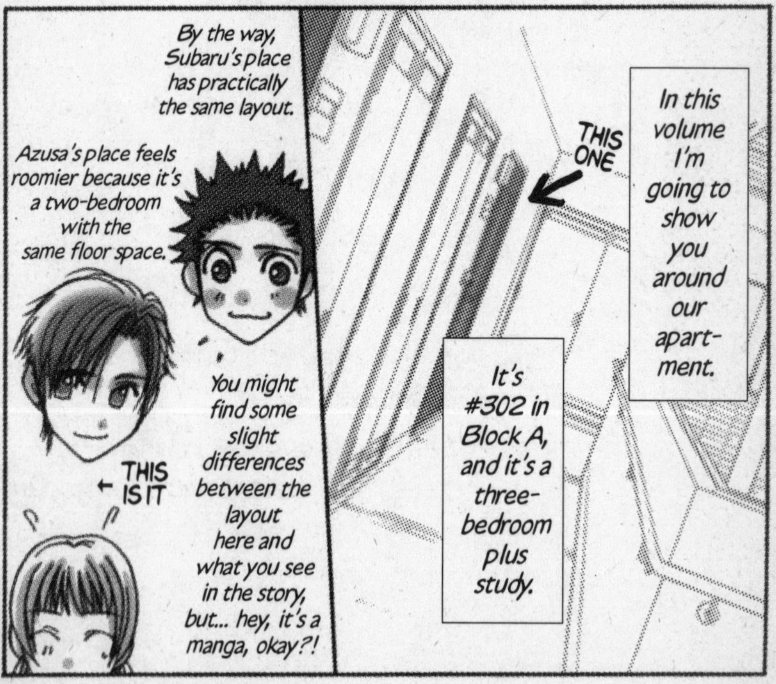
In this volume I'm going to show you around our apartment.
THIS ONE
It's #302 in Block A, and it's a three-bedroom plus study.
By the way, Subaru's place has practically the same layout.
Azusa's place feels roomier because it's a two-bedroom with the same floor space.
You might find some slight differences between the layout here and what you see in the story, but... hey, it's a manga, okay?!
THIS IS IT

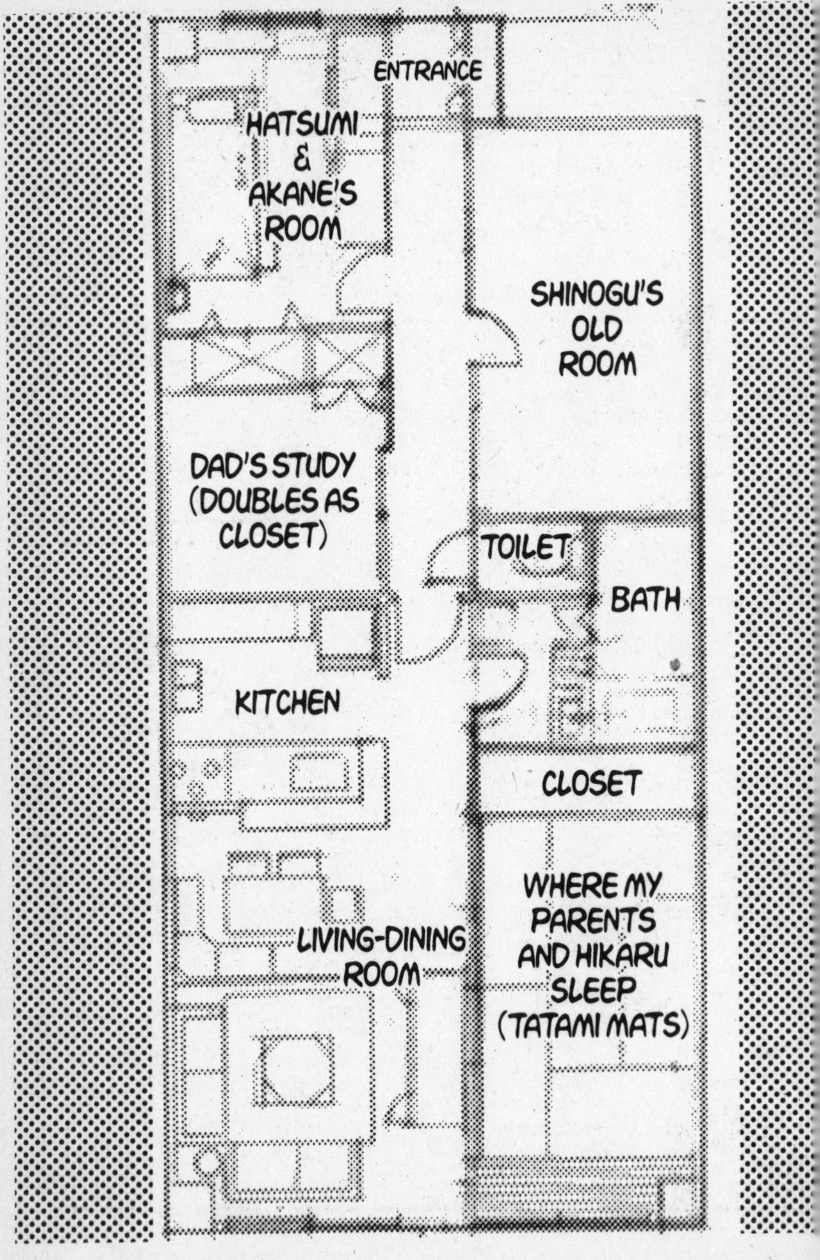
ENTRANCE
HATSUMI & AKANE'S ROOM
SHINOGU'S OLD ROOM
DAD'S STUDY (DOUBLES AS CLOSET)
TOILET
BATH
KITCHEN
CLOSET
WHERE MY PARENTS AND HIKARU SLEEP (TATAMI MATS)
LIVING-DINING ROOM

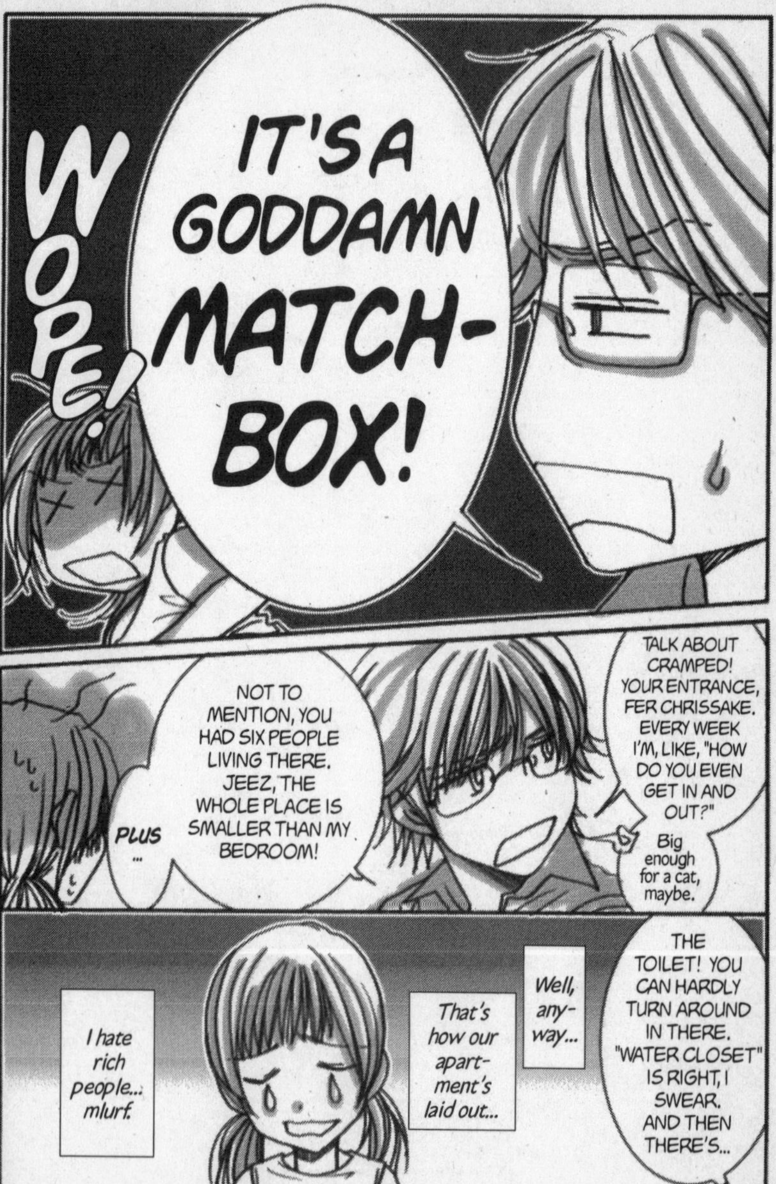
IT'S A GODDAMN MATCH-BOX!
WOPE!
TALK ABOUT CRAMPED! YOUR ENTRANCE, FER CHRISSAKE. EVERY WEEK I'M, LIKE, "HOW DO YOU EVEN GET IN AND OUT?"
Big enough for a cat, maybe.
NOT TO MENTION, YOU HAD SIX PEOPLE LIVING THERE. JEEZ, THE WHOLE PLACE IS SMALLER THAN MY BEDROOM!
PLUS ...
THE TOILET! YOU CAN HARDLY TURN AROUND IN THERE. "WATER CLOSET" IS RIGHT, I SWEAR. AND THEN THERE'S...
Well, anyway...
That's how our apartment's laid out...
I hate rich people... mlurf.